ne
& Hana

1

STORY AND ART BY

Yuki Shiwasu

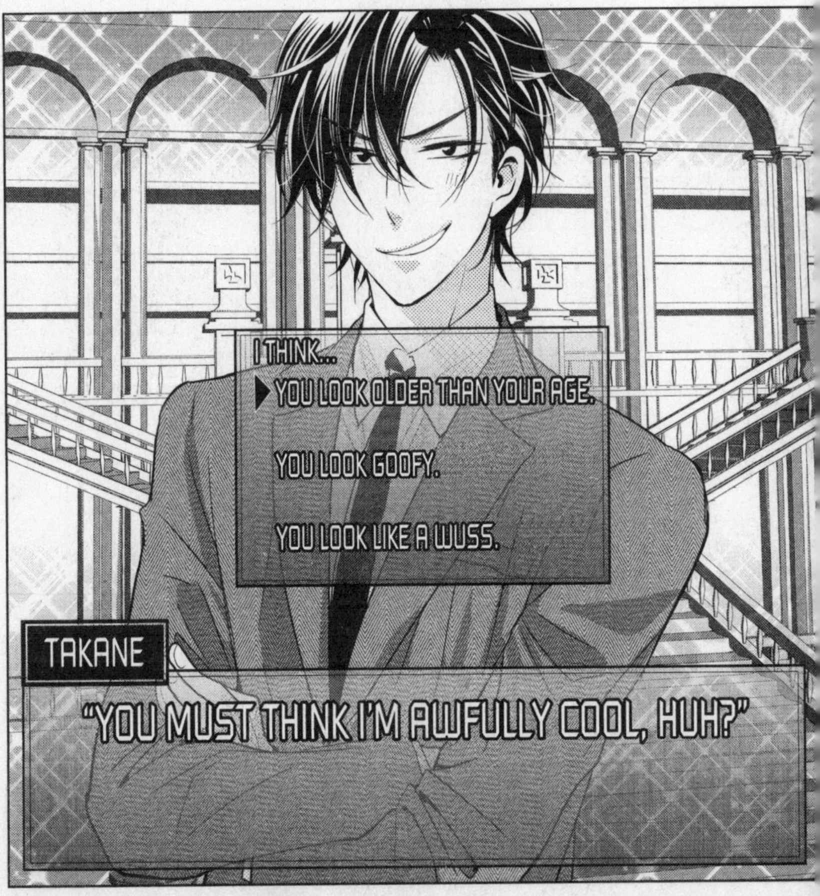
I THINK...
YOU LOOK OLDER THAN YOUR AGE.
YOU LOOK GOOFY.
YOU LOOK LIKE A WUSS.
TAKANE
"YOU MUST THINK I'M AWFULLY COOL, HUH?"

Takane & Hana

1

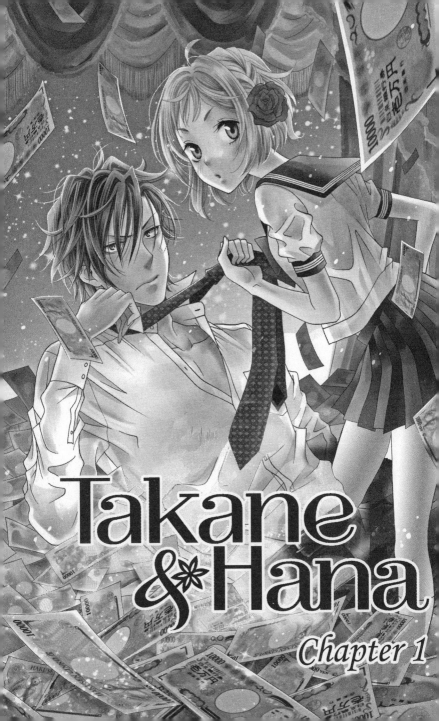

Takane & Hana

Chapter 1

Hello there!

This story started as a one-shot manga, and now it's become an ongoing series. Yay!

My editor used to always tell me to create a manga where "the mere presence of a character is enough to constitute a story line." This time, I feel like I've finally accomplished that.

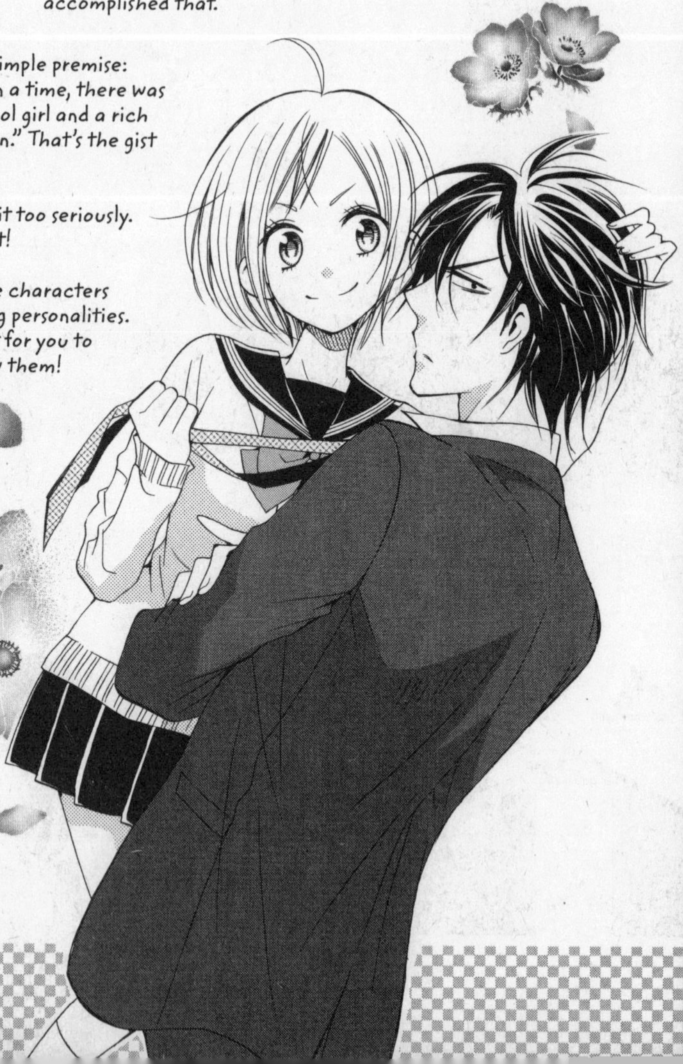

It's a very simple premise: "Once upon a time, there was a high school girl and a rich businessman." That's the gist of it.

Don't take it too seriously. Just enjoy it!

Both of the characters have strong personalities. I can't wait for you to get to know them!

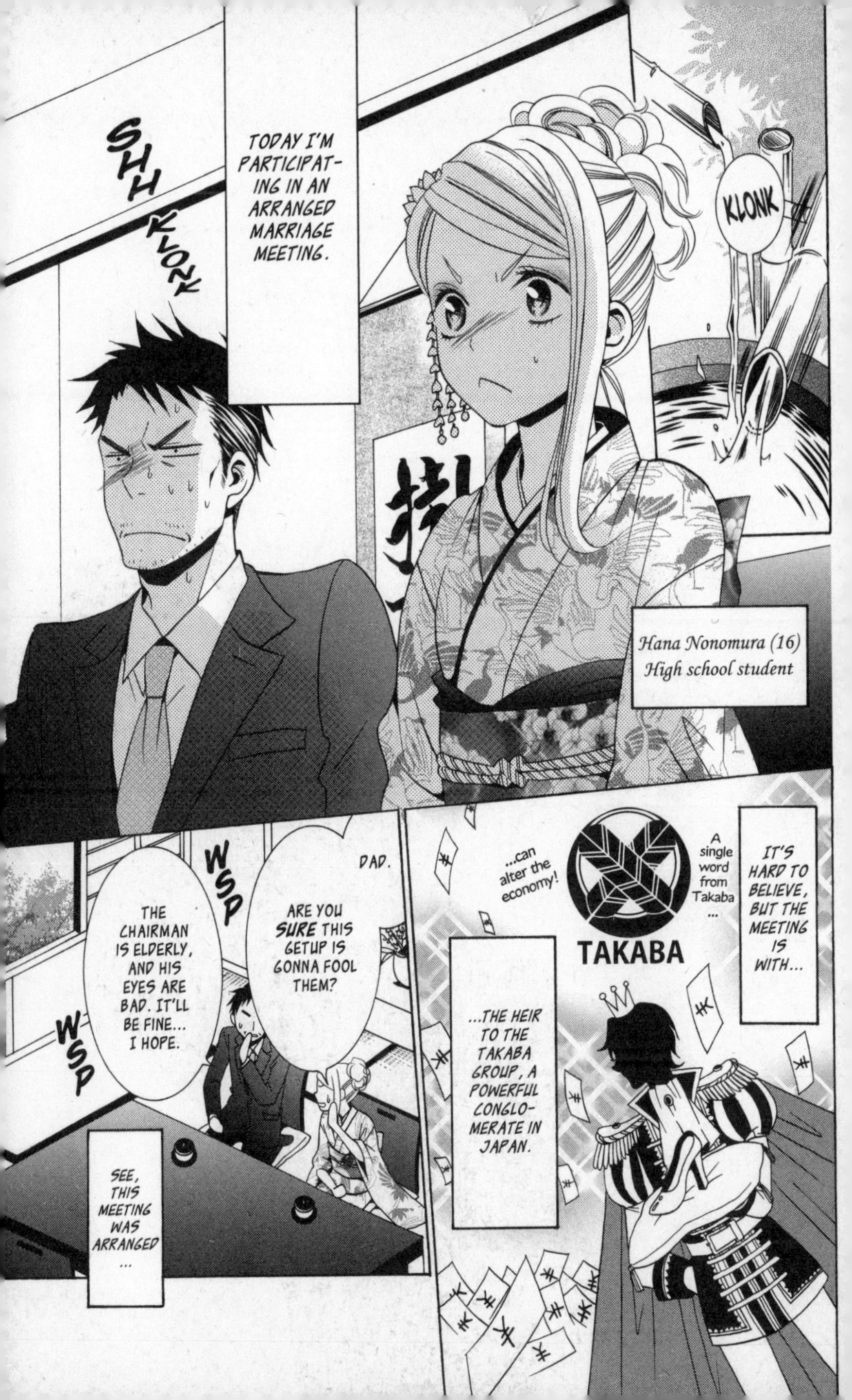
KLONK
TODAY I'M PARTICIPATING IN AN ARRANGED MARRIAGE MEETING.
SHH KLONK
Hana Nonomura (16)
High school student
IT'S HARD TO BELIEVE, BUT THE MEETING IS WITH...
A single word from Takaba...
...can alter the economy!
TAKABA
...THE HEIR TO THE TAKABA GROUP, A POWERFUL CONGLOMERATE IN JAPAN.
DAD.
ARE YOU **SURE** THIS GETUP IS GONNA FOOL THEM?
WSP
THE CHAIRMAN IS ELDERLY, AND HIS EYES ARE BAD. IT'LL BE FINE... I HOPE.
WSP
SEE, THIS MEETING WAS ARRANGED...

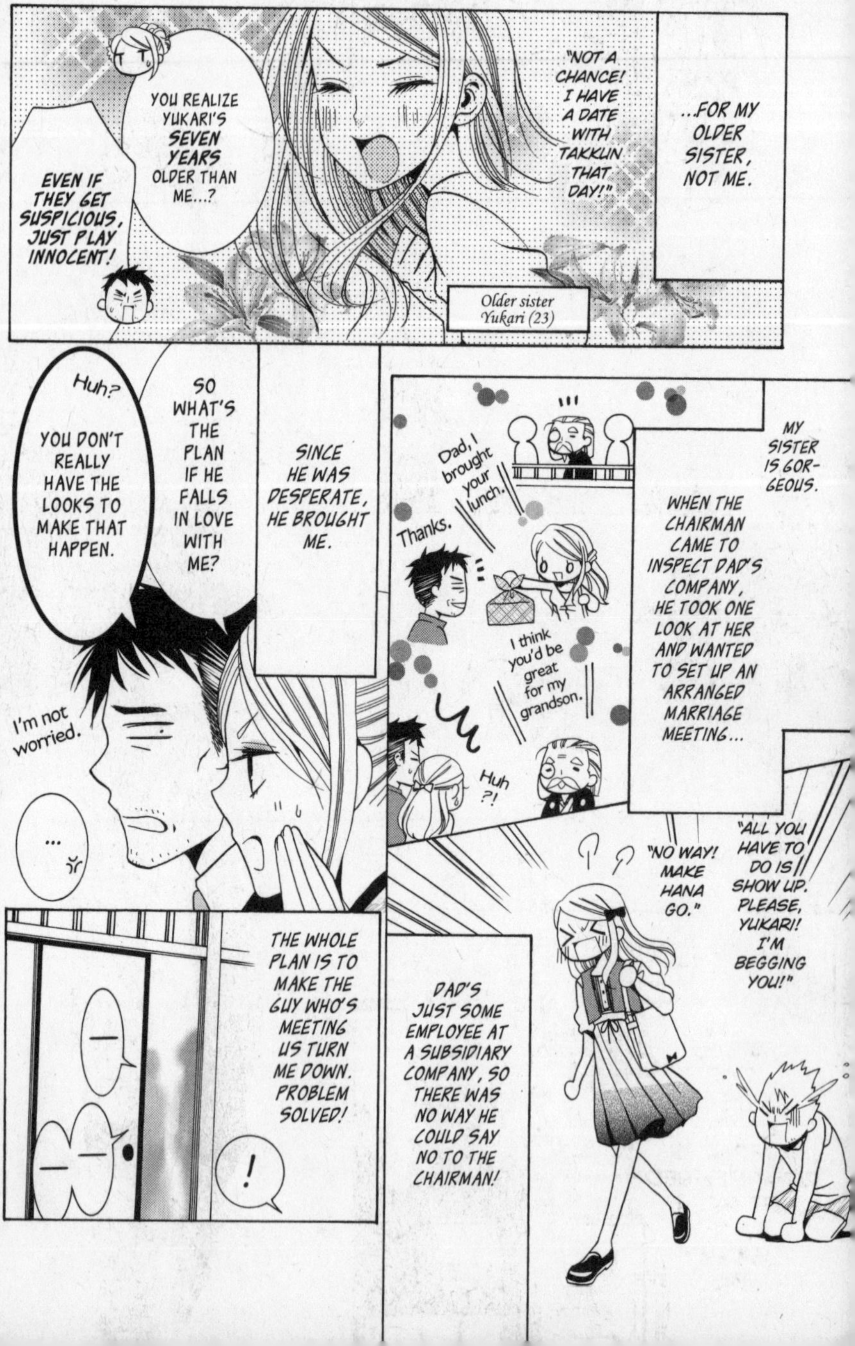
...FOR MY OLDER SISTER, NOT ME.
"NOT A CHANCE! I HAVE A DATE WITH TAKKUN THAT DAY!"
Older sister Yukari (23)
YOU REALIZE YUKARI'S SEVEN YEARS OLDER THAN ME...?
EVEN IF THEY GET SUSPICIOUS, JUST PLAY INNOCENT!
MY SISTER IS GORGEOUS.
WHEN THE CHAIRMAN CAME TO INSPECT DAD'S COMPANY, HE TOOK ONE LOOK AT HER AND WANTED TO SET UP AN ARRANGED MARRIAGE MEETING...
Dad, I brought your lunch.
Thanks.
I think you'd be great for my grandson.
Huh ?!
"ALL YOU HAVE TO DO IS SHOW UP. PLEASE, YUKARI! I'M BEGGING YOU!"
"NO WAY! MAKE HANA GO."
DAD'S JUST SOME EMPLOYEE AT A SUBSIDIARY COMPANY, SO THERE WAS NO WAY HE COULD SAY NO TO THE CHAIRMAN!
SINCE HE WAS DESPERATE, HE BROUGHT ME.
SO WHAT'S THE PLAN IF HE FALLS IN LOVE WITH ME?
Huh?
YOU DON'T REALLY HAVE THE LOOKS TO MAKE THAT HAPPEN.
I'm not worried.
...
THE WHOLE PLAN IS TO MAKE THE GUY WHO'S MEETING US TURN ME DOWN. PROBLEM SOLVED!
—
—
!

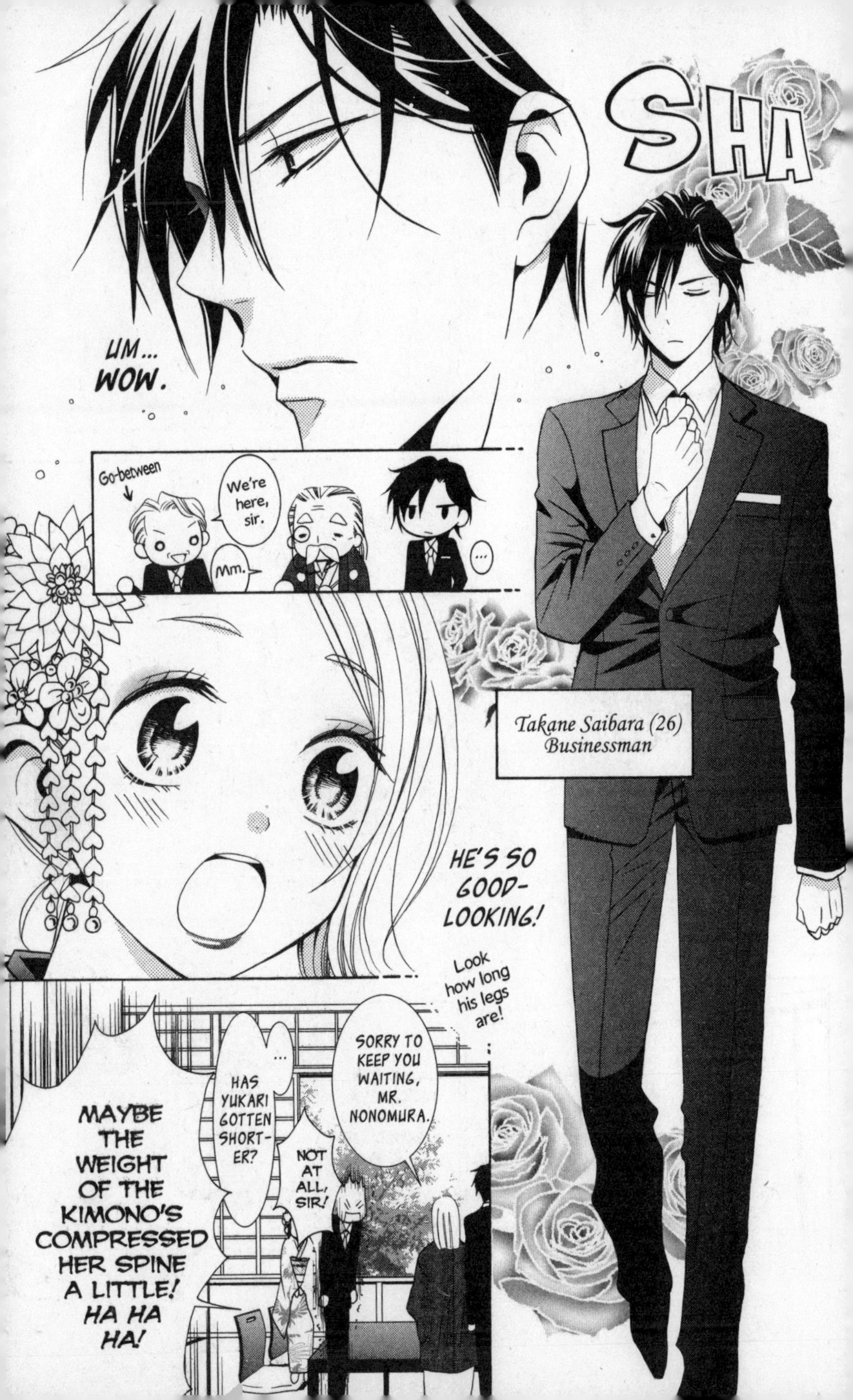
SHA
Takane Saibara (26)
Businessman
HE'S SO GOOD-LOOKING!
Look how long his legs are!
UM... WOW.
...
We're here, sir.
Mm.
Go-between
SORRY TO KEEP YOU WAITING, MR. NONOMURA.
NOT AT ALL, SIR!
... HAS YUKARI GOTTEN SHORTER?
MAYBE THE WEIGHT OF THE KIMONO'S COMPRESSED HER SPINE A LITTLE! HA HA HA!

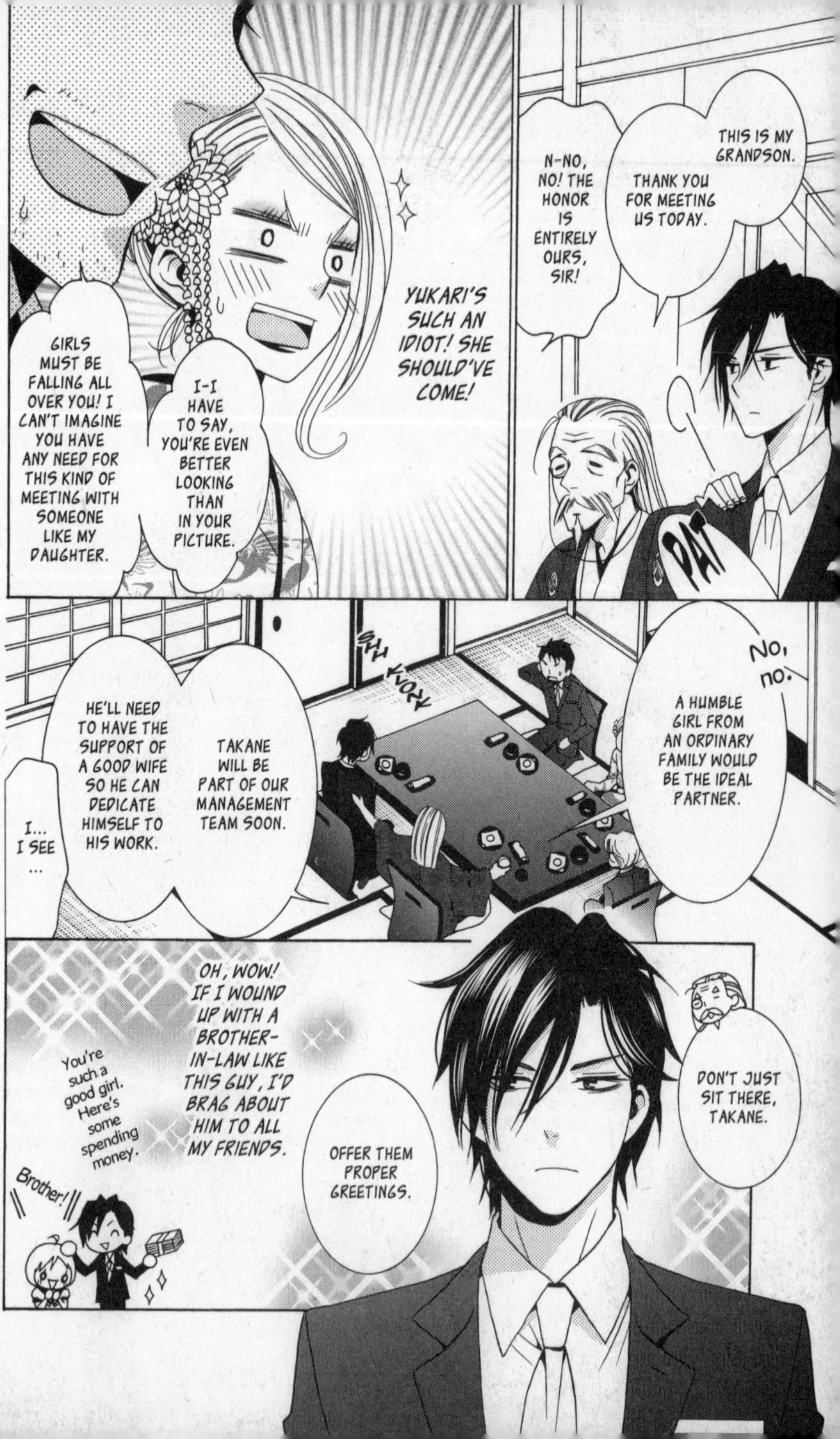
THIS IS MY GRANDSON.
THANK YOU FOR MEETING US TODAY.
N-NO, NO! THE HONOR IS ENTIRELY OURS, SIR!
PAT
YUKARI'S SUCH AN IDIOT! SHE SHOULD'VE COME!
I-I HAVE TO SAY, YOU'RE EVEN BETTER LOOKING THAN IN YOUR PICTURE.
GIRLS MUST BE FALLING ALL OVER YOU! I CAN'T IMAGINE YOU HAVE ANY NEED FOR THIS KIND OF MEETING WITH SOMEONE LIKE MY DAUGHTER.
No, no.
A HUMBLE GIRL FROM AN ORDINARY FAMILY WOULD BE THE IDEAL PARTNER.
SHH KVONK
TAKANE WILL BE PART OF OUR MANAGEMENT TEAM SOON.
HE'LL NEED TO HAVE THE SUPPORT OF A GOOD WIFE SO HE CAN DEDICATE HIMSELF TO HIS WORK.
I... I SEE...
DON'T JUST SIT THERE, TAKANE.
OFFER THEM PROPER GREETINGS.
OH, WOW! IF I WOUND UP WITH A BROTHER-IN-LAW LIKE THIS GUY, I'D BRAG ABOUT HIM TO ALL MY FRIENDS.
You're such a good girl. Here's some spending money.
Brother!

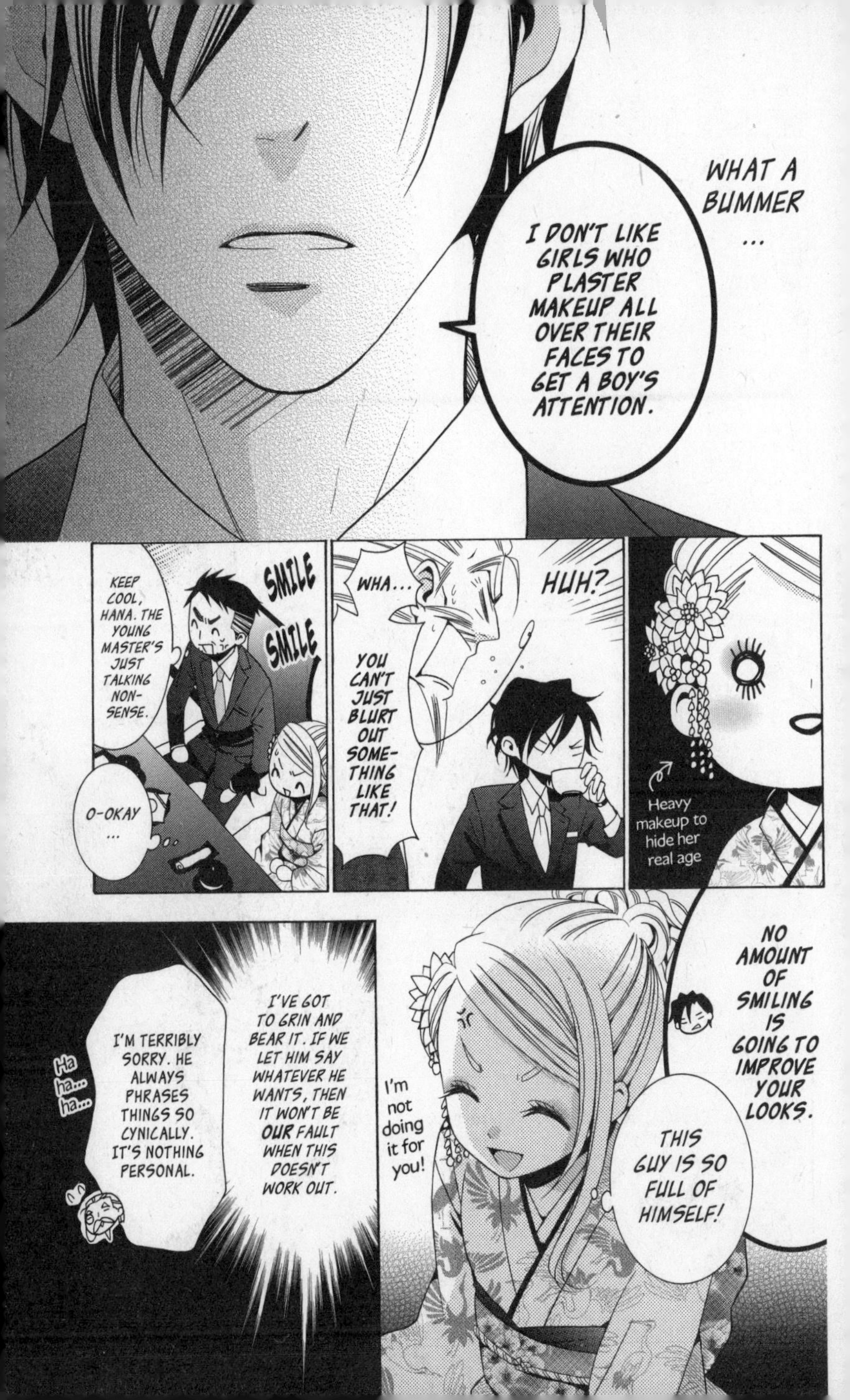
WHAT A BUMMER...
I DON'T LIKE GIRLS WHO PLASTER MAKEUP ALL OVER THEIR FACES TO GET A BOY'S ATTENTION.
Heavy makeup to hide her real age
HUH?
WHA...
YOU CAN'T JUST BLURT OUT SOMETHING LIKE THAT!
SMILE
SMILE
KEEP COOL, HANA. THE YOUNG MASTER'S JUST TALKING NON-SENSE.
O-OKAY...
NO AMOUNT OF SMILING IS GOING TO IMPROVE YOUR LOOKS.
THIS GUY IS SO FULL OF HIMSELF!
I'm not doing it for you!
I'VE GOT TO GRIN AND BEAR IT. IF WE LET HIM SAY WHATEVER HE WANTS, THEN IT WON'T BE OUR FAULT WHEN THIS DOESN'T WORK OUT.
I'M TERRIBLY SORRY. HE ALWAYS PHRASES THINGS SO CYNICALLY. IT'S NOTHING PERSONAL.
Ha ha... ha...

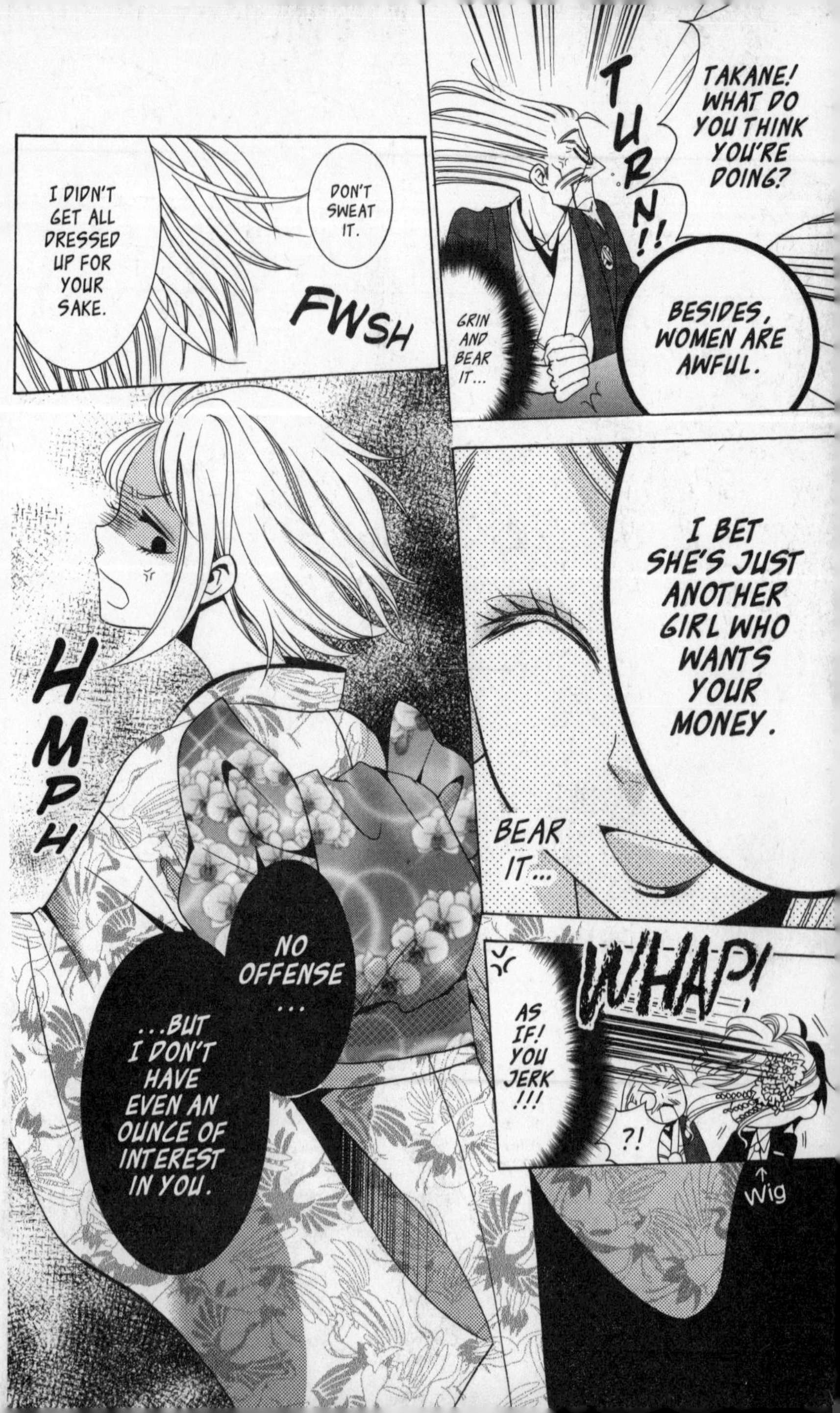
TURN!!
TAKANE! WHAT DO YOU THINK YOU'RE DOING?
BESIDES, WOMEN ARE AWFUL.
GRIN AND BEAR IT...
DON'T SWEAT IT.
I DIDN'T GET ALL DRESSED UP FOR YOUR SAKE.
FWSH
I BET SHE'S JUST ANOTHER GIRL WHO WANTS YOUR MONEY.
BEAR IT...
WHAP!
AS IF! YOU JERK!!!
?!
Wig
HMPH
NO OFFENSE...
...BUT I DON'T HAVE EVEN AN OUNCE OF INTEREST IN YOU.

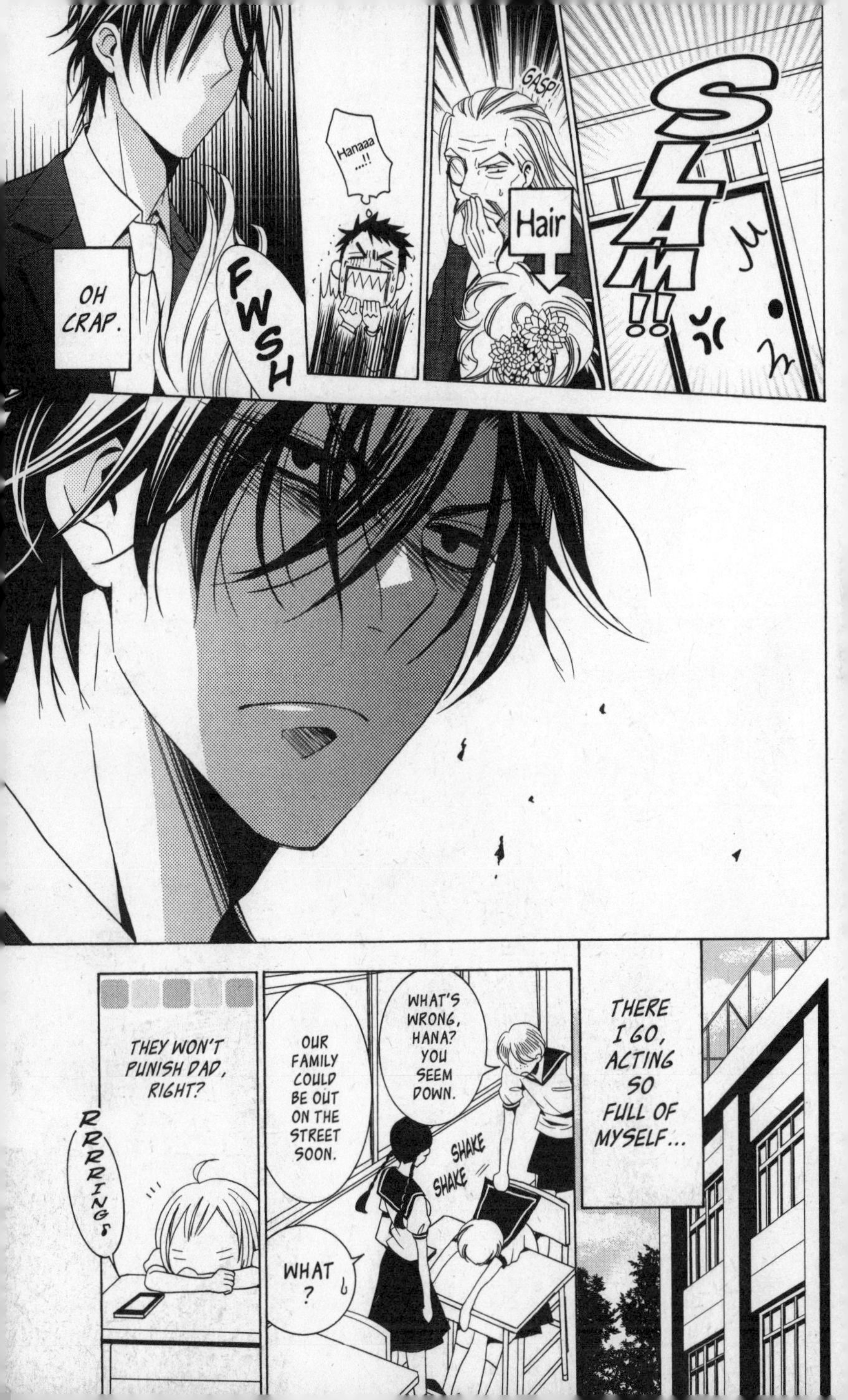
SLAM!!
GASP!
Hair
Hanaaa ...!!
FWSH
OH CRAP.
THERE I GO, ACTING SO FULL OF MYSELF...
WHAT'S WRONG, HANA? YOU SEEM DOWN.
SHAKE
SHAKE
OUR FAMILY COULD BE OUT ON THE STREET SOON.
WHAT?
THEY WON'T PUNISH DAD, RIGHT?
RRRRING

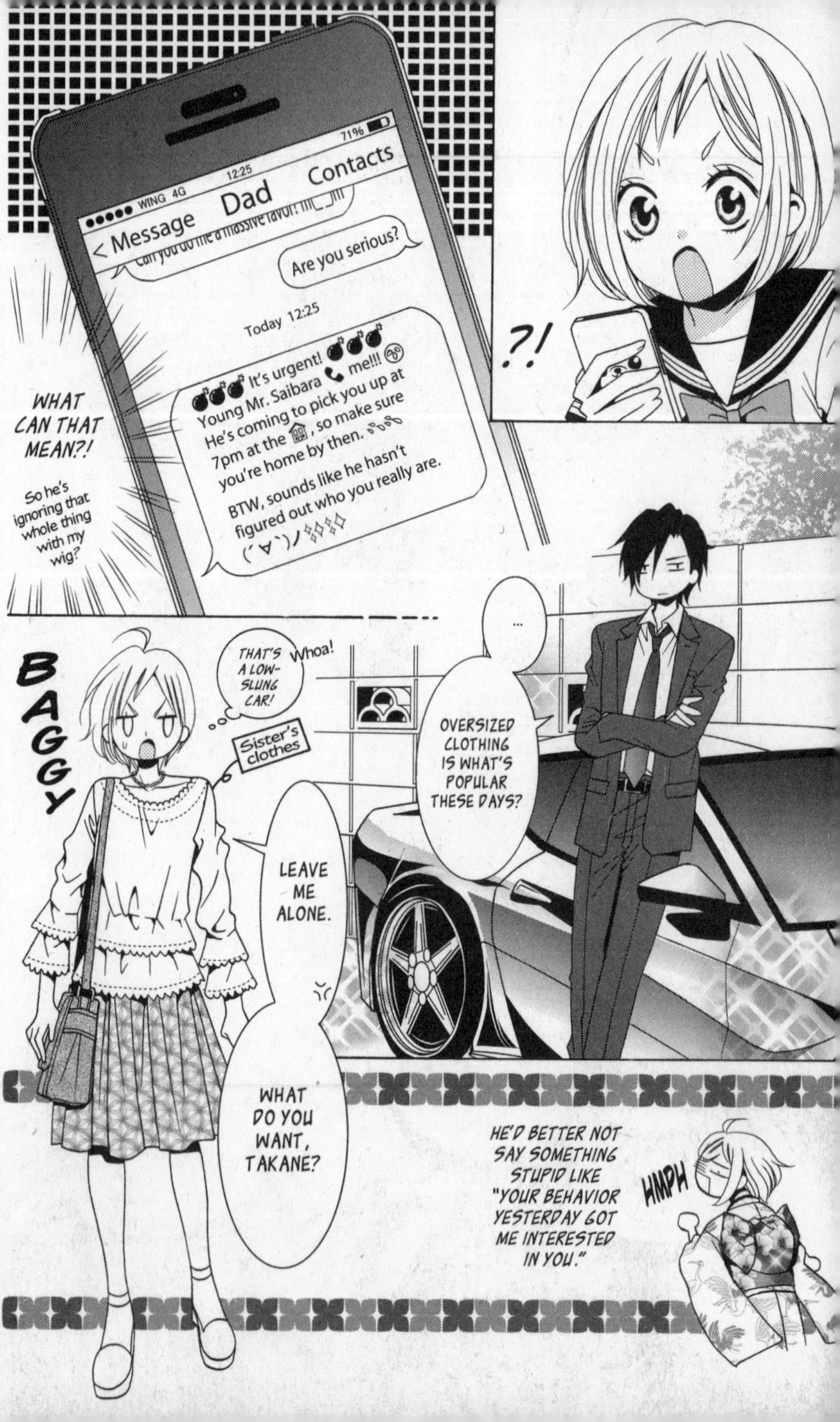
?!
71%
WING 4G
12:25
< Message
Dad
Contacts
Are you serious?
Today 12:25
It's urgent! Young Mr. Saibara me!!! He's coming to pick you up at 7pm at the , so make sure you're home by then.
BTW, sounds like he hasn't figured out who you really are. (´∀`)ノ
WHAT CAN THAT MEAN?!
So he's ignoring that whole thing with my wig?
...
OVERSIZED CLOTHING IS WHAT'S POPULAR THESE DAYS?
THAT'S A LOW-SLUNG CAR!
Whoa!
BAGGY
Sister's clothes
LEAVE ME ALONE.
WHAT DO YOU WANT, TAKANE?
HE'D BETTER NOT SAY SOMETHING STUPID LIKE "YOUR BEHAVIOR YESTERDAY GOT ME INTERESTED IN YOU."
HMPH

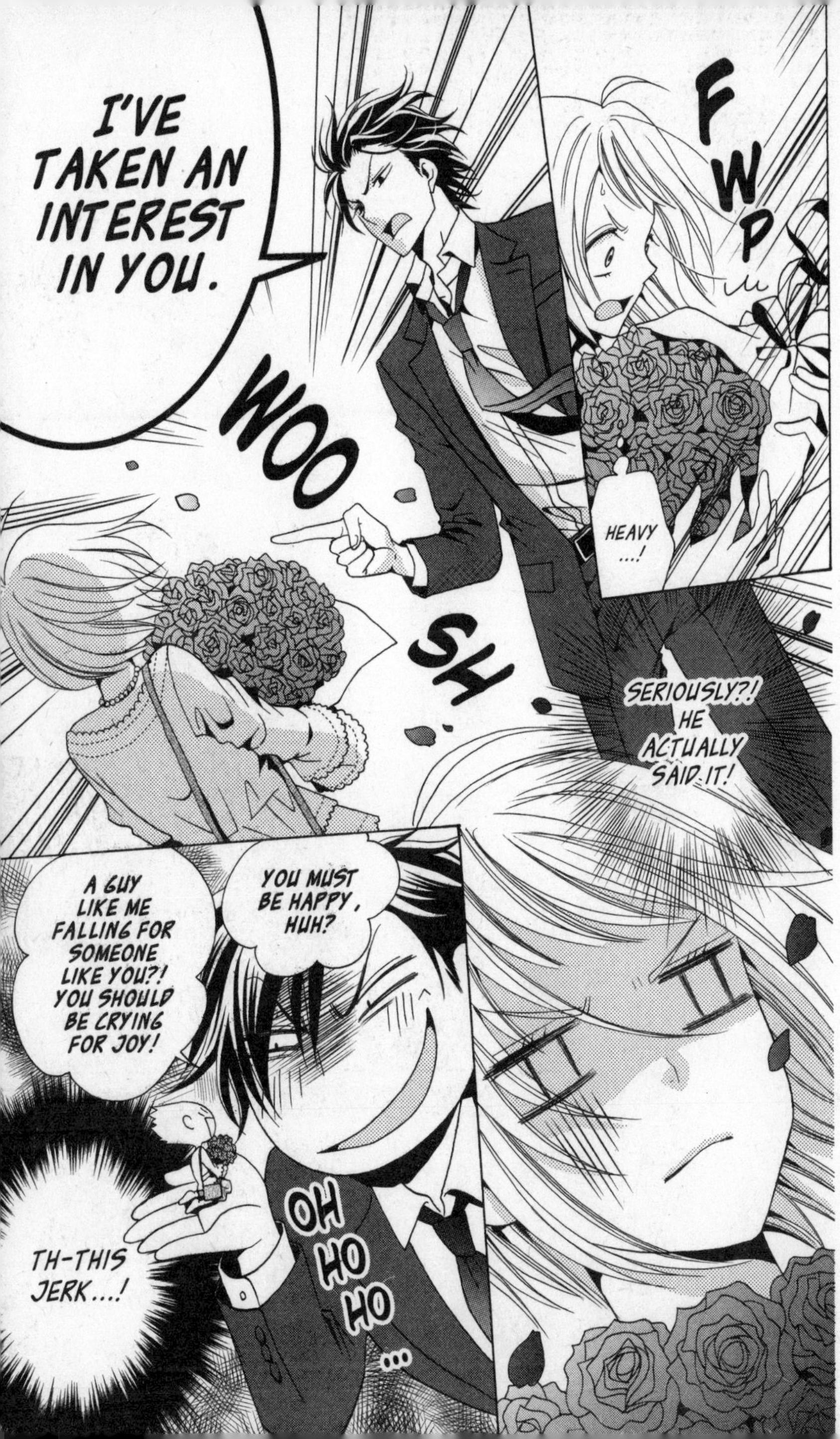
FWP
HEAVY ...!
I'VE TAKEN AN INTEREST IN YOU.
WOOSH
SERIOUSLY?! HE ACTUALLY SAID IT!
YOU MUST BE HAPPY, HUH?
A GUY LIKE ME FALLING FOR SOMEONE LIKE YOU?! YOU SHOULD BE CRYING FOR JOY!
OH HO HO HO...
TH-THIS JERK...!

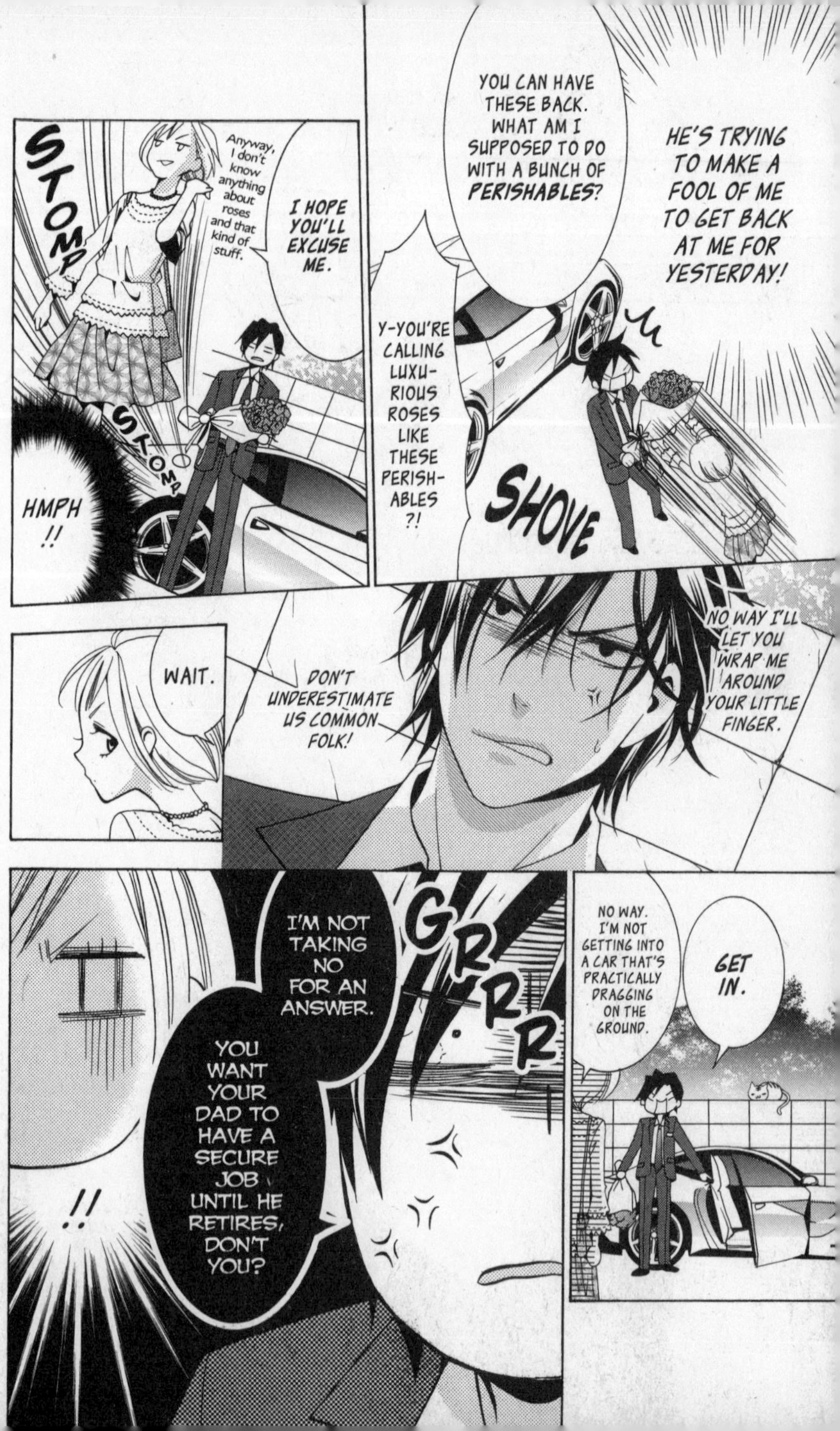
YOU CAN HAVE THESE BACK. WHAT AM I SUPPOSED TO DO WITH A BUNCH OF PERISHABLES?
HE'S TRYING TO MAKE A FOOL OF ME TO GET BACK AT ME FOR YESTERDAY!
Y-YOU'RE CALLING LUXU-RIOUS ROSES LIKE THESE PERISH-ABLES?!
SHOVE
I HOPE YOU'LL EXCUSE ME.
Anyway, I don't know anything about roses and that kind of stuff.
STOMP
STOMP
HMPH!!
NO WAY I'LL LET YOU WRAP ME AROUND YOUR LITTLE FINGER.
DON'T UNDERESTIMATE US COMMON FOLK!
WAIT.
GET IN.
NO WAY. I'M NOT GETTING INTO A CAR THAT'S PRACTICALLY DRAGGING ON THE GROUND.
GRRR
I'M NOT TAKING NO FOR AN ANSWER.
YOU WANT YOUR DAD TO HAVE A SECURE JOB UNTIL HE RETIRES, DON'T YOU?
!!

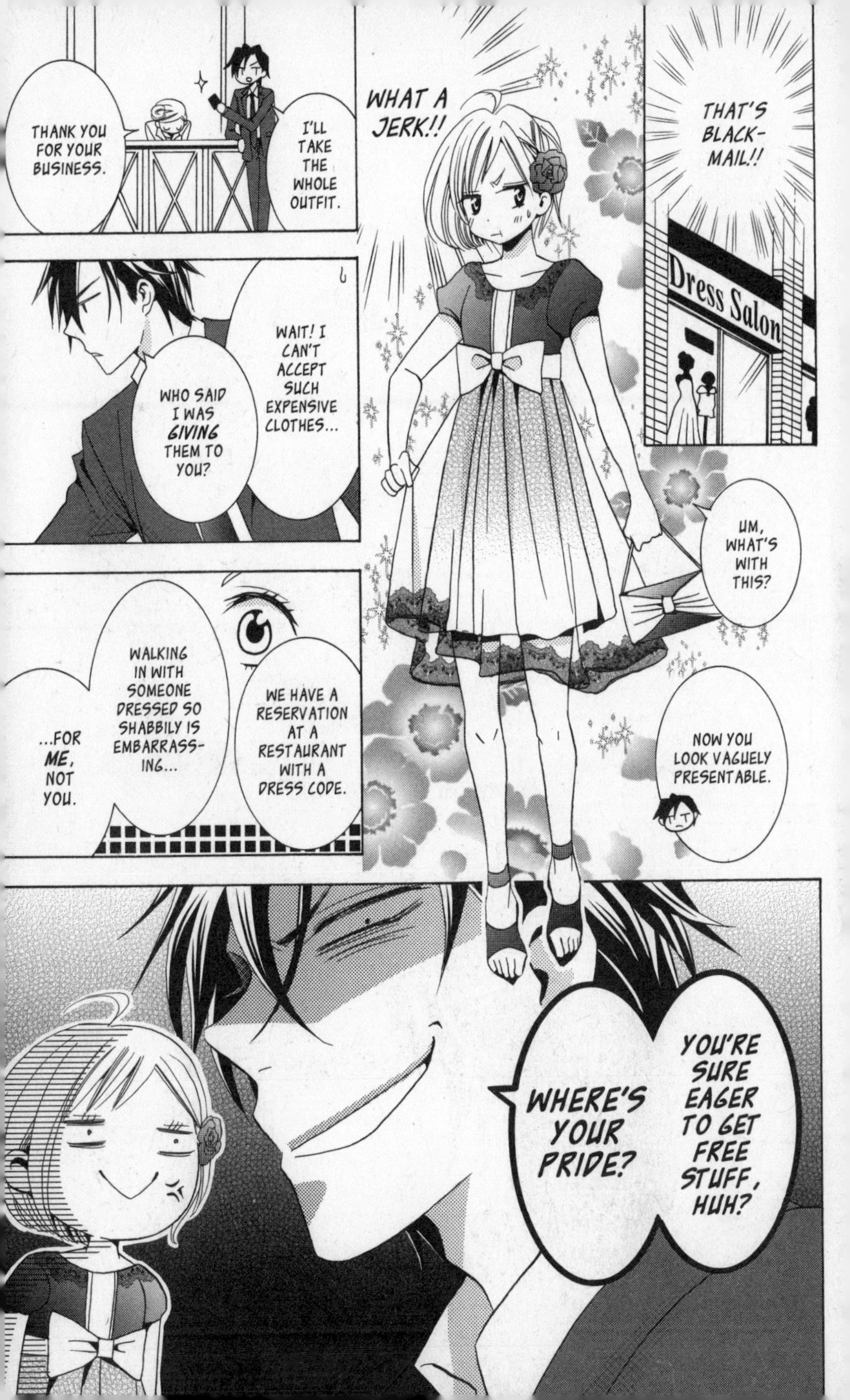
THAT'S BLACK-MAIL!!
Dress Salon
WHAT A JERK!!
UM, WHAT'S WITH THIS?
NOW YOU LOOK VAGUELY PRESENTABLE.
I'LL TAKE THE WHOLE OUTFIT.
THANK YOU FOR YOUR BUSINESS.
WAIT! I CAN'T ACCEPT SUCH EXPENSIVE CLOTHES...
WHO SAID I WAS *GIVING* THEM TO YOU?
WE HAVE A RESERVATION AT A RESTAURANT WITH A DRESS CODE.
WALKING IN WITH SOMEONE DRESSED SO SHABBILY IS EMBARRASS-ING...
...FOR *ME*, NOT YOU.
YOU'RE SURE EAGER TO GET FREE STUFF, HUH?
WHERE'S YOUR PRIDE?

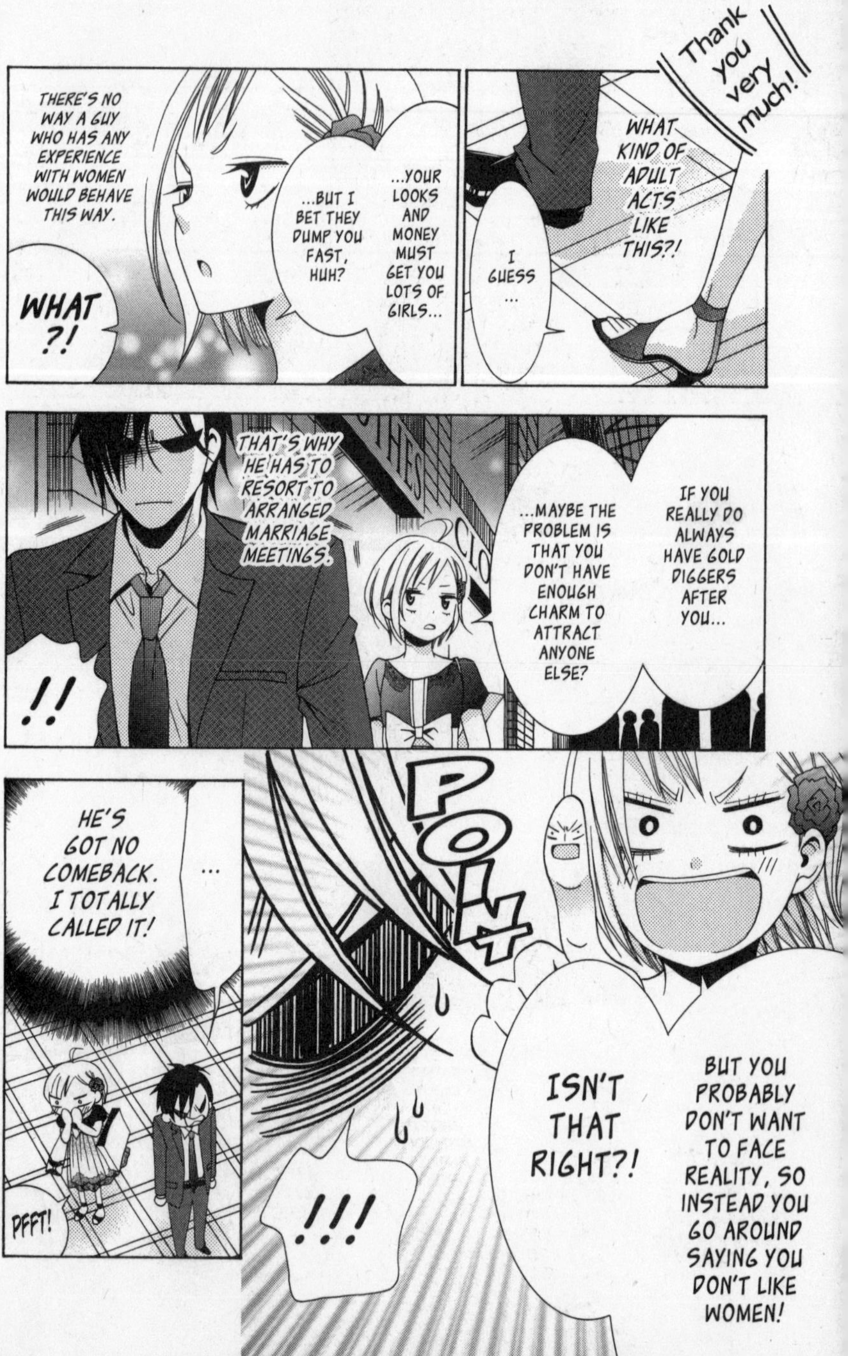
Thank you very much!
WHAT KIND OF ADULT ACTS LIKE THIS?!
I GUESS...
...YOUR LOOKS AND MONEY MUST GET YOU LOTS OF GIRLS...
...BUT I BET THEY DUMP YOU FAST, HUH?
THERE'S NO WAY A GUY WHO HAS ANY EXPERIENCE WITH WOMEN WOULD BEHAVE THIS WAY.
WHAT?!
IF YOU REALLY DO ALWAYS HAVE GOLD DIGGERS AFTER YOU...
...MAYBE THE PROBLEM IS THAT YOU DON'T HAVE ENOUGH CHARM TO ATTRACT ANYONE ELSE?
THAT'S WHY HE HAS TO RESORT TO ARRANGED MARRIAGE MEETINGS.
!!
POINT
BUT YOU PROBABLY DON'T WANT TO FACE REALITY, SO INSTEAD YOU GO AROUND SAYING YOU DON'T LIKE WOMEN!
ISN'T THAT RIGHT?!
!!!
...
HE'S GOT NO COMEBACK. I TOTALLY CALLED IT!
PFFT!

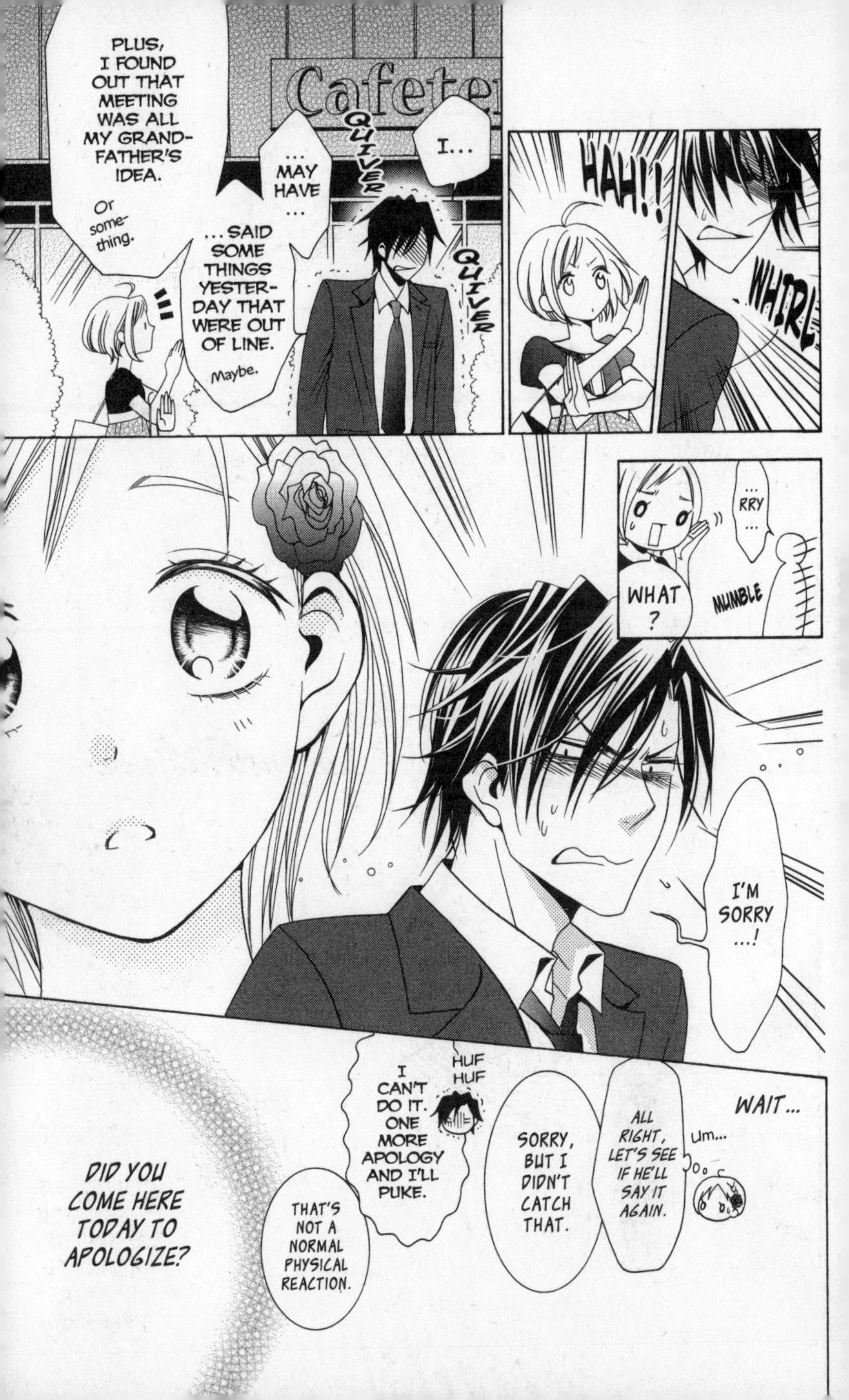
PLUS, I FOUND OUT THAT MEETING WAS ALL MY GRAND-FATHER'S IDEA.
Or some-thing.
I...
QUIVER
...MAY HAVE...
...SAID SOME THINGS YESTER-DAY THAT WERE OUT OF LINE.
Maybe.
QUIVER
WHIRL
HAH!!
...RRY...
MUMBLE
WHAT?
I'M SORRY...!
WAIT...
Um...
ALL RIGHT, LET'S SEE IF HE'LL SAY IT AGAIN.
SORRY, BUT I DIDN'T CATCH THAT.
HUF HUF
I CAN'T DO IT. ONE MORE APOLOGY AND I'LL PUKE.
THAT'S NOT A NORMAL PHYSICAL REACTION.
DID YOU COME HERE TODAY TO APOLOGIZE?

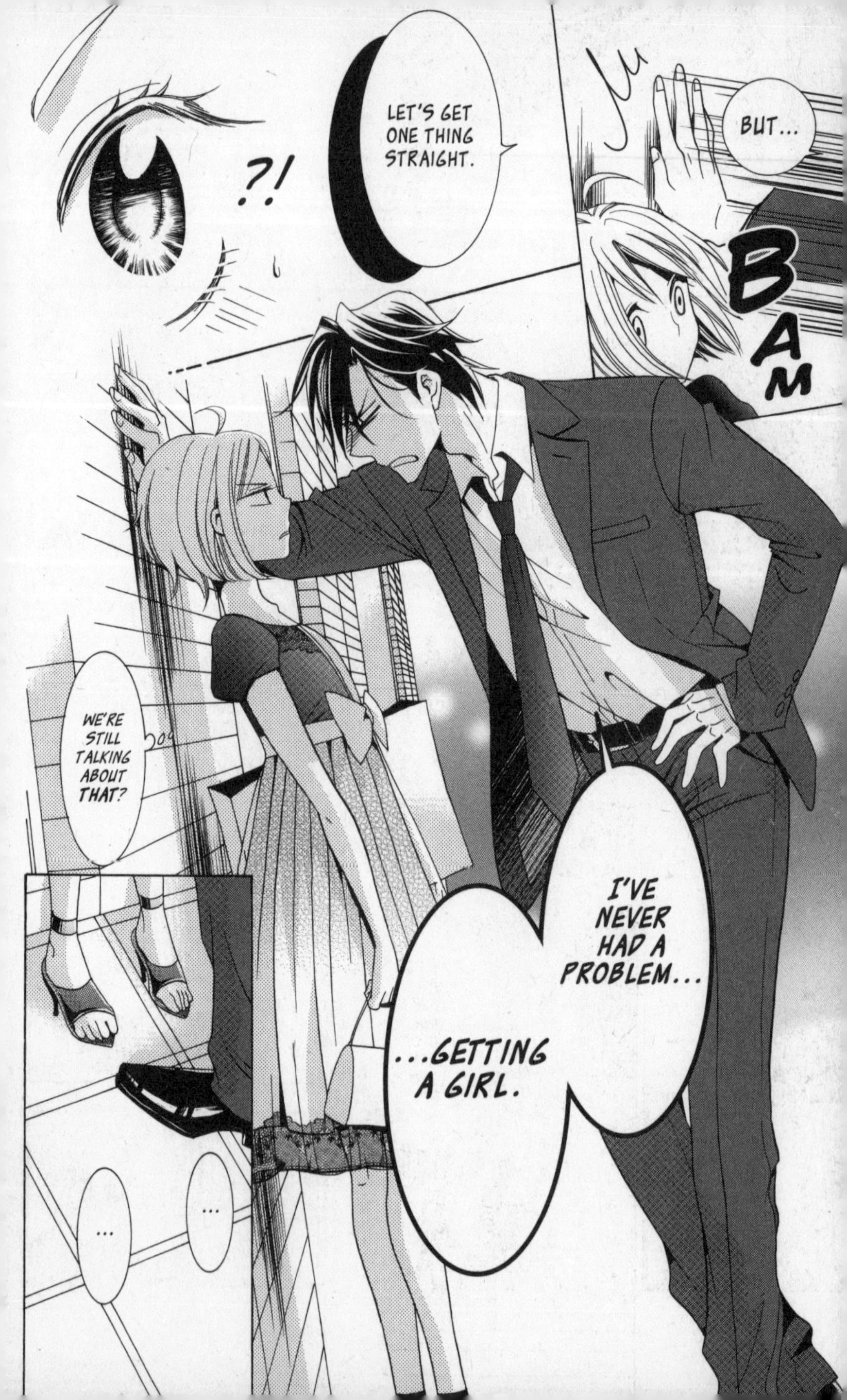
BUT...
BAM
LET'S GET ONE THING STRAIGHT.
?!
I'VE NEVER HAD A PROBLEM...
...GETTING A GIRL.
WE'RE STILL TALKING ABOUT THAT?
...
...

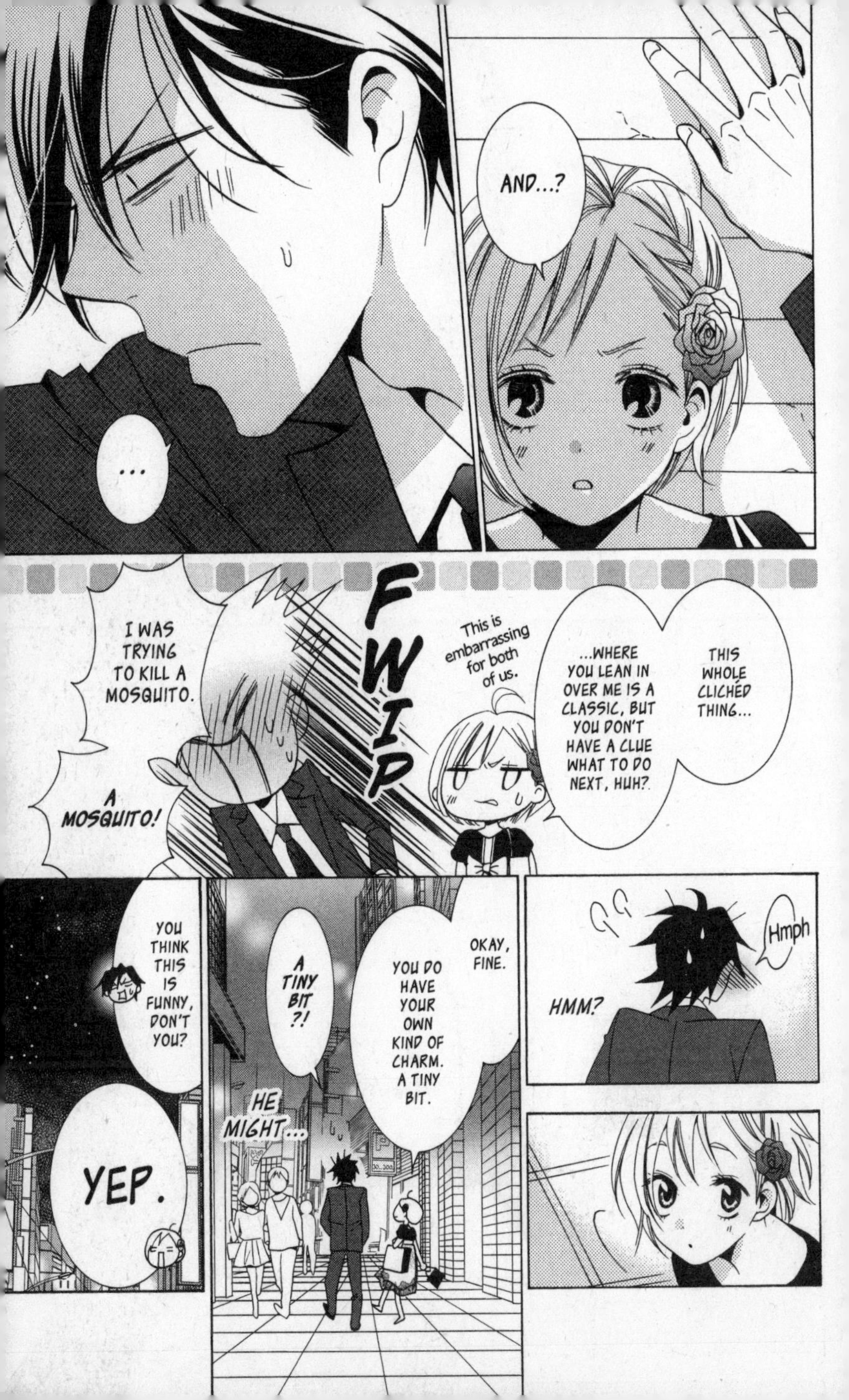
AND...?
...
THIS WHOLE CLICHÉD THING...
...WHERE YOU LEAN IN OVER ME IS A CLASSIC, BUT YOU DON'T HAVE A CLUE WHAT TO DO NEXT, HUH?
This is embarrassing for both of us.
FWIP
I WAS TRYING TO KILL A MOSQUITO.
A MOSQUITO!
Hmph
HMM?
OKAY, FINE.
YOU DO HAVE YOUR OWN KIND OF CHARM. A TINY BIT.
A TINY BIT?!
HE MIGHT...
YOU THINK THIS IS FUNNY, DON'T YOU?
YEP.

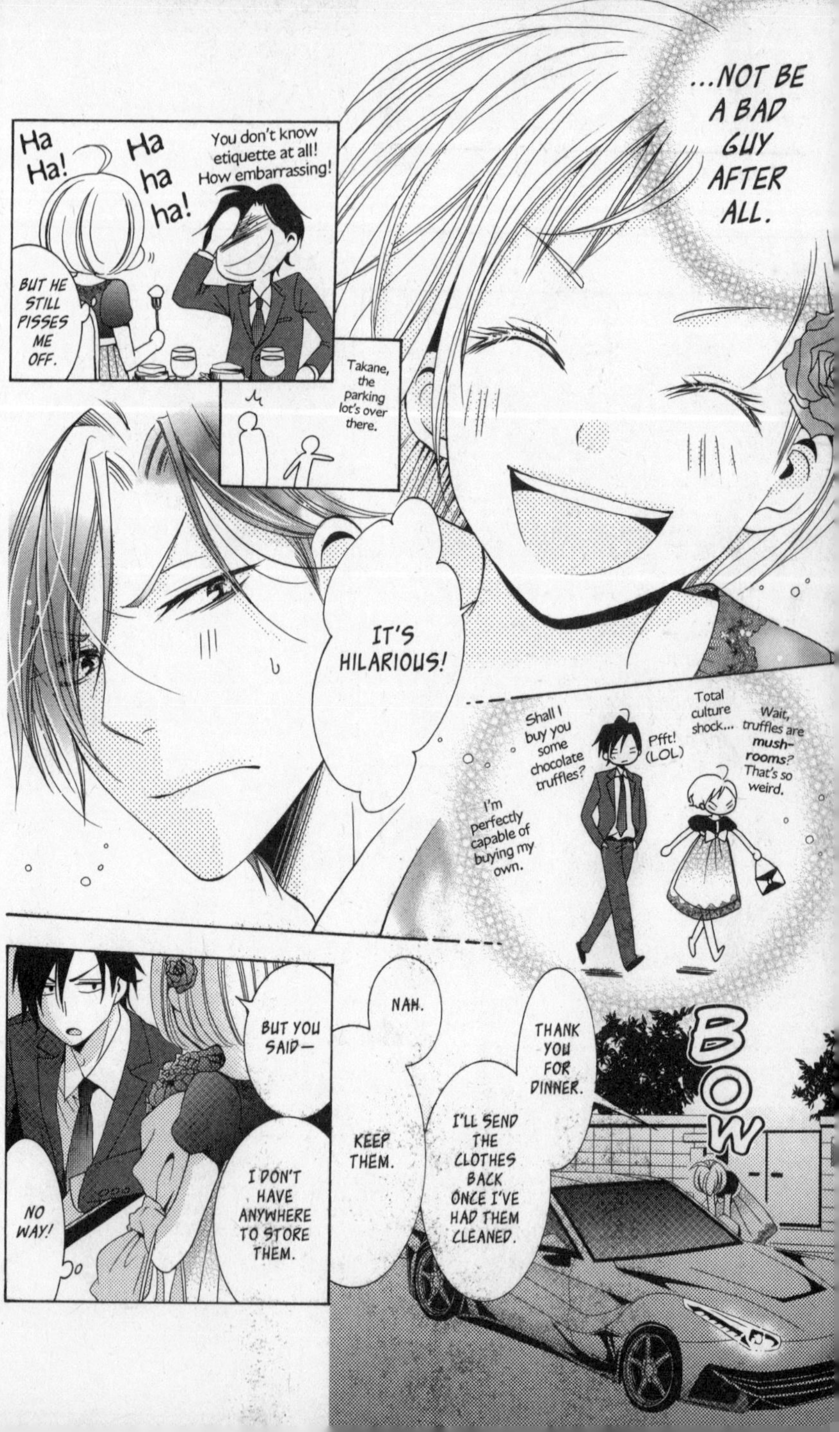
...NOT BE A BAD GUY AFTER ALL.
You don't know etiquette at all! How embarrassing!
Ha ha ha!
Ha Ha!
BUT HE STILL PISSES ME OFF.
Takane, the parking lot's over there.
IT'S HILARIOUS!
Wait, truffles are **mushrooms**? That's so weird.
Total culture shock...
Pfft! (LOL)
Shall I buy you some chocolate truffles?
I'm perfectly capable of buying my own.
BOW
THANK YOU FOR DINNER.
I'LL SEND THE CLOTHES BACK ONCE I'VE HAD THEM CLEANED.
NAH.
KEEP THEM.
BUT YOU SAID—
I DON'T HAVE ANYWHERE TO STORE THEM.
NO WAY!

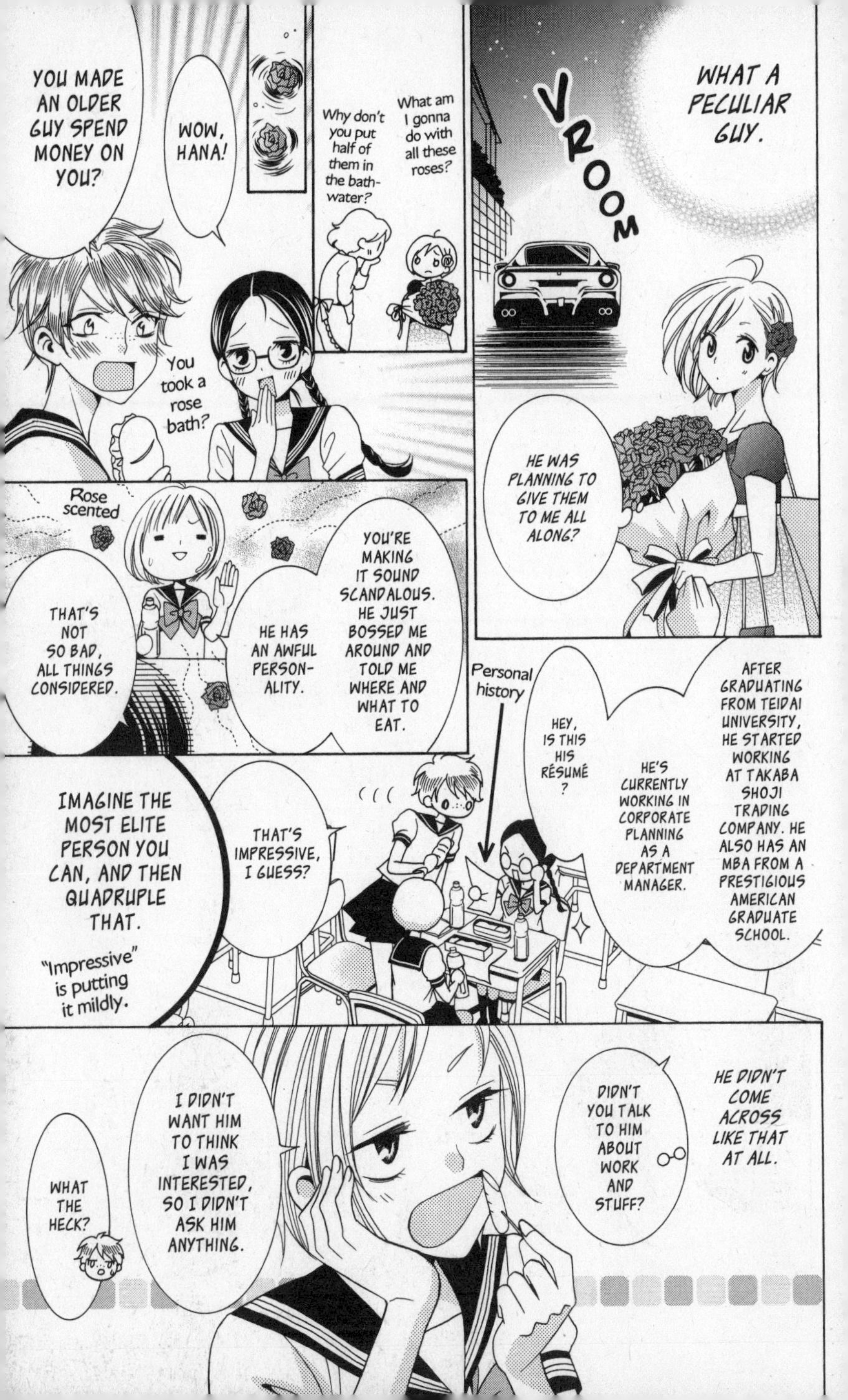
WHAT A PECULIAR GUY.
VROOM
HE WAS PLANNING TO GIVE THEM TO ME ALL ALONG?
What am I gonna do with all these roses?
Why don't you put half of them in the bath-water?
WOW, HANA!
YOU MADE AN OLDER GUY SPEND MONEY ON YOU?
You took a rose bath?
YOU'RE MAKING IT SOUND SCANDALOUS. HE JUST BOSSED ME AROUND AND TOLD ME WHERE AND WHAT TO EAT.
HE HAS AN AWFUL PERSON-ALITY.
Rose scented
THAT'S NOT SO BAD, ALL THINGS CONSIDERED.
AFTER GRADUATING FROM TEIDAI UNIVERSITY, HE STARTED WORKING AT TAKABA SHOJI TRADING COMPANY. HE ALSO HAS AN MBA FROM A PRESTIGIOUS AMERICAN GRADUATE SCHOOL.
HE'S CURRENTLY WORKING IN CORPORATE PLANNING AS A DEPARTMENT MANAGER.
HEY, IS THIS HIS RÉSUMÉ?
Personal history
THAT'S IMPRESSIVE, I GUESS?
IMAGINE THE MOST ELITE PERSON YOU CAN, AND THEN QUADRUPLE THAT.
"Impressive" is putting it mildly.
HE DIDN'T COME ACROSS LIKE THAT AT ALL.
DIDN'T YOU TALK TO HIM ABOUT WORK AND STUFF?
I DIDN'T WANT HIM TO THINK I WAS INTERESTED, SO I DIDN'T ASK HIM ANYTHING.
WHAT THE HECK?

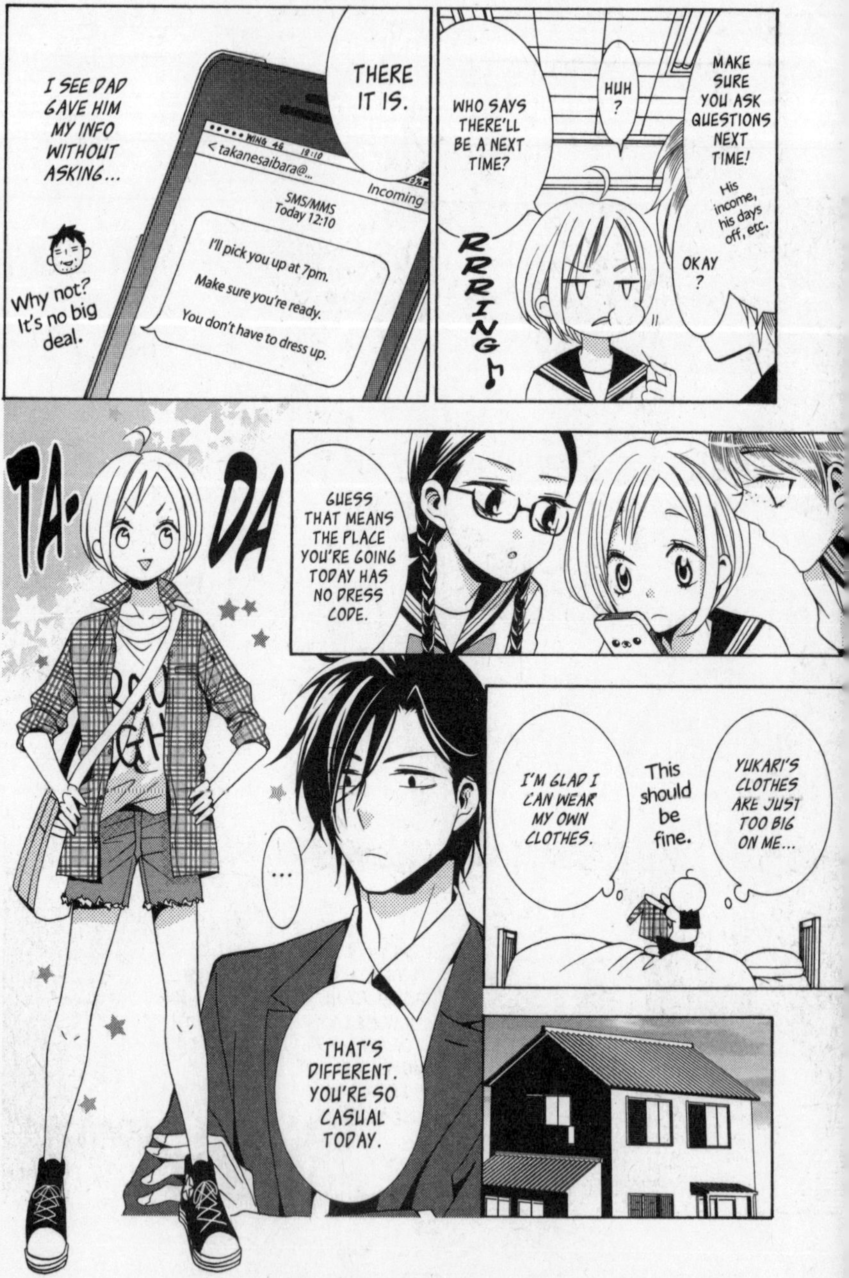
MAKE SURE YOU ASK QUESTIONS NEXT TIME!
His income, his days off, etc.
OKAY?
HUH?
WHO SAYS THERE'LL BE A NEXT TIME?
RRRING♪
THERE IT IS.
WING 4G 12:10
< takanesaibara@...
Incoming
SMS/MMS
Today 12:10
I'll pick you up at 7pm.
Make sure you're ready.
You don't have to dress up.
I SEE DAD GAVE HIM MY INFO WITHOUT ASKING...
Why not? It's no big deal.
GUESS THAT MEANS THE PLACE YOU'RE GOING TODAY HAS NO DRESS CODE.
YUKARI'S CLOTHES ARE JUST TOO BIG ON ME...
This should be fine.
I'M GLAD I CAN WEAR MY OWN CLOTHES.
TA-DA
...
THAT'S DIFFERENT. YOU'RE SO CASUAL TODAY.

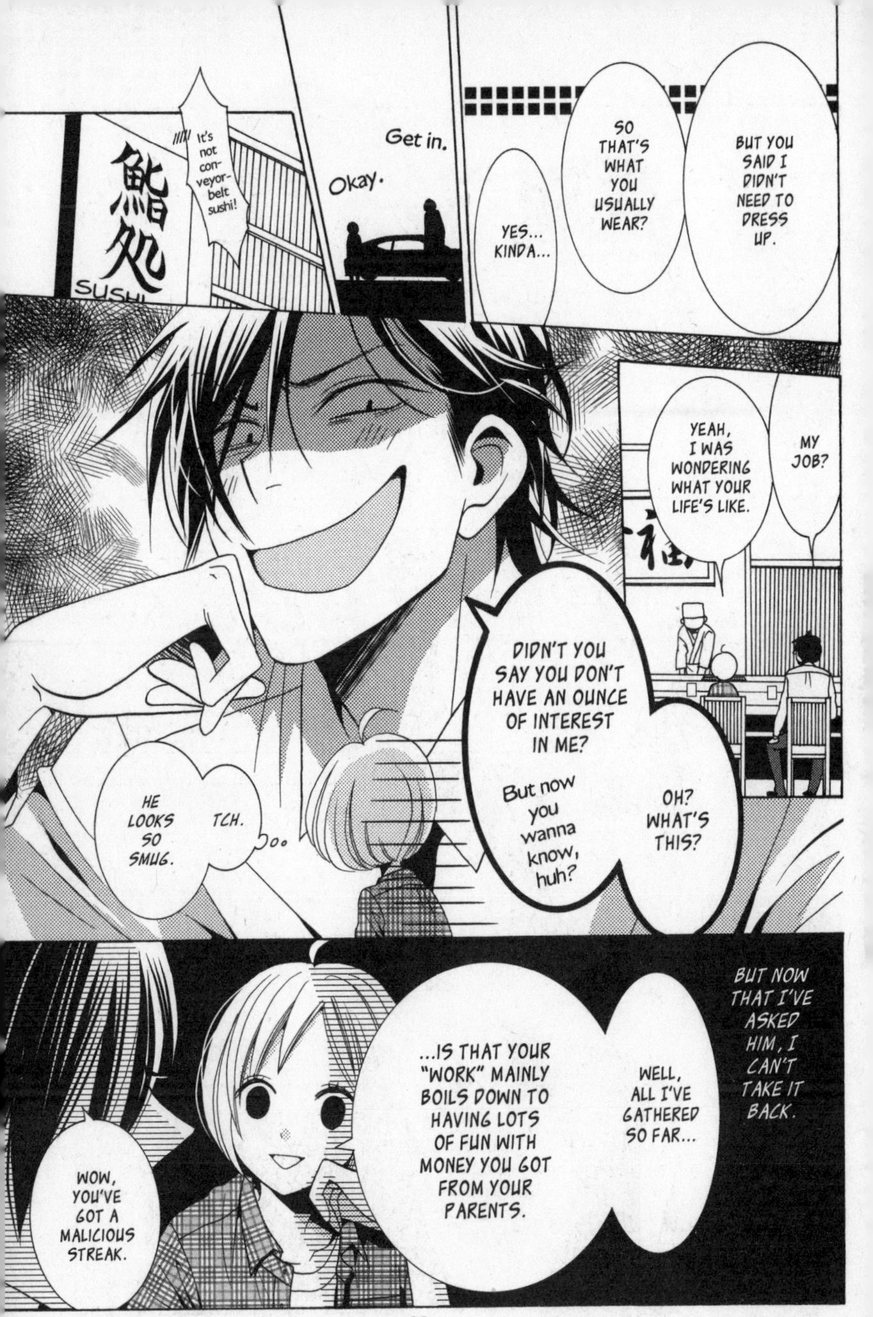
BUT YOU SAID I DIDN'T NEED TO DRESS UP.
SO THAT'S WHAT YOU USUALLY WEAR?
YES... KINDA...
Get in.
Okay.
It's not conveyor-belt sushi!
SUSHI
MY JOB?
YEAH, I WAS WONDERING WHAT YOUR LIFE'S LIKE.
OH? WHAT'S THIS?
DIDN'T YOU SAY YOU DON'T HAVE AN OUNCE OF INTEREST IN ME?
But now you wanna know, huh?
TCH.
HE LOOKS SO SMUG.
BUT NOW THAT I'VE ASKED HIM, I CAN'T TAKE IT BACK.
WELL, ALL I'VE GATHERED SO FAR...
...IS THAT YOUR "WORK" MAINLY BOILS DOWN TO HAVING LOTS OF FUN WITH MONEY YOU GOT FROM YOUR PARENTS.
WOW, YOU'VE GOT A MALICIOUS STREAK.

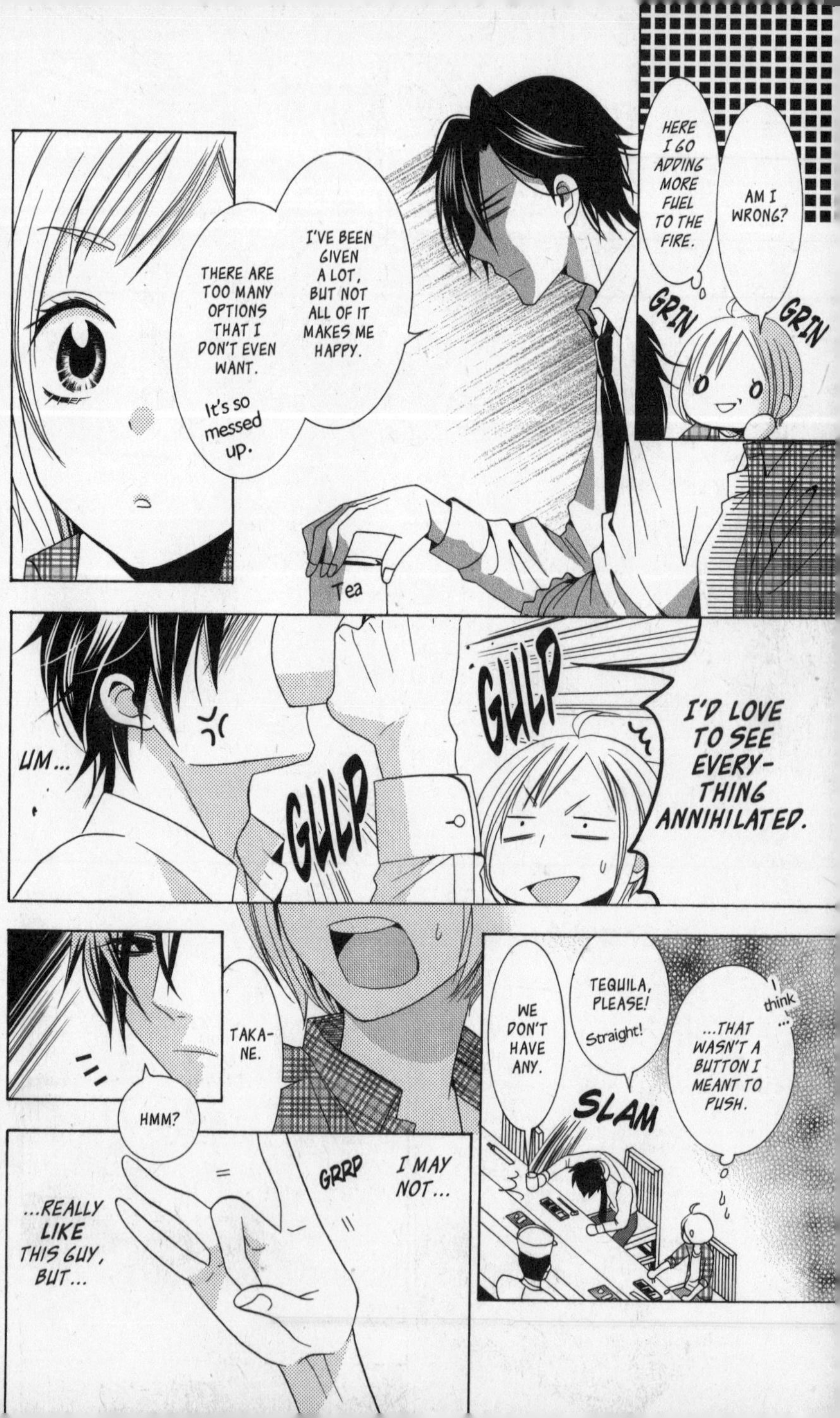
AM I WRONG?
HERE I GO ADDING MORE FUEL TO THE FIRE.
GRIN
GRIN
I'VE BEEN GIVEN A LOT, BUT NOT ALL OF IT MAKES ME HAPPY.
THERE ARE TOO MANY OPTIONS THAT I DON'T EVEN WANT.
It's so messed up.
Tea
I'D LOVE TO SEE EVERY-THING ANNIHILATED.
GULP
GULP
UM...
I think...
...THAT WASN'T A BUTTON I MEANT TO PUSH.
TEQUILA, PLEASE!
Straight!
WE DON'T HAVE ANY.
SLAM
TAKA-NE.
HMM?
I MAY NOT...
GRRP
...REALLY LIKE THIS GUY, BUT...

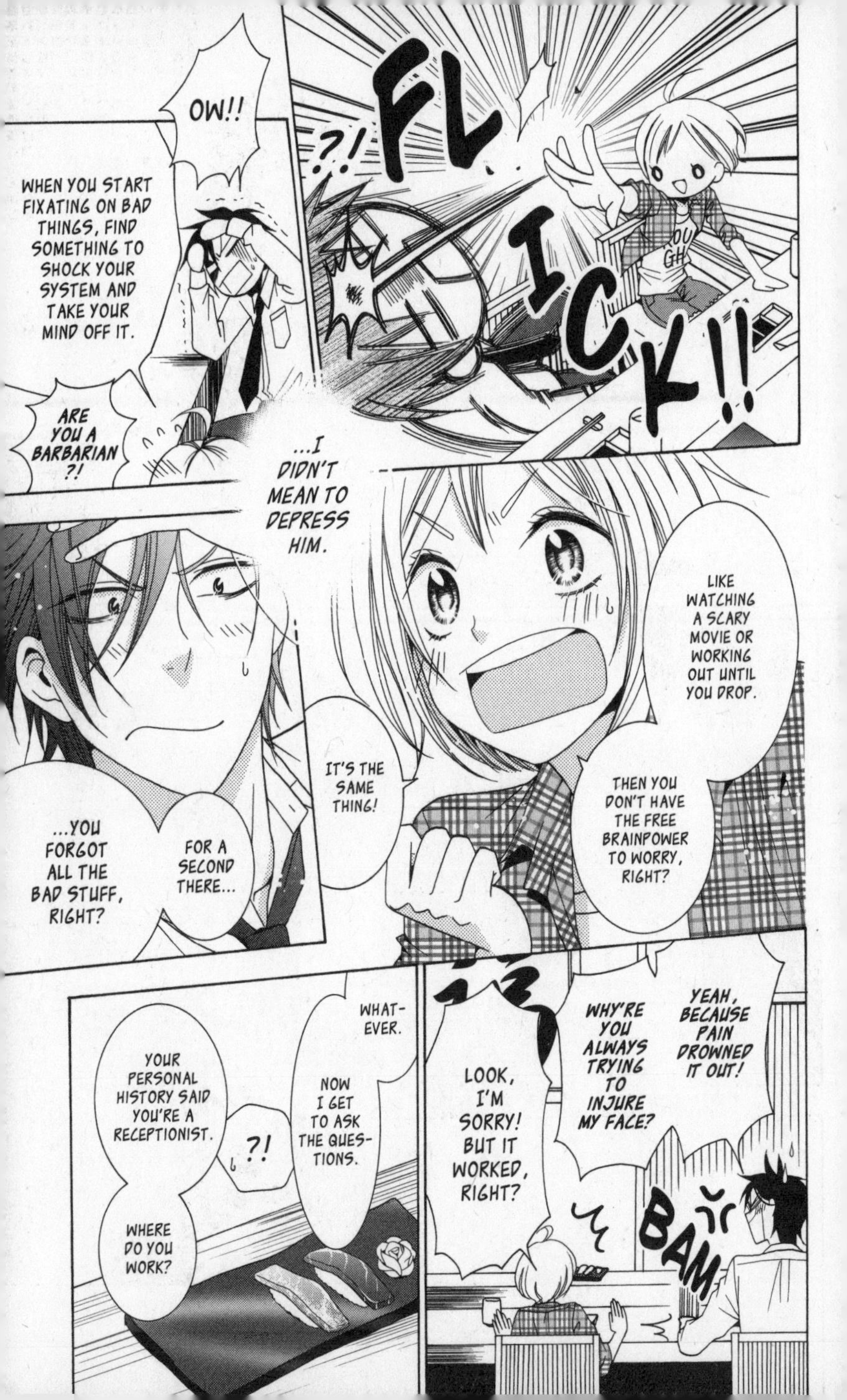

FLICK!!
?!
OW!!
WHEN YOU START FIXATING ON BAD THINGS, FIND SOMETHING TO SHOCK YOUR SYSTEM AND TAKE YOUR MIND OFF IT.
ARE YOU A BARBARIAN ?!
LIKE WATCHING A SCARY MOVIE OR WORKING OUT UNTIL YOU DROP.
THEN YOU DON'T HAVE THE FREE BRAINPOWER TO WORRY, RIGHT?
...I DIDN'T MEAN TO DEPRESS HIM.
IT'S THE SAME THING!
FOR A SECOND THERE...
...YOU FORGOT ALL THE BAD STUFF, RIGHT?
YEAH, BECAUSE PAIN DROWNED IT OUT!
WHY'RE YOU ALWAYS TRYING TO INJURE MY FACE?
LOOK, I'M SORRY! BUT IT WORKED, RIGHT?
BAM
WHAT-EVER.
NOW I GET TO ASK THE QUES-TIONS.
YOUR PERSONAL HISTORY SAID YOU'RE A RECEPTIONIST.
?!
WHERE DO YOU WORK?

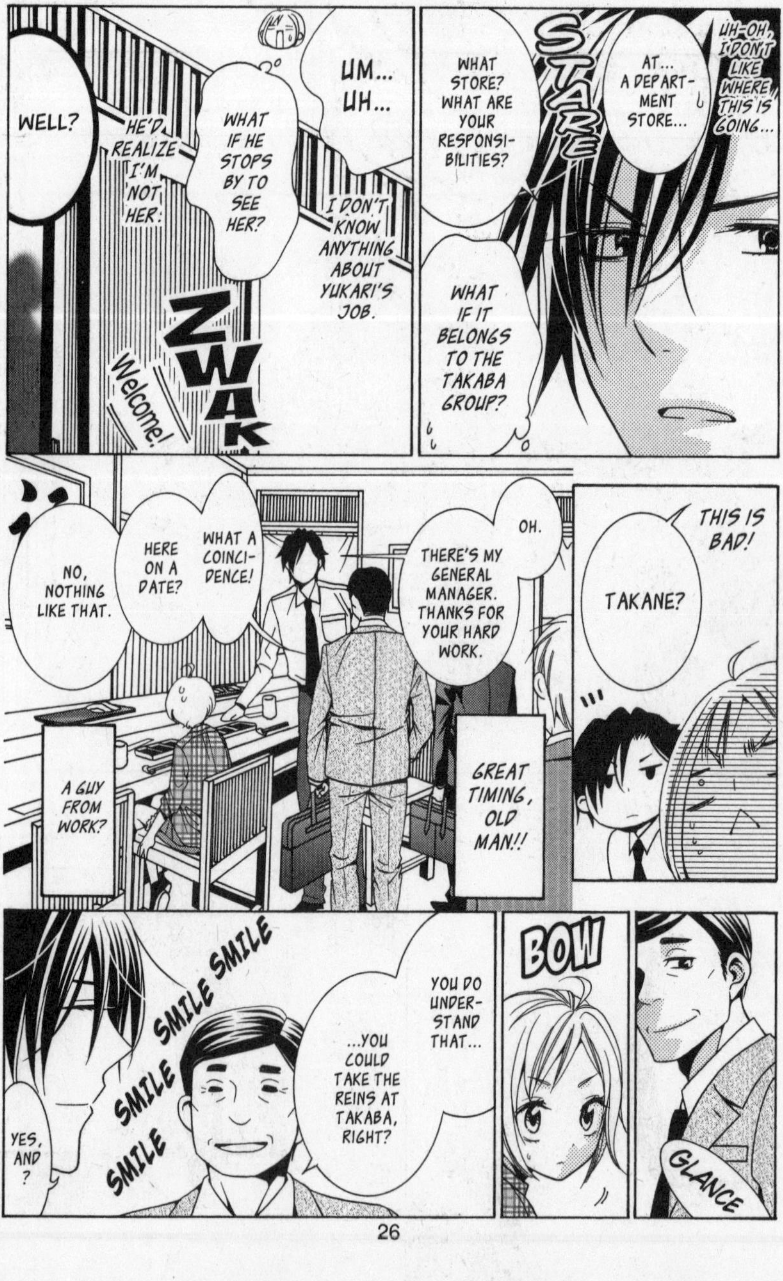
UH-OH, I DON'T LIKE WHERE THIS IS GOING...
STARE
AT... A DEPARTMENT STORE...
WHAT STORE? WHAT ARE YOUR RESPONSIBILITIES?
WHAT IF IT BELONGS TO THE TAKABA GROUP?
UM... UH...
I DON'T KNOW ANYTHING ABOUT YUKARI'S JOB.
WHAT IF HE STOPS BY TO SEE HER?
HE'D REALIZE I'M NOT HER.
WELL?
ZWAK
Welcome!
THIS IS BAD!
TAKANE?
OH.
THERE'S MY GENERAL MANAGER. THANKS FOR YOUR HARD WORK.
GREAT TIMING, OLD MAN!!
WHAT A COINCIDENCE!
HERE ON A DATE?
NO, NOTHING LIKE THAT.
A GUY FROM WORK?
BOW
GLANCE
YOU DO UNDERSTAND THAT...
...YOU COULD TAKE THE REINS AT TAKABA, RIGHT?
SMILE SMILE
SMILE
SMILE
SMILE
YES, AND ?

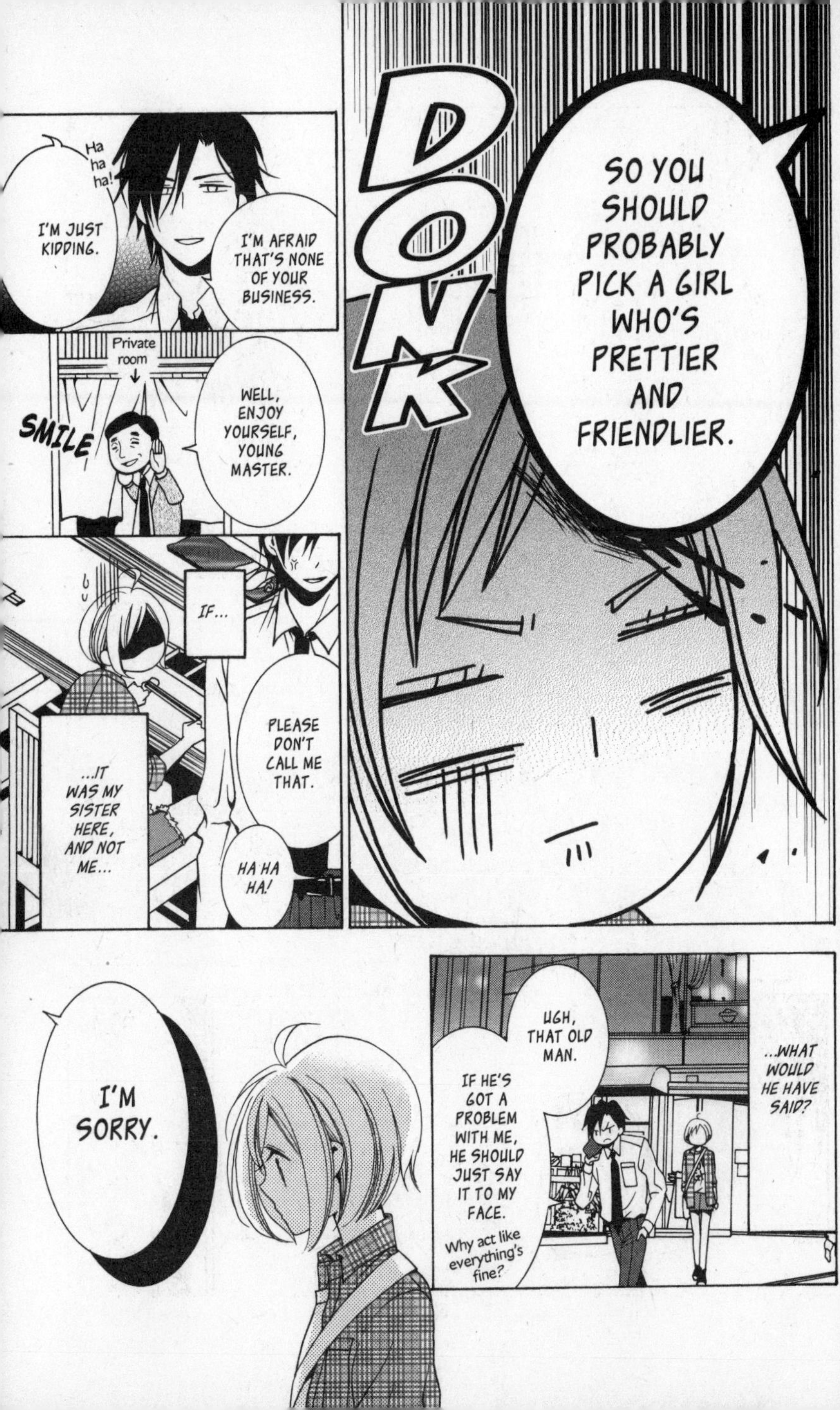
DONK
SO YOU SHOULD PROBABLY PICK A GIRL WHO'S PRETTIER AND FRIENDLIER.
I'M AFRAID THAT'S NONE OF YOUR BUSINESS.
Ha ha ha!
I'M JUST KIDDING.
Private room
WELL, ENJOY YOURSELF, YOUNG MASTER.
SMILE
IF...
PLEASE DON'T CALL ME THAT.
HA HA HA!
...IT WAS MY SISTER HERE, AND NOT ME...
...WHAT WOULD HE HAVE SAID?
UGH, THAT OLD MAN.
IF HE'S GOT A PROBLEM WITH ME, HE SHOULD JUST SAY IT TO MY FACE.
Why act like everything's fine?
I'M SORRY.

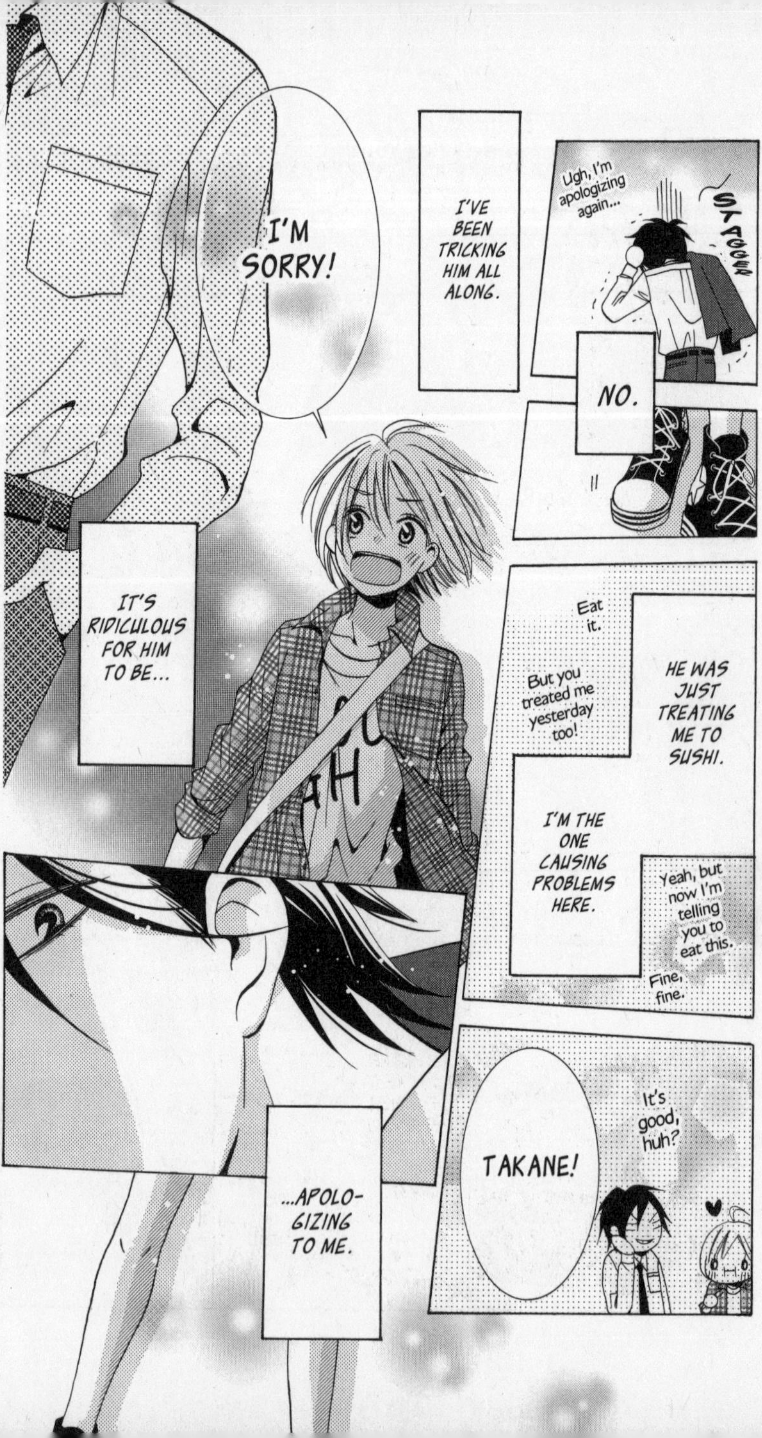

Ugh, I'm apologizing again...
STAGGER
I'VE BEEN TRICKING HIM ALL ALONG.
NO.
HE WAS JUST TREATING ME TO SUSHI.
Eat it.
But you treated me yesterday too!
I'M THE ONE CAUSING PROBLEMS HERE.
Yeah, but now I'm telling you to eat this.
Fine, fine.
It's good, huh?
TAKANE!
I'M SORRY!
IT'S RIDICULOUS FOR HIM TO BE...
...APOLOGIZING TO ME.

FOR WHAT?
OOPS, THAT APOLOGY JUST SLIPPED OUT.
I-IT'S JUST...
...IF I WERE PRETTIER OR FRIENDLIER, LIKE HE SAID...
...HE WOULDN'T HAVE BEEN ABLE TO EMBARRASS YOU LIKE THAT.
AH HA HA HA...
...
SAYING THAT ABOUT MYSELF JUST MAKES ME FEEL PATHETIC.
Has a reputation as "the receptionist too beautiful for words"
IF YUKARI HAD BEEN THE ONE HERE...
...SHE WOULD'VE JUST KEPT SMILING AND BOWING POLITELY, NO MATTER WHAT.
I'M SURPRISED SOMETHING LIKE THAT BOTHERED YOU.
Someone commenting on your looks, I mean.
HEY, I'M STILL A WOMAN!
IS THAT SO WRONG?

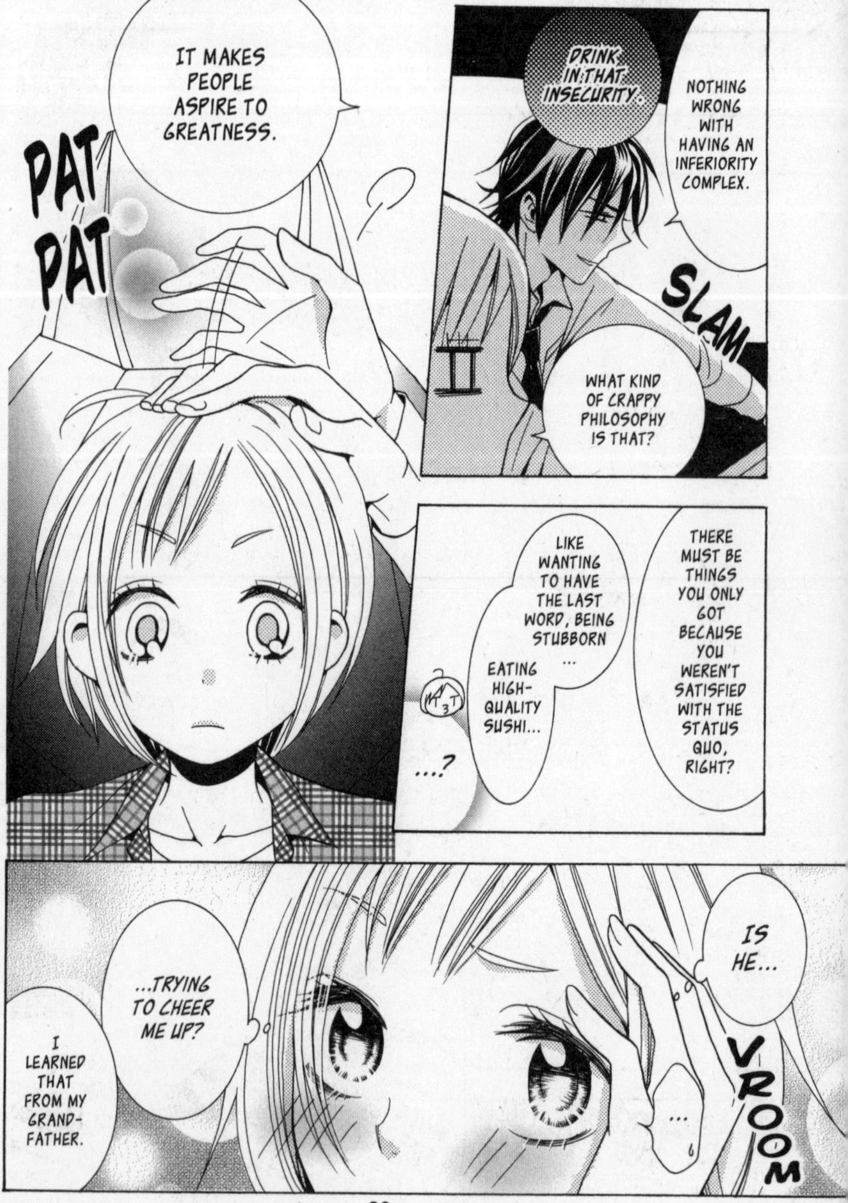
NOTHING WRONG WITH HAVING AN INFERIORITY COMPLEX.
DRINK IN THAT INSECURITY.
SLAM
WHAT KIND OF CRAPPY PHILOSOPHY IS THAT?
THERE MUST BE THINGS YOU ONLY GOT BECAUSE YOU WEREN'T SATISFIED WITH THE STATUS QUO, RIGHT?
LIKE WANTING TO HAVE THE LAST WORD, BEING STUBBORN ...
EATING HIGH-QUALITY SUSHI...
...?
IT MAKES PEOPLE ASPIRE TO GREATNESS.
PAT PAT
?
IS HE...
VROOM
...
...TRYING TO CHEER ME UP?
I LEARNED THAT FROM MY GRANDFATHER.

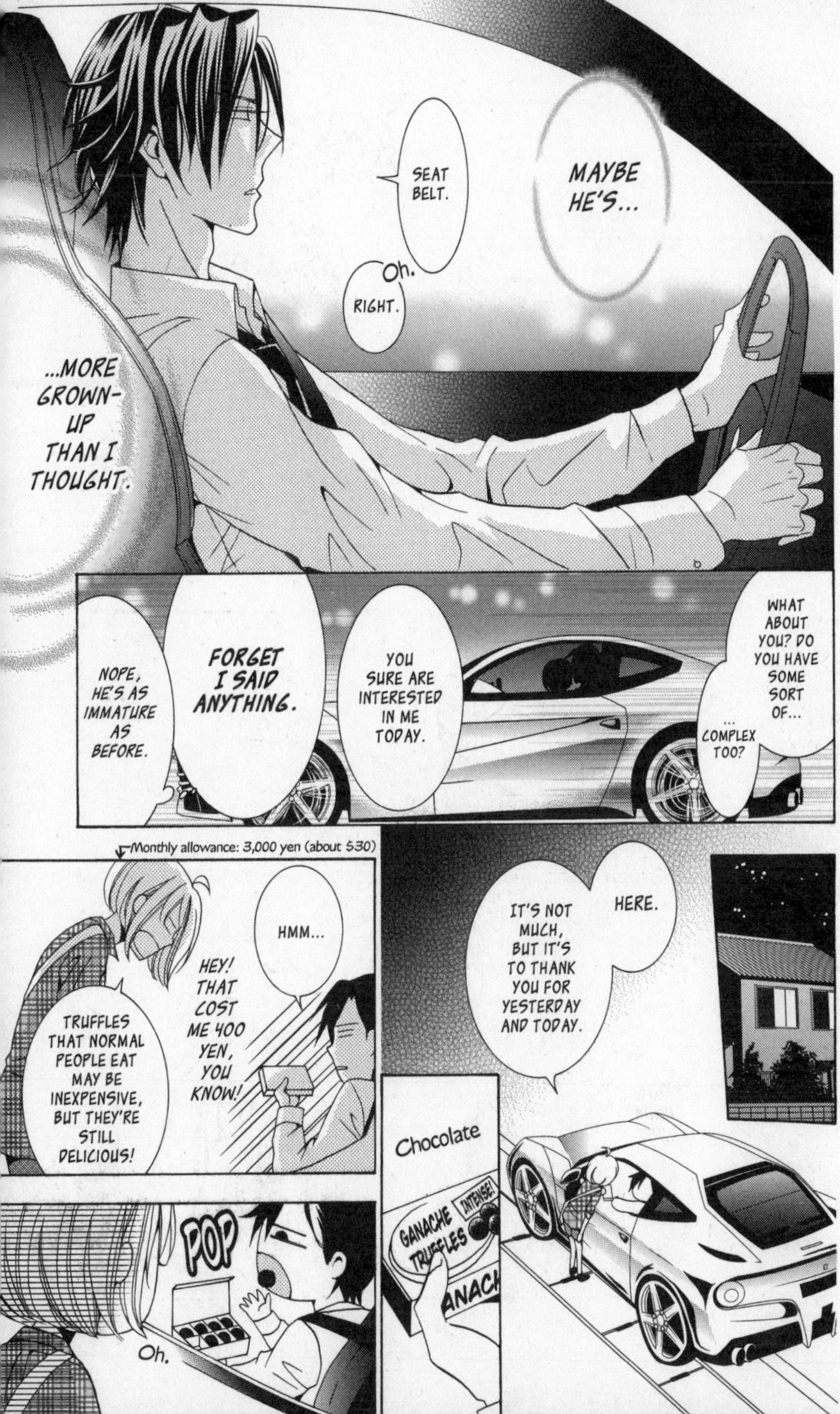
MAYBE HE'S...
SEAT BELT.
Oh.
RIGHT.
...MORE GROWN-UP THAN I THOUGHT.
WHAT ABOUT YOU? DO YOU HAVE SOME SORT OF...
...COMPLEX TOO?
YOU SURE ARE INTERESTED IN ME TODAY.
FORGET I SAID ANYTHING.
NOPE, HE'S AS IMMATURE AS BEFORE.
HERE.
IT'S NOT MUCH, BUT IT'S TO THANK YOU FOR YESTERDAY AND TODAY.
Chocolate
GANACHE TRUFFLES
INTENSE!
ANACH
Monthly allowance: 3,000 yen (about $30)
HMM...
HEY! THAT COST ME 400 YEN, YOU KNOW!
TRUFFLES THAT NORMAL PEOPLE EAT MAY BE INEXPENSIVE, BUT THEY'RE STILL DELICIOUS!
POP
Oh.

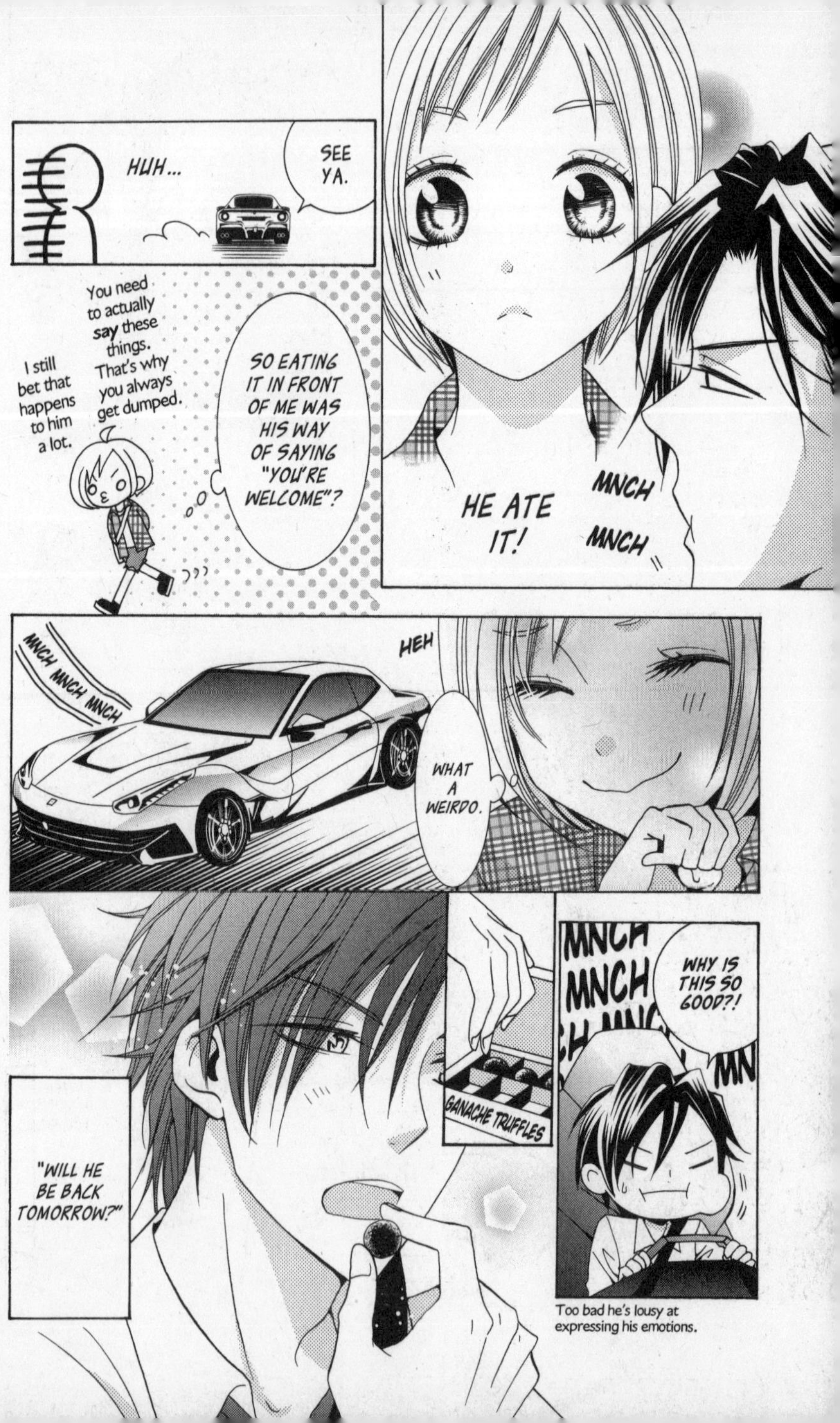
HE ATE IT!
MNCH MNCH
SEE YA.
HUH...
SO EATING IT IN FRONT OF ME WAS HIS WAY OF SAYING "YOU'RE WELCOME"?
You need to actually **say** these things. That's why you always get dumped.
I still bet that happens to him a lot.
HEH
WHAT A WEIRDO.
MNCH MNCH MNCH
MNCH MNCH
WHY IS THIS SO GOOD?!
Too bad he's lousy at expressing his emotions.
GANACHE TRUFFLES
"WILL HE BE BACK TOMORROW?"

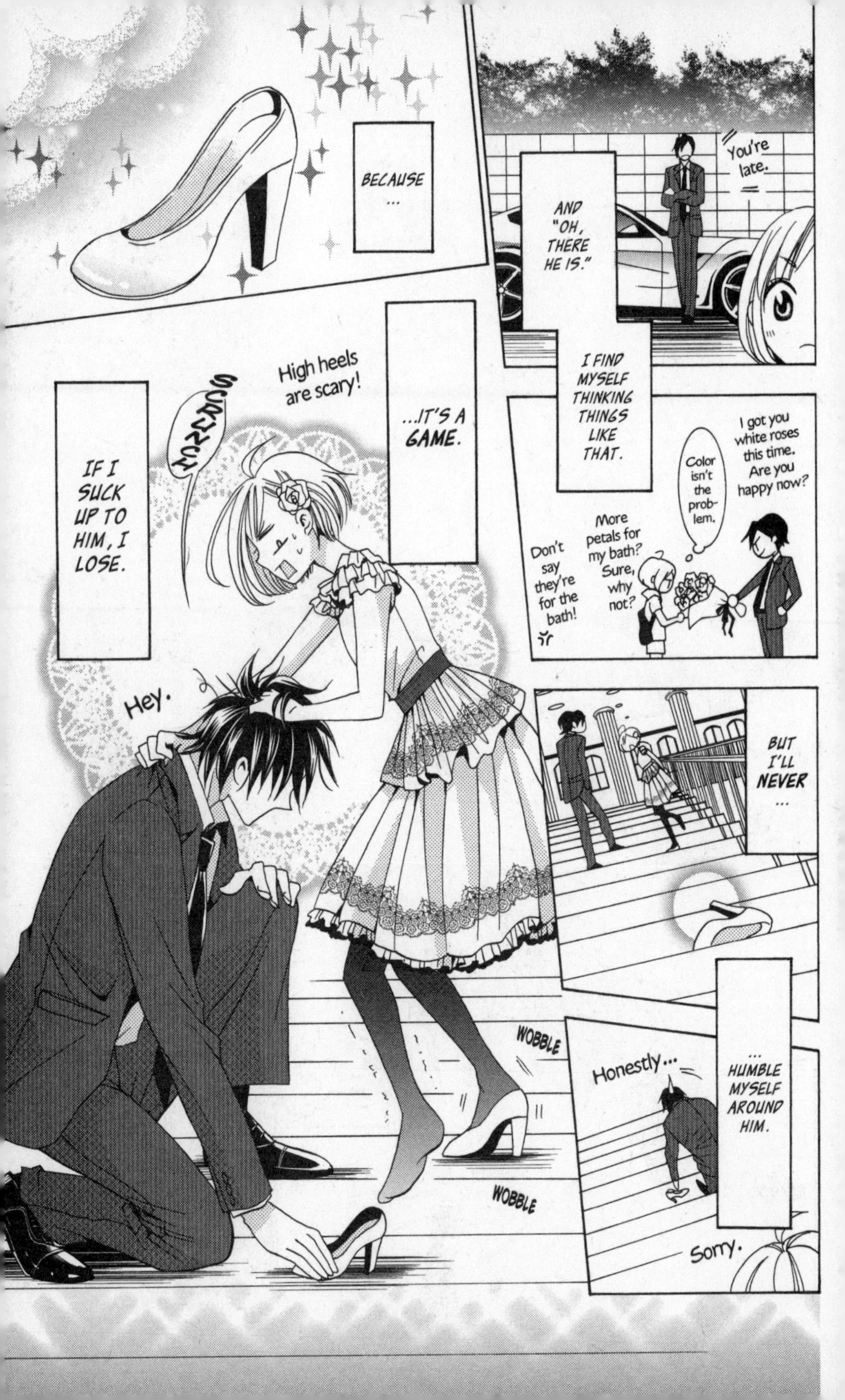
You're late.
AND "OH, THERE HE IS."
BECAUSE ...
I FIND MYSELF THINKING THINGS LIKE THAT.
I got you white roses this time. Are you happy now?
Color isn't the prob-lem.
More petals for my bath? Sure, why not?
Don't say they're for the bath!
BUT I'LL NEVER ...
Honestly...
... HUMBLE MYSELF AROUND HIM.
Sorry.
...IT'S A GAME.
High heels are scary!
SCRUNCH
IF I SUCK UP TO HIM, I LOSE.
Hey.
WOBBLE
WOBBLE

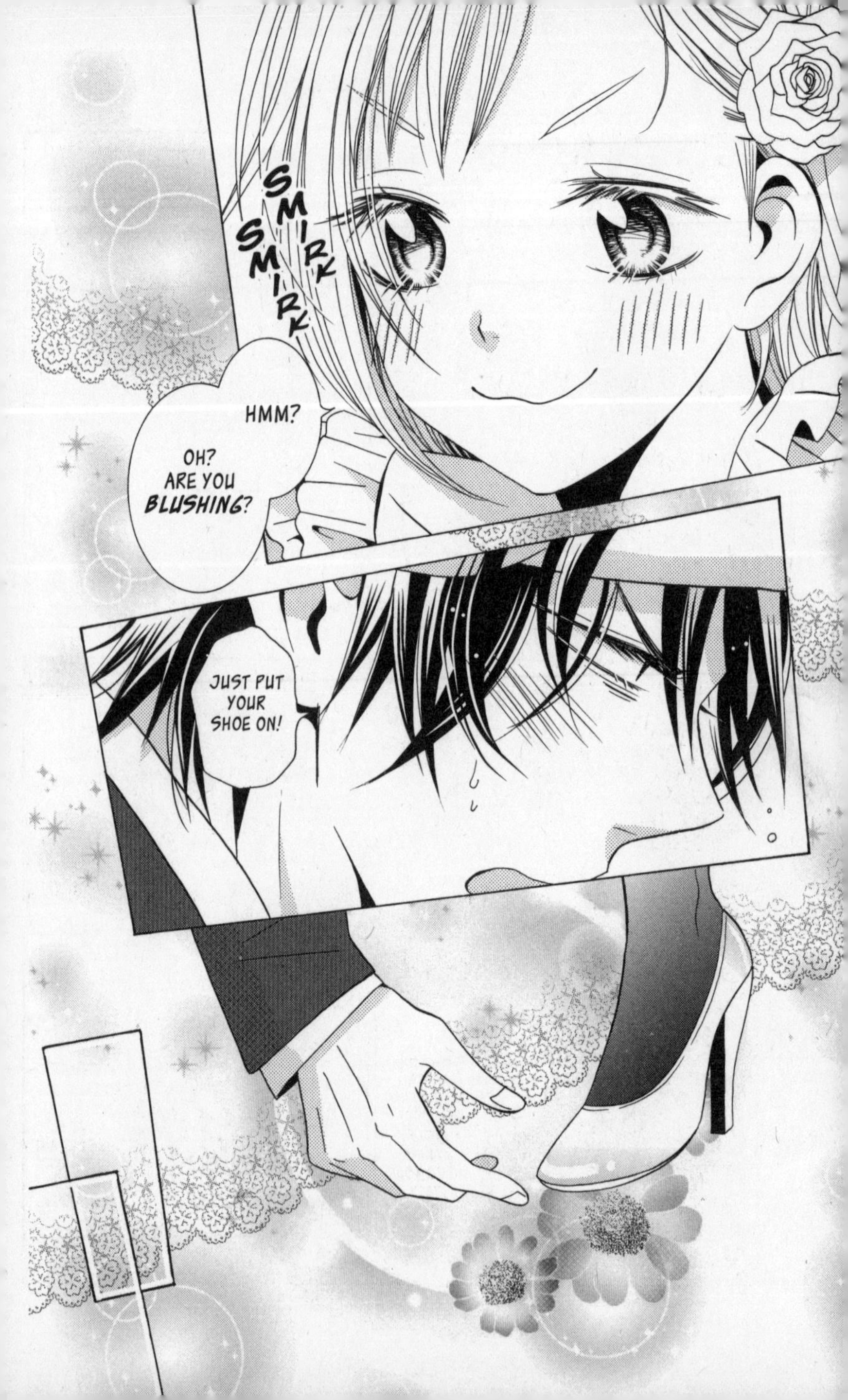
SMIRK SMIRK
HMM?
OH? ARE YOU BLUSHING?
JUST PUT YOUR SHOE ON!

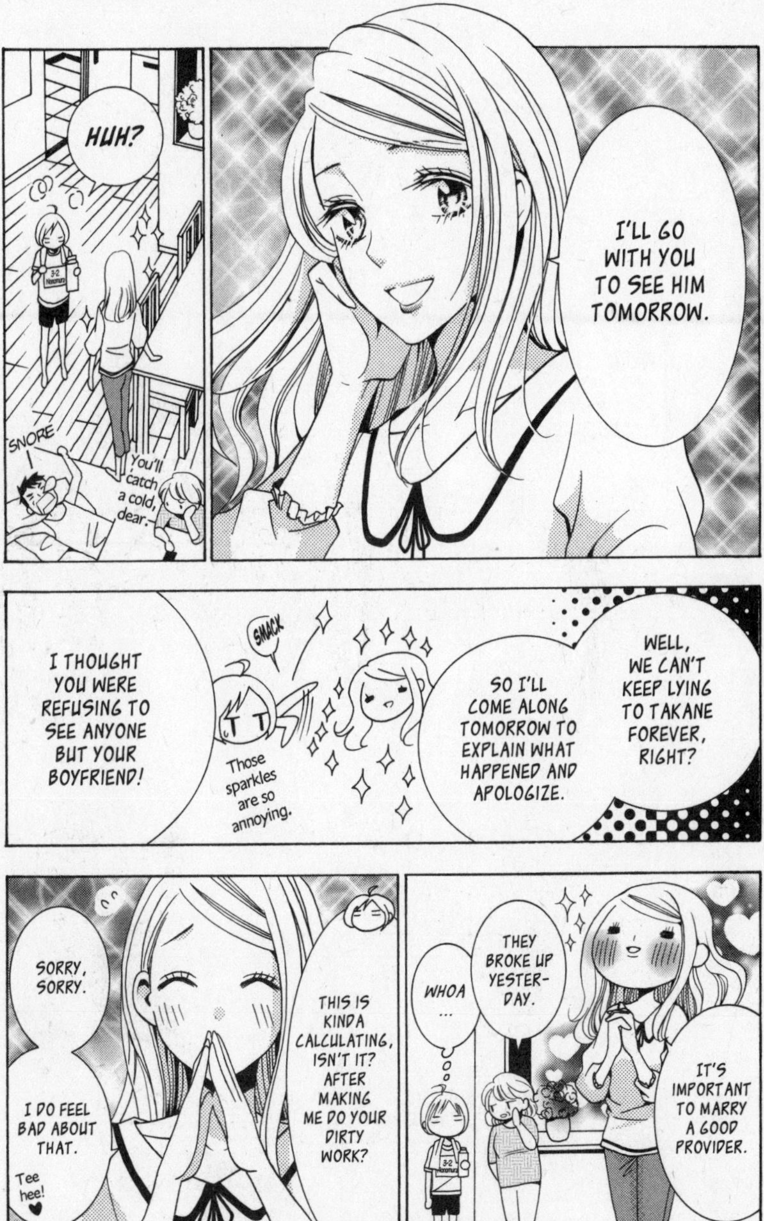
I'LL GO WITH YOU TO SEE HIM TOMORROW.
HUH?
SNORE
You'll catch a cold, dear.
WELL, WE CAN'T KEEP LYING TO TAKANE FOREVER, RIGHT?
SO I'LL COME ALONG TOMORROW TO EXPLAIN WHAT HAPPENED AND APOLOGIZE.
SMACK
Those sparkles are so annoying.
I THOUGHT YOU WERE REFUSING TO SEE ANYONE BUT YOUR BOYFRIEND!
IT'S IMPORTANT TO MARRY A GOOD PROVIDER.
THEY BROKE UP YESTER-DAY.
WHOA...
THIS IS KINDA CALCULATING, ISN'T IT? AFTER MAKING ME DO YOUR DIRTY WORK?
SORRY, SORRY.
I DO FEEL BAD ABOUT THAT.
Tee hee! ♥

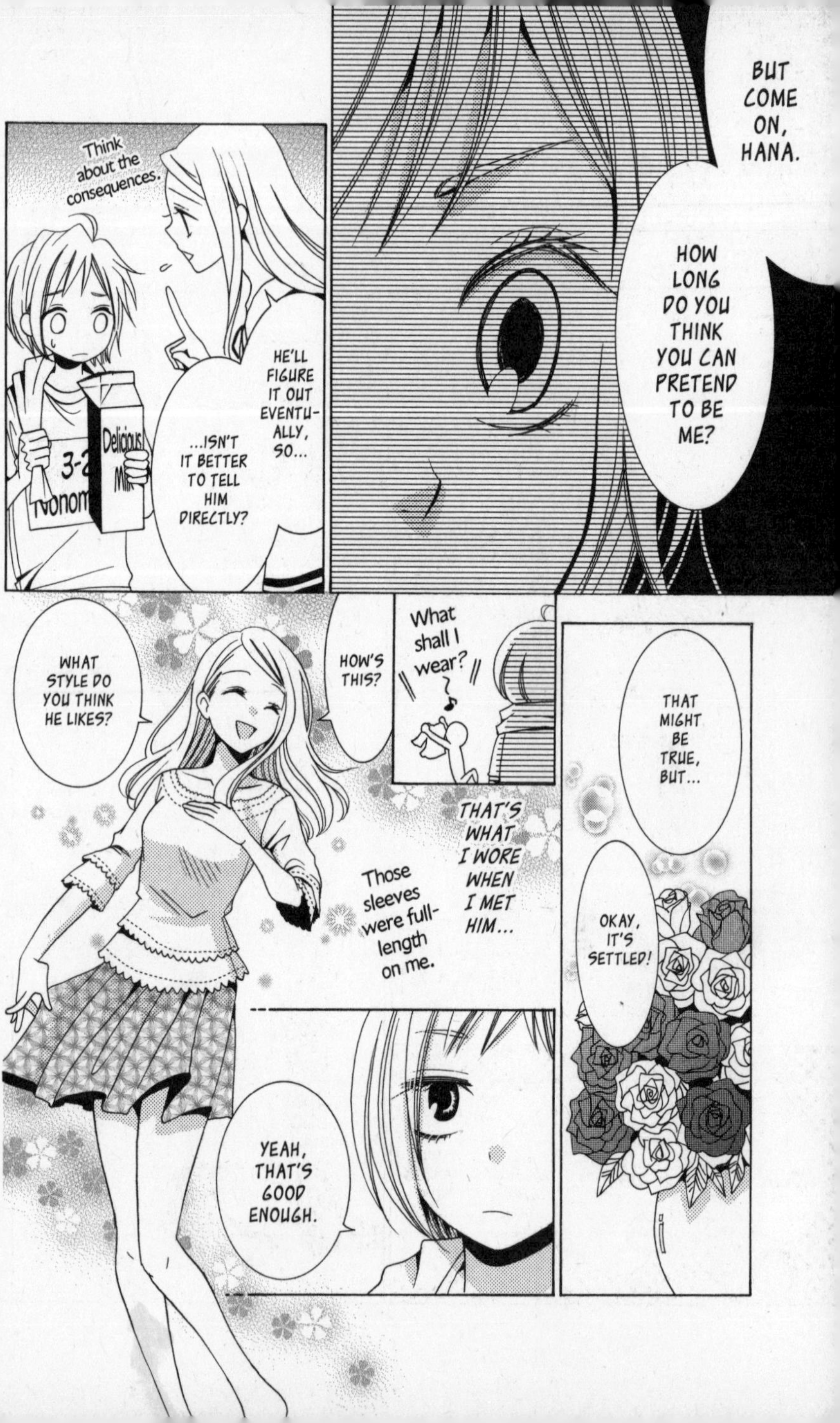
BUT COME ON, HANA.
HOW LONG DO YOU THINK YOU CAN PRETEND TO BE ME?
Think about the consequences.
HE'LL FIGURE IT OUT EVENTUALLY, SO...
...ISN'T IT BETTER TO TELL HIM DIRECTLY?
THAT MIGHT BE TRUE, BUT...
OKAY, IT'S SETTLED!
What shall I wear?
HOW'S THIS?
WHAT STYLE DO YOU THINK HE LIKES?
THAT'S WHAT I WORE WHEN I MET HIM...
Those sleeves were full-length on me.
YEAH, THAT'S GOOD ENOUGH.

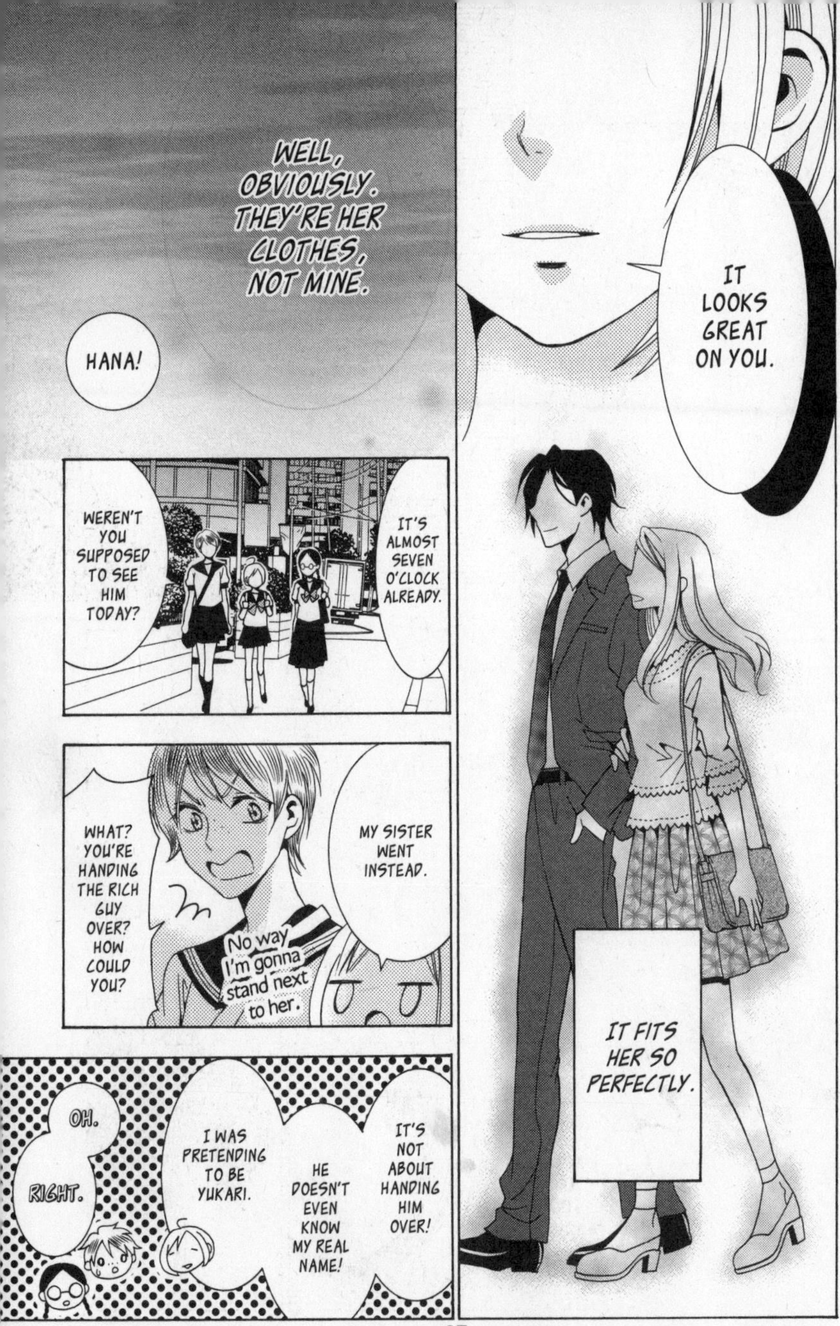
IT LOOKS GREAT ON YOU.
IT FITS HER SO PERFECTLY.
WELL, OBVIOUSLY. THEY'RE HER CLOTHES, NOT MINE.
HANA!
IT'S ALMOST SEVEN O'CLOCK ALREADY.
WEREN'T YOU SUPPOSED TO SEE HIM TODAY?
MY SISTER WENT INSTEAD.
WHAT? YOU'RE HANDING THE RICH GUY OVER? HOW COULD YOU?
No way I'm gonna stand next to her.
IT'S NOT ABOUT HANDING HIM OVER!
HE DOESN'T EVEN KNOW MY REAL NAME!
I WAS PRETENDING TO BE YUKARI.
OH.
RIGHT.

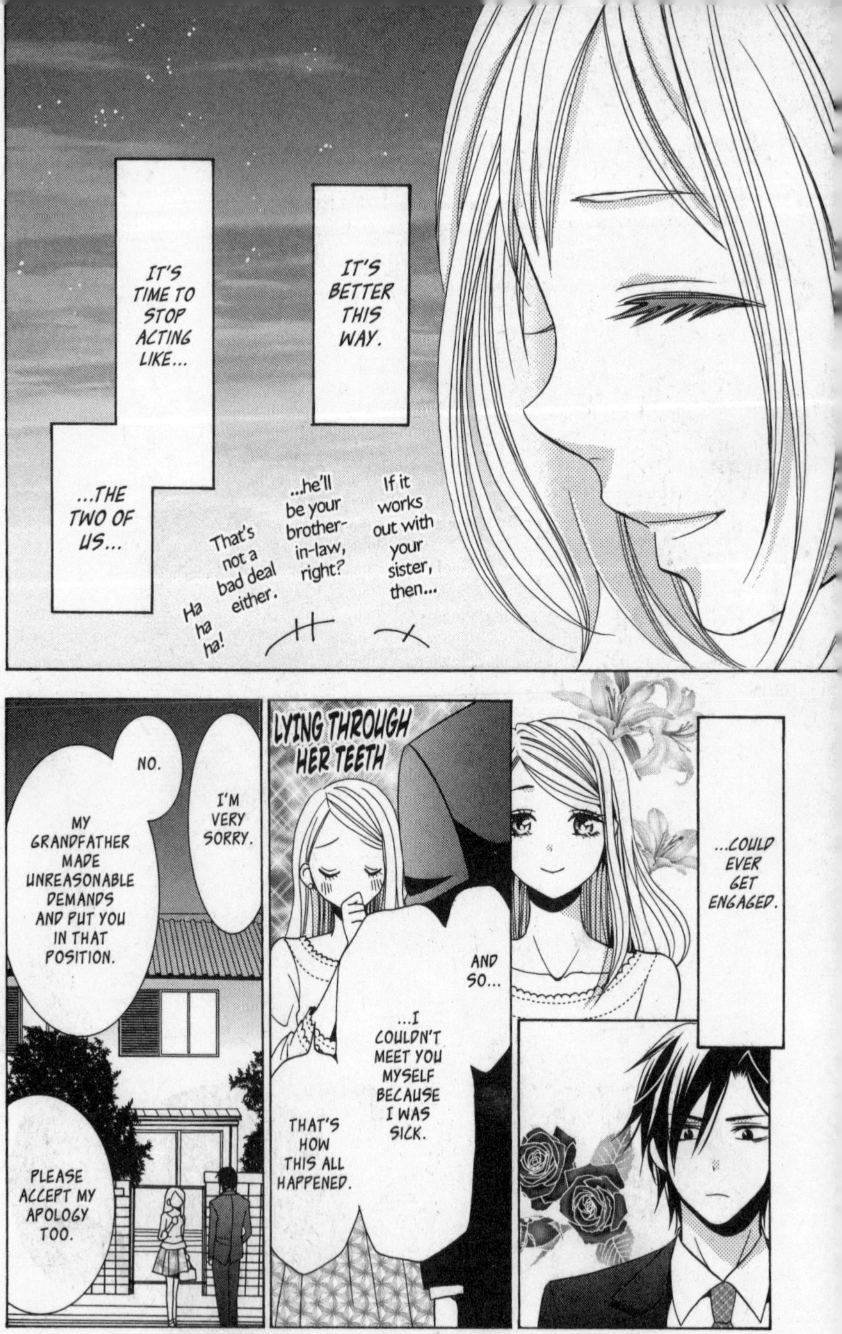
If it works out with your sister, then...
...he'll be your brother-in-law, right?
That's not a bad deal either.
Ha ha ha!
IT'S BETTER THIS WAY.
IT'S TIME TO STOP ACTING LIKE...
...THE TWO OF US...
...COULD EVER GET ENGAGED.
LYING THROUGH HER TEETH
AND SO...
...I COULDN'T MEET YOU MYSELF BECAUSE I WAS SICK.
THAT'S HOW THIS ALL HAPPENED.
NO.
I'M VERY SORRY.
MY GRANDFATHER MADE UNREASONABLE DEMANDS AND PUT YOU IN THAT POSITION.
PLEASE ACCEPT MY APOLOGY TOO.

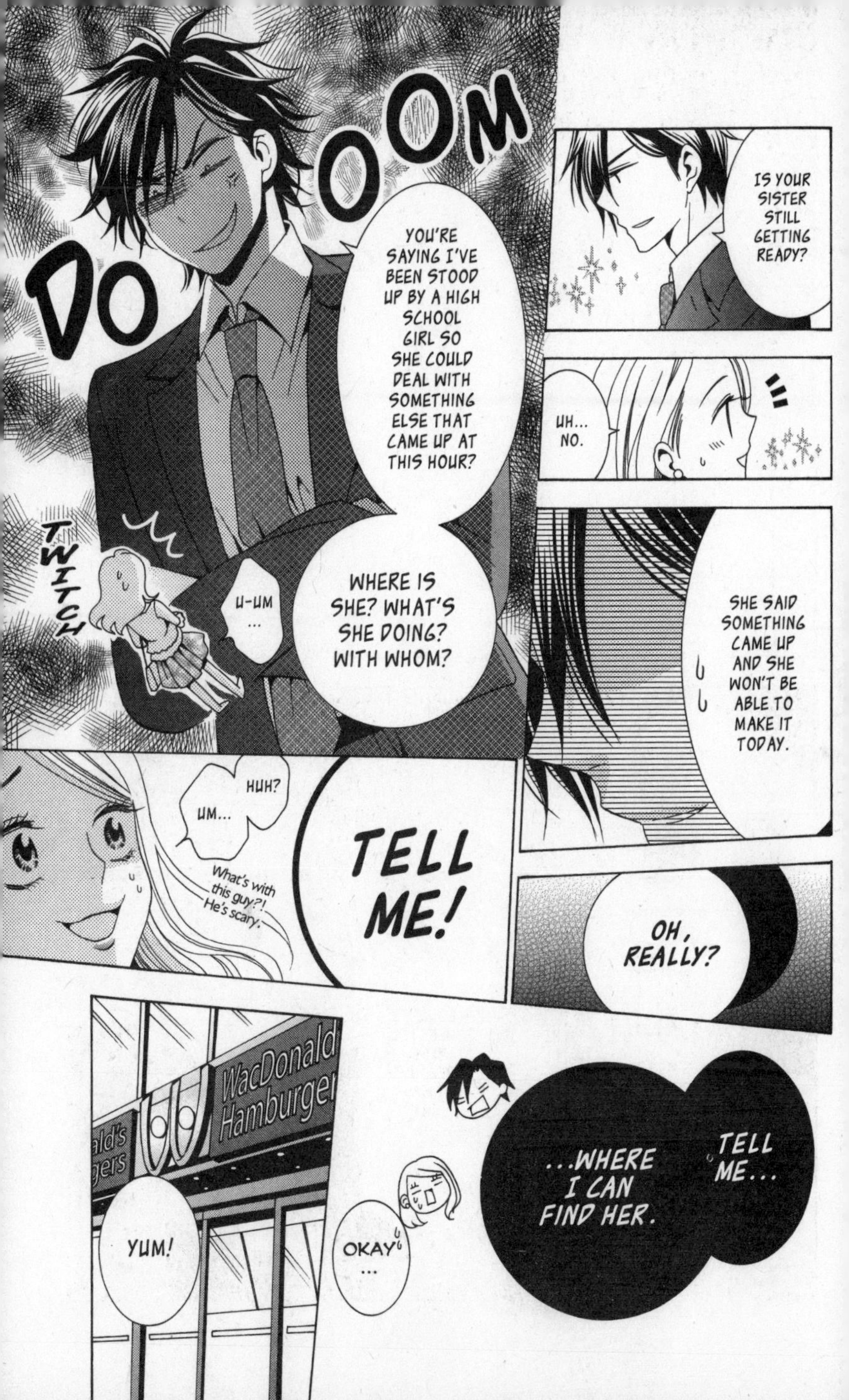
IS YOUR SISTER STILL GETTING READY?
UH... NO.
SHE SAID SOMETHING CAME UP AND SHE WON'T BE ABLE TO MAKE IT TODAY.
OH, REALLY?
DOOOM
YOU'RE SAYING I'VE BEEN STOOD UP BY A HIGH SCHOOL GIRL SO SHE COULD DEAL WITH SOMETHING ELSE THAT CAME UP AT THIS HOUR?
WHERE IS SHE? WHAT'S SHE DOING? WITH WHOM?
U-UM...
TWITCH
TELL ME!
HUH?
UM...
What's with this guy?! He's scary.
TELL ME...
...WHERE I CAN FIND HER.
OKAY...
YUM!
WacDonald Hamburger
ald's gers

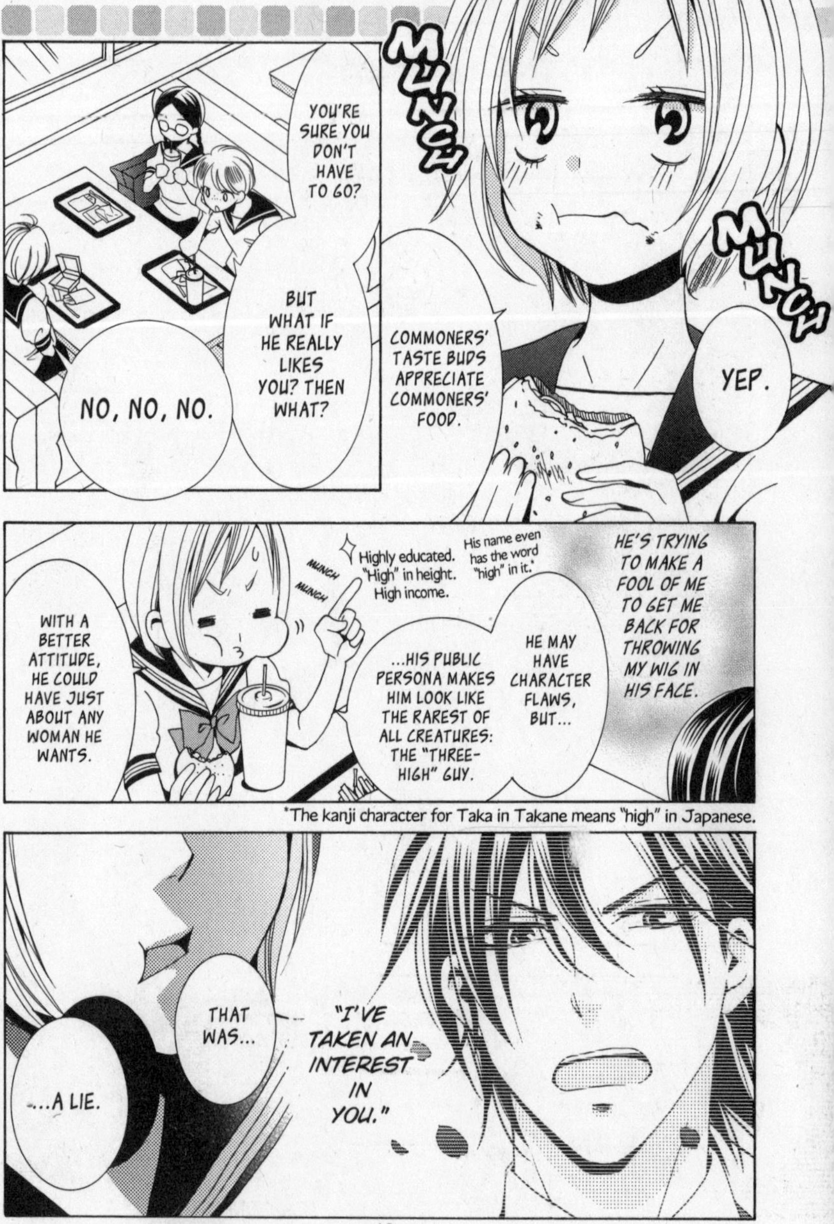
MUNCH
MUNCH
YEP.
COMMONERS' TASTE BUDS APPRECIATE COMMONERS' FOOD.
YOU'RE SURE YOU DON'T HAVE TO GO?
BUT WHAT IF HE REALLY LIKES YOU? THEN WHAT?
NO, NO, NO.
HE'S TRYING TO MAKE A FOOL OF ME TO GET ME BACK FOR THROWING MY WIG IN HIS FACE.
His name even has the word "high" in it.*
Highly educated. "High" in height. High income.
HE MAY HAVE CHARACTER FLAWS, BUT...
...HIS PUBLIC PERSONA MAKES HIM LOOK LIKE THE RAREST OF ALL CREATURES: THE "THREE-HIGH" GUY.
MUNCH
MUNCH
WITH A BETTER ATTITUDE, HE COULD HAVE JUST ABOUT ANY WOMAN HE WANTS.
"I'VE TAKEN AN INTEREST IN YOU."
THAT WAS...
...A LIE.

*The kanji character for Taka in Takane means "high" in Japanese.

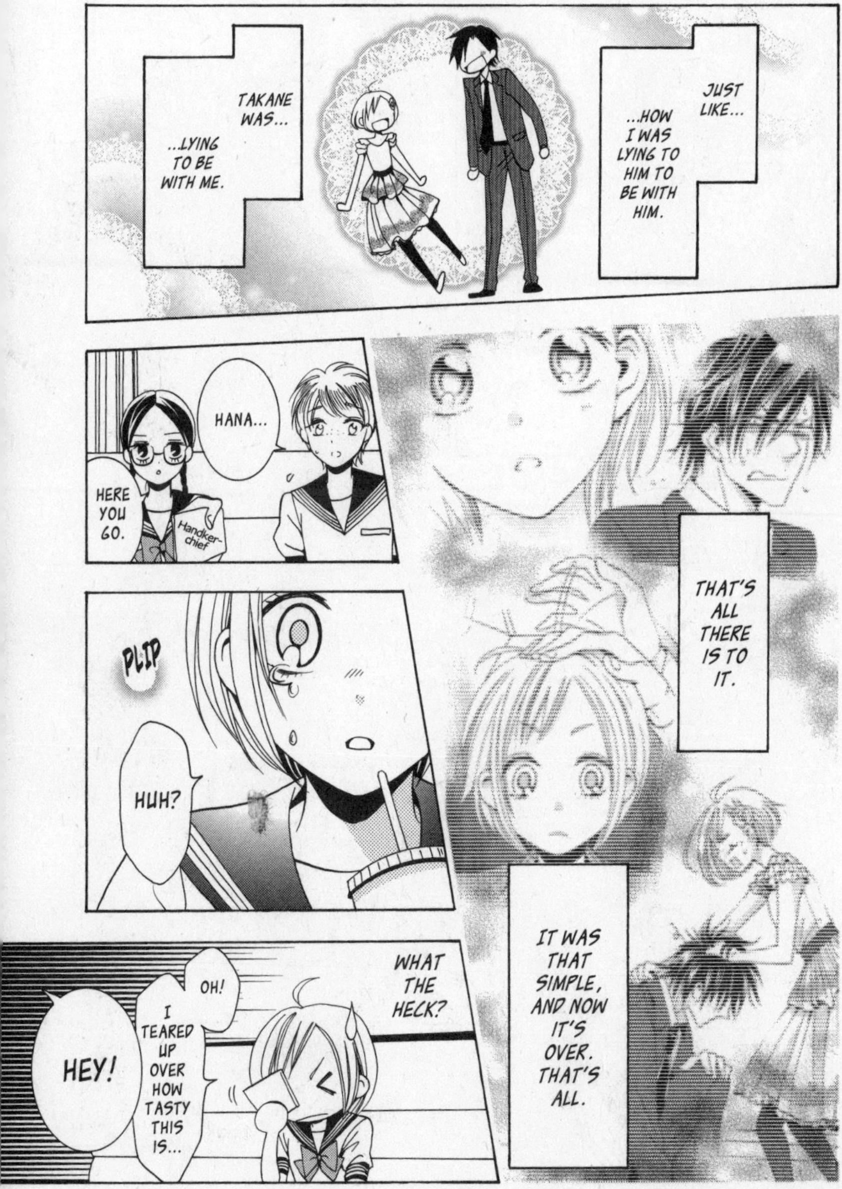

JUST LIKE...
...HOW I WAS LYING TO HIM TO BE WITH HIM.
TAKANE WAS...
...LYING TO BE WITH ME.
THAT'S ALL THERE IS TO IT.
IT WAS THAT SIMPLE, AND NOW IT'S OVER. THAT'S ALL.
HANA...
HERE YOU GO.
Handkerchief
PLIP
HUH?
WHAT THE HECK?
OH!
I TEARED UP OVER HOW TASTY THIS IS...
HEY!

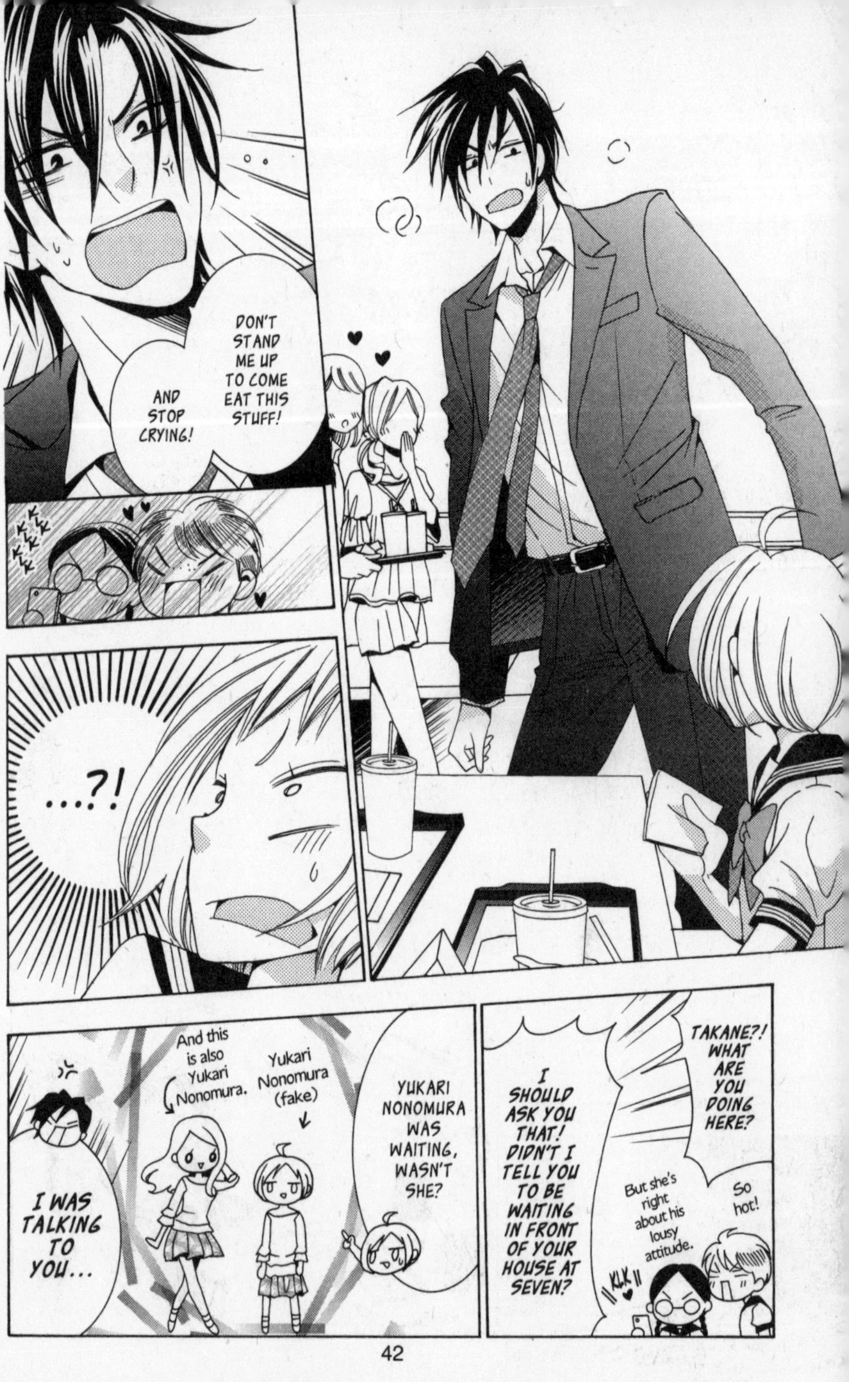
DON'T STAND ME UP TO COME EAT THIS STUFF!
AND STOP CRYING!
KLK KLK KLK
...?!
TAKANE?! WHAT ARE YOU DOING HERE?
I SHOULD ASK YOU THAT! DIDN'T I TELL YOU TO BE WAITING IN FRONT OF YOUR HOUSE AT SEVEN?
So hot!
But she's right about his lousy attitude.
KLK
YUKARI NONOMURA WAS WAITING, WASN'T SHE?
Yukari Nonomura (fake)
And this is also Yukari Nonomura.
I WAS TALKING TO YOU...

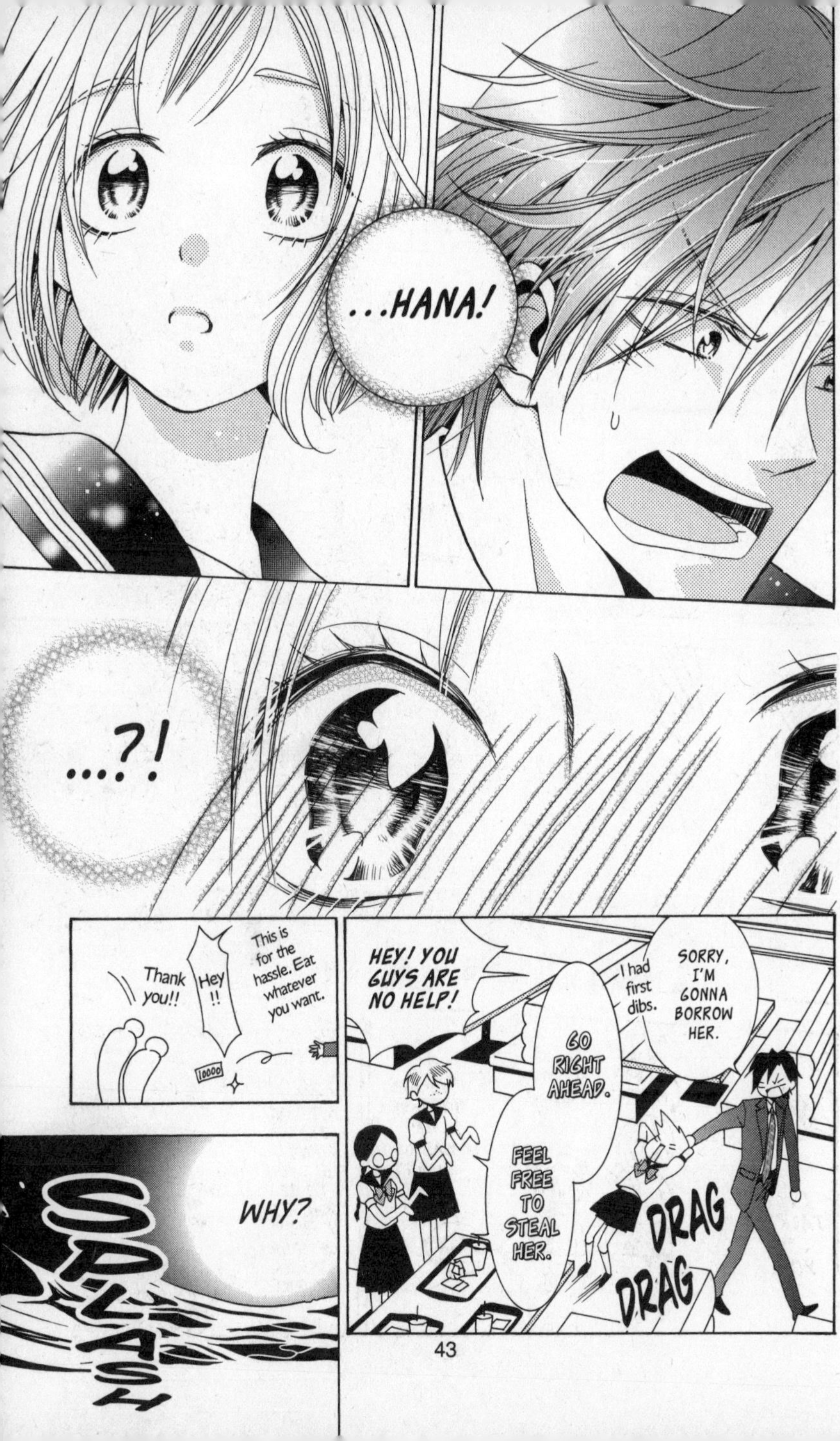
...HANA!
...?!
SORRY, I'M GONNA BORROW HER.
I had first dibs.
HEY! YOU GUYS ARE NO HELP!
GO RIGHT AHEAD.
FEEL FREE TO STEAL HER.
DRAG
DRAG
This is for the hassle. Eat whatever you want.
Hey!!
Thank you!!
10000
WHY?
SPLASH

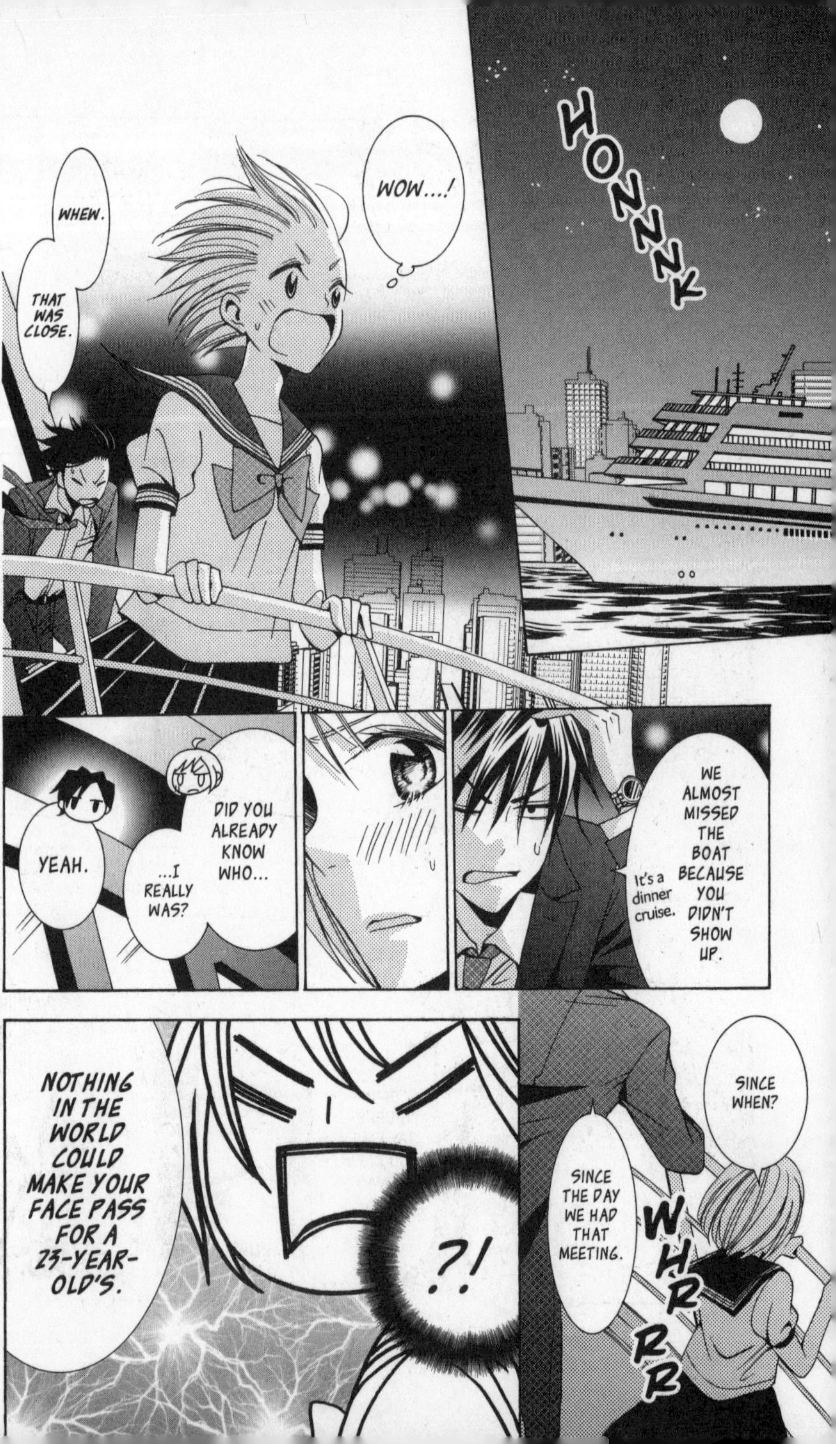
HONNNK
WOW...!
WHEW.
THAT WAS CLOSE.
WE ALMOST MISSED THE BOAT BECAUSE YOU DIDN'T SHOW UP.
It's a dinner cruise.
DID YOU ALREADY KNOW WHO...
...I REALLY WAS?
YEAH.
SINCE WHEN?
SINCE THE DAY WE HAD THAT MEETING.
WHRRR
?!
NOTHING IN THE WORLD COULD MAKE YOUR FACE PASS FOR A 23-YEAR-OLD'S.

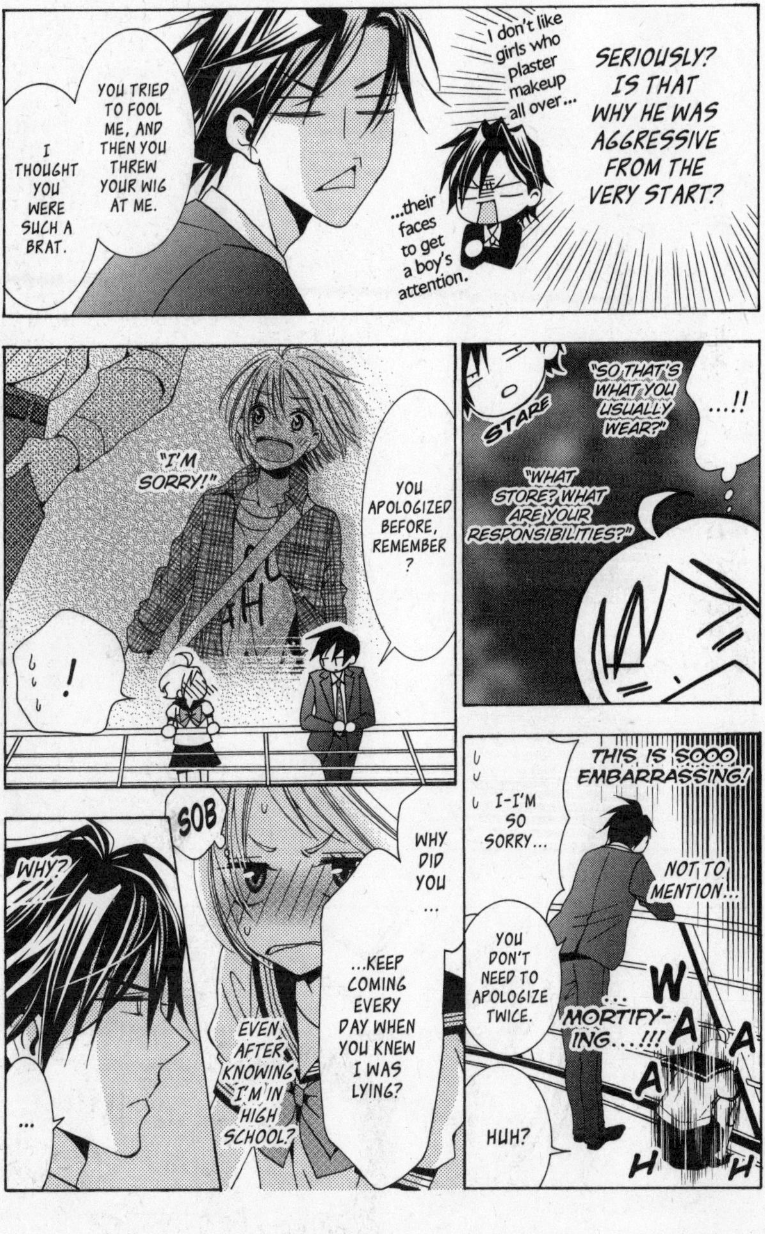
SERIOUSLY? IS THAT WHY HE WAS AGGRESSIVE FROM THE VERY START?
I don't like girls who plaster makeup all over...
...their faces to get a boy's attention.
YOU TRIED TO FOOL ME, AND THEN YOU THREW YOUR WIG AT ME.
I THOUGHT YOU WERE SUCH A BRAT.
...!!
STARE
"SO THAT'S WHAT YOU USUALLY WEAR?"
"WHAT STORE? WHAT ARE YOUR RESPONSIBILITIES?"
YOU APOLOGIZED BEFORE, REMEMBER?
"I'M SORRY!"
!
THIS IS SOOO EMBARRASSING!
I-I'M SO SORRY...
NOT TO MENTION...
YOU DON'T NEED TO APOLOGIZE TWICE.
...MORTIFY-ING...!!!
WAAAHH
HUH?
SOB
WHY DID YOU ...
...KEEP COMING EVERY DAY WHEN YOU KNEW I WAS LYING?
EVEN AFTER KNOWING I'M IN HIGH SCHOOL?
WHY?
...

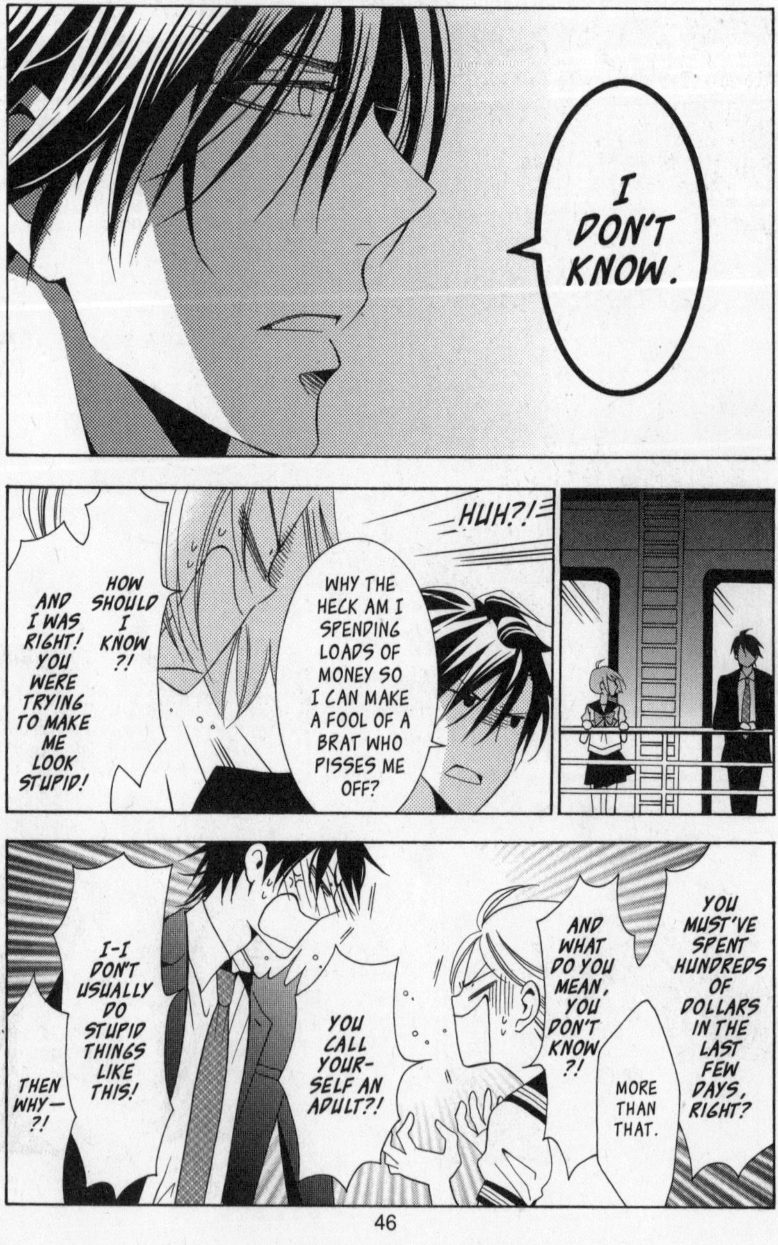
I DON'T KNOW.
HUH?!
WHY THE HECK AM I SPENDING LOADS OF MONEY SO I CAN MAKE A FOOL OF A BRAT WHO PISSES ME OFF?
HOW SHOULD I KNOW?!
AND I WAS RIGHT! YOU WERE TRYING TO MAKE ME LOOK STUPID!
YOU MUST'VE SPENT HUNDREDS OF DOLLARS IN THE LAST FEW DAYS, RIGHT?
MORE THAN THAT.
AND WHAT DO YOU MEAN, YOU DON'T KNOW?!
YOU CALL YOUR-SELF AN ADULT?!
I-I DON'T USUALLY DO STUPID THINGS LIKE THIS!
THEN WHY—?!

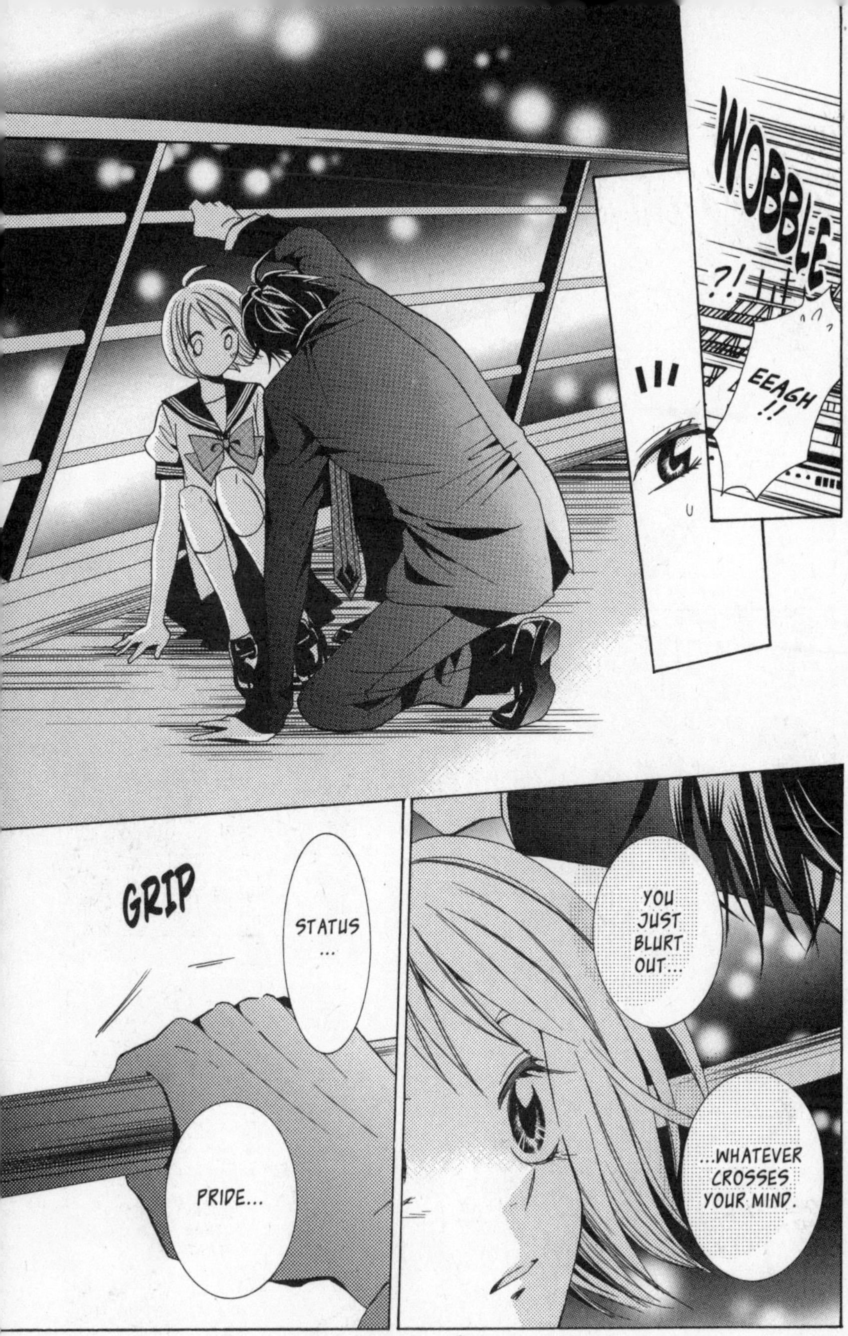
WOBBLE
?!
EEAGH!!
YOU JUST BLURT OUT...
...WHATEVER CROSSES YOUR MIND.
GRIP
STATUS...
PRIDE...

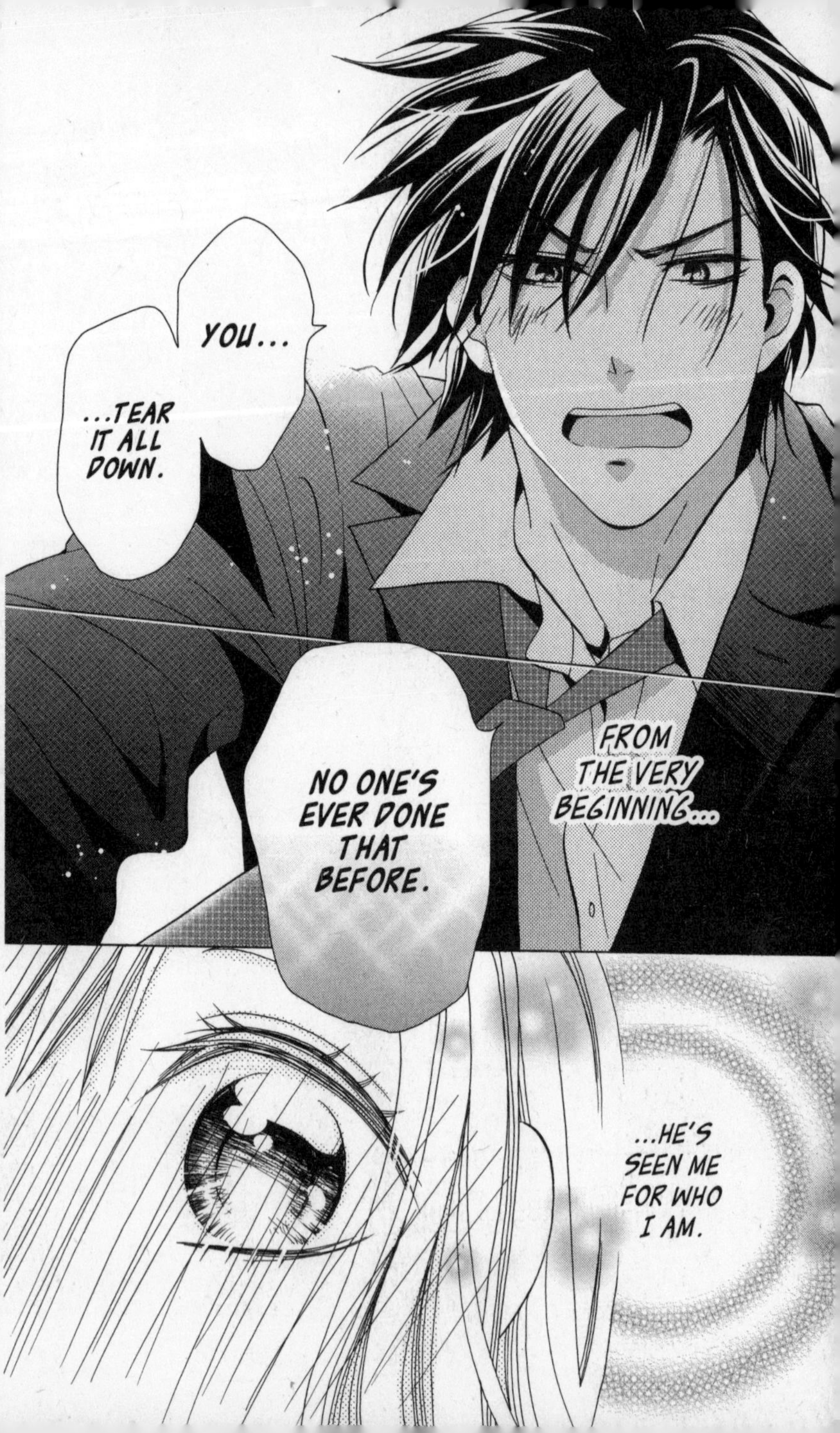
YOU...
...TEAR IT ALL DOWN.
FROM THE VERY BEGINNING...
NO ONE'S EVER DONE THAT BEFORE.
...HE'S SEEN ME FOR WHO I AM.

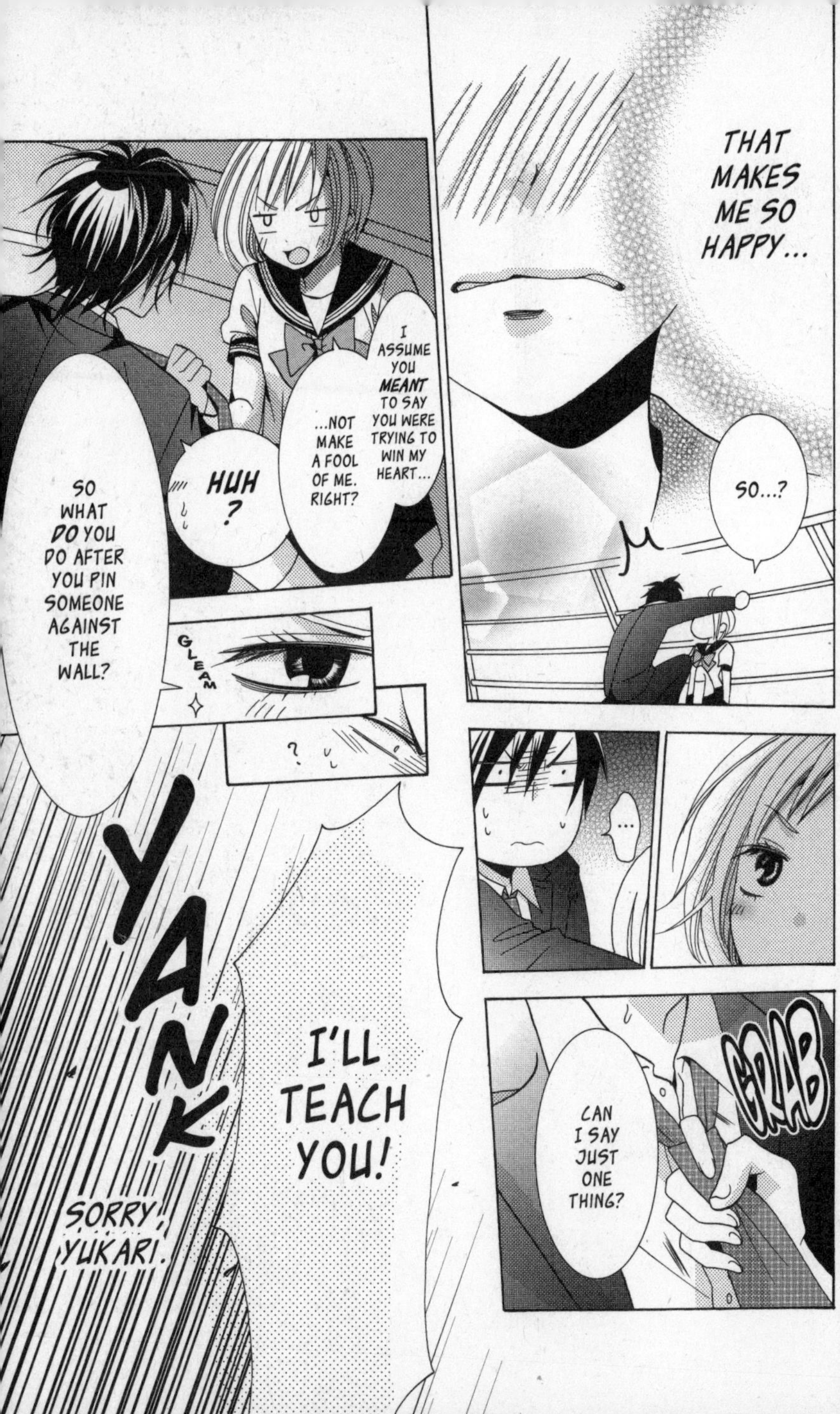
THAT MAKES ME SO HAPPY...
SO...?
I ASSUME YOU MEANT TO SAY YOU WERE TRYING TO WIN MY HEART...
...NOT MAKE A FOOL OF ME. RIGHT?
HUH?
SO WHAT DO YOU DO AFTER YOU PIN SOMEONE AGAINST THE WALL?
GLEAM
...
GRAB
CAN I SAY JUST ONE THING?
YANK
I'LL TEACH YOU!
SORRY, YUKARI.

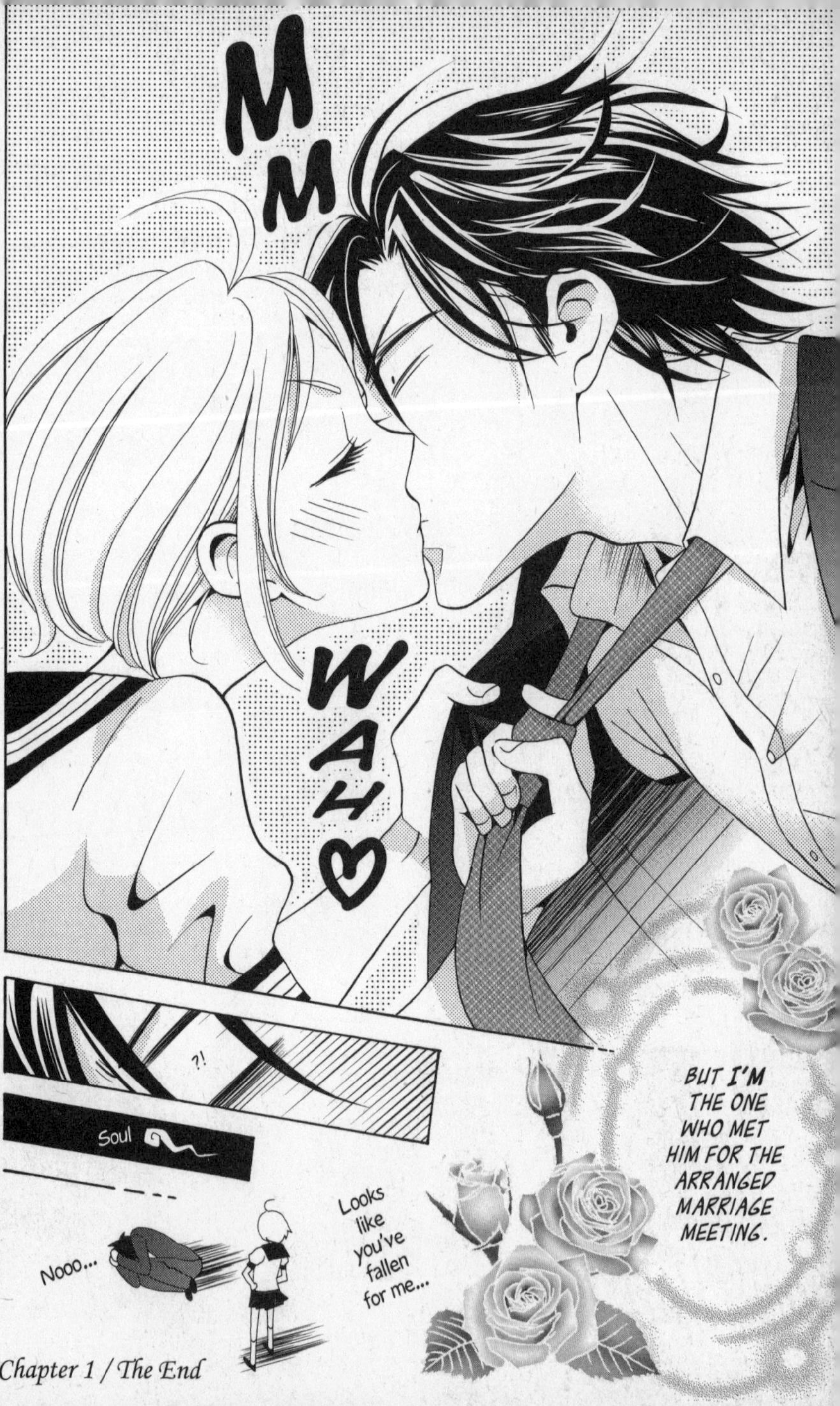
MMWAH♥
BUT I'M THE ONE WHO MET HIM FOR THE ARRANGED MARRIAGE MEETING.
?!
Soul
Looks like you've fallen for me...
Nooo...

Chapter 1 / The End

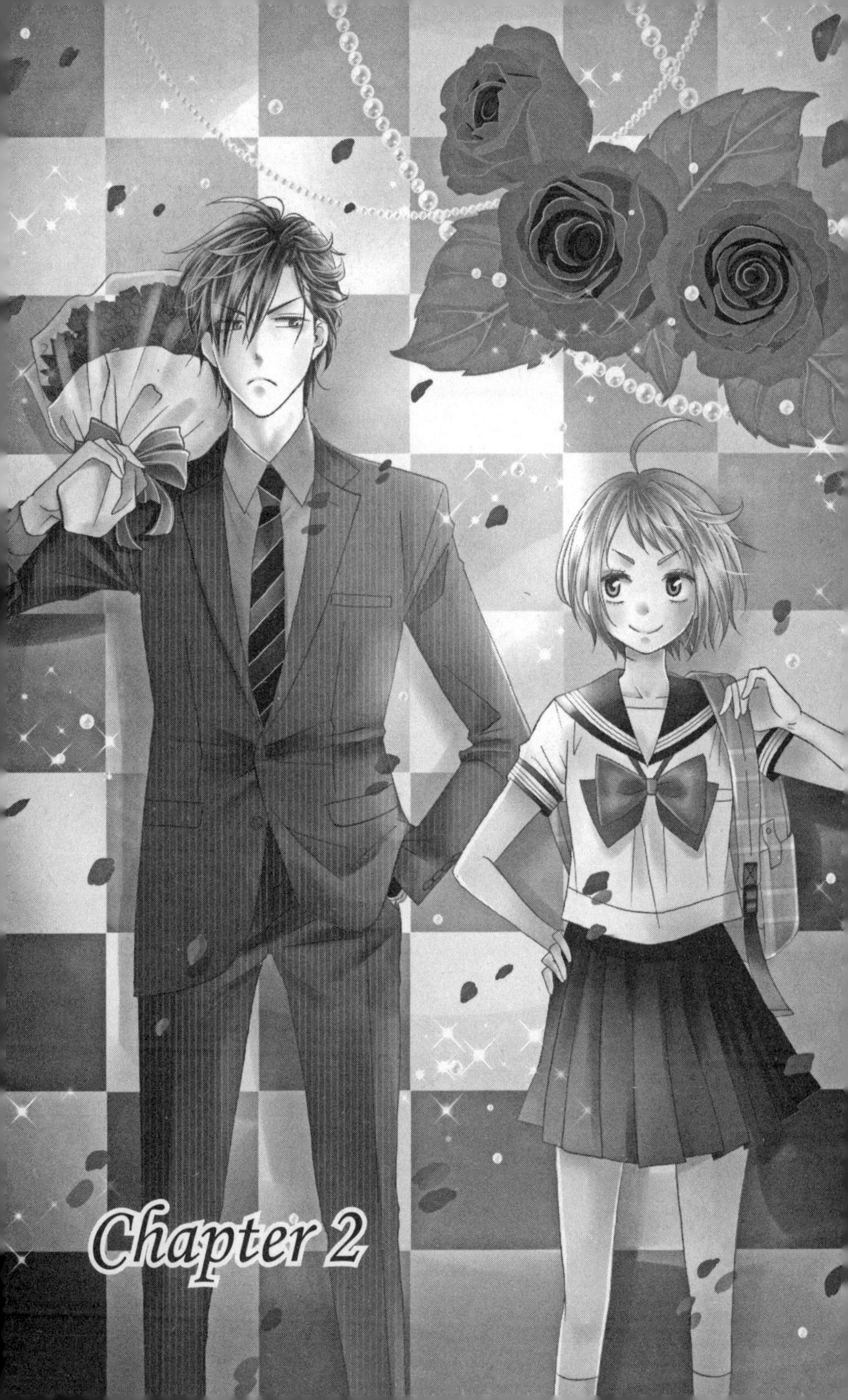
Chapter 2

Afterward

SHE STOLE A KISS.
SHE STOLE A KISS.
SHE STOLE A KISS.
SHE'S SO YOUNG.
A COMMONER.
A HIGH SCHOOL STUDENT.
YOU'RE AN ADULT. THAT'S DISGRACE-FUL.
YOU KISSING HER WOULD BE ONE THING, BUT HER KISSING YOU...
IT'S JUST SAD.
*AUDITORY HALLUCINATIONS
I HEAR HE FROZE UP AFTER IT HAPPENED.
PATHETIC.
*AUDITORY HALLUCINATIONS
SOB SOB SOB SOB SOB
COULDN'T GET OUT OF BED FOR TWO DAYS

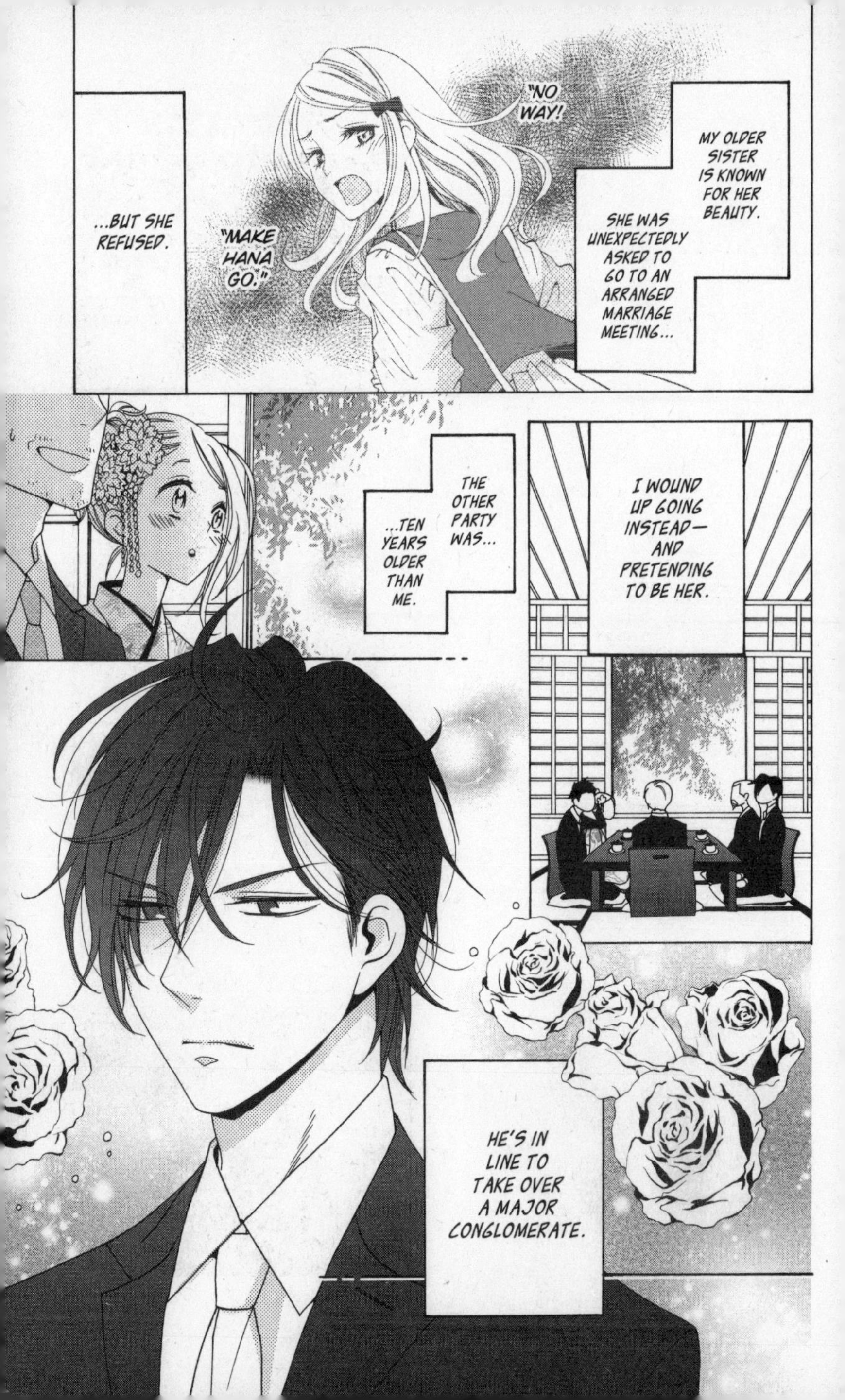
MY OLDER SISTER IS KNOWN FOR HER BEAUTY.
SHE WAS UNEXPECTEDLY ASKED TO GO TO AN ARRANGED MARRIAGE MEETING...
"NO WAY!
MAKE HANA GO."
...BUT SHE REFUSED.
I WOUND UP GOING INSTEAD—AND PRETENDING TO BE HER.
THE OTHER PARTY WAS...
...TEN YEARS OLDER THAN ME.
HE'S IN LINE TO TAKE OVER A MAJOR CONGLOMERATE.

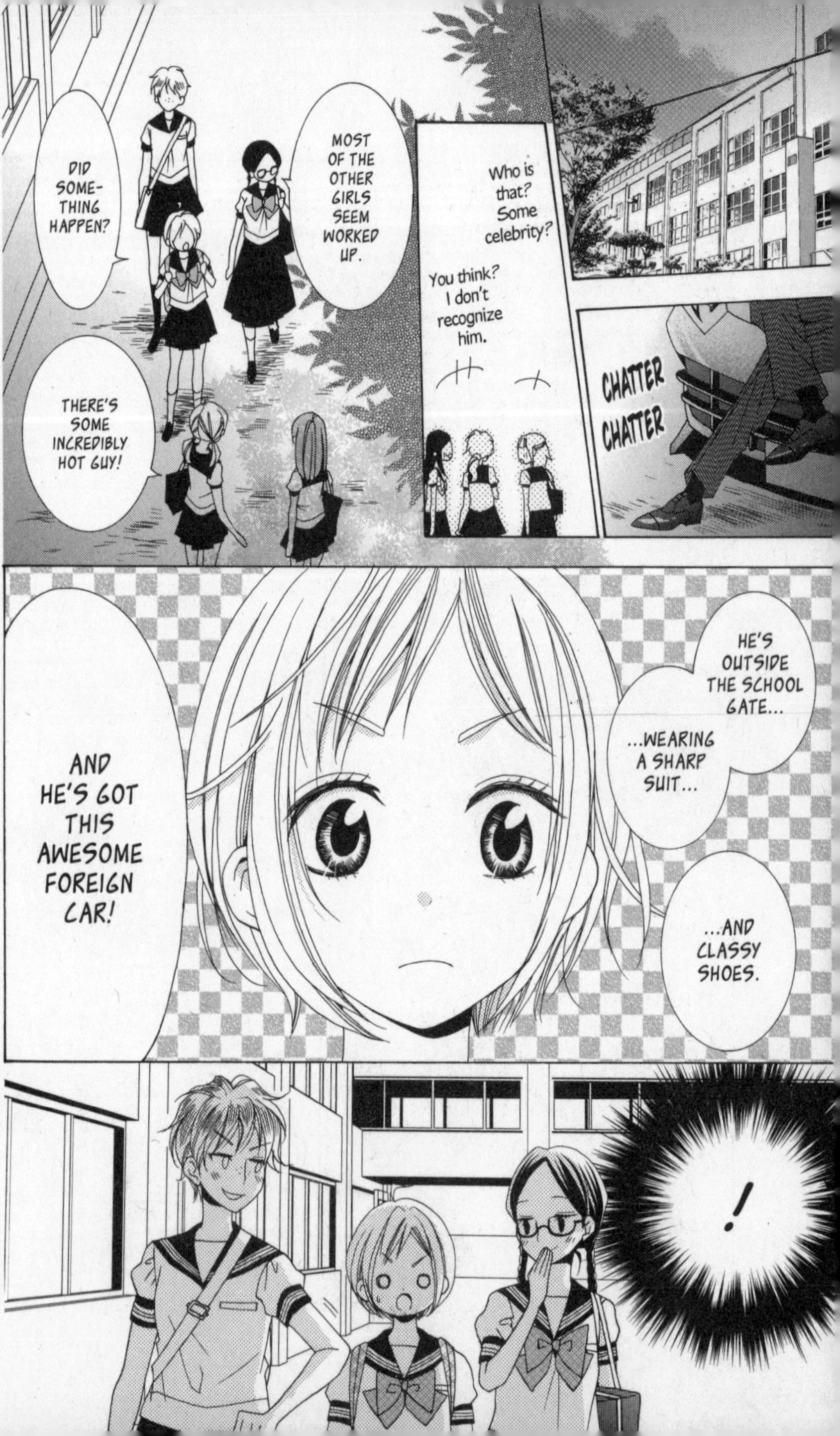
CHATTER CHATTER
Who is that? Some celebrity?
You think? I don't recognize him.
MOST OF THE OTHER GIRLS SEEM WORKED UP.
DID SOMETHING HAPPEN?
THERE'S SOME INCREDIBLY HOT GUY!
HE'S OUTSIDE THE SCHOOL GATE...
...WEARING A SHARP SUIT...
...AND CLASSY SHOES.
AND HE'S GOT THIS AWESOME FOREIGN CAR!
!

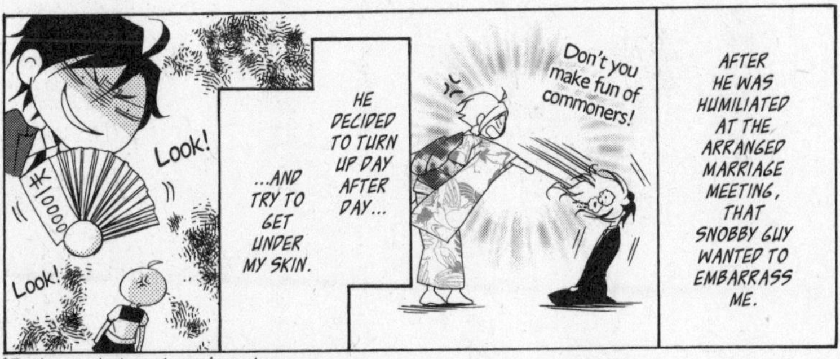
AFTER HE WAS HUMILIATED AT THE ARRANGED MARRIAGE MEETING, THAT SNOBBY GUY WANTED TO EMBARRASS ME.
Don't you make fun of commoners!
HE DECIDED TO TURN UP DAY AFTER DAY...
...AND TRY TO GET UNDER MY SKIN.
Look!
Look!

*By the way, he knew I wasn't my sister.

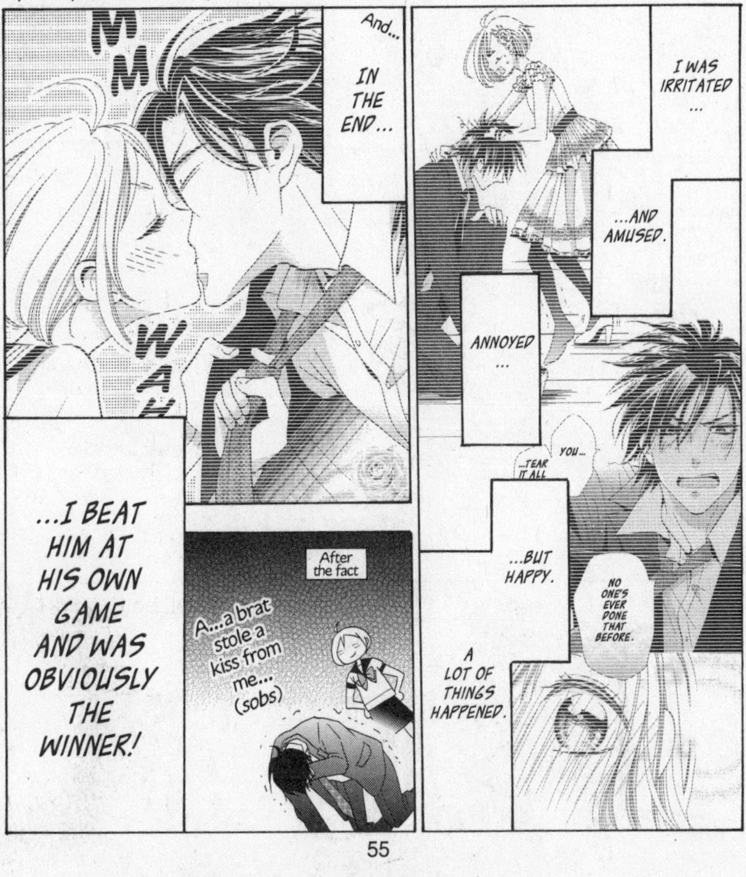
I WAS IRRITATED...
...AND AMUSED.
ANNOYED...
YOU...
...TEAR IT ALL
...BUT HAPPY.
NO ONE'S EVER DONE THAT BEFORE.
A LOT OF THINGS HAPPENED.
And...
IN THE END...
MMWAH
After the fact
A...a brat stole a kiss from me... (sobs)
...I BEAT HIM AT HIS OWN GAME AND WAS OBVIOUSLY THE WINNER!

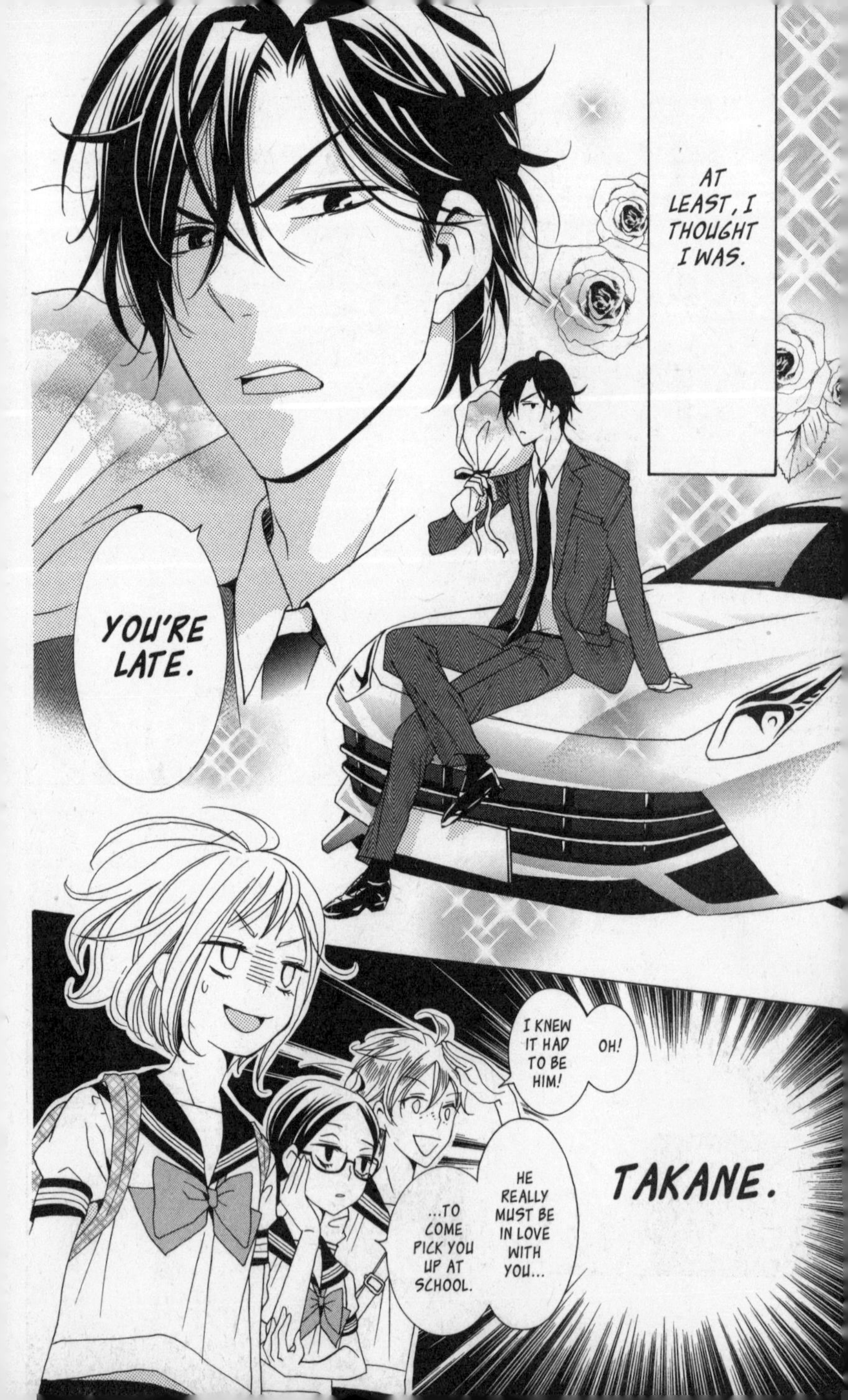
AT LEAST, I THOUGHT I WAS.
YOU'RE LATE.
TAKANE.
OH!
I KNEW IT HAD TO BE HIM!
HE REALLY MUST BE IN LOVE WITH YOU...
...TO COME PICK YOU UP AT SCHOOL.

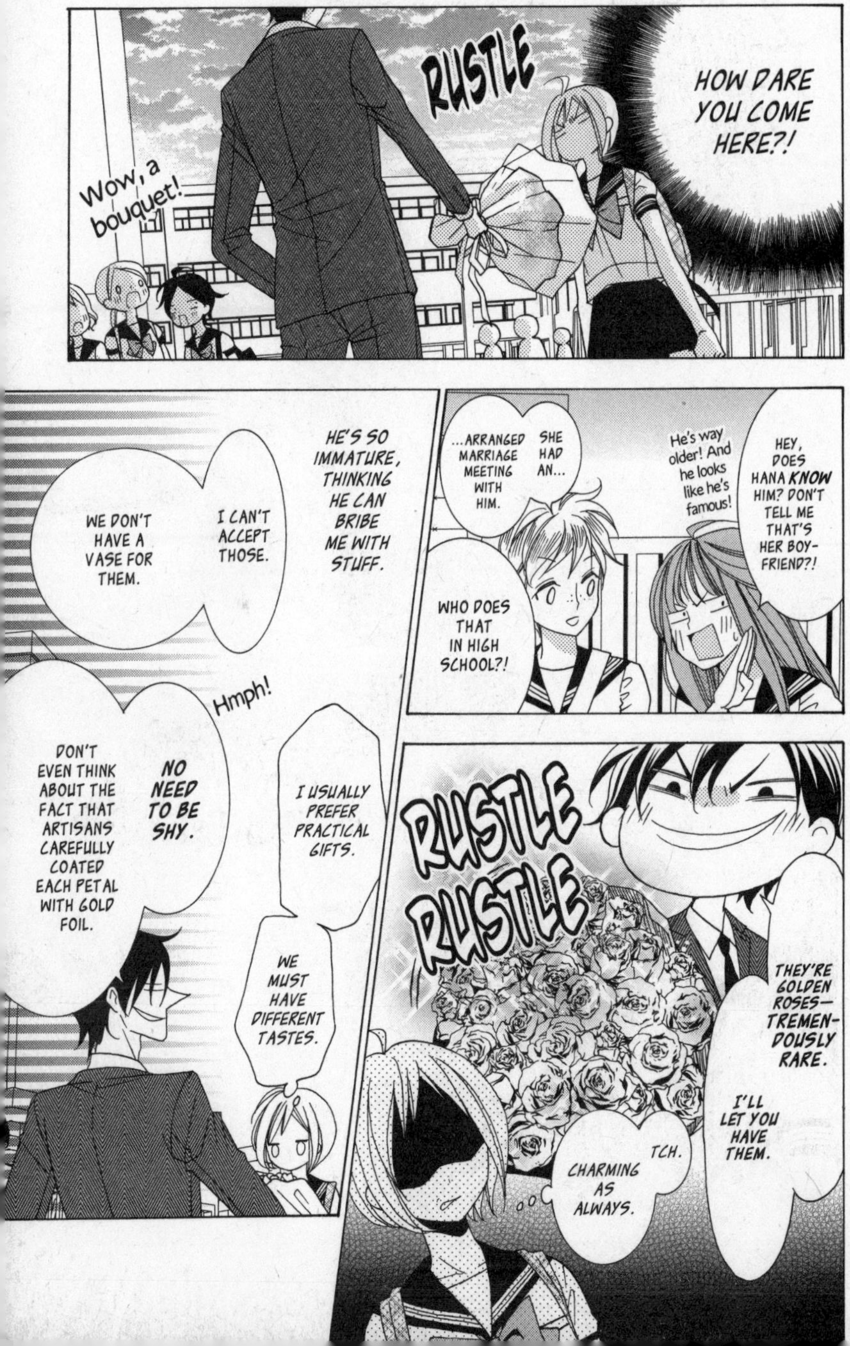
HOW DARE YOU COME HERE?!
RUSTLE
Wow, a bouquet!
HEY, DOES HANA KNOW HIM? DON'T TELL ME THAT'S HER BOY-FRIEND?!
He's way older! And he looks like he's famous!
SHE HAD AN...
...ARRANGED MARRIAGE MEETING WITH HIM.
WHO DOES THAT IN HIGH SCHOOL?!
RUSTLE RUSTLE
THEY'RE GOLDEN ROSES—TREMEN-DOUSLY RARE.
I'LL LET YOU HAVE THEM.
TCH.
CHARMING AS ALWAYS.
HE'S SO IMMATURE, THINKING HE CAN BRIBE ME WITH STUFF.
I CAN'T ACCEPT THOSE.
WE DON'T HAVE A VASE FOR THEM.
Hmph!
NO NEED TO BE SHY.
DON'T EVEN THINK ABOUT THE FACT THAT ARTISANS CAREFULLY COATED EACH PETAL WITH GOLD FOIL.
I USUALLY PREFER PRACTICAL GIFTS.
WE MUST HAVE DIFFERENT TASTES.

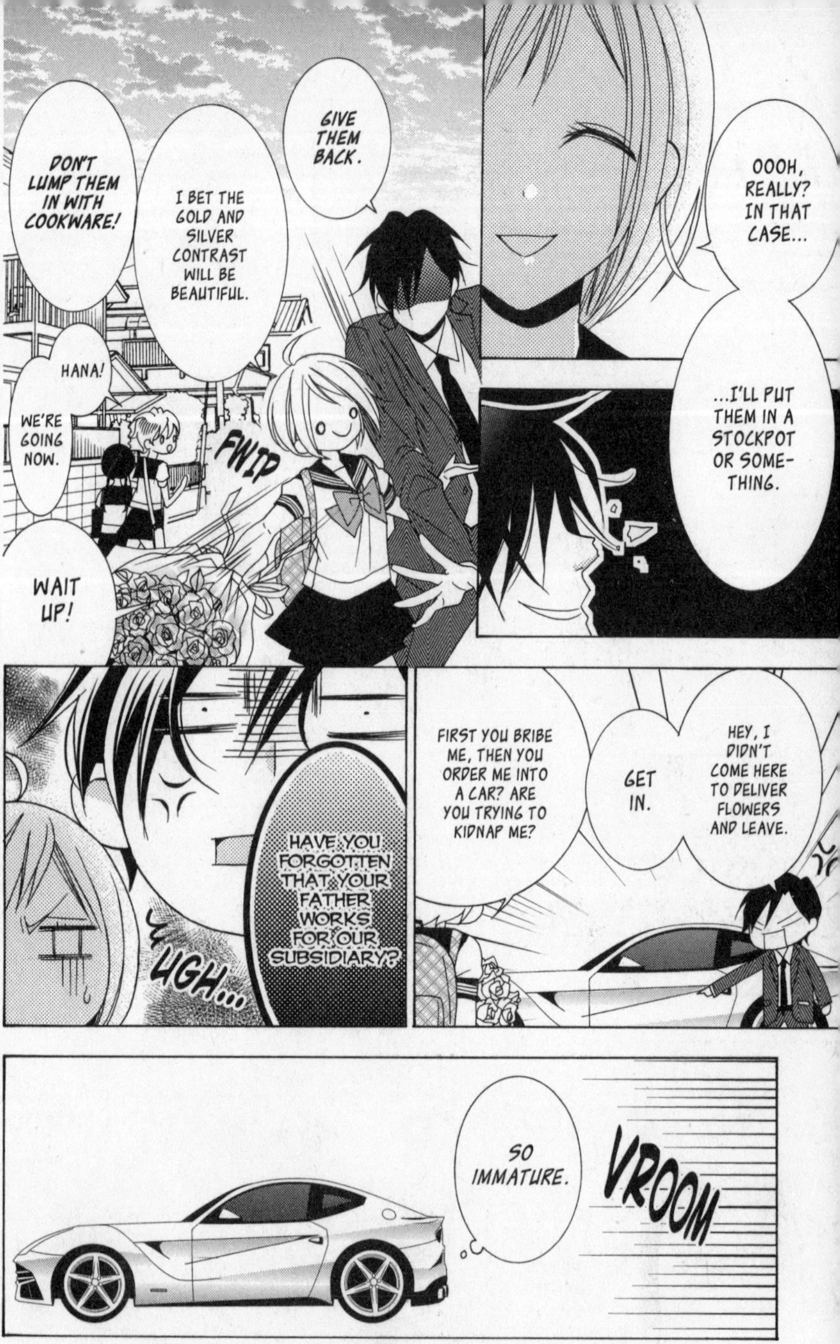
OOOH, REALLY? IN THAT CASE...
...I'LL PUT THEM IN A STOCKPOT OR SOME-THING.
GIVE THEM BACK.
FWIP
I BET THE GOLD AND SILVER CONTRAST WILL BE BEAUTIFUL.
DON'T LUMP THEM IN WITH COOKWARE!
HANA! WE'RE GOING NOW.
WAIT UP!
HEY, I DIDN'T COME HERE TO DELIVER FLOWERS AND LEAVE.
GET IN.
FIRST YOU BRIBE ME, THEN YOU ORDER ME INTO A CAR? ARE YOU TRYING TO KIDNAP ME?
HAVE YOU FORGOTTEN THAT YOUR FATHER WORKS FOR OUR SUBSIDIARY?
UGH...
VROOM
SO IMMATURE.

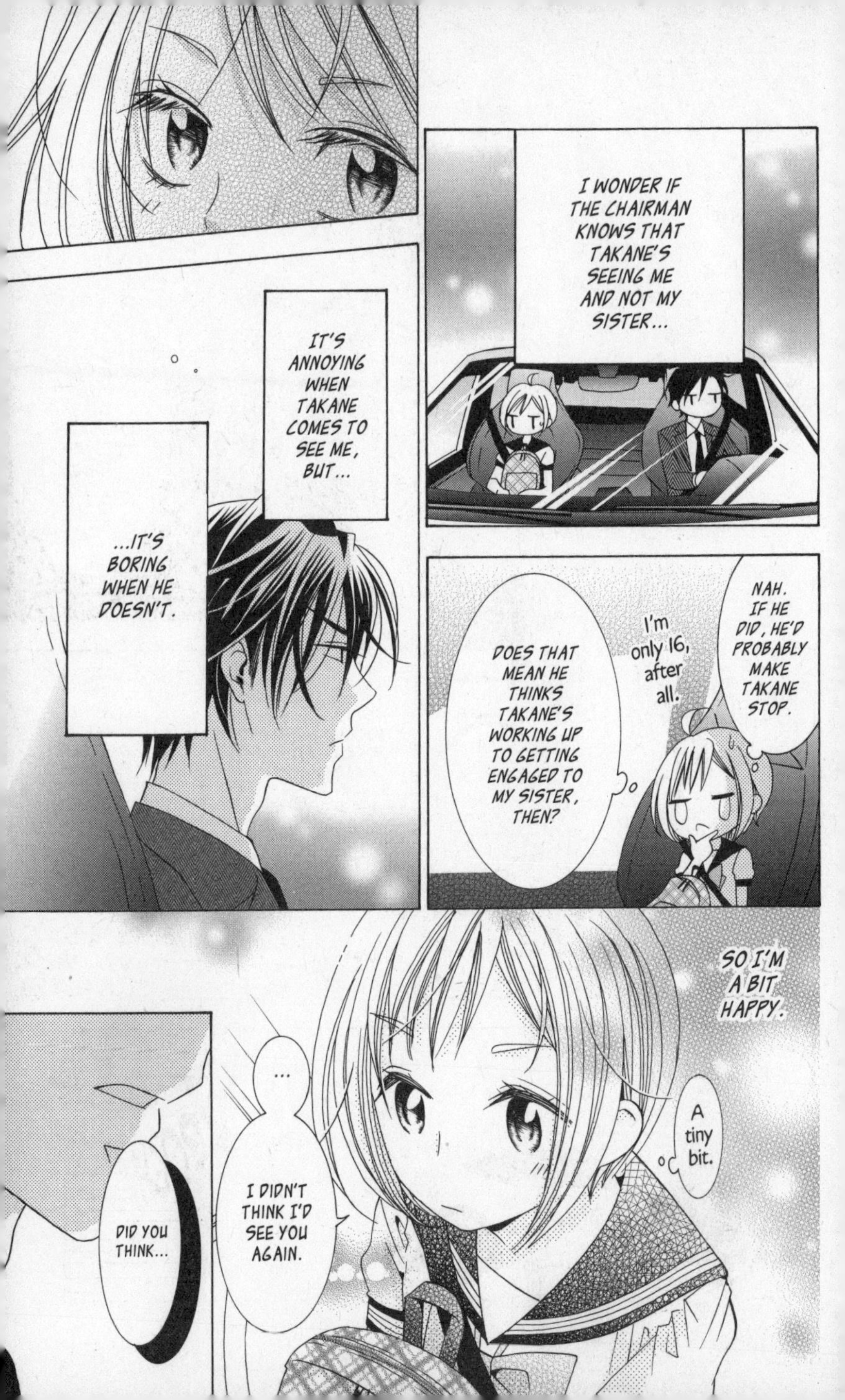
I WONDER IF THE CHAIRMAN KNOWS THAT TAKANE'S SEEING ME AND NOT MY SISTER...
NAH. IF HE DID, HE'D PROBABLY MAKE TAKANE STOP.
I'm only 16, after all.
DOES THAT MEAN HE THINKS TAKANE'S WORKING UP TO GETTING ENGAGED TO MY SISTER, THEN?
IT'S ANNOYING WHEN TAKANE COMES TO SEE ME, BUT...
...IT'S BORING WHEN HE DOESN'T.
SO I'M A BIT HAPPY.
A tiny bit.
...
I DIDN'T THINK I'D SEE YOU AGAIN.
DID YOU THINK...

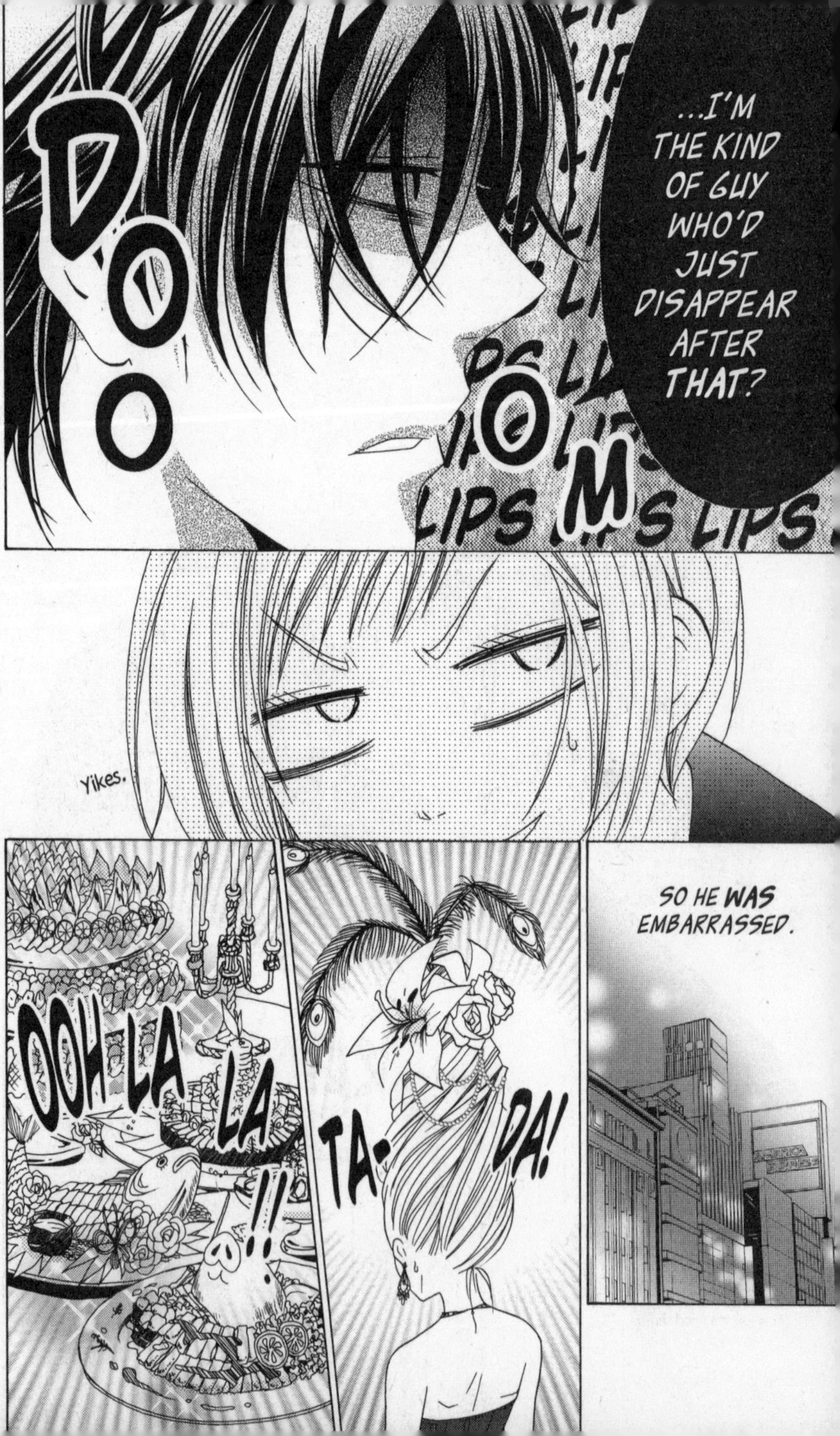
...I'M THE KIND OF GUY WHO'D JUST DISAPPEAR AFTER THAT?
DOOOM
LIPS LIPS
Yikes.
SO HE WAS EMBARRASSED.
TA-DA!
OOH LA LA!!

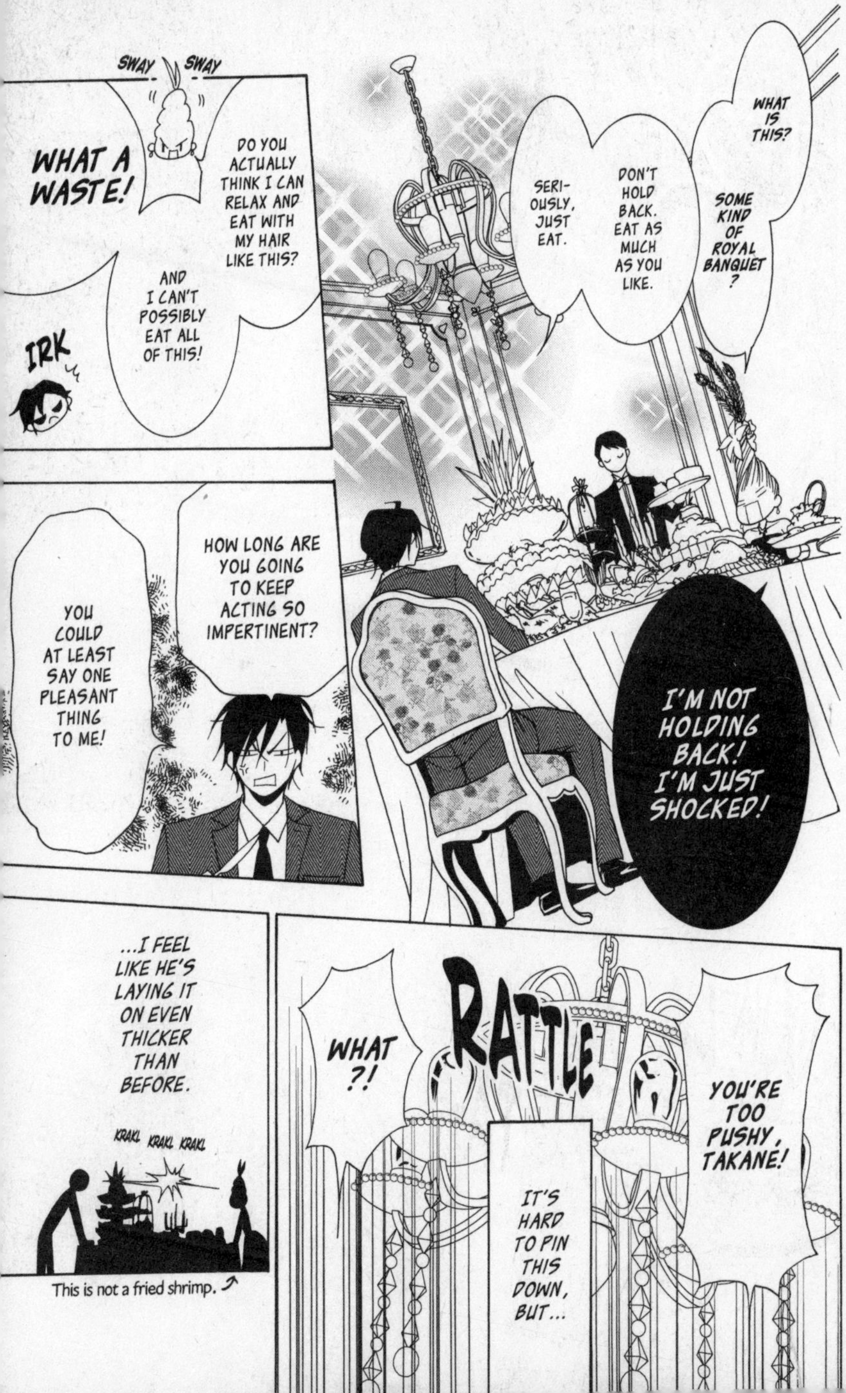
WHAT IS THIS?
SOME KIND OF ROYAL BANQUET?
DON'T HOLD BACK. EAT AS MUCH AS YOU LIKE.
SERIOUSLY, JUST EAT.
I'M NOT HOLDING BACK! I'M JUST SHOCKED!
SWAY SWAY
DO YOU ACTUALLY THINK I CAN RELAX AND EAT WITH MY HAIR LIKE THIS?
AND I CAN'T POSSIBLY EAT ALL OF THIS!
WHAT A WASTE!
IRK
HOW LONG ARE YOU GOING TO KEEP ACTING SO IMPERTINENT?
YOU COULD AT LEAST SAY ONE PLEASANT THING TO ME!
YOU'RE TOO PUSHY, TAKANE!
RATTLE
WHAT?!
IT'S HARD TO PIN THIS DOWN, BUT...
...I FEEL LIKE HE'S LAYING IT ON EVEN THICKER THAN BEFORE.
KRAKL KRAKL KRAKL
This is not a fried shrimp.

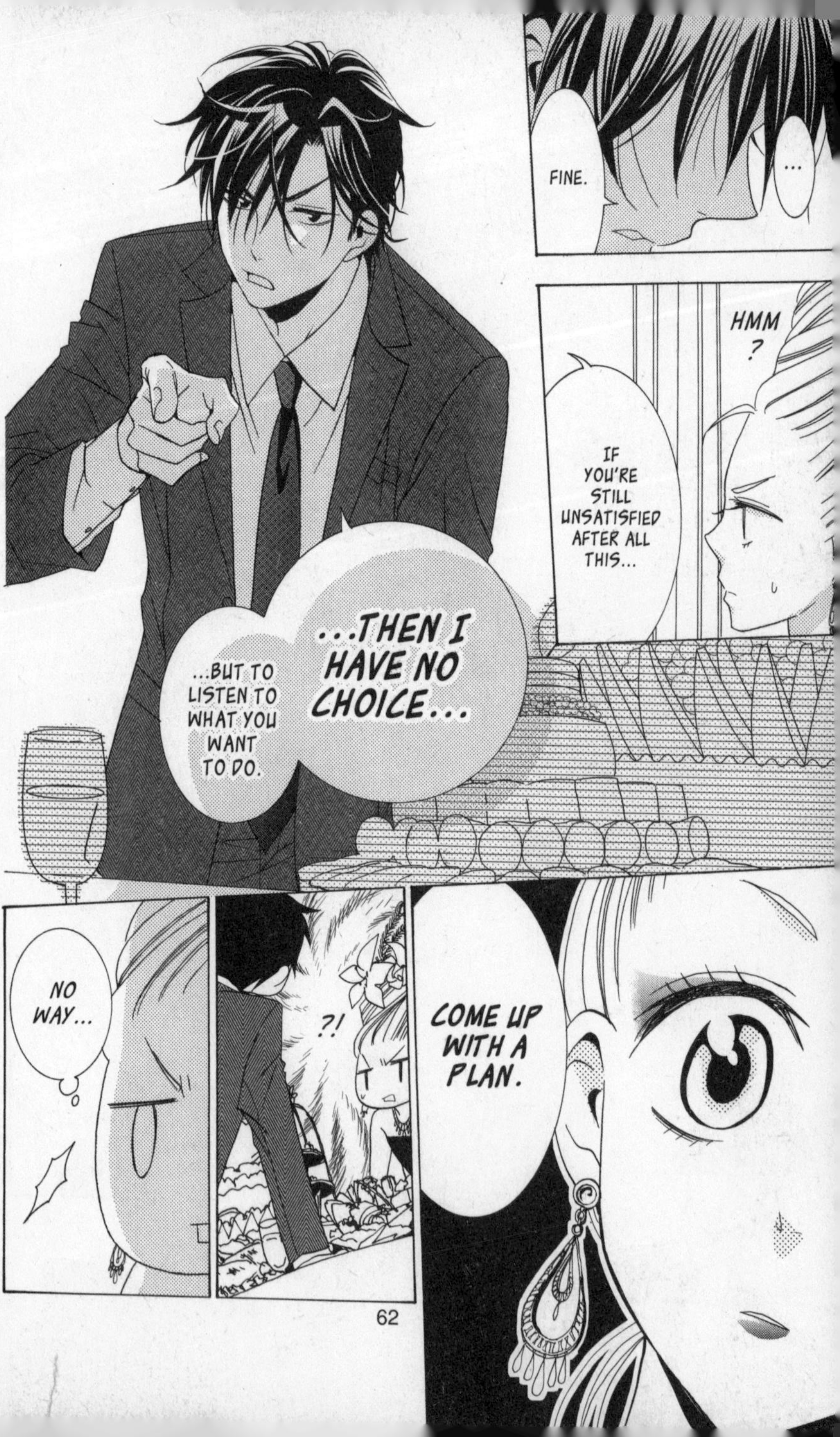
...
FINE.
HMM?
IF YOU'RE STILL UNSATISFIED AFTER ALL THIS...
...THEN I HAVE NO CHOICE...
...BUT TO LISTEN TO WHAT YOU WANT TO DO.
COME UP WITH A PLAN.
?!
NO WAY...

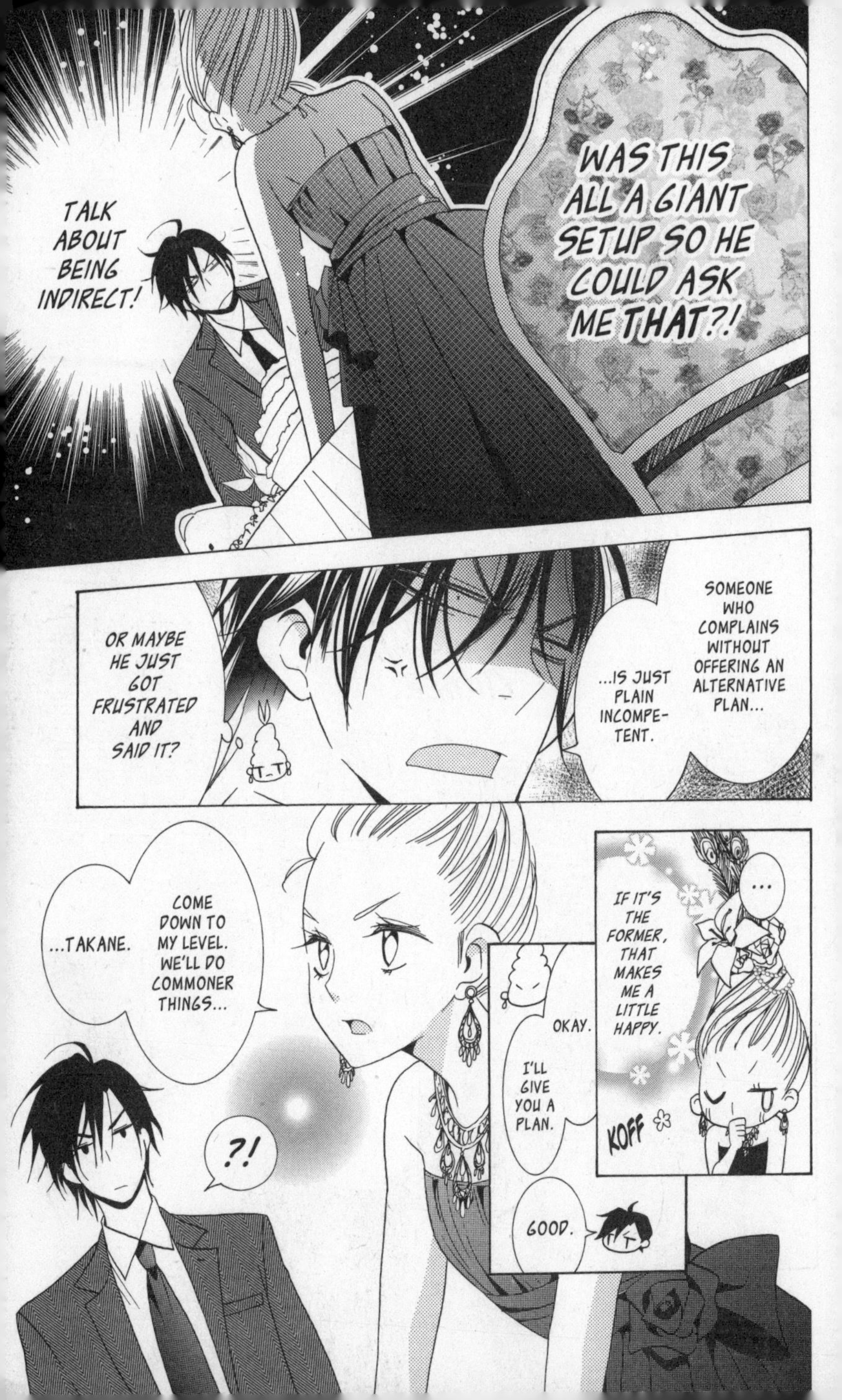
WAS THIS ALL A GIANT SETUP SO HE COULD ASK ME THAT?!
TALK ABOUT BEING INDIRECT!
SOMEONE WHO COMPLAINS WITHOUT OFFERING AN ALTERNATIVE PLAN...
...IS JUST PLAIN INCOMPETENT.
OR MAYBE HE JUST GOT FRUSTRATED AND SAID IT?
...
IF IT'S THE FORMER, THAT MAKES ME A LITTLE HAPPY.
KOFF
OKAY.
I'LL GIVE YOU A PLAN.
GOOD.
COME DOWN TO MY LEVEL. WE'LL DO COMMONER THINGS...
...TAKANE.
?!

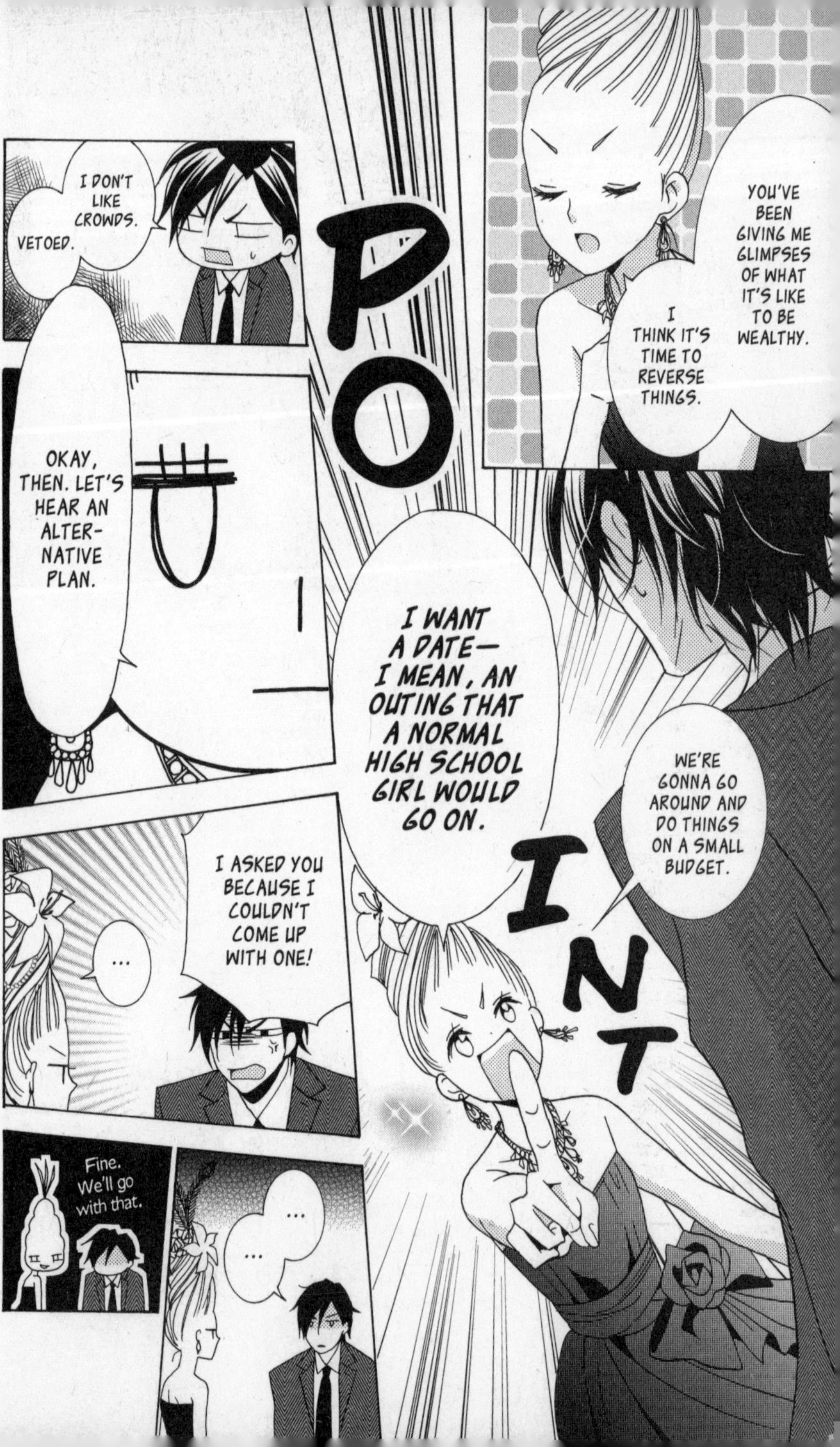
YOU'VE BEEN GIVING ME GLIMPSES OF WHAT IT'S LIKE TO BE WEALTHY.
I THINK IT'S TIME TO REVERSE THINGS.
POINT
I WANT A DATE— I MEAN, AN OUTING THAT A NORMAL HIGH SCHOOL GIRL WOULD GO ON.
WE'RE GONNA GO AROUND AND DO THINGS ON A SMALL BUDGET.
I DON'T LIKE CROWDS.
VETOED.
OKAY, THEN. LET'S HEAR AN ALTER-NATIVE PLAN.
I ASKED YOU BECAUSE I COULDN'T COME UP WITH ONE!
...
...
...
Fine. We'll go with that.

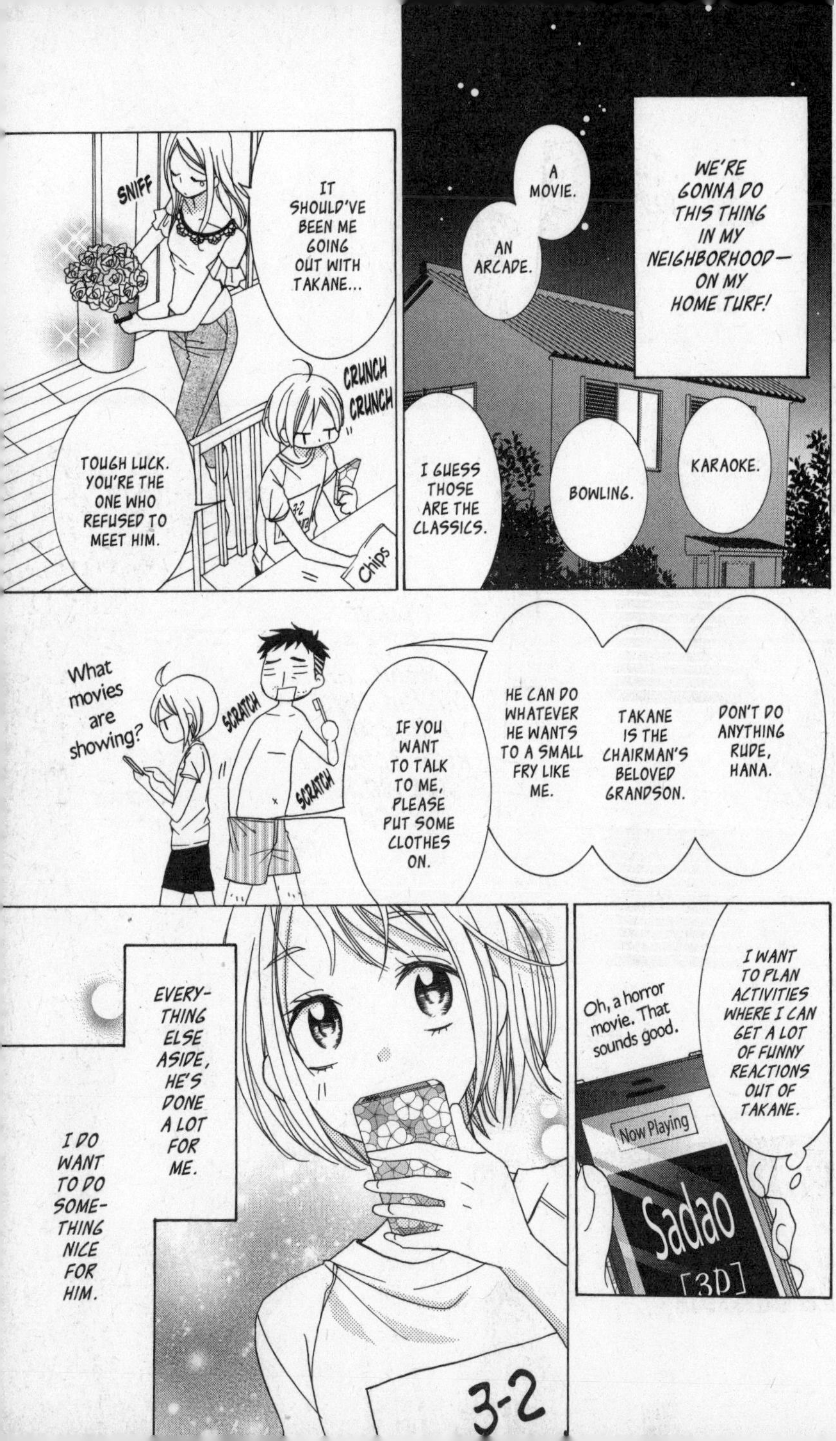
WE'RE GONNA DO THIS THING IN MY NEIGHBORHOOD—ON MY HOME TURF!
A MOVIE.
AN ARCADE.
KARAOKE.
BOWLING.
I GUESS THOSE ARE THE CLASSICS.
IT SHOULD'VE BEEN ME GOING OUT WITH TAKANE...
SNIFF
CRUNCH CRUNCH
TOUGH LUCK. YOU'RE THE ONE WHO REFUSED TO MEET HIM.
Chips
DON'T DO ANYTHING RUDE, HANA.
TAKANE IS THE CHAIRMAN'S BELOVED GRANDSON.
HE CAN DO WHATEVER HE WANTS TO A SMALL FRY LIKE ME.
IF YOU WANT TO TALK TO ME, PLEASE PUT SOME CLOTHES ON.
SCRATCH
SCRATCH
What movies are showing?
I WANT TO PLAN ACTIVITIES WHERE I CAN GET A LOT OF FUNNY REACTIONS OUT OF TAKANE.
Oh, a horror movie. That sounds good.
Now Playing
Sadao
[3D]
EVERY-THING ELSE ASIDE, HE'S DONE A LOT FOR ME.
I DO WANT TO DO SOME-THING NICE FOR HIM.
3-2

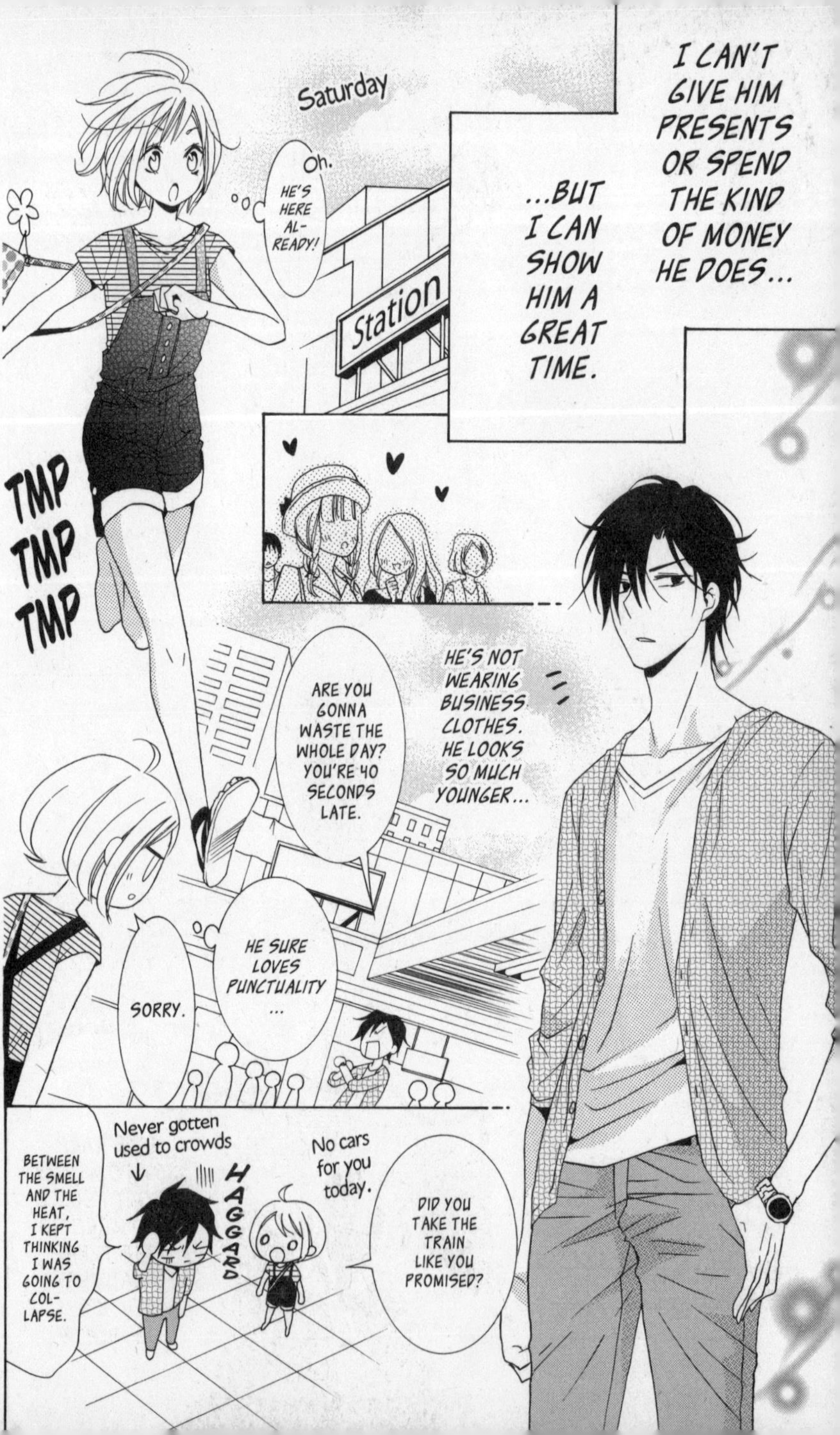

I CAN'T GIVE HIM PRESENTS OR SPEND THE KIND OF MONEY HE DOES...
...BUT I CAN SHOW HIM A GREAT TIME.
Saturday
Station
Oh.
HE'S HERE AL-READY!
TMP TMP TMP
HE'S NOT WEARING BUSINESS CLOTHES. HE LOOKS SO MUCH YOUNGER...
ARE YOU GONNA WASTE THE WHOLE DAY? YOU'RE 40 SECONDS LATE.
HE SURE LOVES PUNCTUALITY...
SORRY.
DID YOU TAKE THE TRAIN LIKE YOU PROMISED?
No cars for you today.
HAGGARD
Never gotten used to crowds
BETWEEN THE SMELL AND THE HEAT, I KEPT THINKING I WAS GOING TO COL-LAPSE.

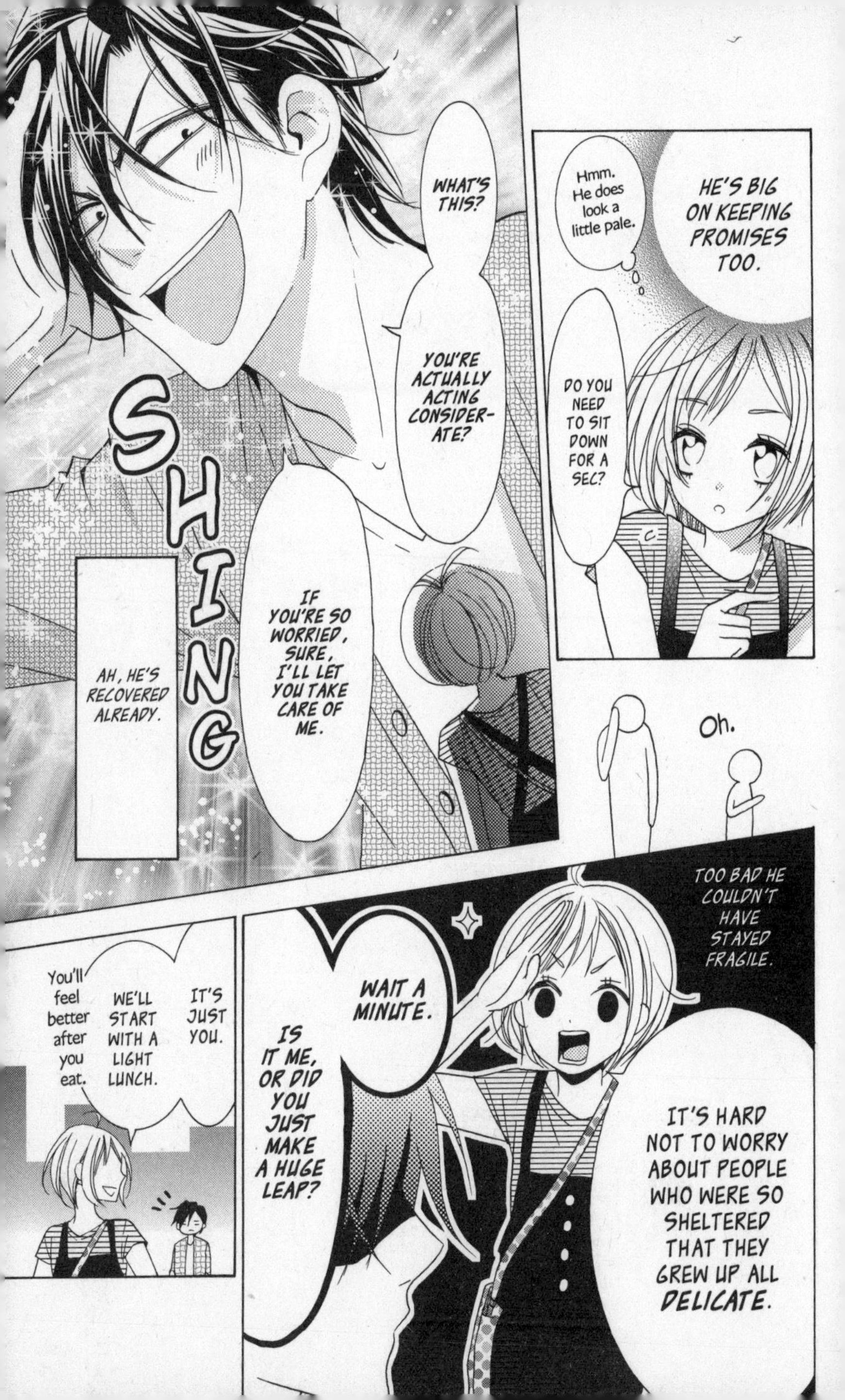
HE'S BIG ON KEEPING PROMISES TOO.
Hmm. He does look a little pale.
DO YOU NEED TO SIT DOWN FOR A SEC?
Oh.
WHAT'S THIS?
YOU'RE ACTUALLY ACTING CONSIDER-ATE?
IF YOU'RE SO WORRIED, SURE, I'LL LET YOU TAKE CARE OF ME.
SHING
AH, HE'S RECOVERED ALREADY.
TOO BAD HE COULDN'T HAVE STAYED FRAGILE.
IT'S HARD NOT TO WORRY ABOUT PEOPLE WHO WERE SO SHELTERED THAT THEY GREW UP ALL DELICATE.
WAIT A MINUTE.
IS IT ME, OR DID YOU JUST MAKE A HUGE LEAP?
IT'S JUST YOU.
WE'LL START WITH A LIGHT LUNCH.
You'll feel better after you eat.

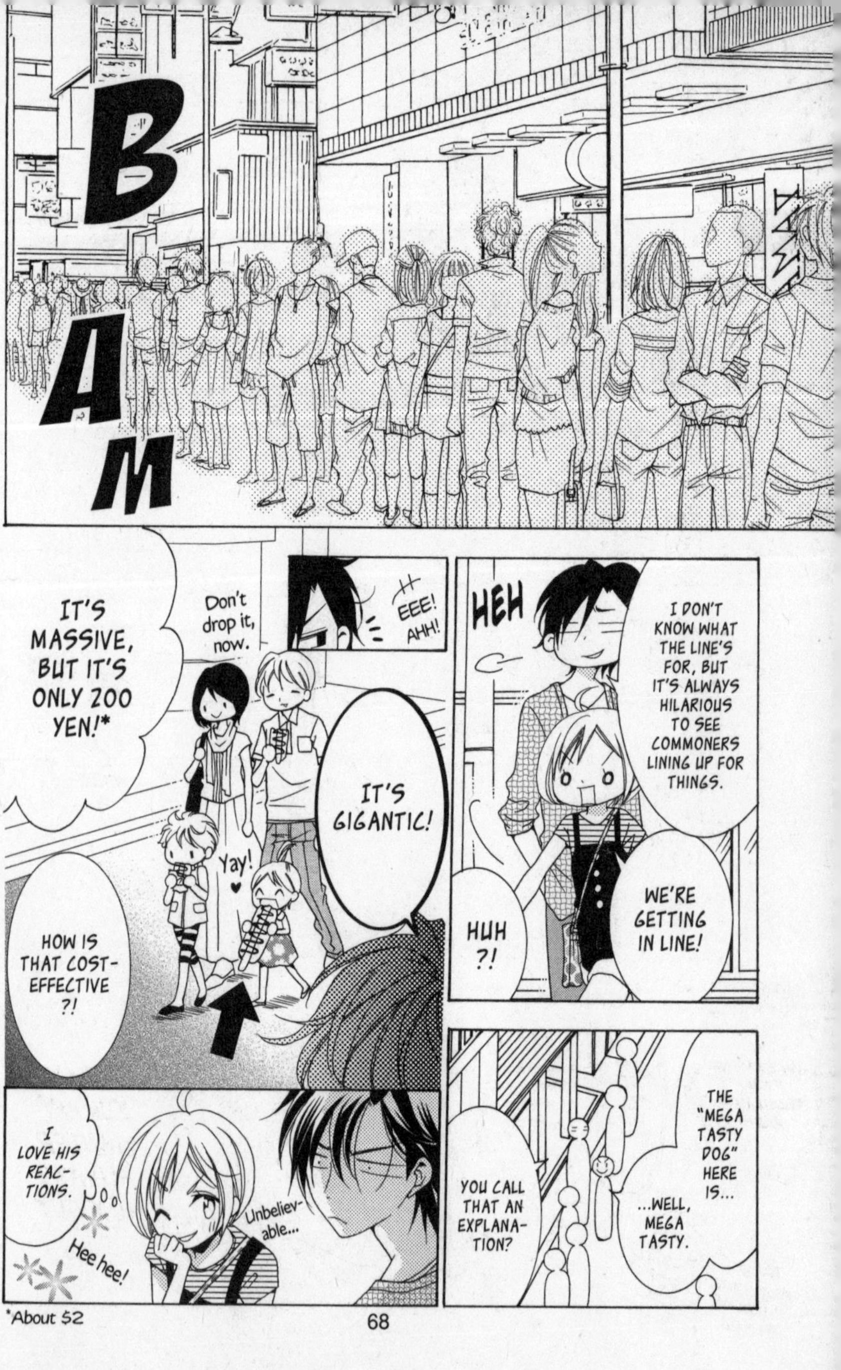
BAM
HEH
I DON'T KNOW WHAT THE LINE'S FOR, BUT IT'S ALWAYS HILARIOUS TO SEE COMMONERS LINING UP FOR THINGS.
WE'RE GETTING IN LINE!
HUH?!
EEE! AHH!
Don't drop it, now.
IT'S MASSIVE, BUT IT'S ONLY 200 YEN!*
IT'S GIGANTIC!
Yay!
HOW IS THAT COST-EFFECTIVE?!
THE "MEGA TASTY DOG" HERE IS...
...WELL, MEGA TASTY.
YOU CALL THAT AN EXPLANATION?
Unbeliev-able...
I LOVE HIS REAC-TIONS.
Hee hee!

*About $2

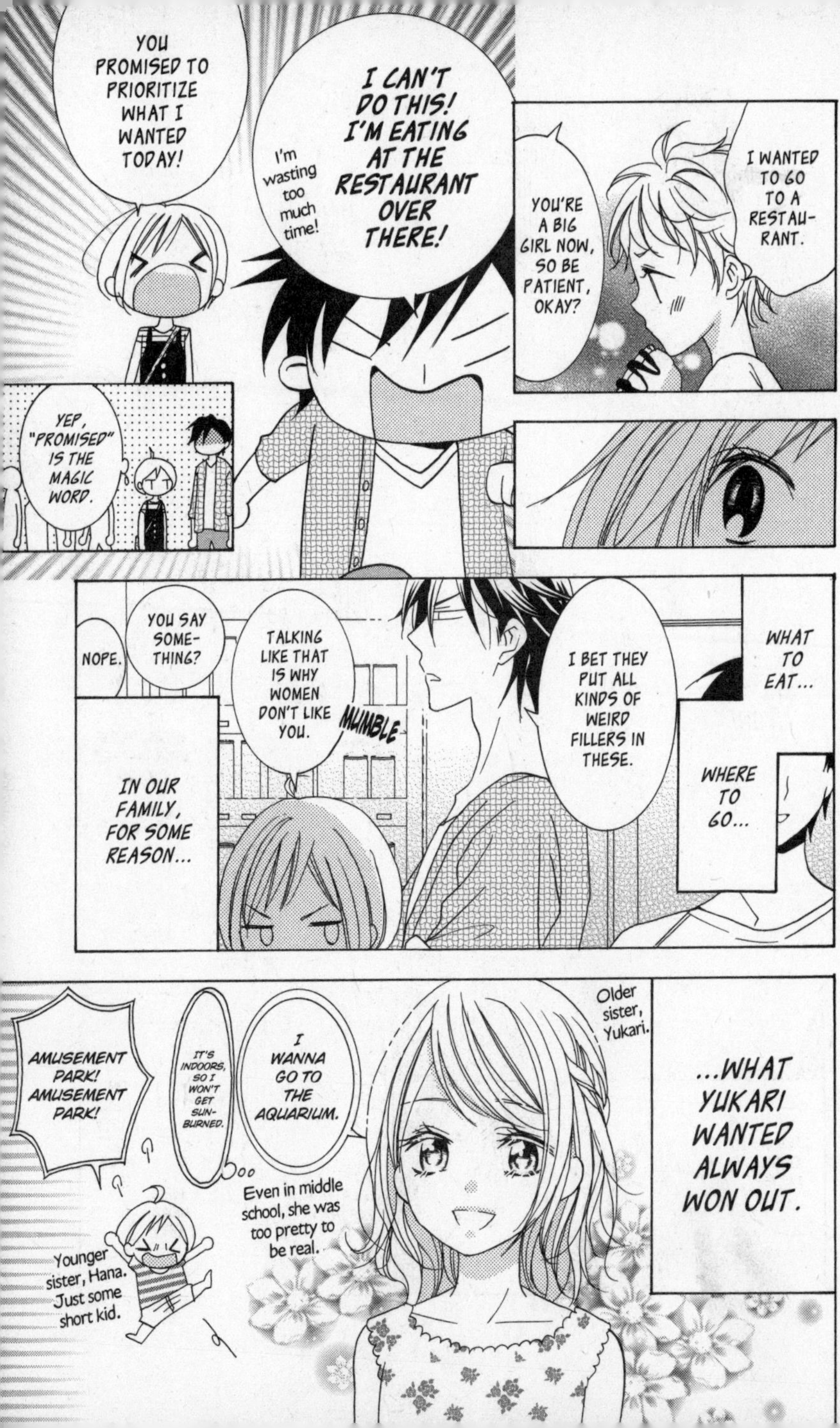
I WANTED TO GO TO A RESTAURANT.
YOU'RE A BIG GIRL NOW, SO BE PATIENT, OKAY?
I CAN'T DO THIS! I'M EATING AT THE RESTAURANT OVER THERE!
I'm wasting too much time!
YOU PROMISED TO PRIORITIZE WHAT I WANTED TODAY!
YEP, "PROMISED" IS THE MAGIC WORD.
WHAT TO EAT...
WHERE TO GO...
I BET THEY PUT ALL KINDS OF WEIRD FILLERS IN THESE.
MUMBLE
TALKING LIKE THAT IS WHY WOMEN DON'T LIKE YOU.
YOU SAY SOME-THING?
NOPE.
IN OUR FAMILY, FOR SOME REASON...
...WHAT YUKARI WANTED ALWAYS WON OUT.
Older sister, Yukari.
I WANNA GO TO THE AQUARIUM.
IT'S INDOORS, SO I WON'T GET SUN-BURNED.
Even in middle school, she was too pretty to be real.
AMUSEMENT PARK! AMUSEMENT PARK!
Younger sister, Hana. Just some short kid.

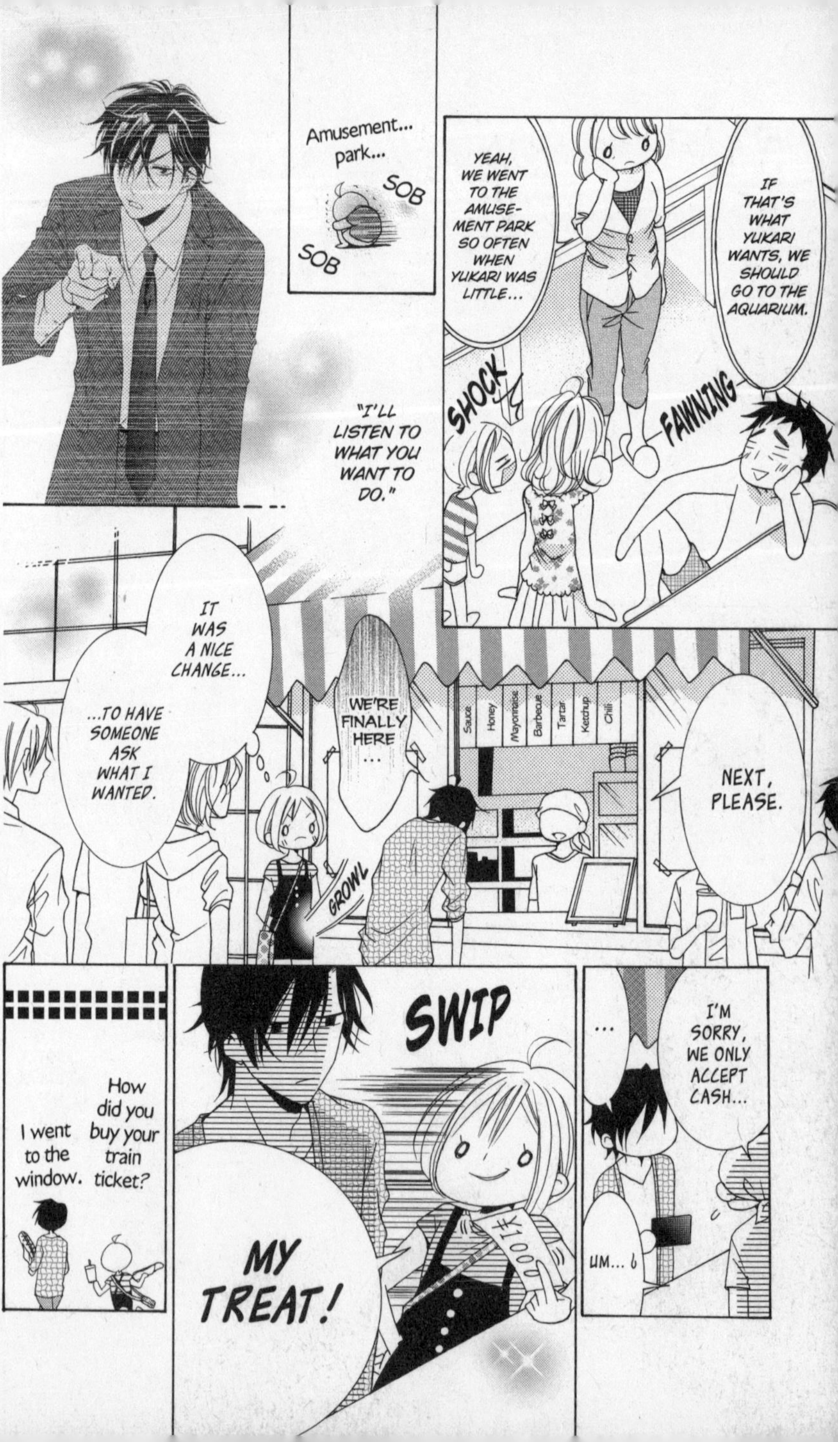
Amusement... park...
SOB
SOB
IF THAT'S WHAT YUKARI WANTS, WE SHOULD GO TO THE AQUARIUM.
YEAH, WE WENT TO THE AMUSEMENT PARK SO OFTEN WHEN YUKARI WAS LITTLE...
FAWNING
SHOCK
"I'LL LISTEN TO WHAT YOU WANT TO DO."
NEXT, PLEASE.
Sauce
Honey
Mayonnaise
Barbecue
Tartar
Ketchup
Chili
WE'RE FINALLY HERE...
GROWL
IT WAS A NICE CHANGE...
...TO HAVE SOMEONE ASK WHAT I WANTED.
I'M SORRY, WE ONLY ACCEPT CASH...
...
UM...
SWIP
¥1000
MY TREAT!
How did you buy your train ticket?
I went to the window.

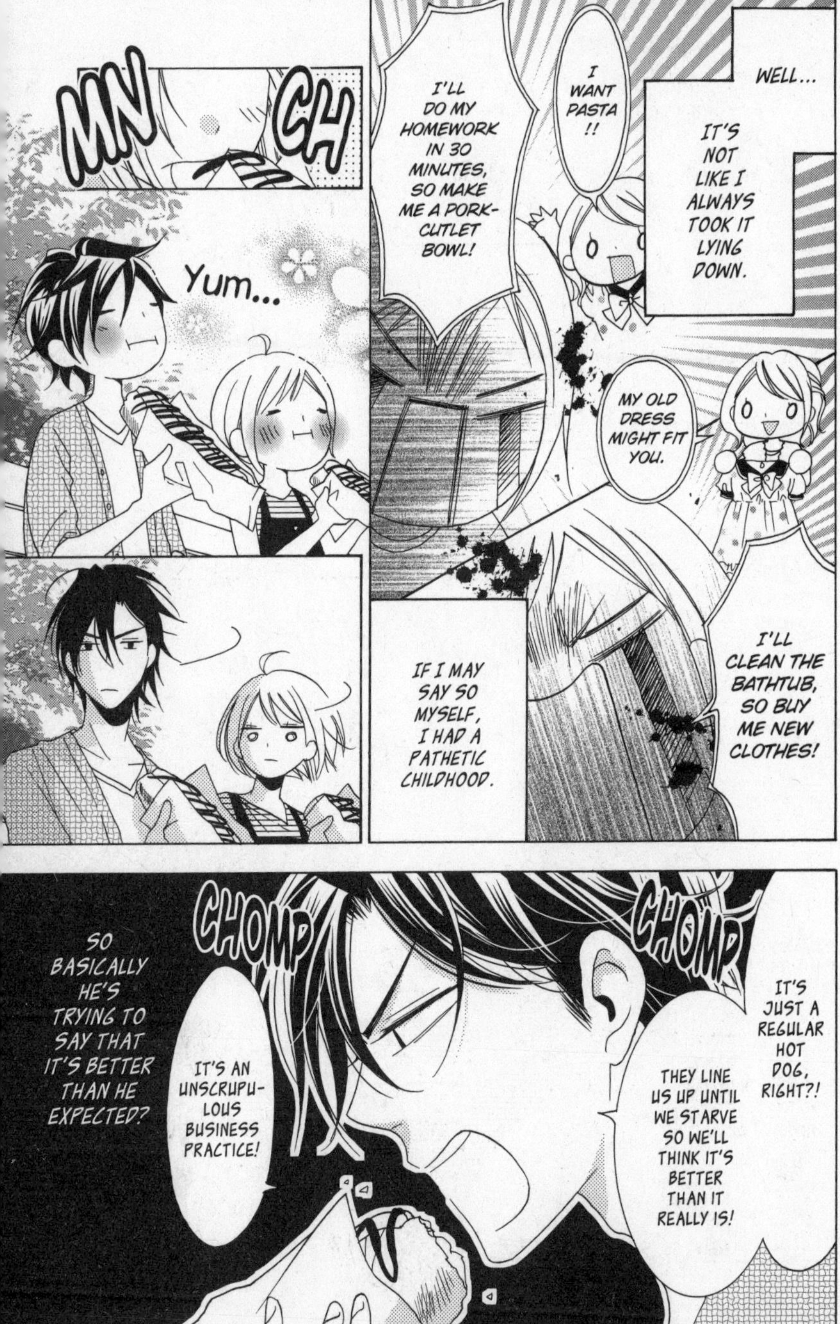
WELL...
IT'S NOT LIKE I ALWAYS TOOK IT LYING DOWN.
I WANT PASTA!!
I'LL DO MY HOMEWORK IN 30 MINUTES, SO MAKE ME A PORK-CUTLET BOWL!
MY OLD DRESS MIGHT FIT YOU.
I'LL CLEAN THE BATHTUB, SO BUY ME NEW CLOTHES!
IF I MAY SAY SO MYSELF, I HAD A PATHETIC CHILDHOOD.
MN
CH
Yum...
CHOMP
CHOMP
IT'S JUST A REGULAR HOT DOG, RIGHT?!
THEY LINE US UP UNTIL WE STARVE SO WE'LL THINK IT'S BETTER THAN IT REALLY IS!
IT'S AN UNSCRUPULOUS BUSINESS PRACTICE!
SO BASICALLY HE'S TRYING TO SAY THAT IT'S BETTER THAN HE EXPECTED?

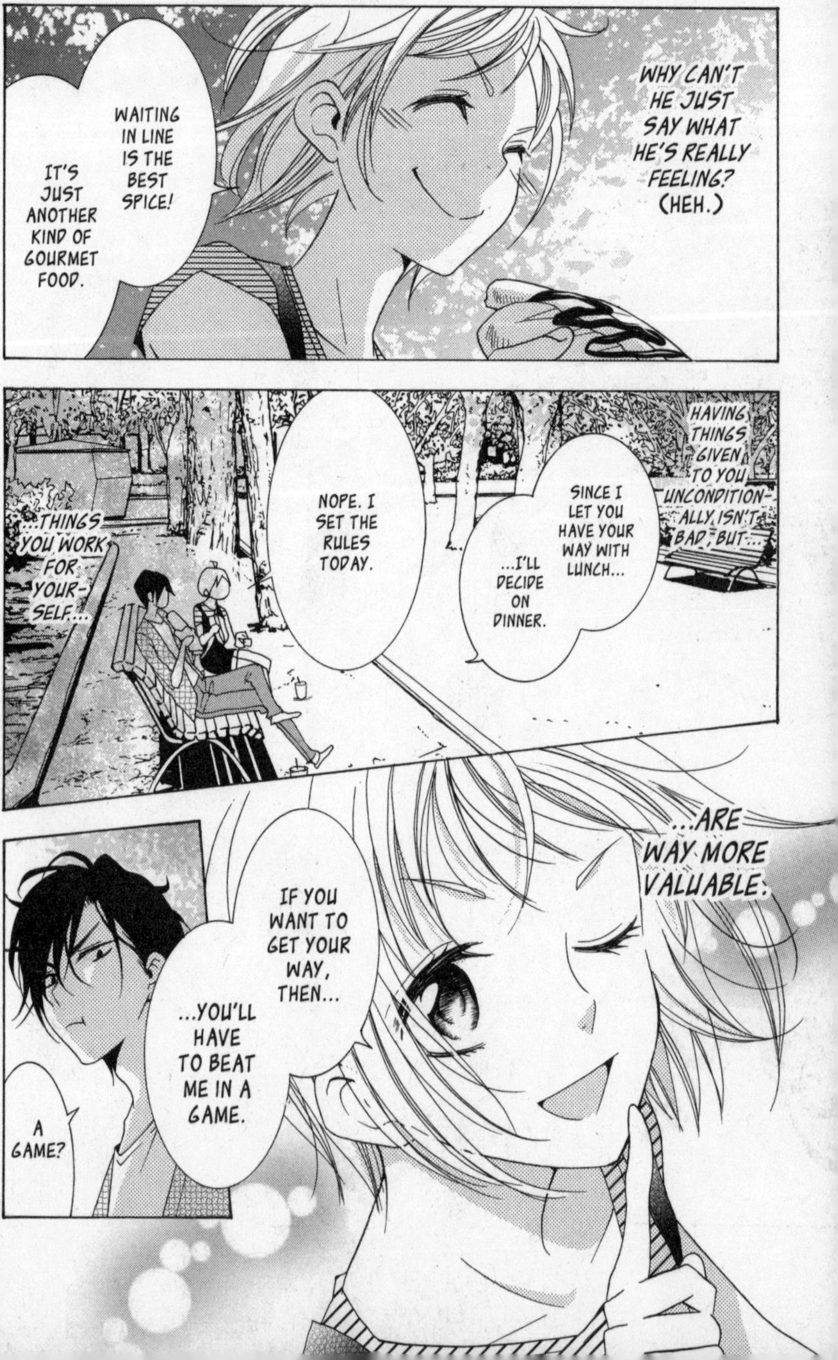
WHY CAN'T HE JUST SAY WHAT HE'S REALLY FEELING? (HEH.)
WAITING IN LINE IS THE BEST SPICE!
IT'S JUST ANOTHER KIND OF GOURMET FOOD.
HAVING THINGS GIVEN TO YOU UNCONDITION-ALLY ISN'T BAD, BUT...
SINCE I LET YOU HAVE YOUR WAY WITH LUNCH...
...I'LL DECIDE ON DINNER.
NOPE. I SET THE RULES TODAY.
...THINGS YOU WORK FOR YOUR-SELF...
...ARE WAY MORE VALUABLE.
IF YOU WANT TO GET YOUR WAY, THEN...
...YOU'LL HAVE TO BEAT ME IN A GAME.
A GAME?

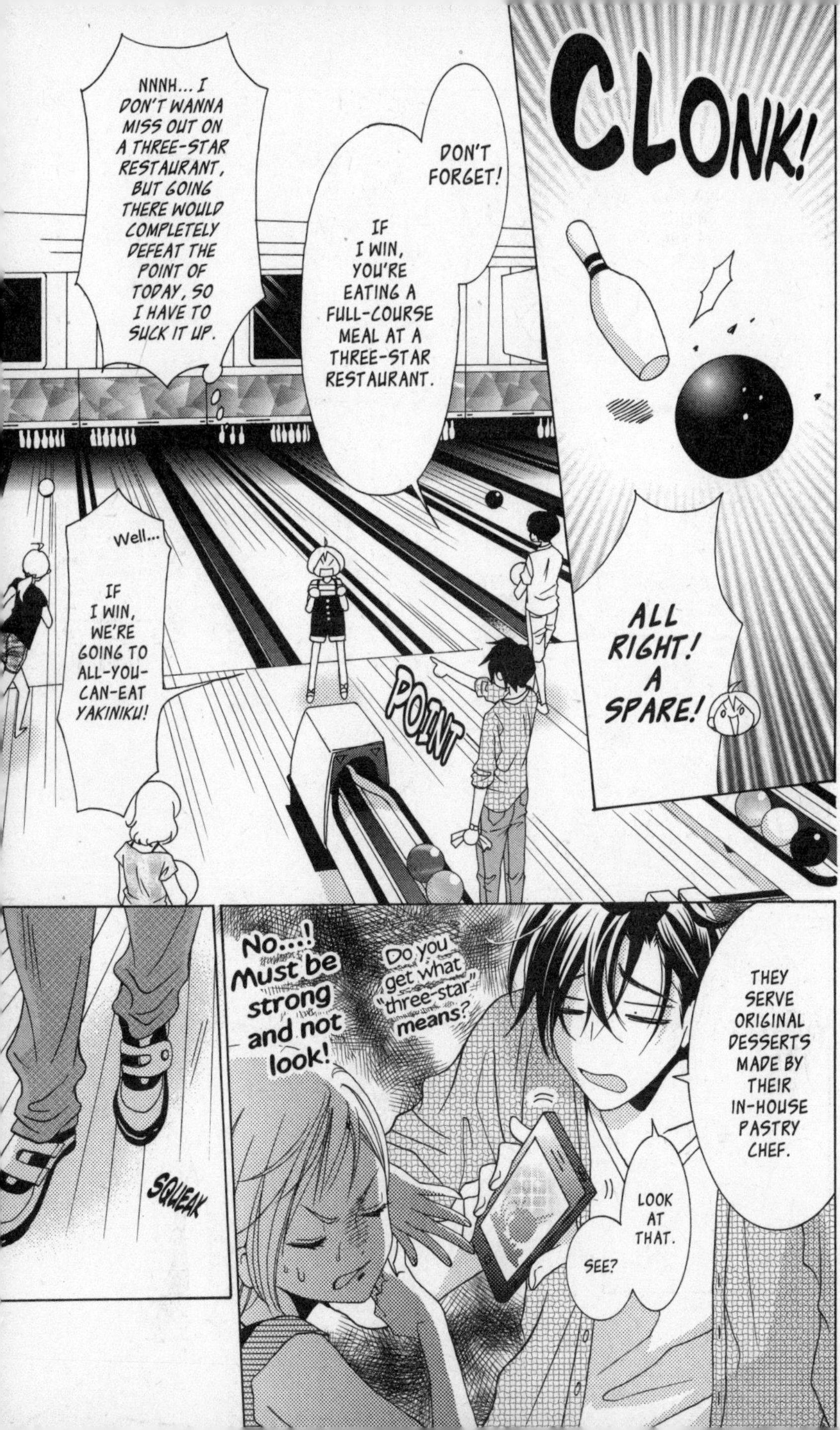

CLONK!
ALL RIGHT! A SPARE!
DON'T FORGET!
IF I WIN, YOU'RE EATING A FULL-COURSE MEAL AT A THREE-STAR RESTAURANT.
NNNH... I DON'T WANNA MISS OUT ON A THREE-STAR RESTAURANT, BUT GOING THERE WOULD COMPLETELY DEFEAT THE POINT OF TODAY, SO I HAVE TO SUCK IT UP.
POINT
Well...
IF I WIN, WE'RE GOING TO ALL-YOU-CAN-EAT YAKINIKU!
THEY SERVE ORIGINAL DESSERTS MADE BY THEIR IN-HOUSE PASTRY CHEF.
LOOK AT THAT.
SEE?
Do you get what "three-star" means?
No...! Must be strong and not look!
SQUEAK

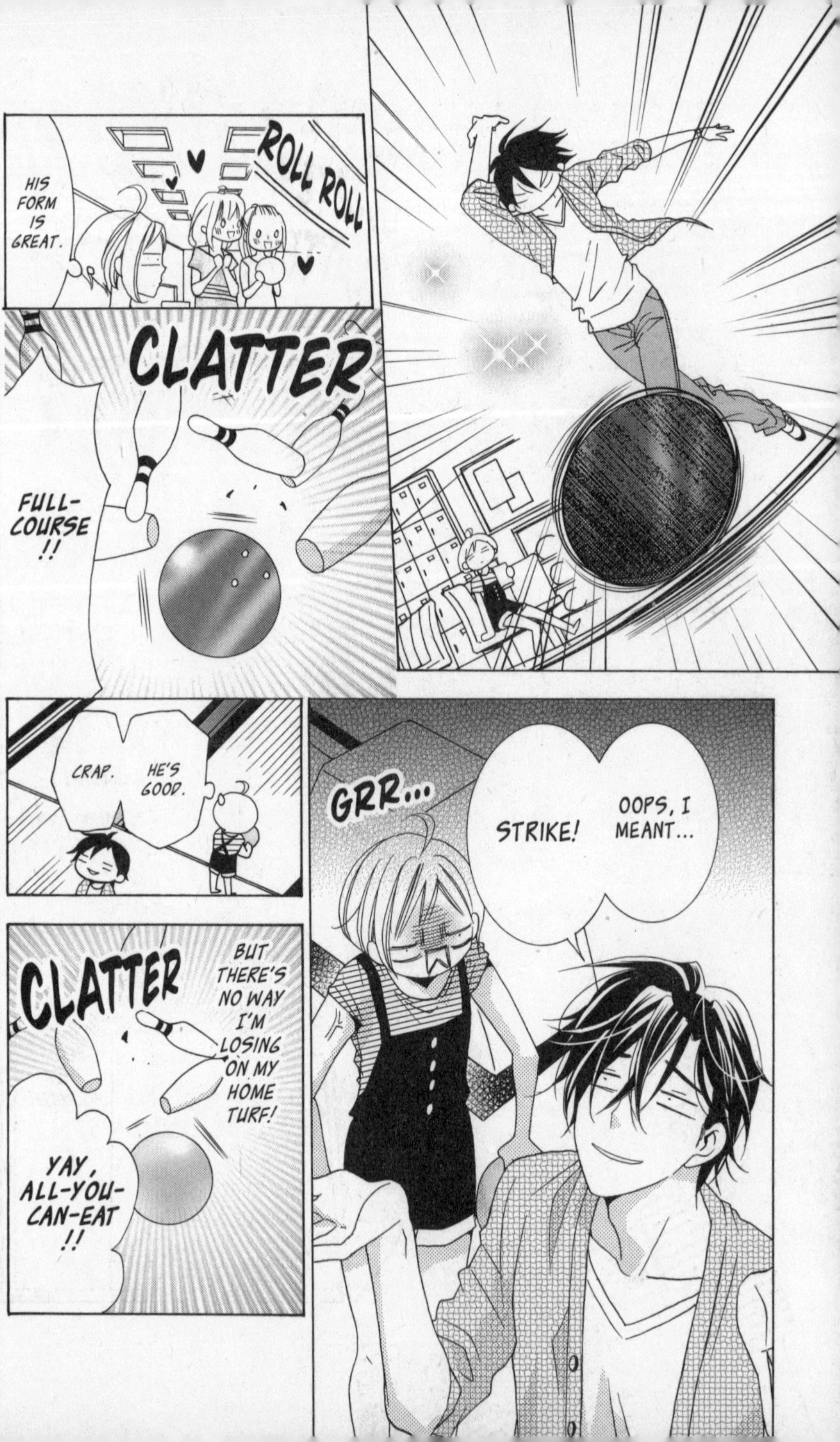
ROLL ROLL
HIS FORM IS GREAT.
CLATTER
FULL-COURSE!!
OOPS, I MEANT...
STRIKE!
GRR...
HE'S GOOD.
CRAP.
BUT THERE'S NO WAY I'M LOSING ON MY HOME TURF!
CLATTER
YAY, ALL-YOU-CAN-EAT!!

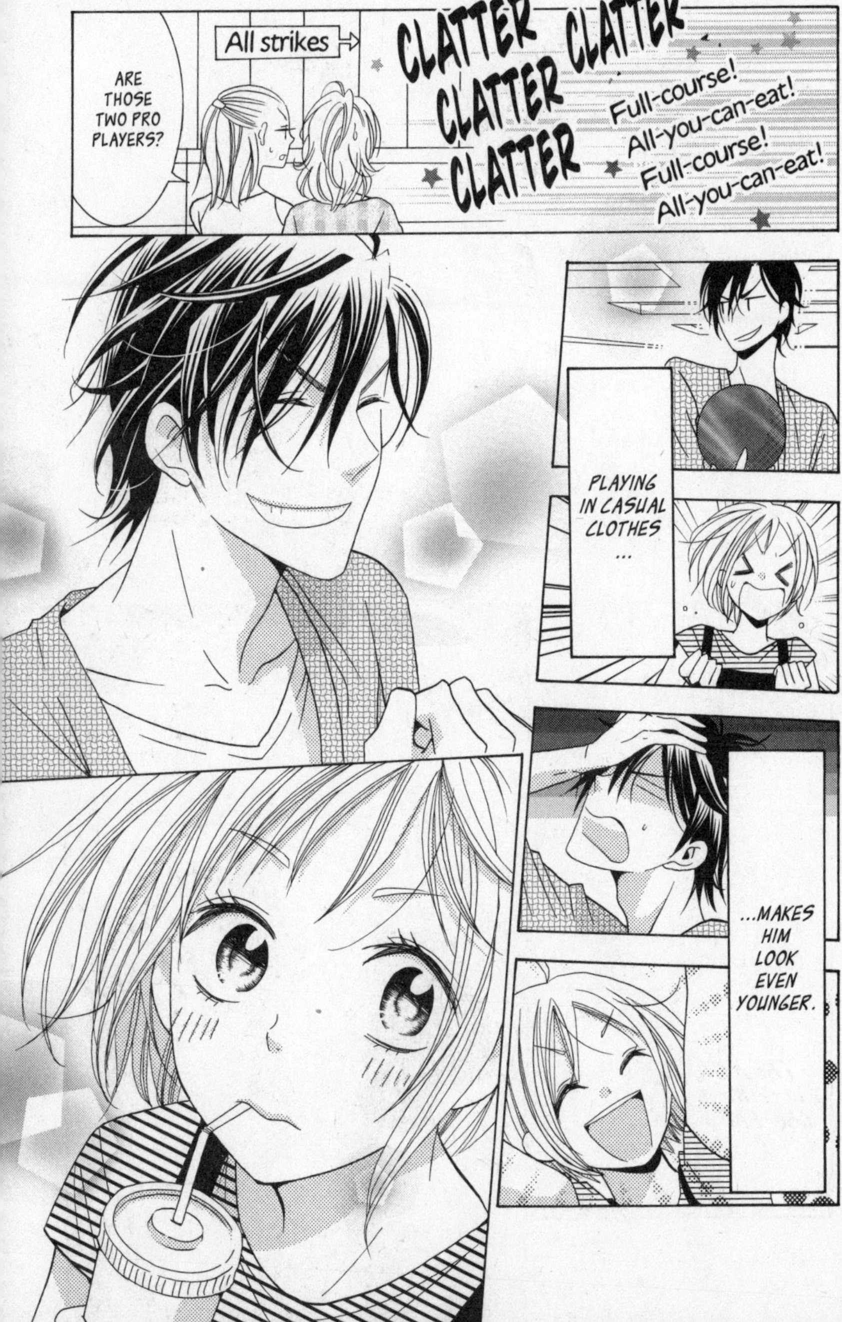
Full-course! All-you-can-eat! Full-course! All-you-can-eat!
CLATTER CLATTER CLATTER CLATTER
All strikes
ARE THOSE TWO PRO PLAYERS?
PLAYING IN CASUAL CLOTHES ...
...MAKES HIM LOOK EVEN YOUNGER.

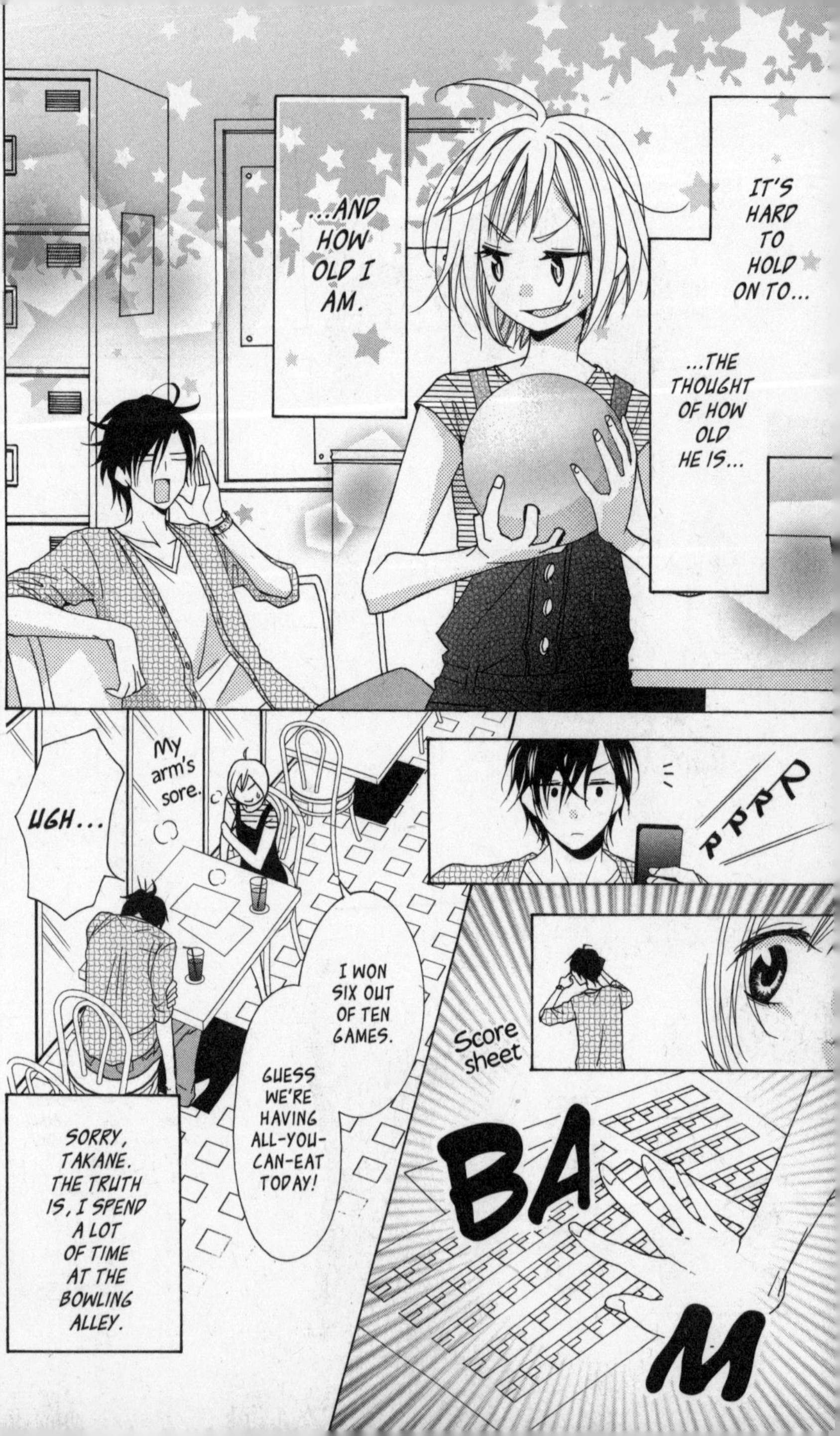
IT'S HARD TO HOLD ON TO...
...THE THOUGHT OF HOW OLD HE IS...
...AND HOW OLD I AM.
PRRR
Score sheet
BAM
My arm's sore.
UGH...
I WON SIX OUT OF TEN GAMES.
GUESS WE'RE HAVING ALL-YOU-CAN-EAT TODAY!
SORRY, TAKANE. THE TRUTH IS, I SPEND A LOT OF TIME AT THE BOWLING ALLEY.

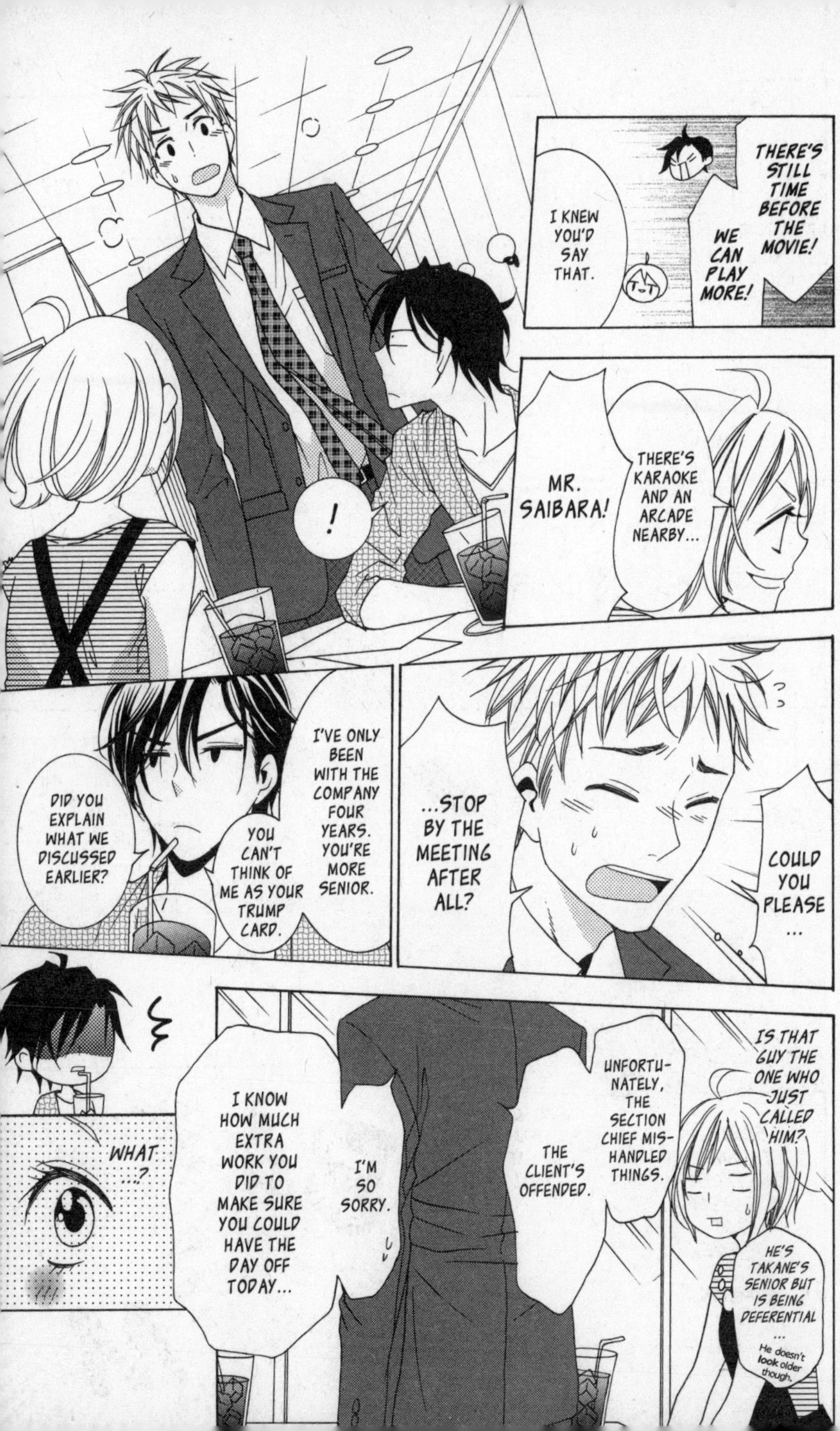
THERE'S STILL TIME BEFORE THE MOVIE!
WE CAN PLAY MORE!
I KNEW YOU'D SAY THAT.
THERE'S KARAOKE AND AN ARCADE NEARBY...
MR. SAIBARA!
!
COULD YOU PLEASE ...
...STOP BY THE MEETING AFTER ALL?
I'VE ONLY BEEN WITH THE COMPANY FOUR YEARS. YOU'RE MORE SENIOR.
YOU CAN'T THINK OF ME AS YOUR TRUMP CARD.
DID YOU EXPLAIN WHAT WE DISCUSSED EARLIER?
IS THAT GUY THE ONE WHO JUST CALLED HIM?
UNFORTU-NATELY, THE SECTION CHIEF MIS-HANDLED THINGS.
THE CLIENT'S OFFENDED.
HE'S TAKANE'S SENIOR BUT IS BEING DEFERENTIAL ...
He doesn't look older though.
I'M SO SORRY.
I KNOW HOW MUCH EXTRA WORK YOU DID TO MAKE SURE YOU COULD HAVE THE DAY OFF TODAY...
WHAT ...?

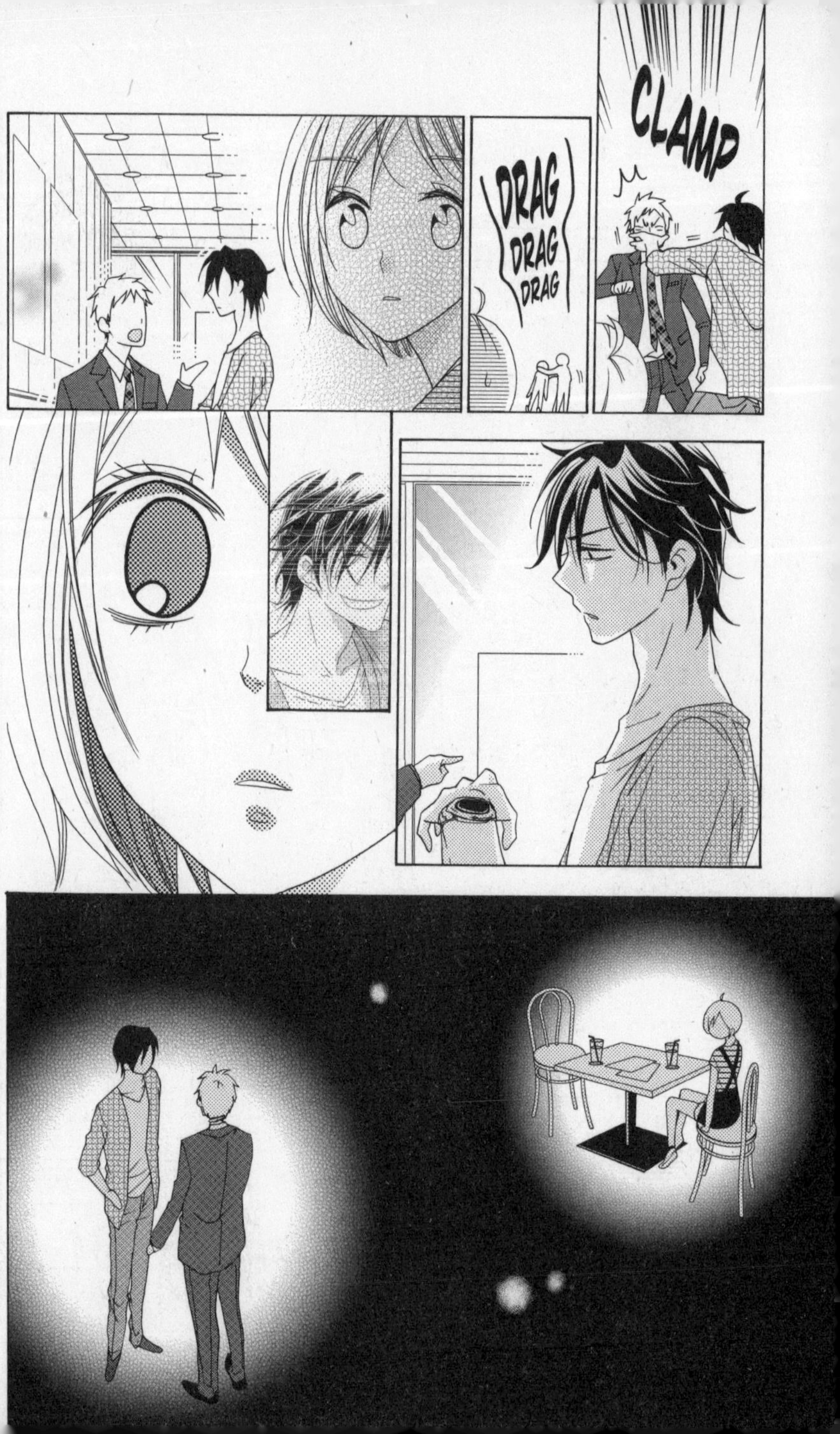
CLAMP
DRAG
DRAG
DRAG

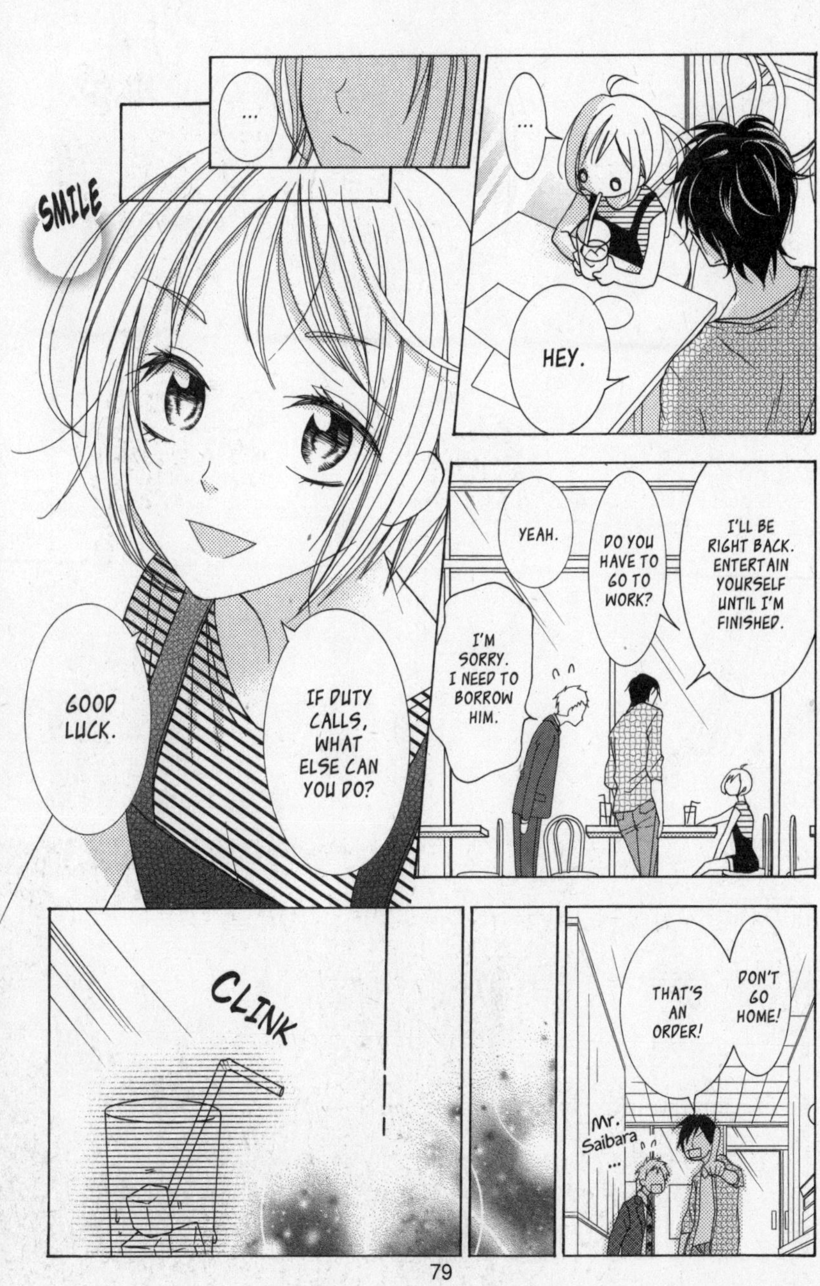
...
HEY.
I'LL BE RIGHT BACK. ENTERTAIN YOURSELF UNTIL I'M FINISHED.
DO YOU HAVE TO GO TO WORK?
YEAH.
I'M SORRY. I NEED TO BORROW HIM.
...
SMILE
IF DUTY CALLS, WHAT ELSE CAN YOU DO?
GOOD LUCK.
DON'T GO HOME!
THAT'S AN ORDER!
Mr. Saibara ...
CLINK

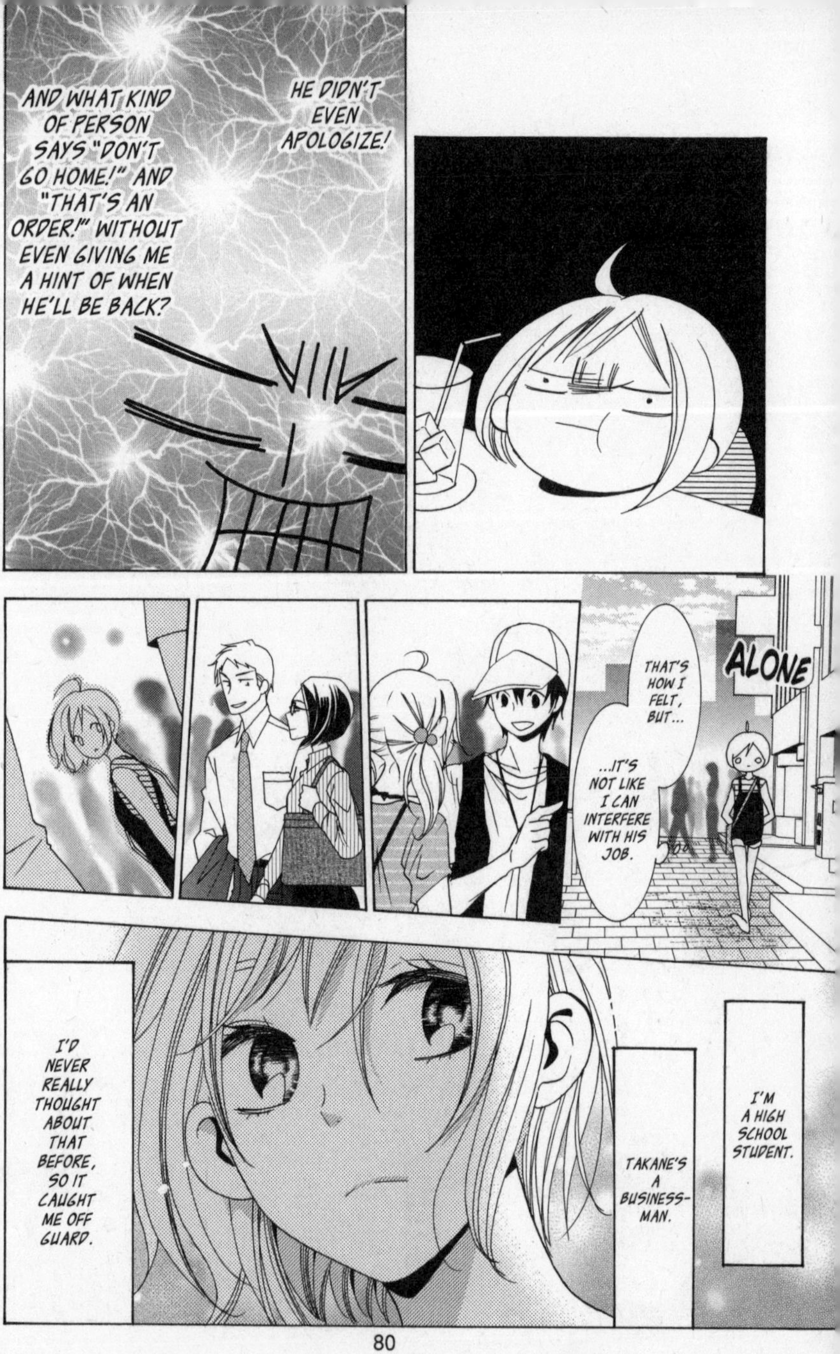
HE DIDN'T EVEN APOLOGIZE!
AND WHAT KIND OF PERSON SAYS "DON'T GO HOME!" AND "THAT'S AN ORDER!" WITHOUT EVEN GIVING ME A HINT OF WHEN HE'LL BE BACK?
ALONE
THAT'S HOW I FELT, BUT...
...IT'S NOT LIKE I CAN INTERFERE WITH HIS JOB.
I'M A HIGH SCHOOL STUDENT.
TAKANE'S A BUSINESS-MAN.
I'D NEVER REALLY THOUGHT ABOUT THAT BEFORE, SO IT CAUGHT ME OFF GUARD.

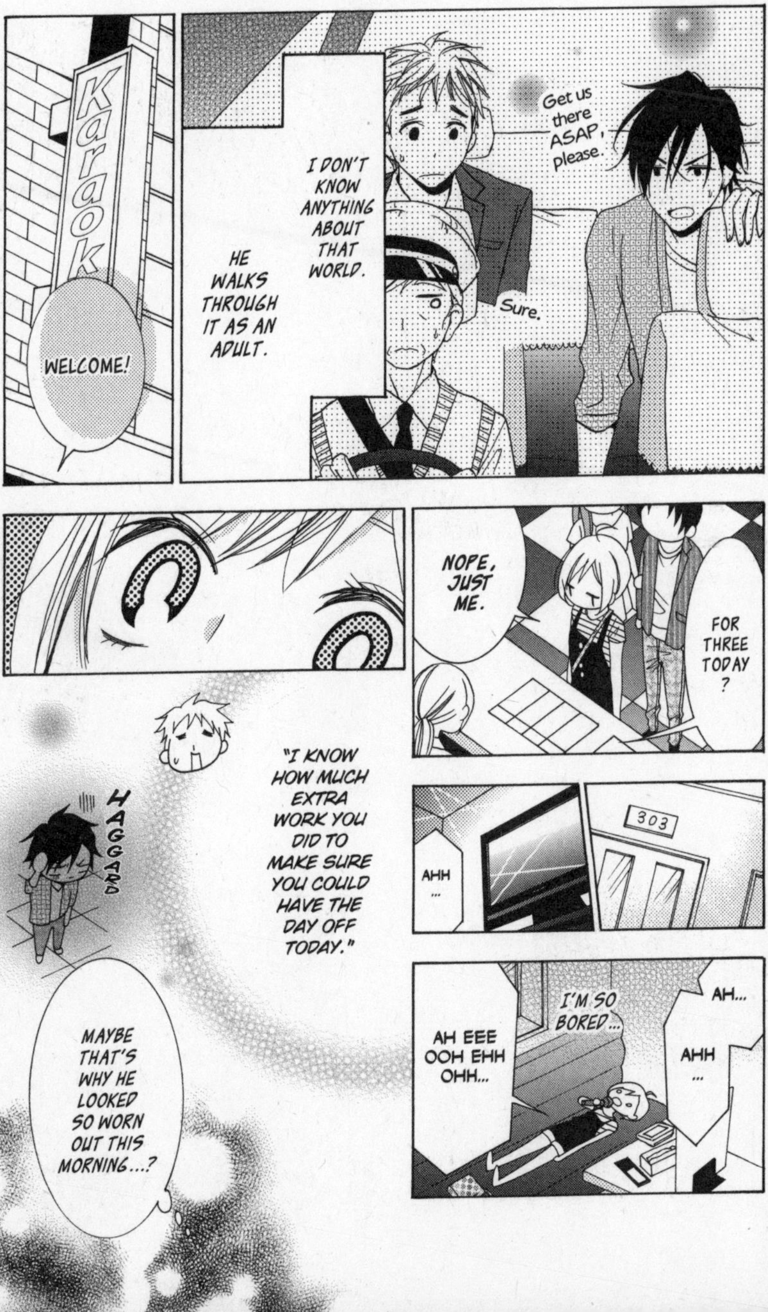
Get us there ASAP, please.
I DON'T KNOW ANYTHING ABOUT THAT WORLD.
Sure.
HE WALKS THROUGH IT AS AN ADULT.
Karaok
WELCOME!
FOR THREE TODAY?
NOPE, JUST ME.
AHH...
AH...
AHH...
I'M SO BORED...
AH EEE OOH EHH OHH...
"I KNOW HOW MUCH EXTRA WORK YOU DID TO MAKE SURE YOU COULD HAVE THE DAY OFF TODAY."
HAGGARD
MAYBE THAT'S WHY HE LOOKED SO WORN OUT THIS MORNING...?

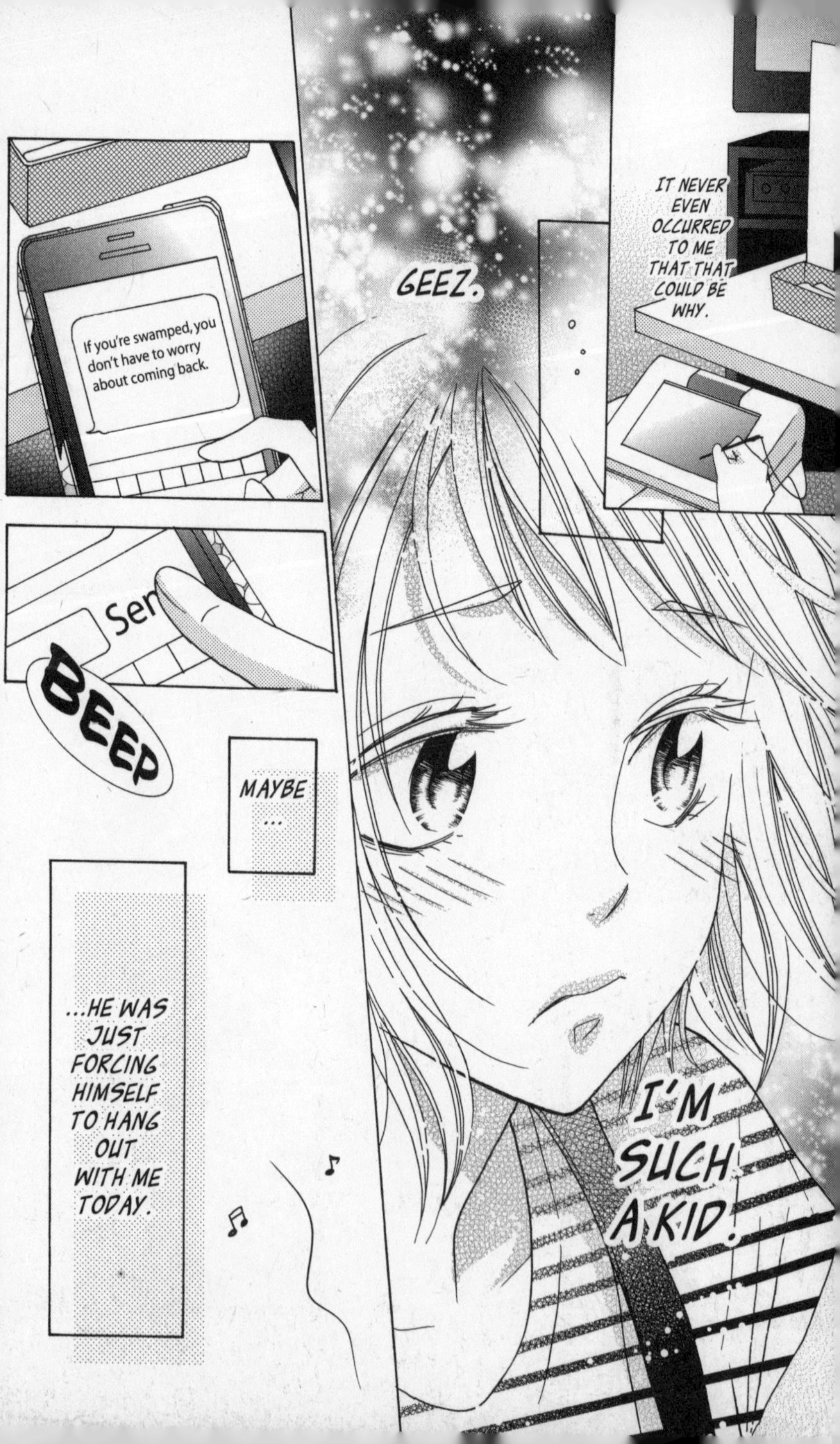
IT NEVER EVEN OCCURRED TO ME THAT THAT COULD BE WHY.
GEEZ.
If you're swamped, you don't have to worry about coming back.
Sen
BEEP
MAYBE ...
...HE WAS JUST FORCING HIMSELF TO HANG OUT WITH ME TODAY.
I'M SUCH A KID!

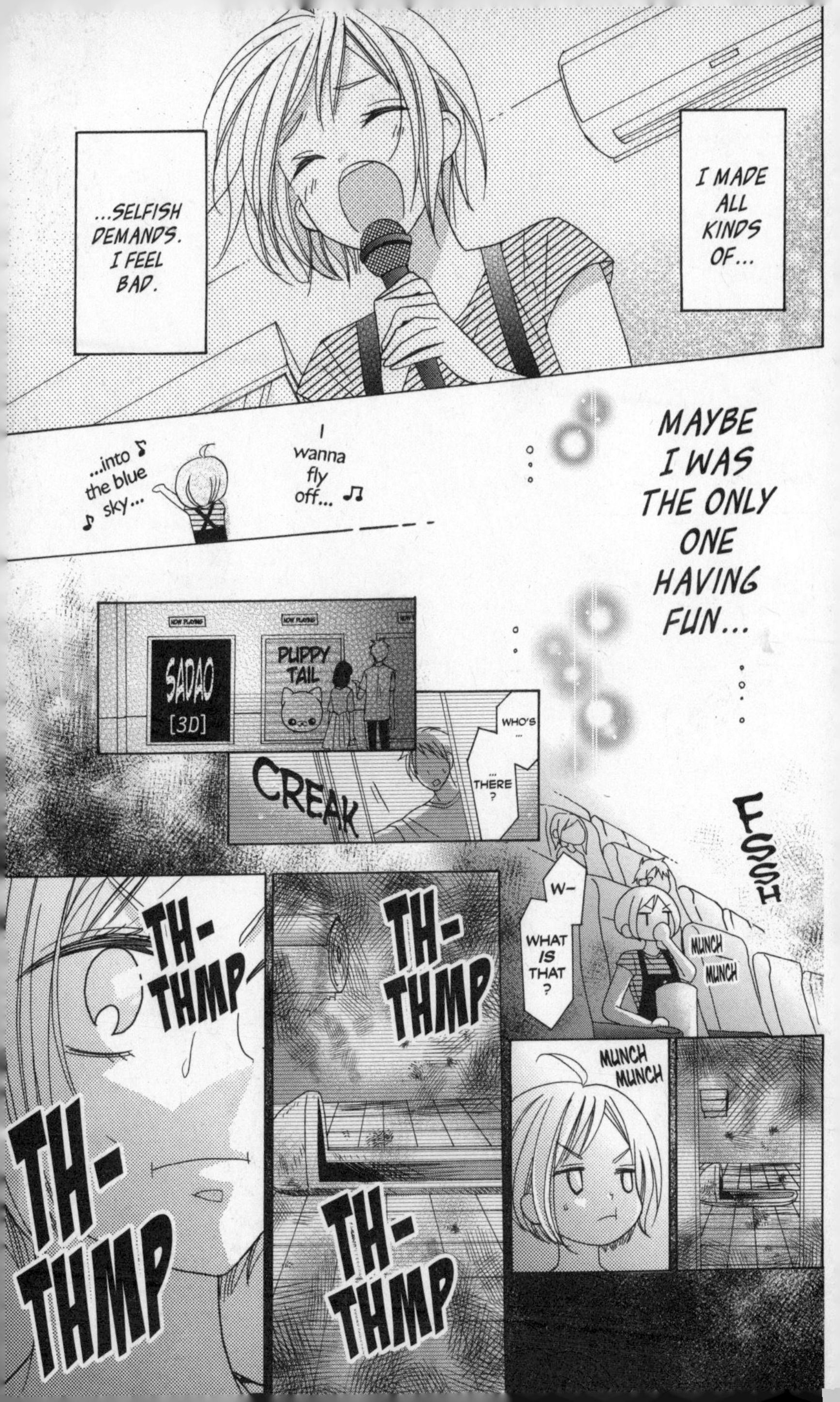
I MADE ALL KINDS OF...
...SELFISH DEMANDS. I FEEL BAD.
I wanna fly off... ♫
...into ♪ the blue ♪ sky...
MAYBE I WAS THE ONLY ONE HAVING FUN...
NOW PLAYING
NOW PLAYING
PUPPY TAIL
SADAO [3D]
WHO'S ... ... THERE?
CREAK
FSSH
MUNCH MUNCH
W- WHAT IS THAT?
MUNCH MUNCH
TH-THMP
TH-THMP
TH-THMP
TH-THMP

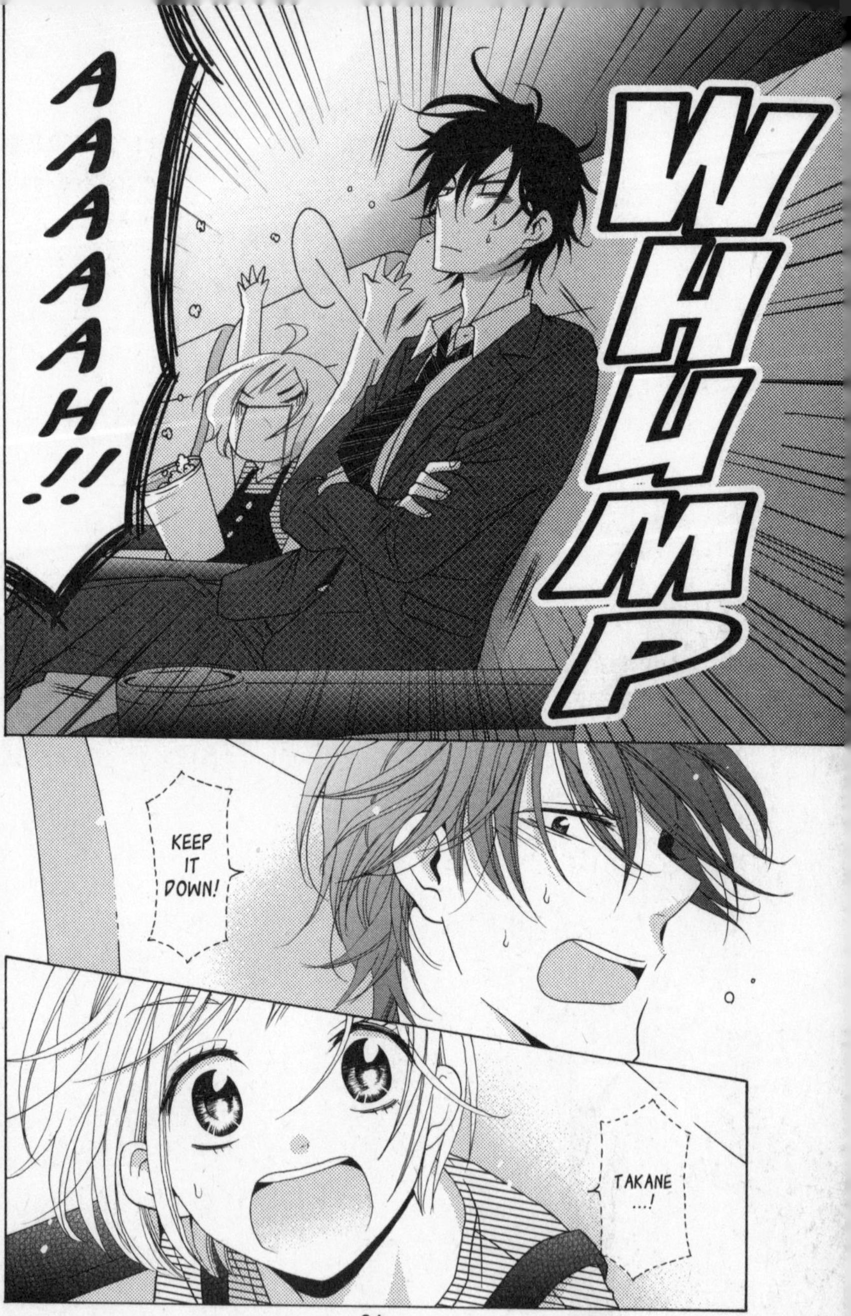
WHUMP
AAAAAAH!!
KEEP IT DOWN!
TAKANE ...!

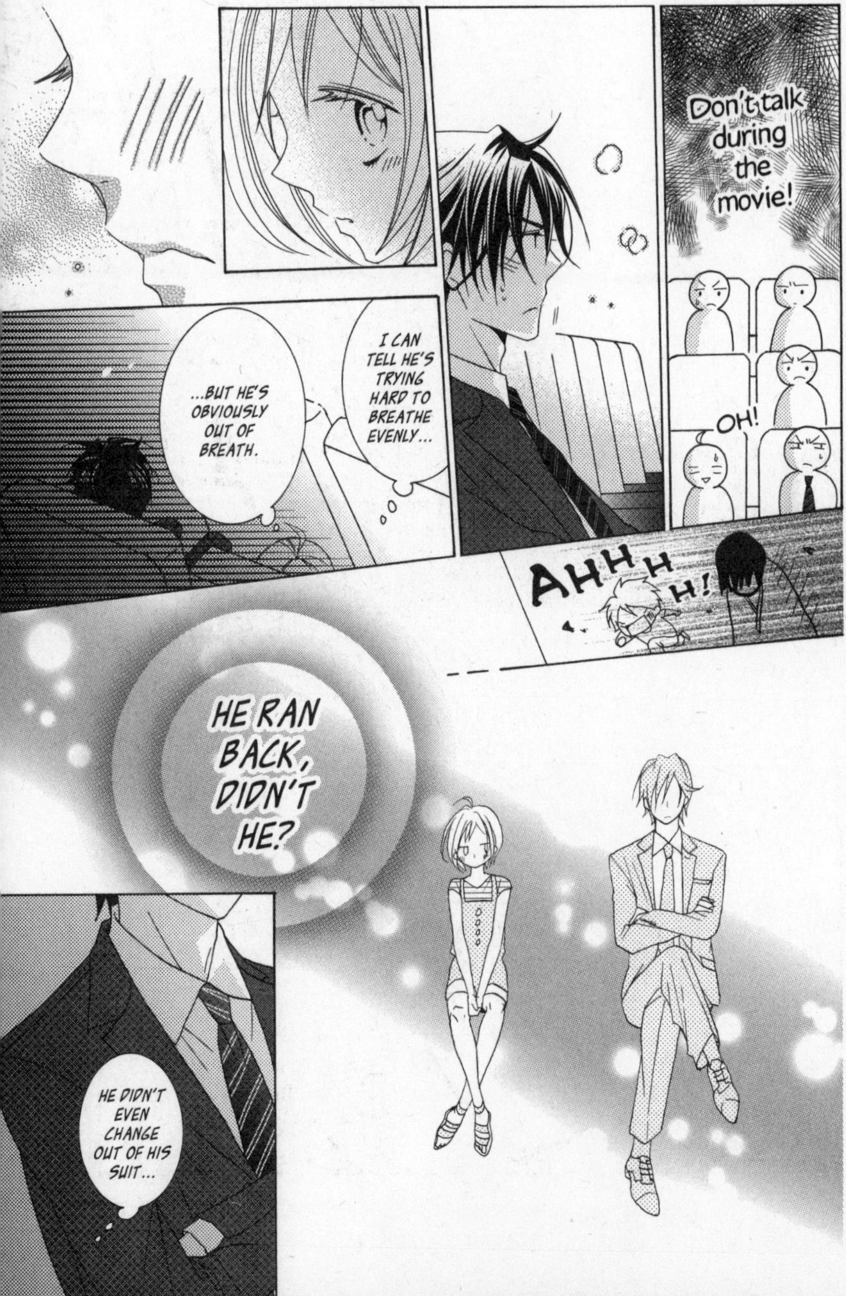
Don't talk during the movie!
OH!
AHHHH!
I CAN TELL HE'S TRYING HARD TO BREATHE EVENLY...
...BUT HE'S OBVIOUSLY OUT OF BREATH.
HE RAN BACK, DIDN'T HE?
HE DIDN'T EVEN CHANGE OUT OF HIS SUIT...

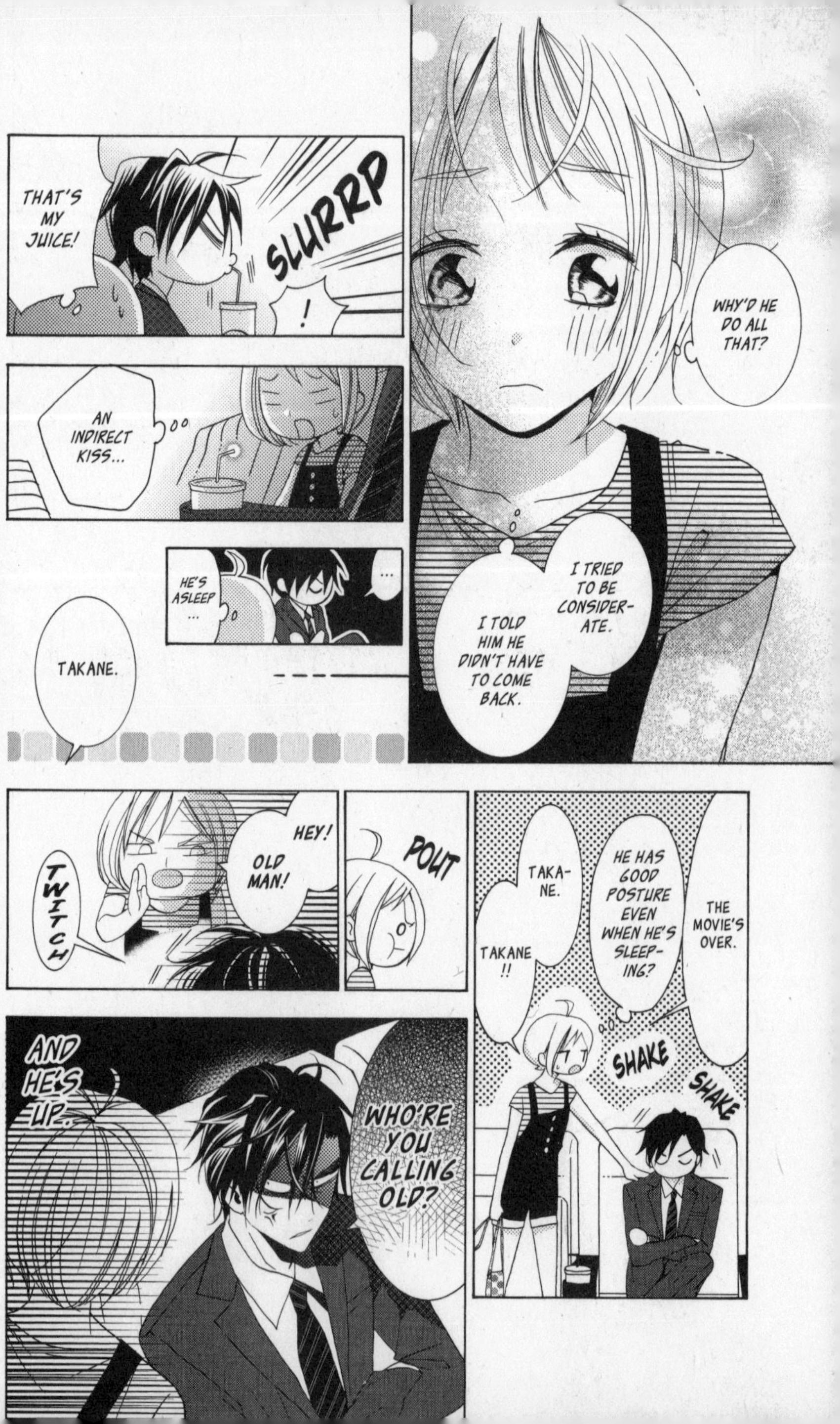
WHY'D HE DO ALL THAT?
I TRIED TO BE CONSIDER-ATE.
I TOLD HIM HE DIDN'T HAVE TO COME BACK.
SLURRP
!
THAT'S MY JUICE!
AN INDIRECT KISS...
...
HE'S ASLEEP ...
TAKANE.
THE MOVIE'S OVER.
HE HAS GOOD POSTURE EVEN WHEN HE'S SLEEP-ING?
TAKA-NE.
TAKANE !!
SHAKE
SHAKE
POUT
HEY!
OLD MAN!
TWITCH
WHO'RE YOU CALLING OLD?
AND HE'S UP...

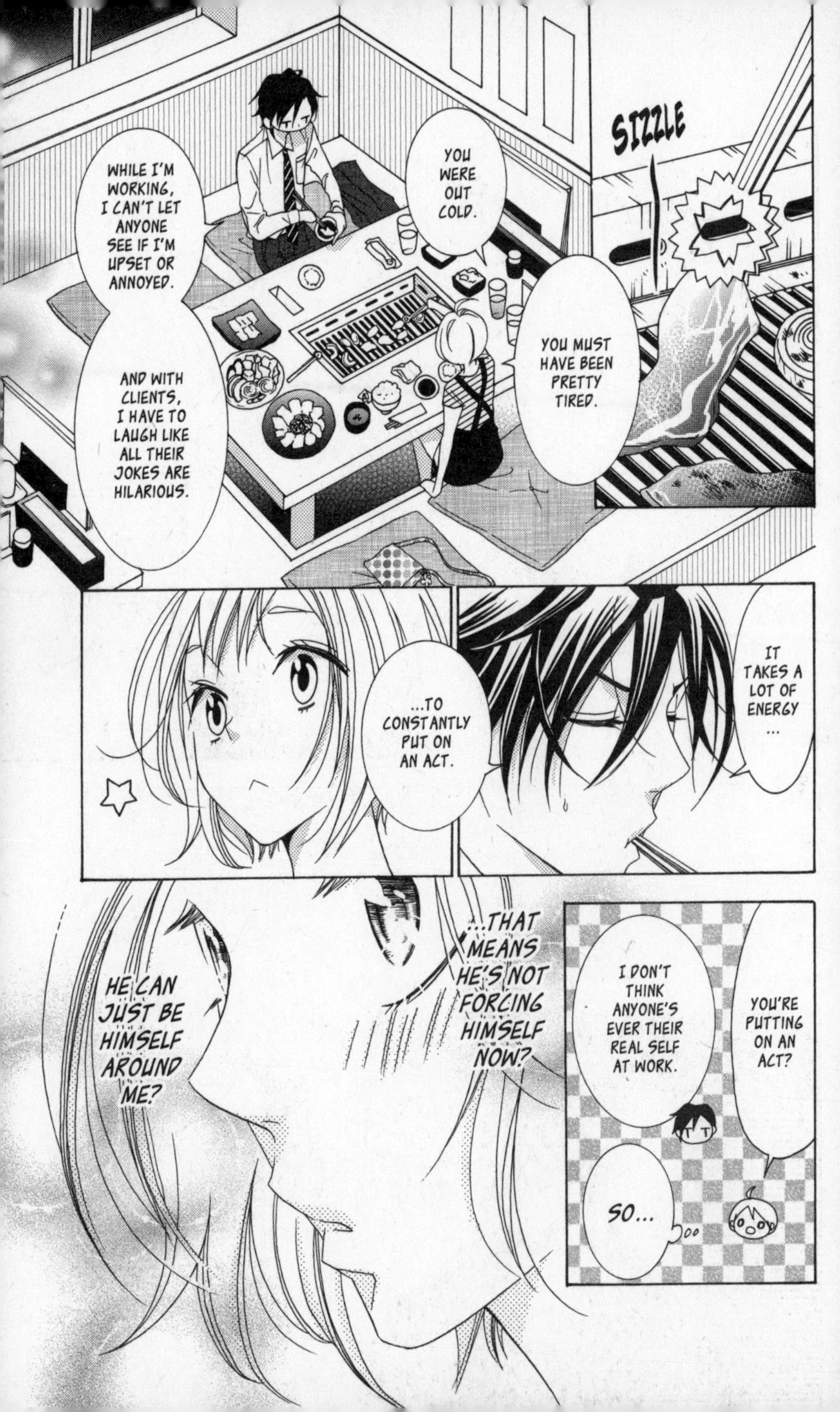
SIZZLE
YOU WERE OUT COLD.
YOU MUST HAVE BEEN PRETTY TIRED.
WHILE I'M WORKING, I CAN'T LET ANYONE SEE IF I'M UPSET OR ANNOYED.
AND WITH CLIENTS, I HAVE TO LAUGH LIKE ALL THEIR JOKES ARE HILARIOUS.
IT TAKES A LOT OF ENERGY ...
...TO CONSTANTLY PUT ON AN ACT.
YOU'RE PUTTING ON AN ACT?
I DON'T THINK ANYONE'S EVER THEIR REAL SELF AT WORK.
SO...
...THAT MEANS HE'S NOT FORCING HIMSELF NOW?
HE CAN JUST BE HIMSELF AROUND ME?

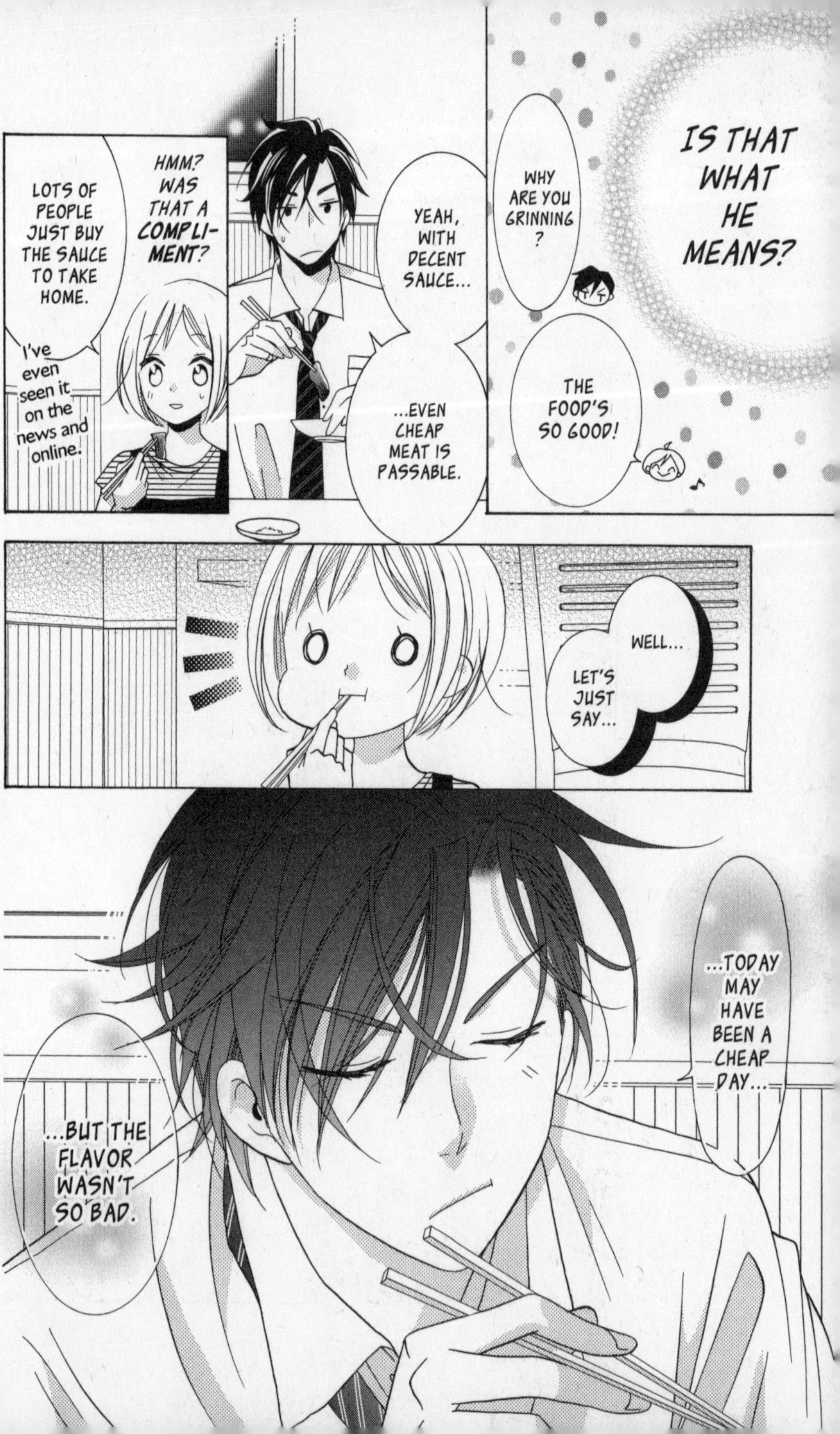
IS THAT WHAT HE MEANS?
WHY ARE YOU GRINNING?
THE FOOD'S SO GOOD!
YEAH, WITH DECENT SAUCE...
...EVEN CHEAP MEAT IS PASSABLE.
HMM? WAS THAT A COMPLIMENT?
LOTS OF PEOPLE JUST BUY THE SAUCE TO TAKE HOME.
I've even seen it on the news and online.
WELL...
LET'S JUST SAY...
...TODAY MAY HAVE BEEN A CHEAP DAY...
...BUT THE FLAVOR WASN'T SO BAD.

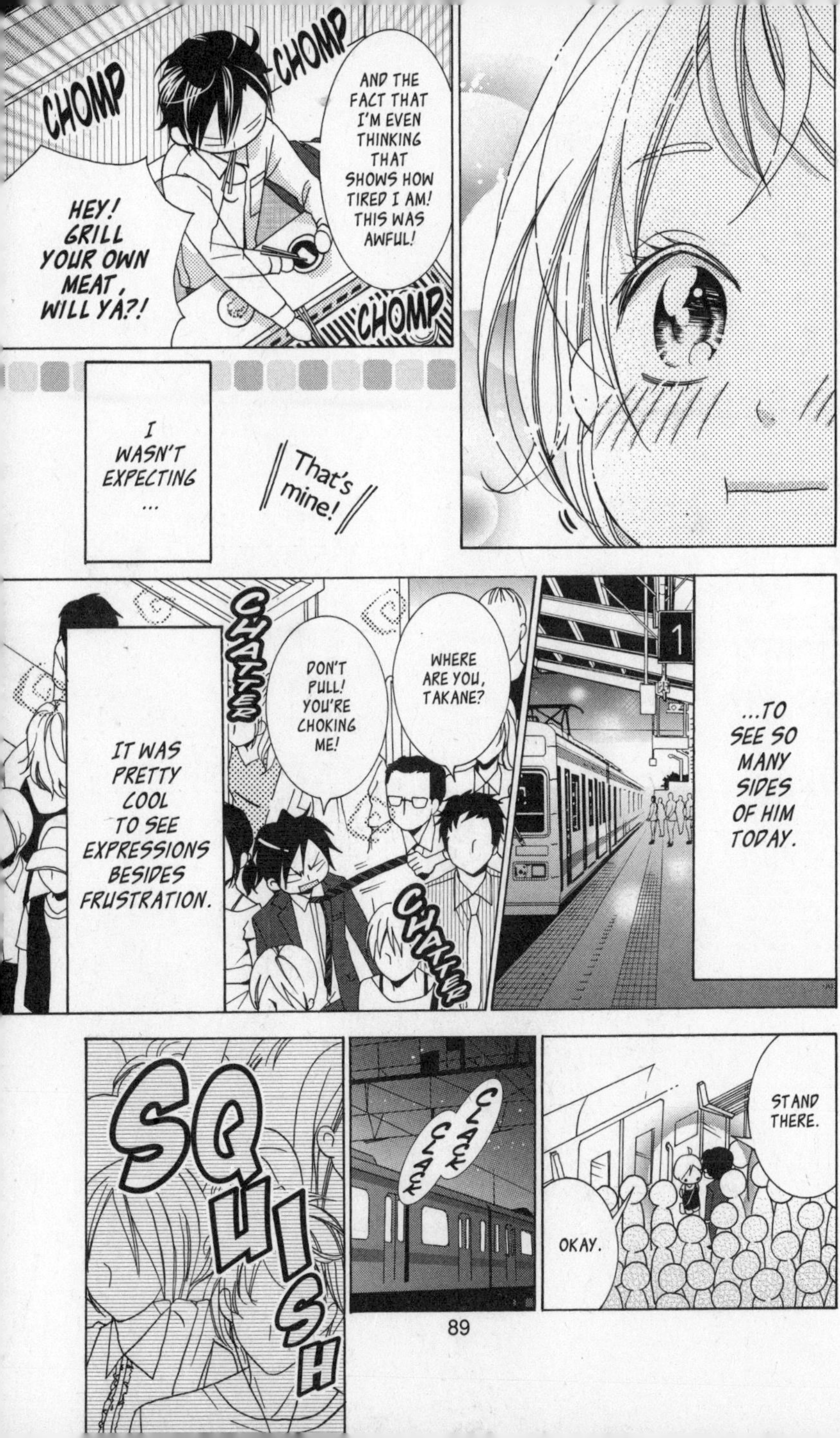
CHOMP
AND THE FACT THAT I'M EVEN THINKING THAT SHOWS HOW TIRED I AM! THIS WAS AWFUL!
CHOMP
CHOMP
HEY! GRILL YOUR OWN MEAT, WILL YA?!
That's mine!
I WASN'T EXPECTING ...
...TO SEE SO MANY SIDES OF HIM TODAY.
WHERE ARE YOU, TAKANE?
DON'T PULL! YOU'RE CHOKING ME!
CHATTER
CHATTER
IT WAS PRETTY COOL TO SEE EXPRESSIONS BESIDES FRUSTRATION.
STAND THERE.
OKAY.
CLACK CLACK CLACK
SQUISH

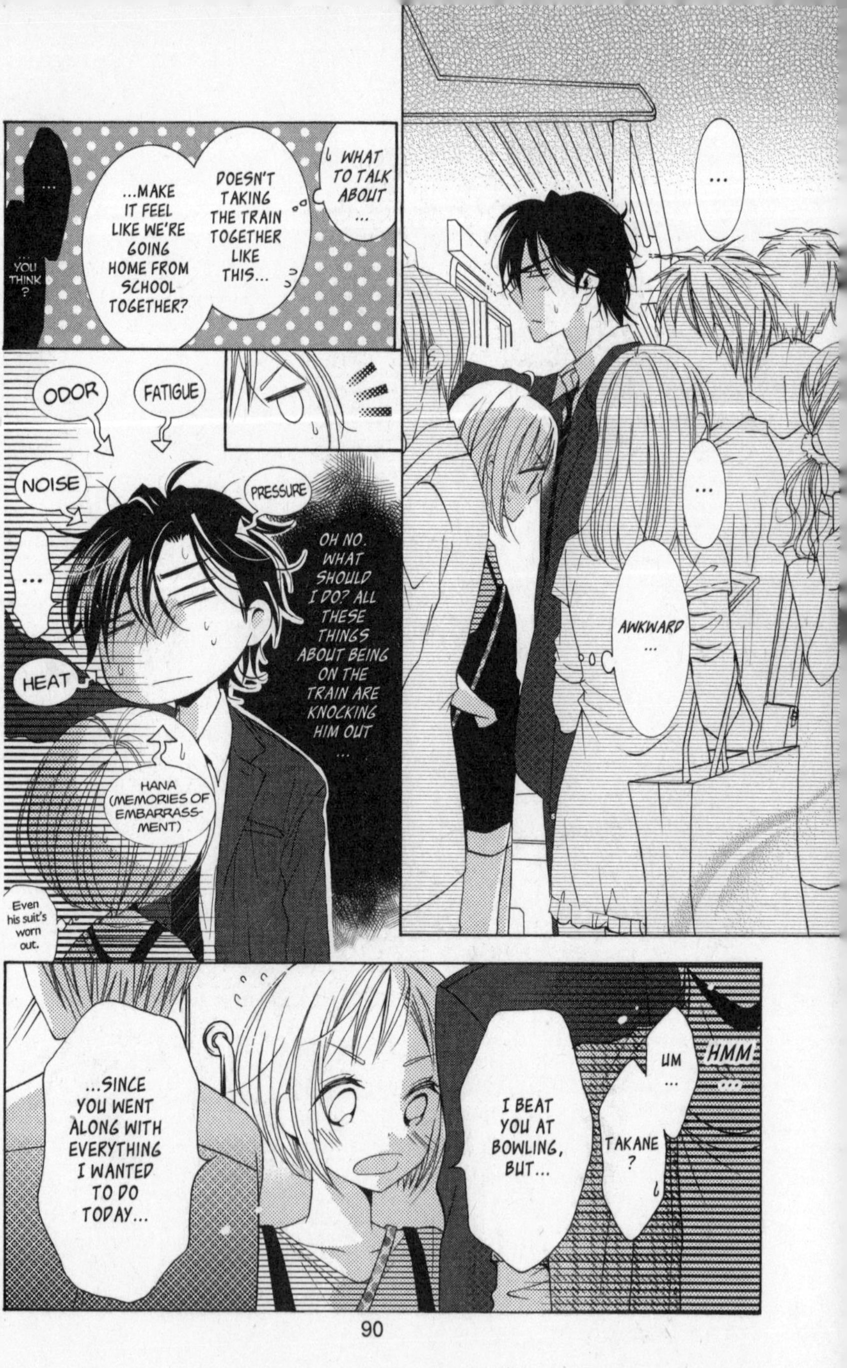

...
...
AWKWARD ...
WHAT TO TALK ABOUT ...
DOESN'T TAKING THE TRAIN TOGETHER LIKE THIS...
...MAKE IT FEEL LIKE WE'RE GOING HOME FROM SCHOOL TOGETHER?
...
... YOU THINK ?
OH NO. WHAT SHOULD I DO? ALL THESE THINGS ABOUT BEING ON THE TRAIN ARE KNOCKING HIM OUT ...
PRESSURE
FATIGUE
ODOR
NOISE
...
HEAT
HANA (MEMORIES OF EMBARRASSMENT)
Even his suit's worn out.
HMM ...
UM ... TAKANE?
I BEAT YOU AT BOWLING, BUT...
...SINCE YOU WENT ALONG WITH EVERYTHING I WANTED TO DO TODAY...

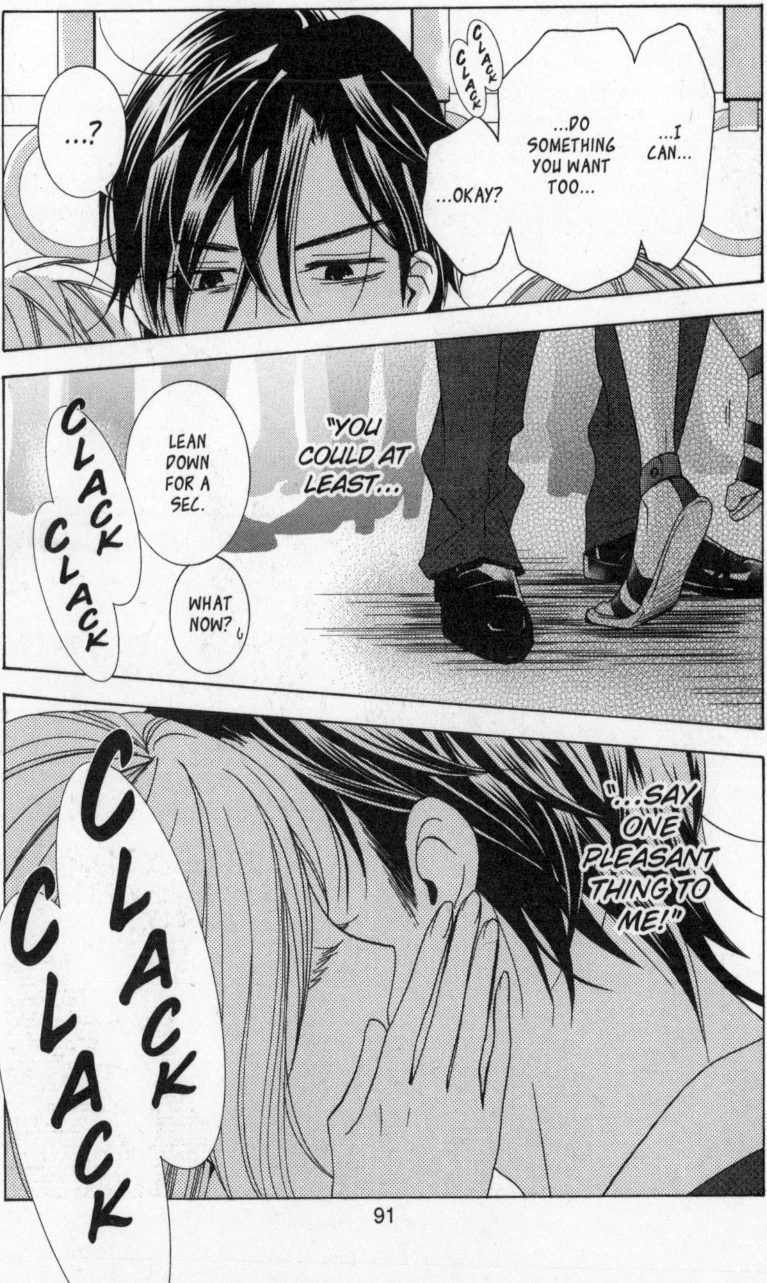
...I CAN...
...DO SOMETHING YOU WANT TOO...
...OKAY?
CLACK CLACK
...?
"YOU COULD AT LEAST...
LEAN DOWN FOR A SEC.
WHAT NOW?
CLACK CLACK
"...SAY ONE PLEASANT THING TO ME!"
CLACK CLACK

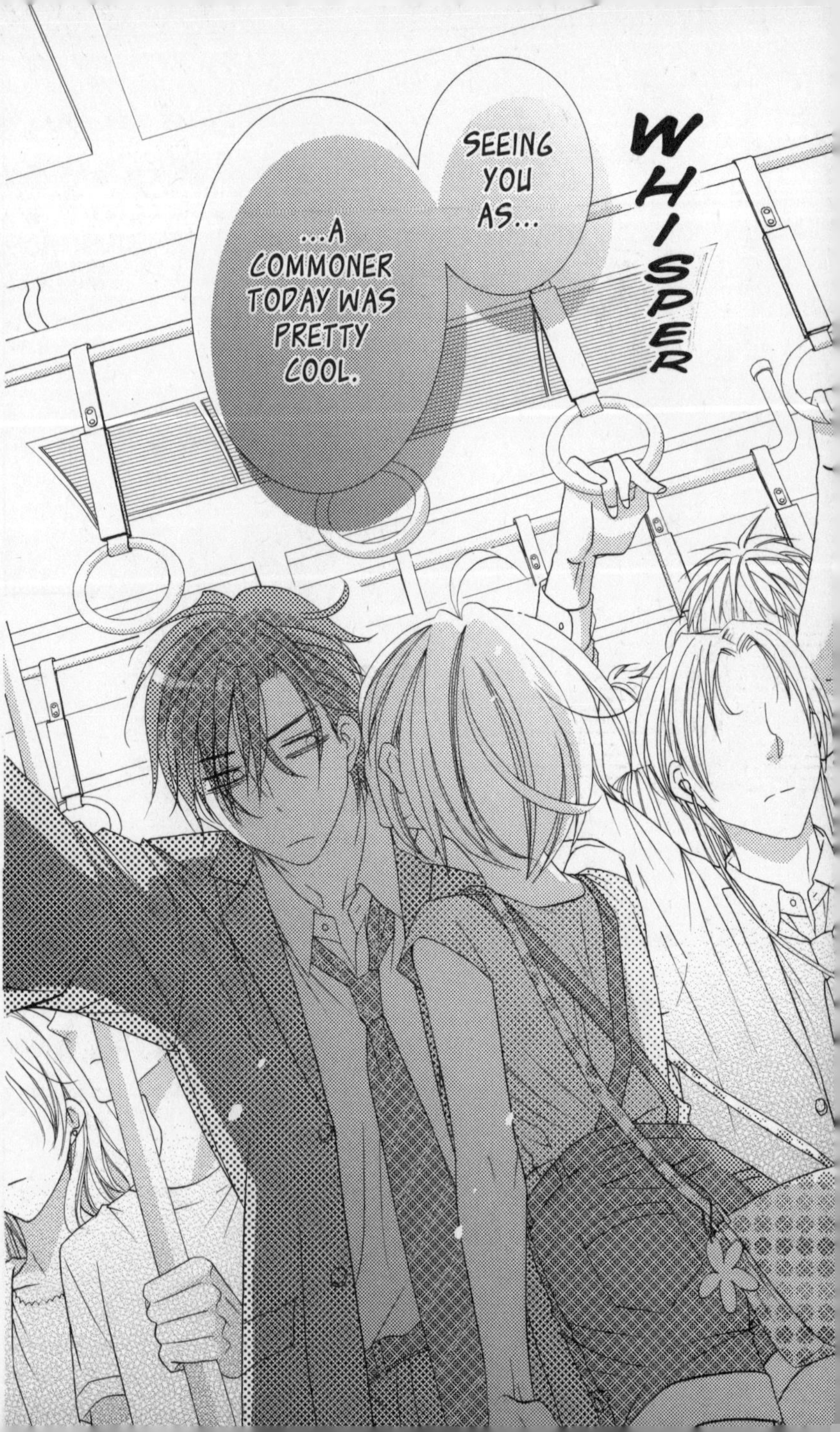
WHISPER
SEEING YOU AS...
...A COMMONER TODAY WAS PRETTY COOL.

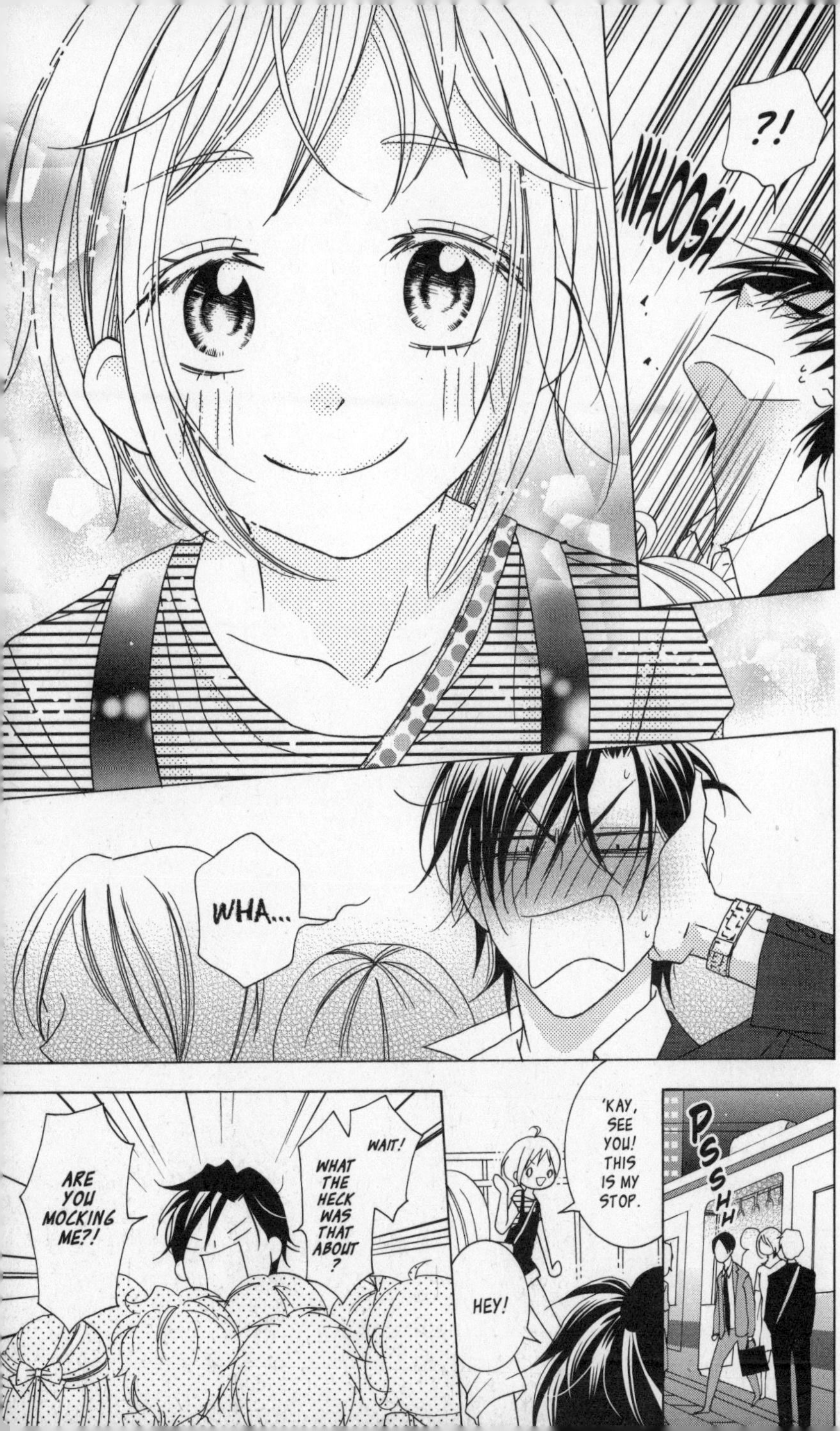
?!
WHOOSH
WHA...
PSSHH
'KAY, SEE YOU! THIS IS MY STOP.
HEY!
WAIT!
WHAT THE HECK WAS THAT ABOUT?
ARE YOU MOCKING ME?!

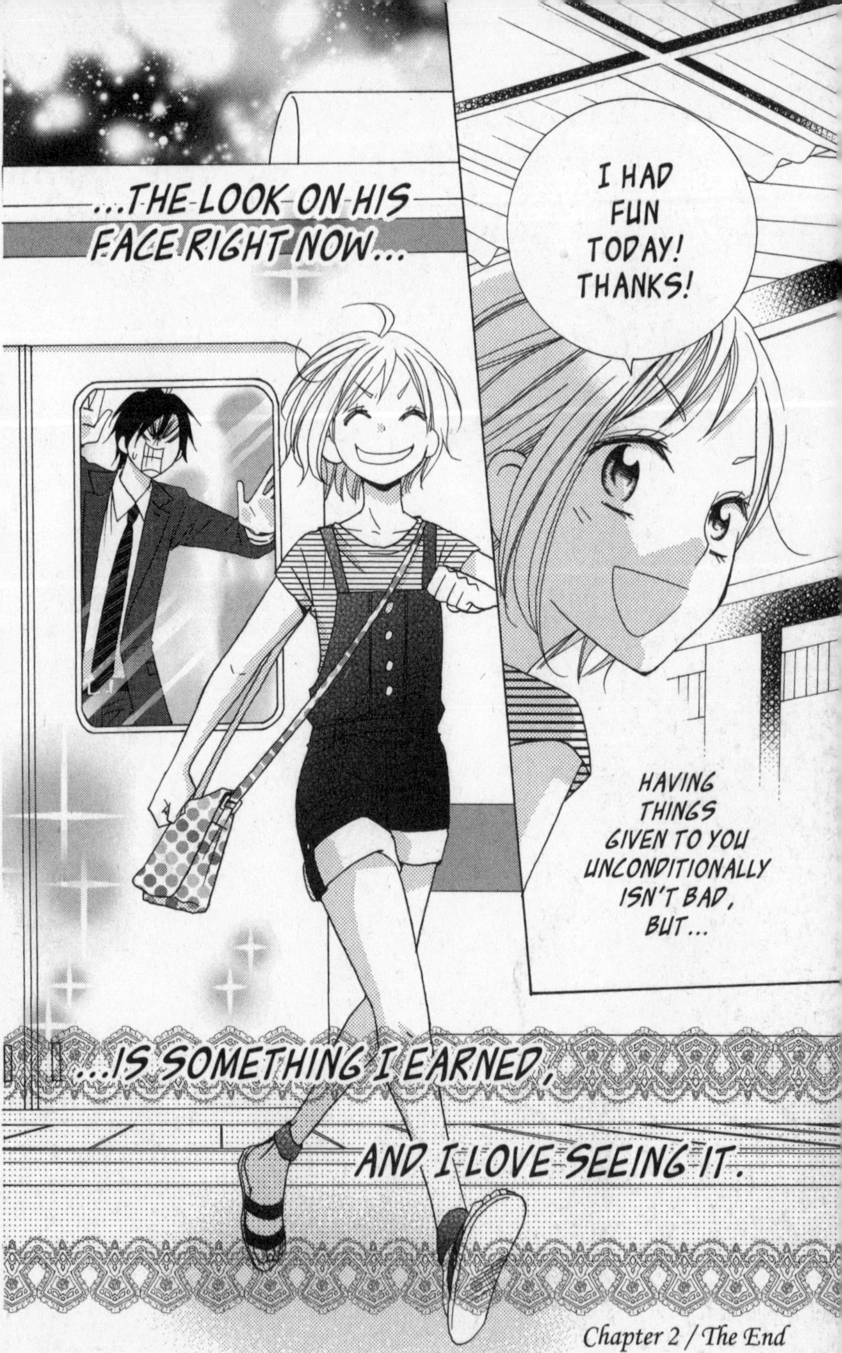
I HAD FUN TODAY! THANKS!
HAVING THINGS GIVEN TO YOU UNCONDITIONALLY ISN'T BAD, BUT...
...THE LOOK ON HIS FACE RIGHT NOW...
...IS SOMETHING I EARNED,
AND I LOVE SEEING IT.

Chapter 2 / The End

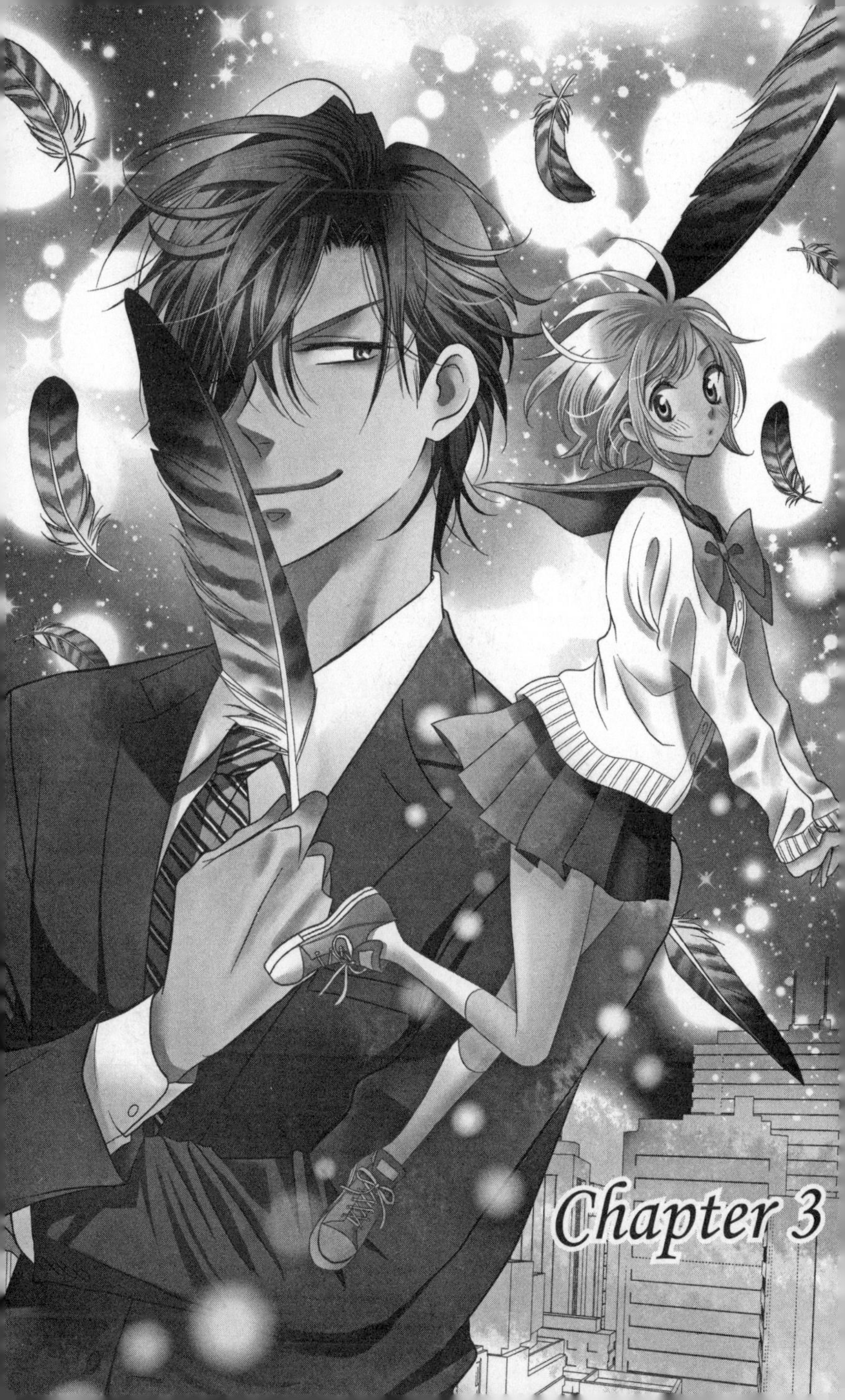
Chapter 3

At the Movie Theater

I'M THIRSTY!
SLURP
I DON'T CARE WHAT IT IS, I JUST NEED TO HYDRATE.
!!
HM?
OH.
AN INDIRECT KISS!!
...
I'M JUST GONNA GO TO SLEEP...

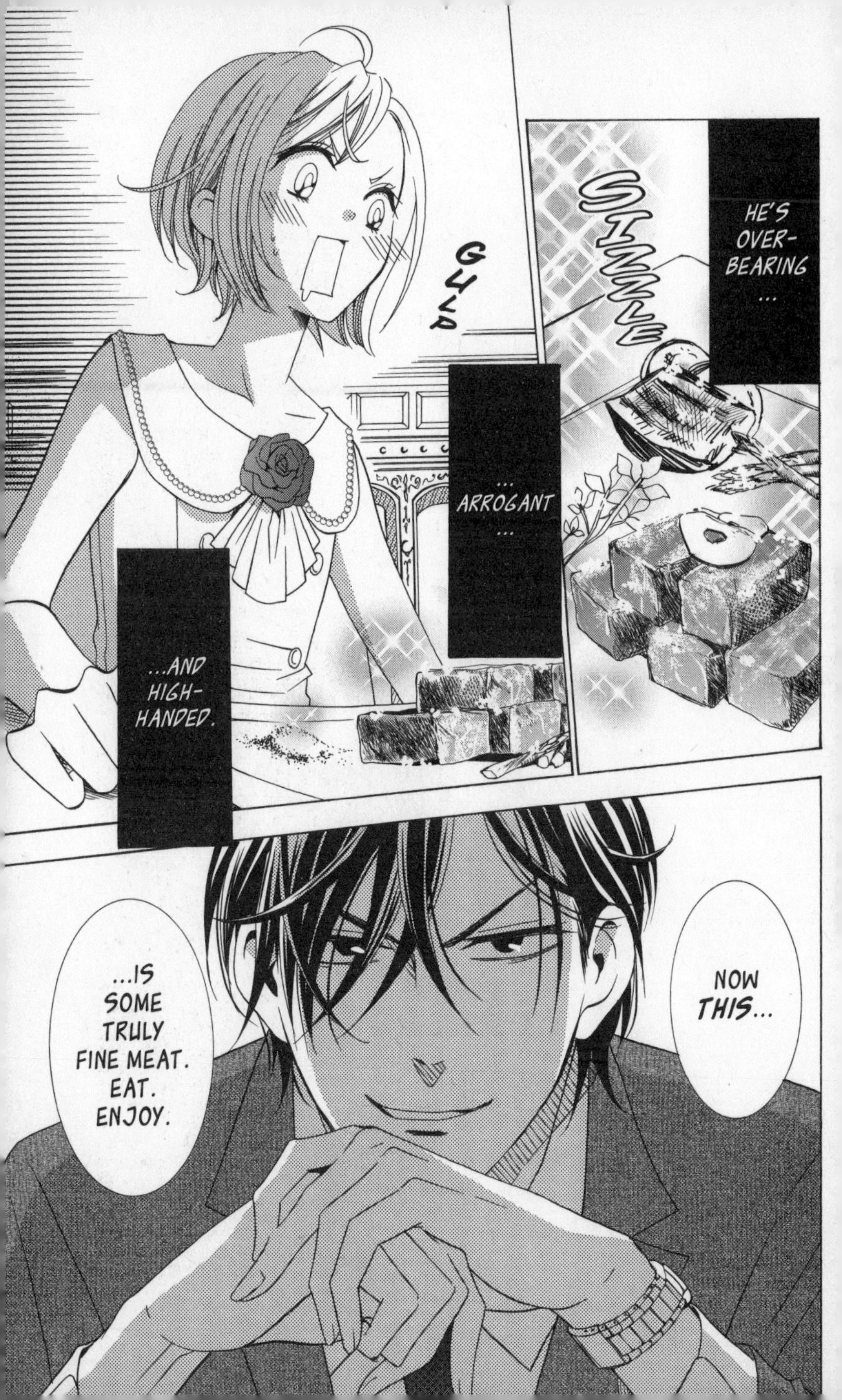
SIZZLE
HE'S OVER-BEARING...
GULP
...ARROGANT...
...AND HIGH-HANDED.
NOW THIS...
...IS SOME TRULY FINE MEAT. EAT. ENJOY.

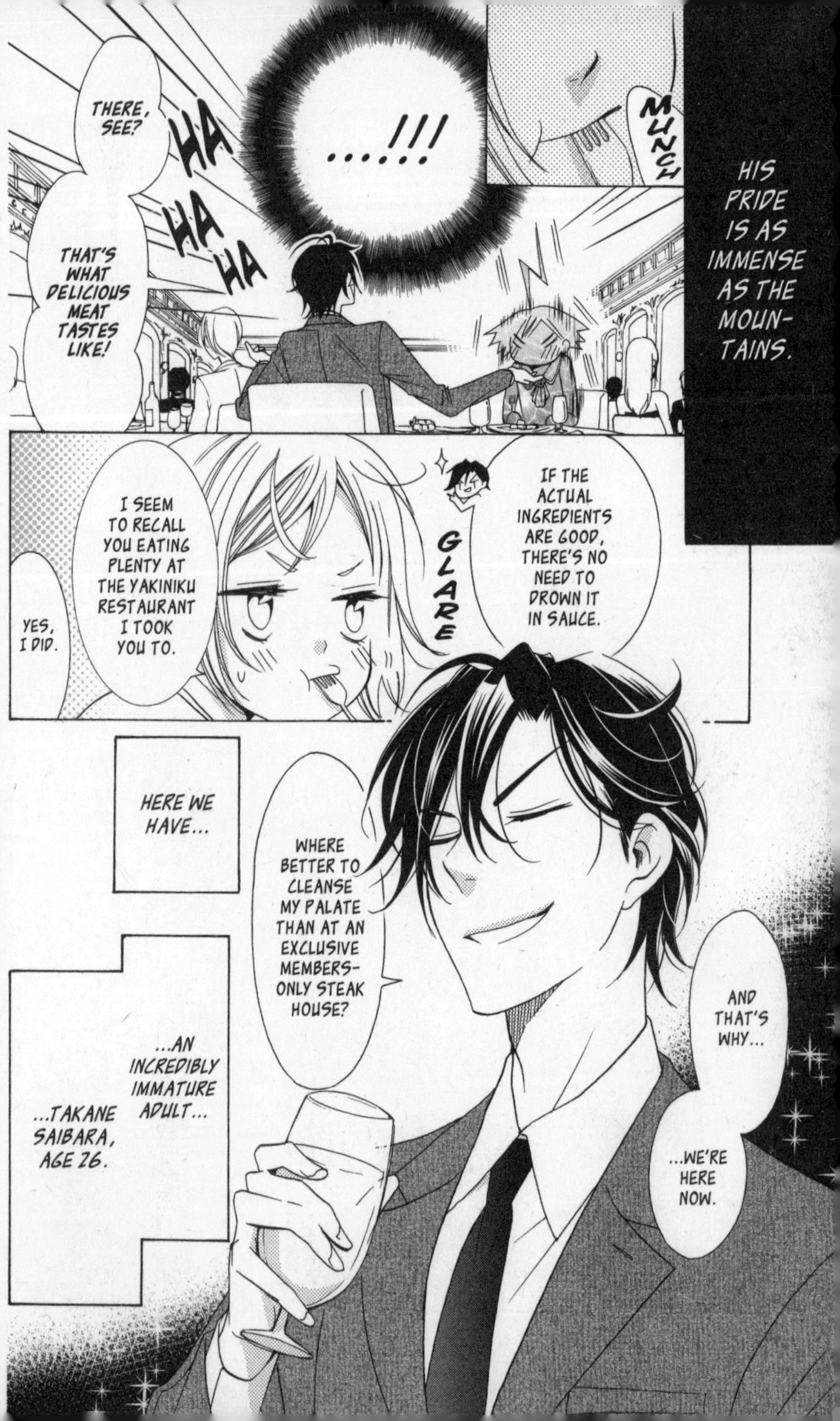
HIS PRIDE IS AS IMMENSE AS THE MOUNTAINS.
MUNCH
...!!!
HA HA HA
THERE, SEE?
THAT'S WHAT DELICIOUS MEAT TASTES LIKE!
IF THE ACTUAL INGREDIENTS ARE GOOD, THERE'S NO NEED TO DROWN IT IN SAUCE.
GLARE
I SEEM TO RECALL YOU EATING PLENTY AT THE YAKINIKU RESTAURANT I TOOK YOU TO.
YES, I DID.
AND THAT'S WHY...
...WE'RE HERE NOW.
WHERE BETTER TO CLEANSE MY PALATE THAN AT AN EXCLUSIVE MEMBERS-ONLY STEAK HOUSE?
HERE WE HAVE...
...AN INCREDIBLY IMMATURE ADULT...
...TAKANE SAIBARA, AGE 26.

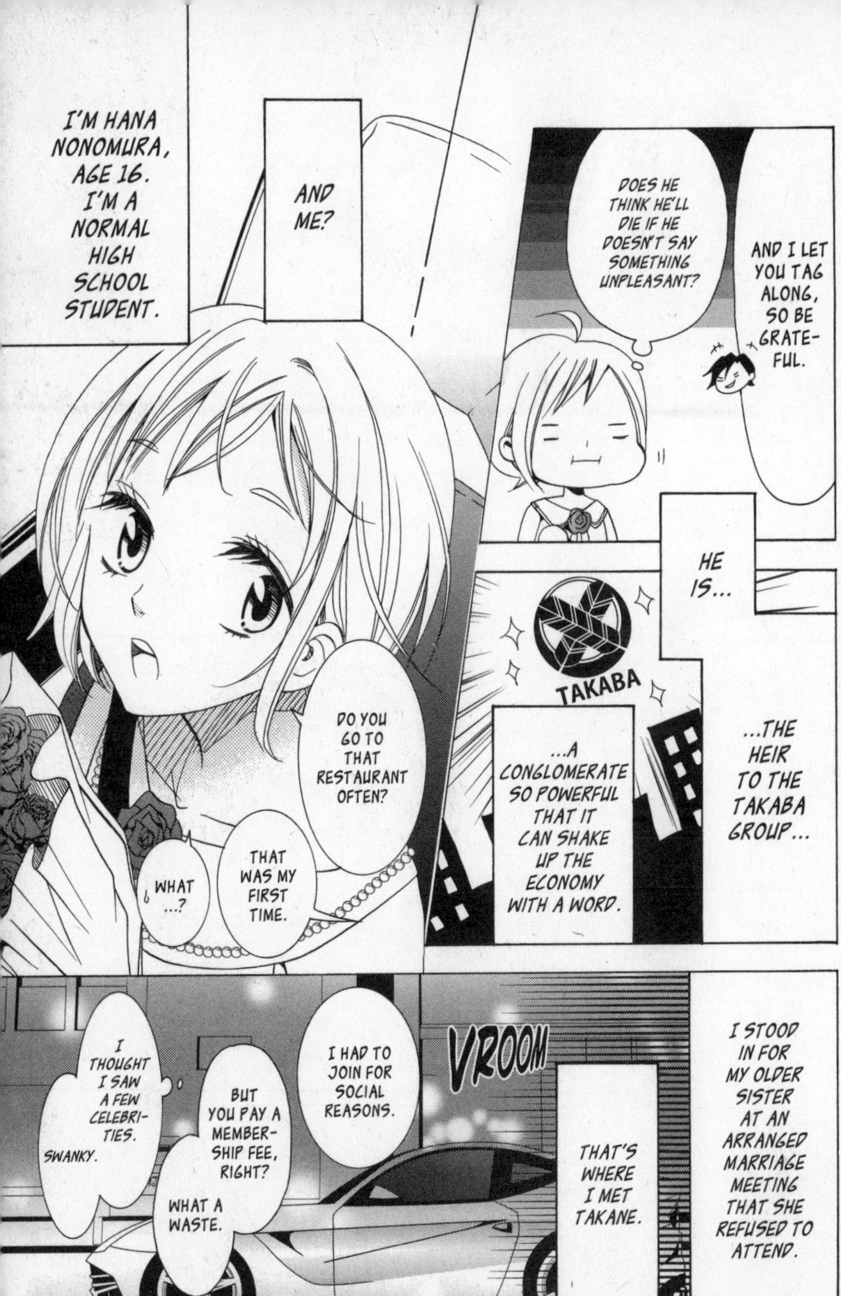

AND I LET YOU TAG ALONG, SO BE GRATE-FUL.
DOES HE THINK HE'LL DIE IF HE DOESN'T SAY SOMETHING UNPLEASANT?
HE IS...
...THE HEIR TO THE TAKABA GROUP...
TAKABA
...A CONGLOMERATE SO POWERFUL THAT IT CAN SHAKE UP THE ECONOMY WITH A WORD.
AND ME?
I'M HANA NONOMURA, AGE 16. I'M A NORMAL HIGH SCHOOL STUDENT.
DO YOU GO TO THAT RESTAURANT OFTEN?
THAT WAS MY FIRST TIME.
WHAT ...?
I STOOD IN FOR MY OLDER SISTER AT AN ARRANGED MARRIAGE MEETING THAT SHE REFUSED TO ATTEND.
THAT'S WHERE I MET TAKANE.
VROOM
I HAD TO JOIN FOR SOCIAL REASONS.
BUT YOU PAY A MEMBER-SHIP FEE, RIGHT?
WHAT A WASTE.
I THOUGHT I SAW A FEW CELEBRI-TIES.
SWANKY.

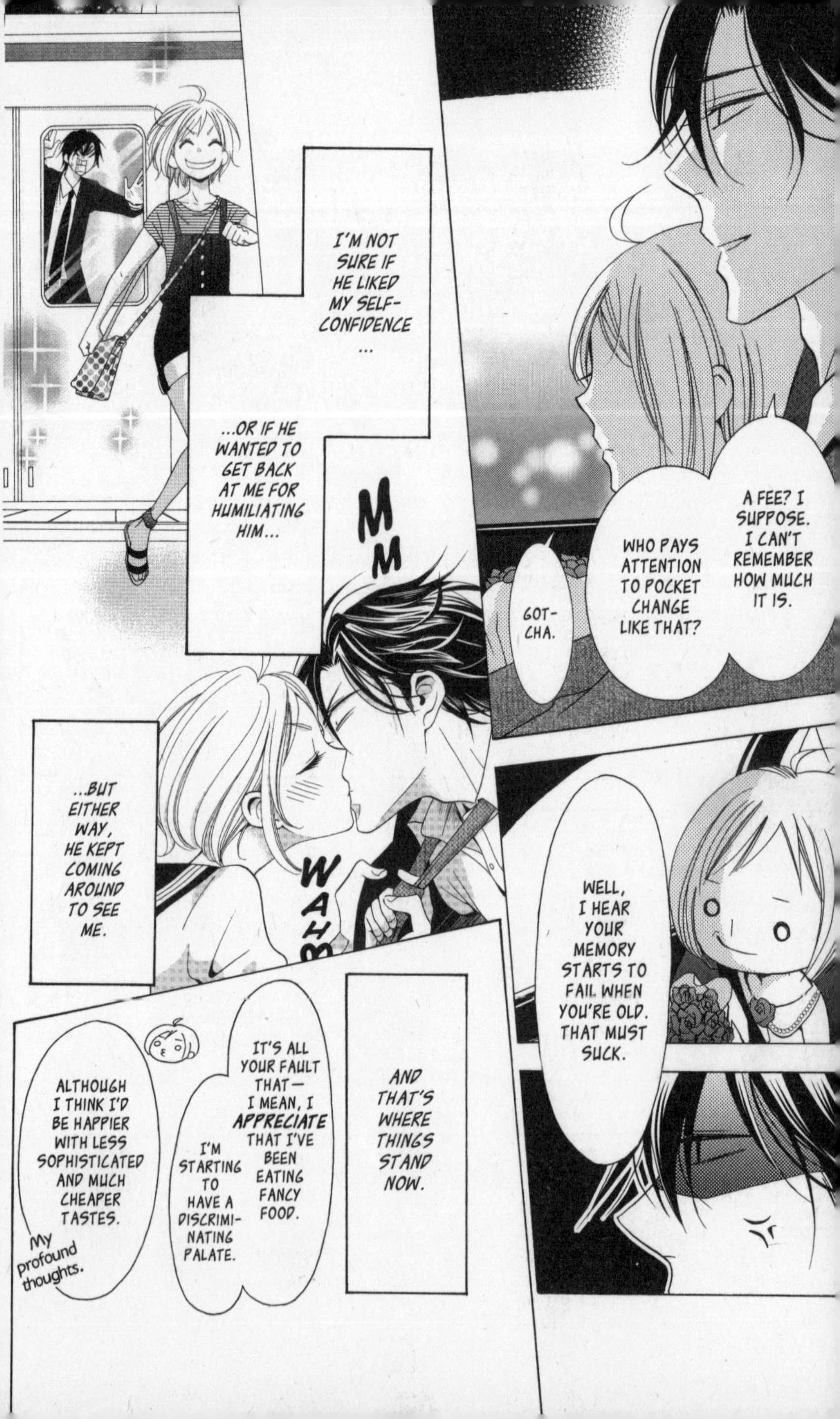
A FEE? I SUPPOSE. I CAN'T REMEMBER HOW MUCH IT IS.
WHO PAYS ATTENTION TO POCKET CHANGE LIKE THAT?
GOT-CHA.
WELL, I HEAR YOUR MEMORY STARTS TO FAIL WHEN YOU'RE OLD. THAT MUST SUCK.
I'M NOT SURE IF HE LIKED MY SELF-CONFIDENCE...
...OR IF HE WANTED TO GET BACK AT ME FOR HUMILIATING HIM...
MM
...BUT EITHER WAY, HE KEPT COMING AROUND TO SEE ME.
WAH
AND THAT'S WHERE THINGS STAND NOW.
IT'S ALL YOUR FAULT THAT— I MEAN, I *APPRECIATE* THAT I'VE BEEN EATING FANCY FOOD.
I'M STARTING TO HAVE A DISCRIMINATING PALATE.
ALTHOUGH I THINK I'D BE HAPPIER WITH LESS SOPHISTICATED AND MUCH CHEAPER TASTES.
My profound thoughts.

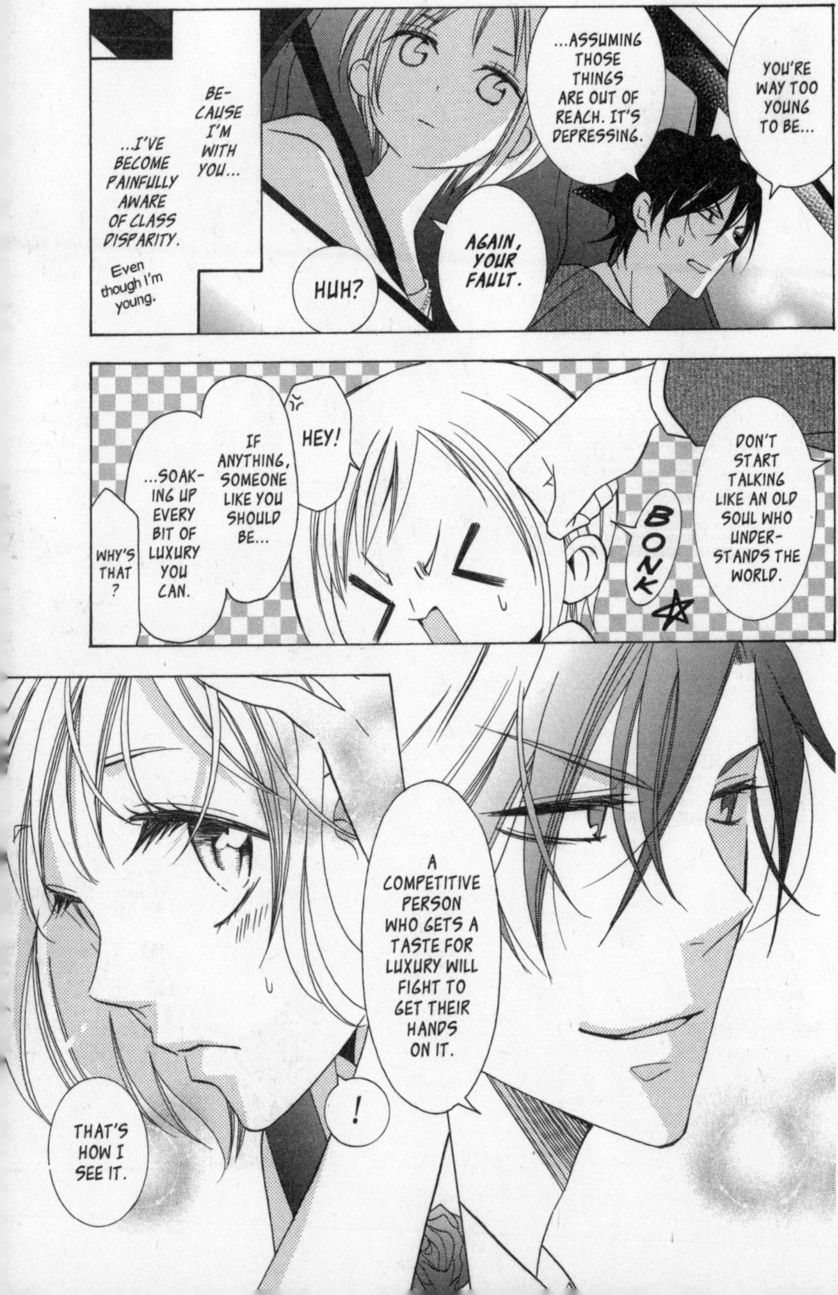
YOU'RE WAY TOO YOUNG TO BE...
...ASSUMING THOSE THINGS ARE OUT OF REACH. IT'S DEPRESSING.
AGAIN, YOUR FAULT.
HUH?
BE-CAUSE I'M WITH YOU...
...I'VE BECOME PAINFULLY AWARE OF CLASS DISPARITY.
Even though I'm young.
DON'T START TALKING LIKE AN OLD SOUL WHO UNDER-STANDS THE WORLD.
BONK
HEY!
IF ANYTHING, SOMEONE LIKE YOU SHOULD BE...
...SOAK-ING UP EVERY BIT OF LUXURY YOU CAN.
WHY'S THAT?
A COMPETITIVE PERSON WHO GETS A TASTE FOR LUXURY WILL FIGHT TO GET THEIR HANDS ON IT.
!
THAT'S HOW I SEE IT.

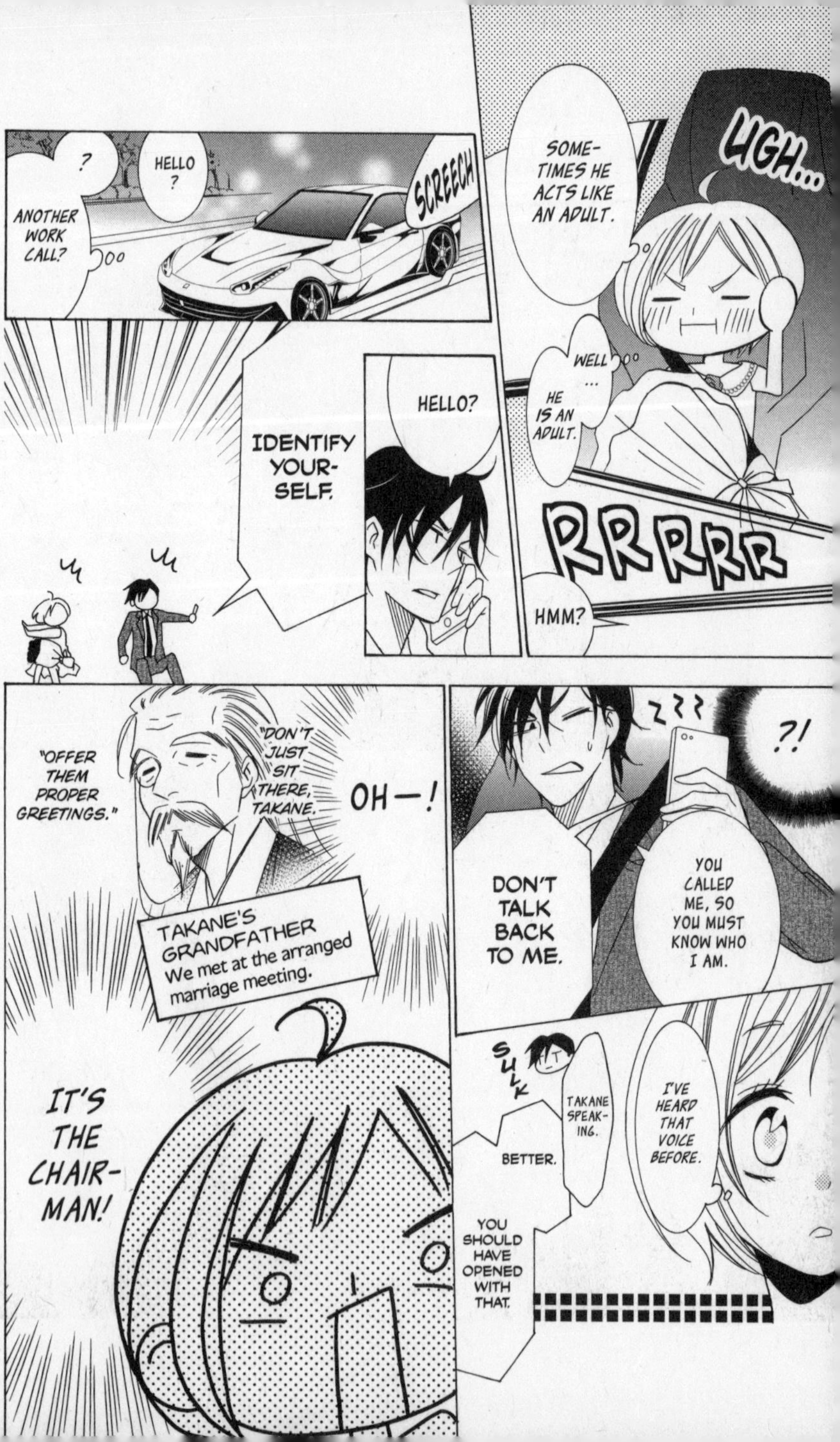
UGH...
SOME-TIMES HE ACTS LIKE AN ADULT.
WELL ...
HE IS AN ADULT.
RRRRR
HMM?
SCREECH
HELLO ?
?
ANOTHER WORK CALL?
HELLO?
IDENTIFY YOUR-SELF.
?!
YOU CALLED ME, SO YOU MUST KNOW WHO I AM.
DON'T TALK BACK TO ME.
"DON'T JUST SIT THERE, TAKANE.
OH—!
"OFFER THEM PROPER GREETINGS."
TAKANE'S GRANDFATHER
We met at the arranged marriage meeting.
I'VE HEARD THAT VOICE BEFORE.
SULK
TAKANE SPEAK-ING.
BETTER.
YOU SHOULD HAVE OPENED WITH THAT.
IT'S THE CHAIR-MAN!

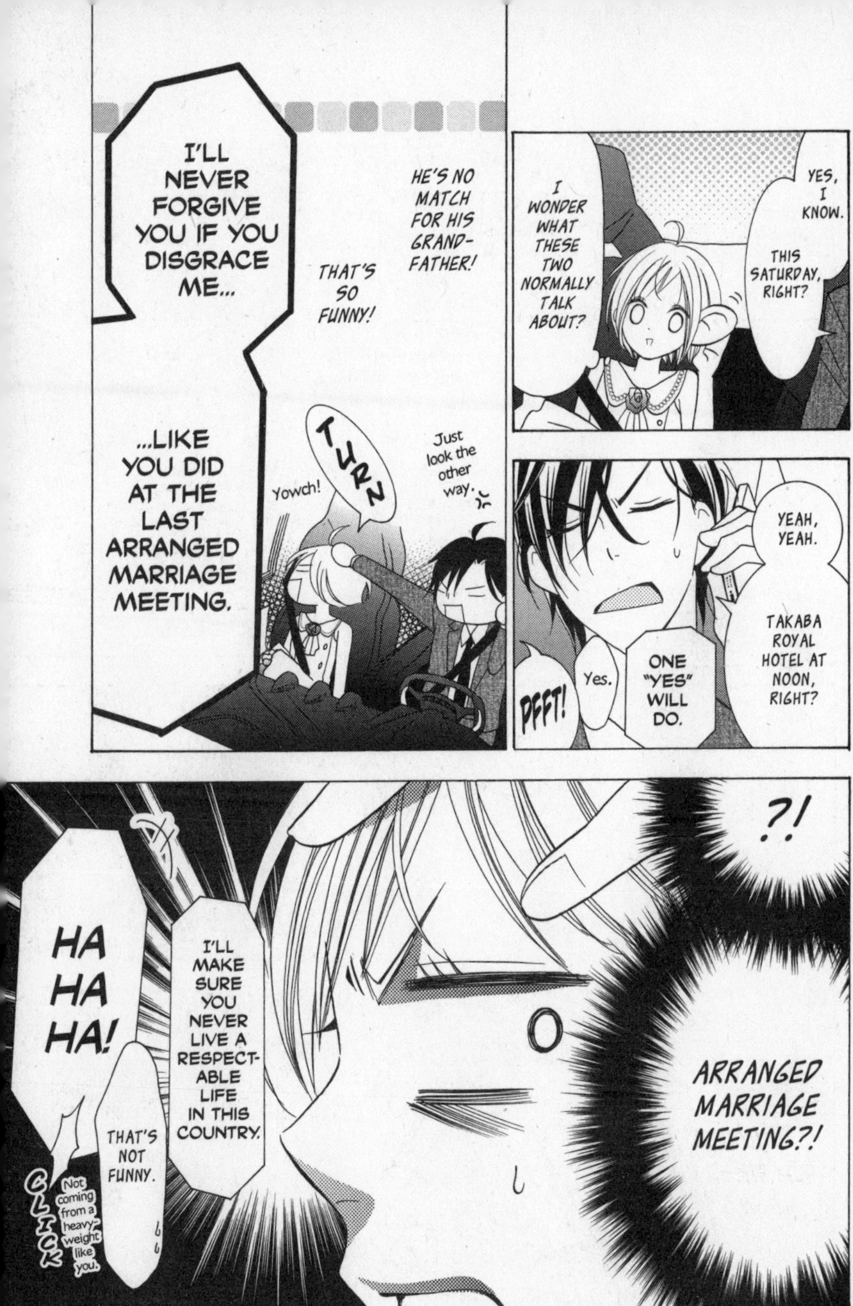
YES, I KNOW.
THIS SATURDAY, RIGHT?
I WONDER WHAT THESE TWO NORMALLY TALK ABOUT?
YEAH, YEAH.
TAKABA ROYAL HOTEL AT NOON, RIGHT?
ONE "YES" WILL DO.
Yes.
PFFT!
I'LL NEVER FORGIVE YOU IF YOU DISGRACE ME...
HE'S NO MATCH FOR HIS GRAND-FATHER!
THAT'S SO FUNNY!
...LIKE YOU DID AT THE LAST ARRANGED MARRIAGE MEETING.
Just look the other way.
TURN
Yowch!
?!
ARRANGED MARRIAGE MEETING?!
I'LL MAKE SURE YOU NEVER LIVE A RESPECT-ABLE LIFE IN THIS COUNTRY.
HA HA HA!
THAT'S NOT FUNNY.
Not coming from a heavy-weight like you.
CLICK

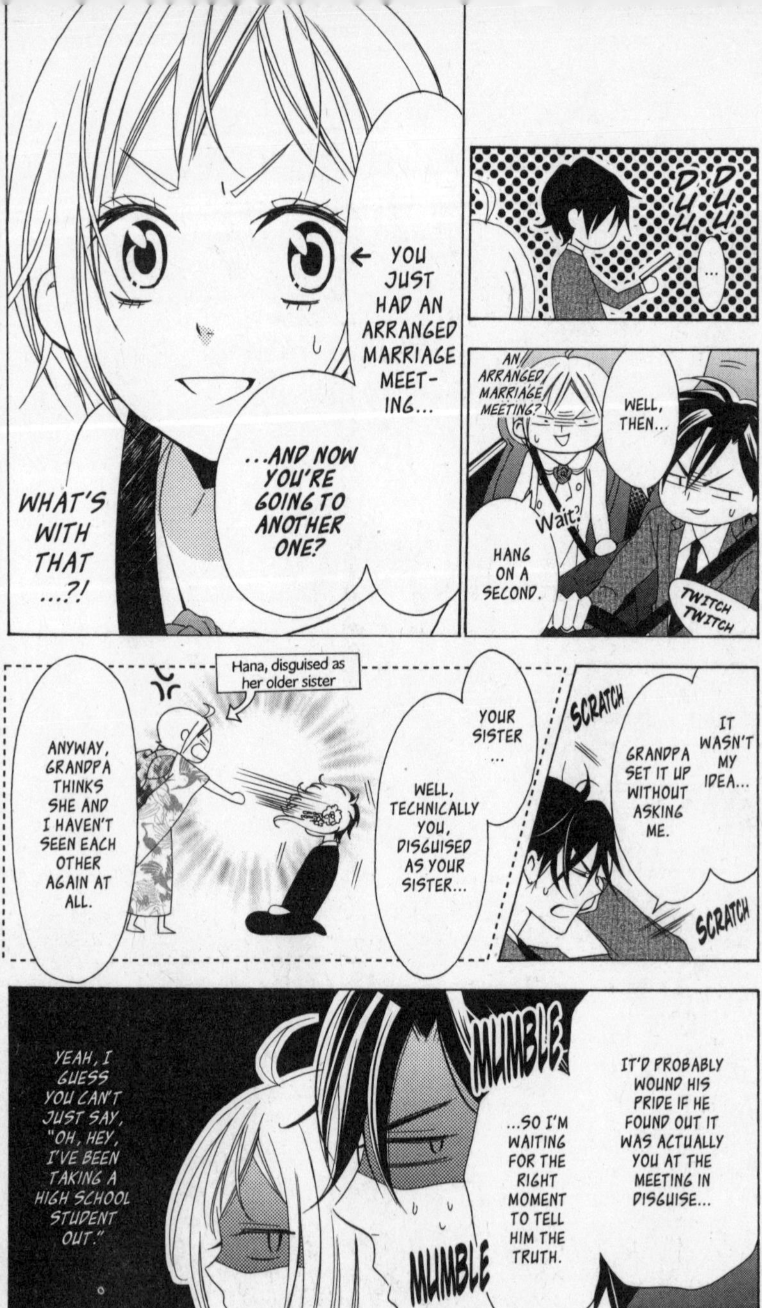
DUUU DUUU
...
WELL, THEN...
AN ARRANGED MARRIAGE MEETING?
Wait?
HANG ON A SECOND.
TWITCH TWITCH
YOU JUST HAD AN ARRANGED MARRIAGE MEET-ING...
...AND NOW YOU'RE GOING TO ANOTHER ONE?
WHAT'S WITH THAT ...?!
SCRATCH
IT WASN'T MY IDEA...
GRANDPA SET IT UP WITHOUT ASKING ME.
SCRATCH
YOUR SISTER ...
WELL, TECHNICALLY YOU, DISGUISED AS YOUR SISTER...
Hana, disguised as her older sister
ANYWAY, GRANDPA THINKS SHE AND I HAVEN'T SEEN EACH OTHER AGAIN AT ALL.
IT'D PROBABLY WOUND HIS PRIDE IF HE FOUND OUT IT WAS ACTUALLY YOU AT THE MEETING IN DISGUISE...
MUMBLE
...SO I'M WAITING FOR THE RIGHT MOMENT TO TELL HIM THE TRUTH.
MUMBLE
YEAH, I GUESS YOU CAN'T JUST SAY, "OH, HEY, I'VE BEEN TAKING A HIGH SCHOOL STUDENT OUT."

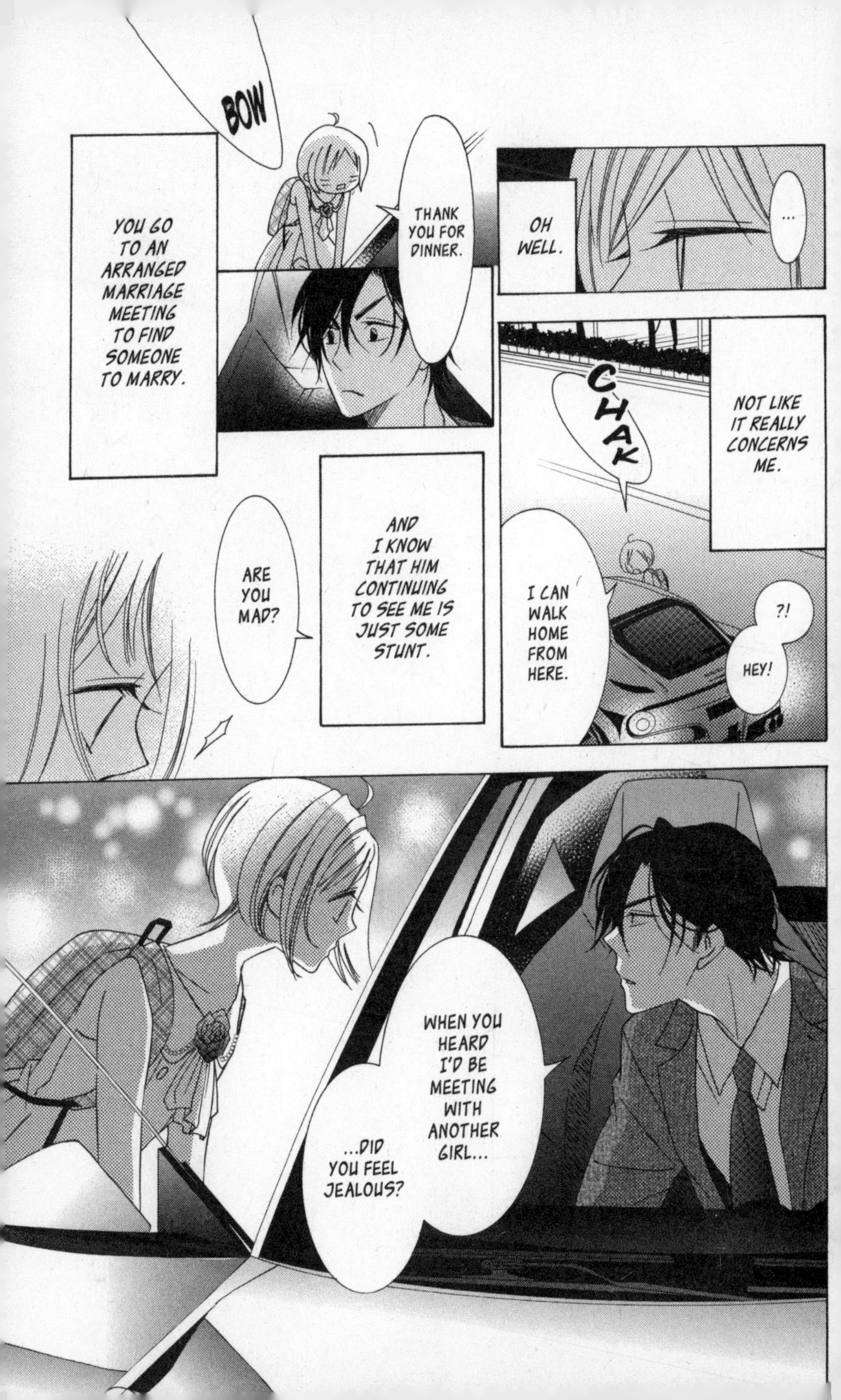
...
OH WELL.
BOW
THANK YOU FOR DINNER.
YOU GO TO AN ARRANGED MARRIAGE MEETING TO FIND SOMEONE TO MARRY.
NOT LIKE IT REALLY CONCERNS ME.
CHAK
I CAN WALK HOME FROM HERE.
?!
HEY!
AND I KNOW THAT HIM CONTINUING TO SEE ME IS JUST SOME STUNT.
ARE YOU MAD?
WHEN YOU HEARD I'D BE MEETING WITH ANOTHER GIRL...
...DID YOU FEEL JEALOUS?

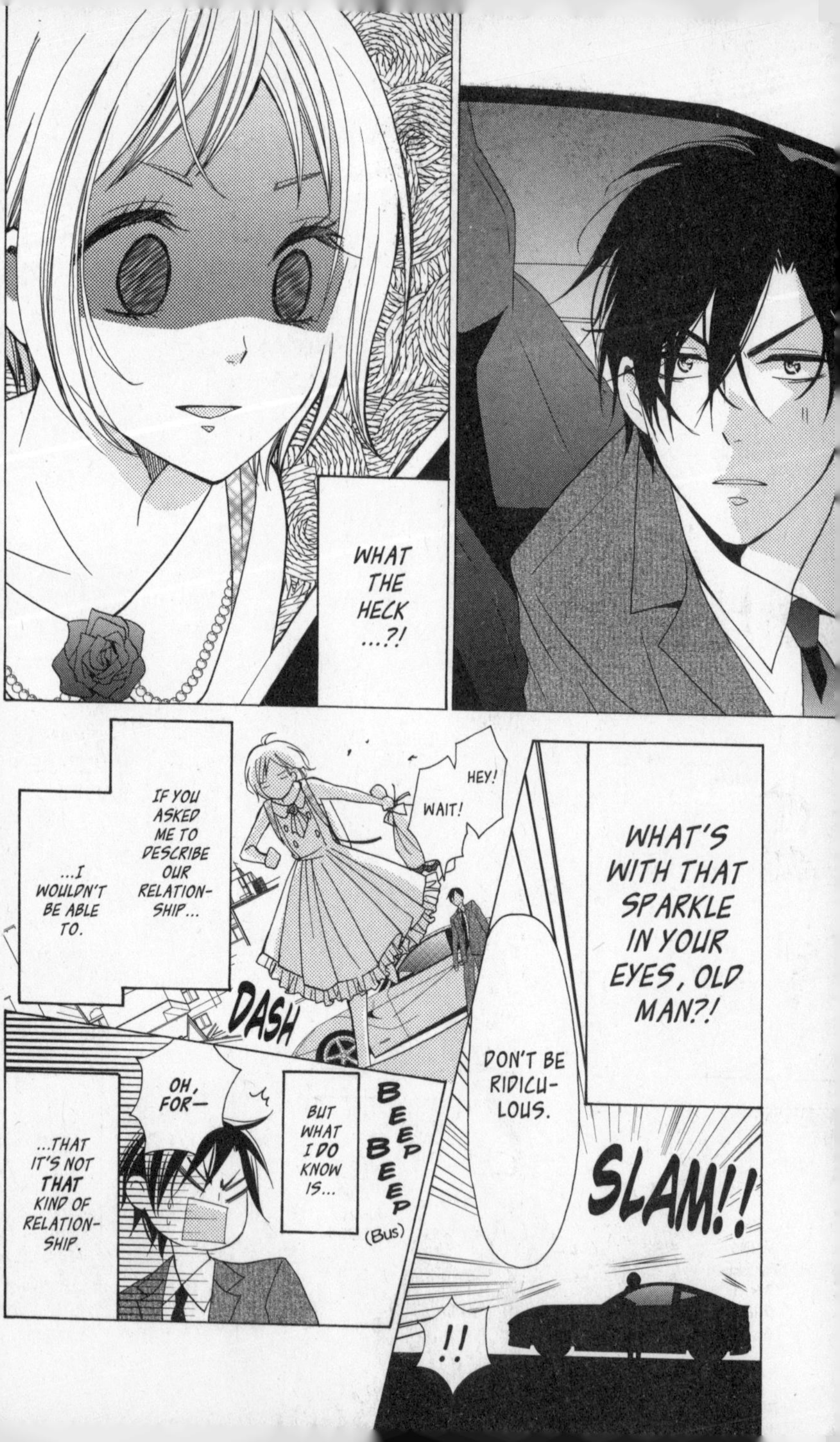
WHAT THE HECK ...?!
WHAT'S WITH THAT SPARKLE IN YOUR EYES, OLD MAN?!
DON'T BE RIDICULOUS.
SLAM!!
!!
HEY! WAIT!
IF YOU ASKED ME TO DESCRIBE OUR RELATION-SHIP...
...I WOULDN'T BE ABLE TO.
DASH
BEEP BEEP
(Bus)
BUT WHAT I DO KNOW IS...
OH, FOR—
...THAT IT'S NOT THAT KIND OF RELATION-SHIP.

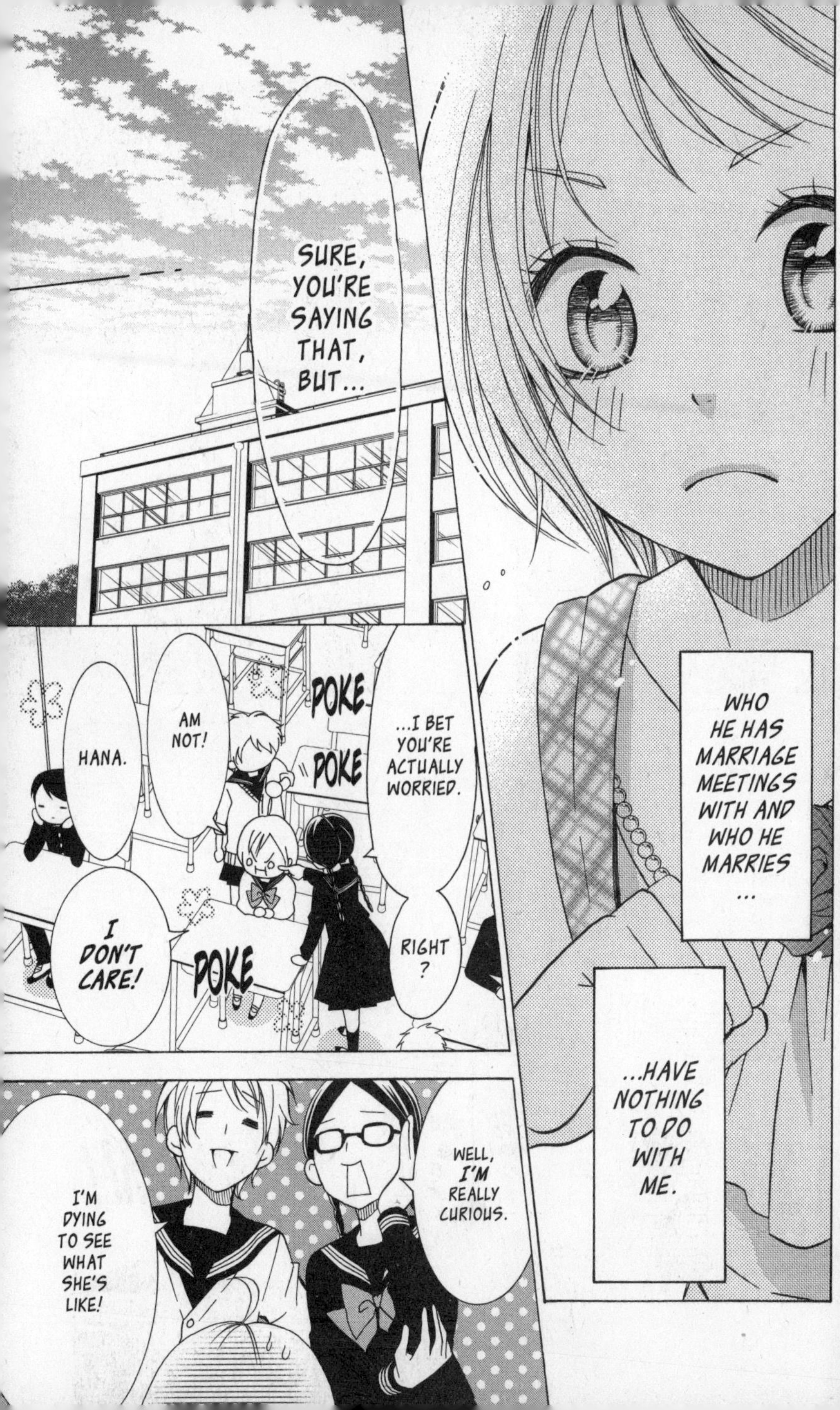
WHO HE HAS MARRIAGE MEETINGS WITH AND WHO HE MARRIES...
...HAVE NOTHING TO DO WITH ME.
SURE, YOU'RE SAYING THAT, BUT...
POKE
...I BET YOU'RE ACTUALLY WORRIED.
POKE
RIGHT?
AM NOT!
HANA.
I DON'T CARE!
POKE
WELL, I'M REALLY CURIOUS.
I'M DYING TO SEE WHAT SHE'S LIKE!

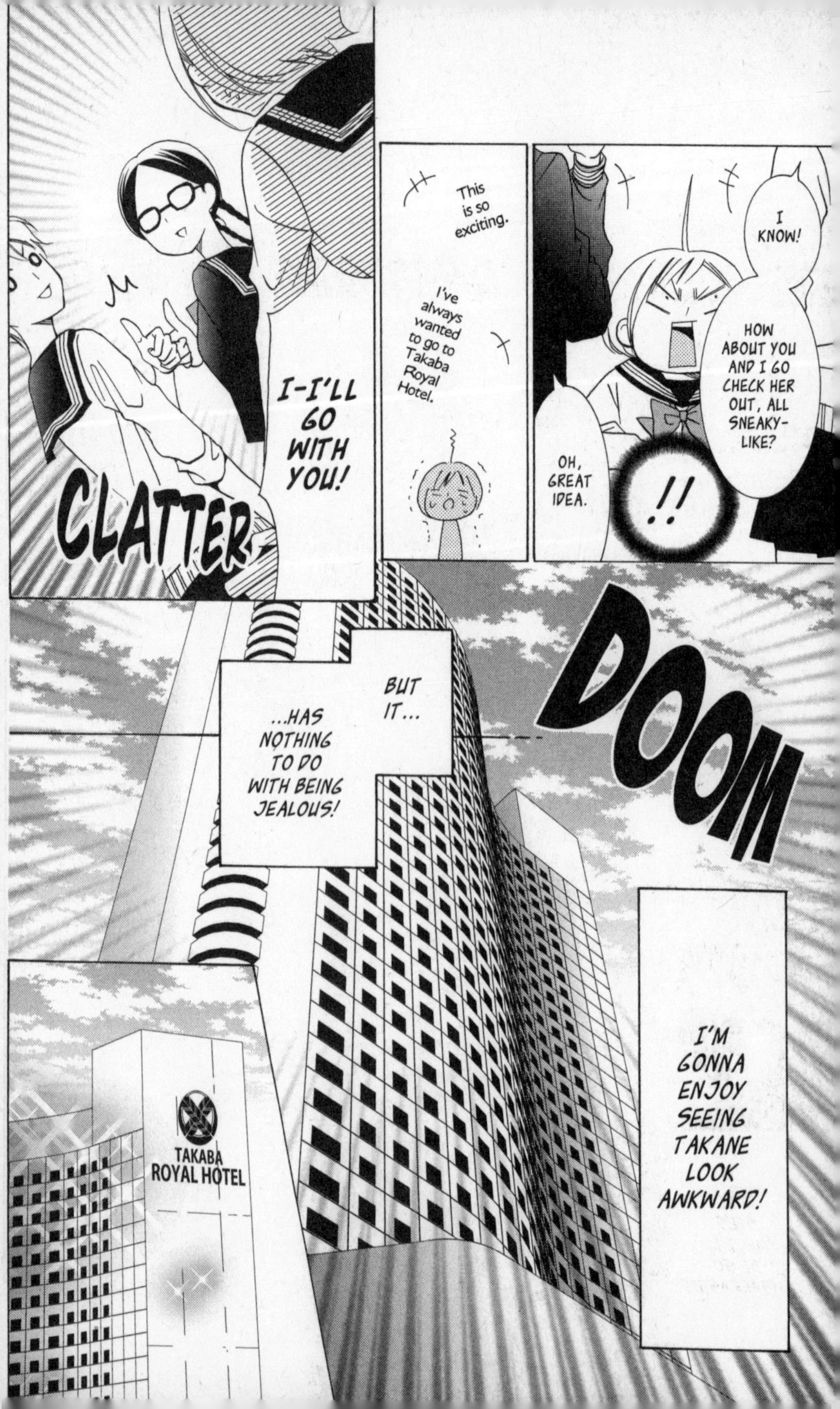
I KNOW!
HOW ABOUT YOU AND I GO CHECK HER OUT, ALL SNEAKY-LIKE?
!!
OH, GREAT IDEA.
This is so exciting.
I've always wanted to go to Takaba Royal Hotel.
I-I'LL GO WITH YOU!
CLATTER
DOOM
BUT IT...
...HAS NOTHING TO DO WITH BEING JEALOUS!
I'M GONNA ENJOY SEEING TAKANE LOOK AWKWARD!
TAKABA ROYAL HOTEL

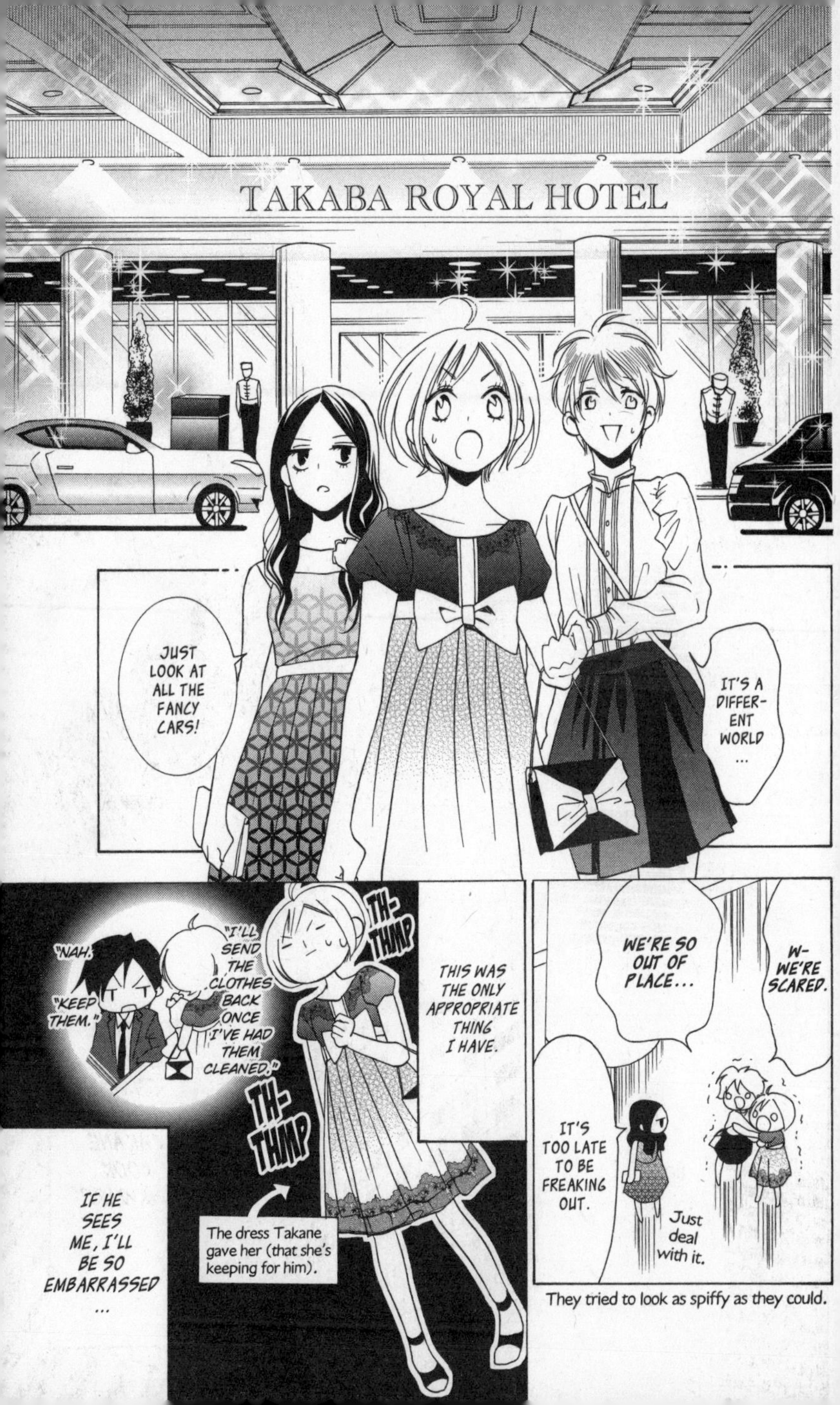
TAKABA ROYAL HOTEL
IT'S A DIFFERENT WORLD...
JUST LOOK AT ALL THE FANCY CARS!
W-WE'RE SCARED.
WE'RE SO OUT OF PLACE...
IT'S TOO LATE TO BE FREAKING OUT.
Just deal with it.
They tried to look as spiffy as they could.
THIS WAS THE ONLY APPROPRIATE THING I HAVE.
TH-THMP
"I'LL SEND THE CLOTHES BACK ONCE I'VE HAD THEM CLEANED."
"NAH."
"KEEP THEM."
TH-THMP
The dress Takane gave her (that she's keeping for him).
IF HE SEES ME, I'LL BE SO EMBARRASSED...

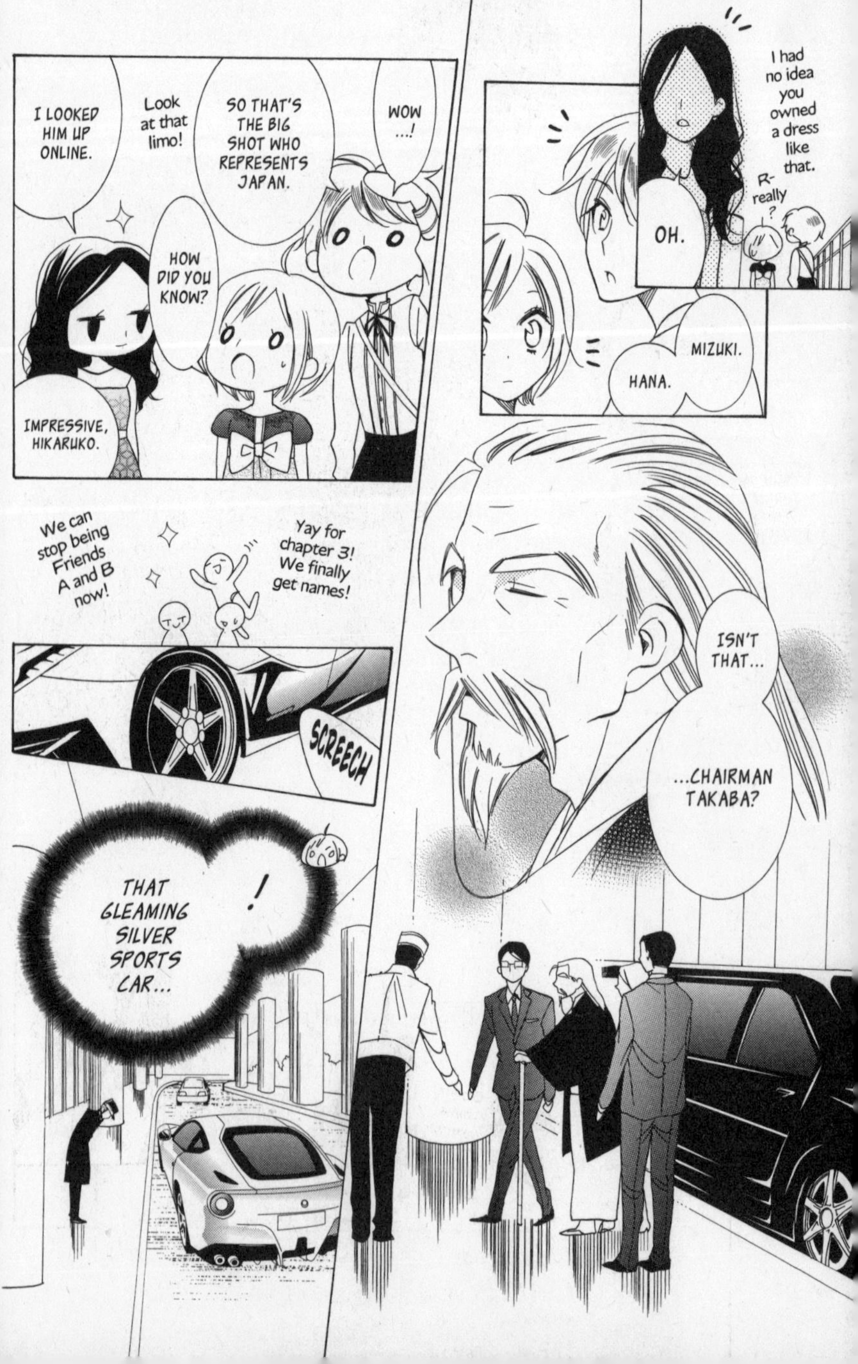
I had no idea you owned a dress like that.
R-really?
OH.
MIZUKI.
HANA.
ISN'T THAT...
...CHAIRMAN TAKABA?
WOW ...!
SO THAT'S THE BIG SHOT WHO REPRESENTS JAPAN.
Look at that limo!
I LOOKED HIM UP ONLINE.
HOW DID YOU KNOW?
IMPRESSIVE, HIKARUKO.
Yay for chapter 3! We finally get names!
We can stop being Friends A and B now!
SCREECH
THAT GLEAMING SILVER SPORTS CAR...
!

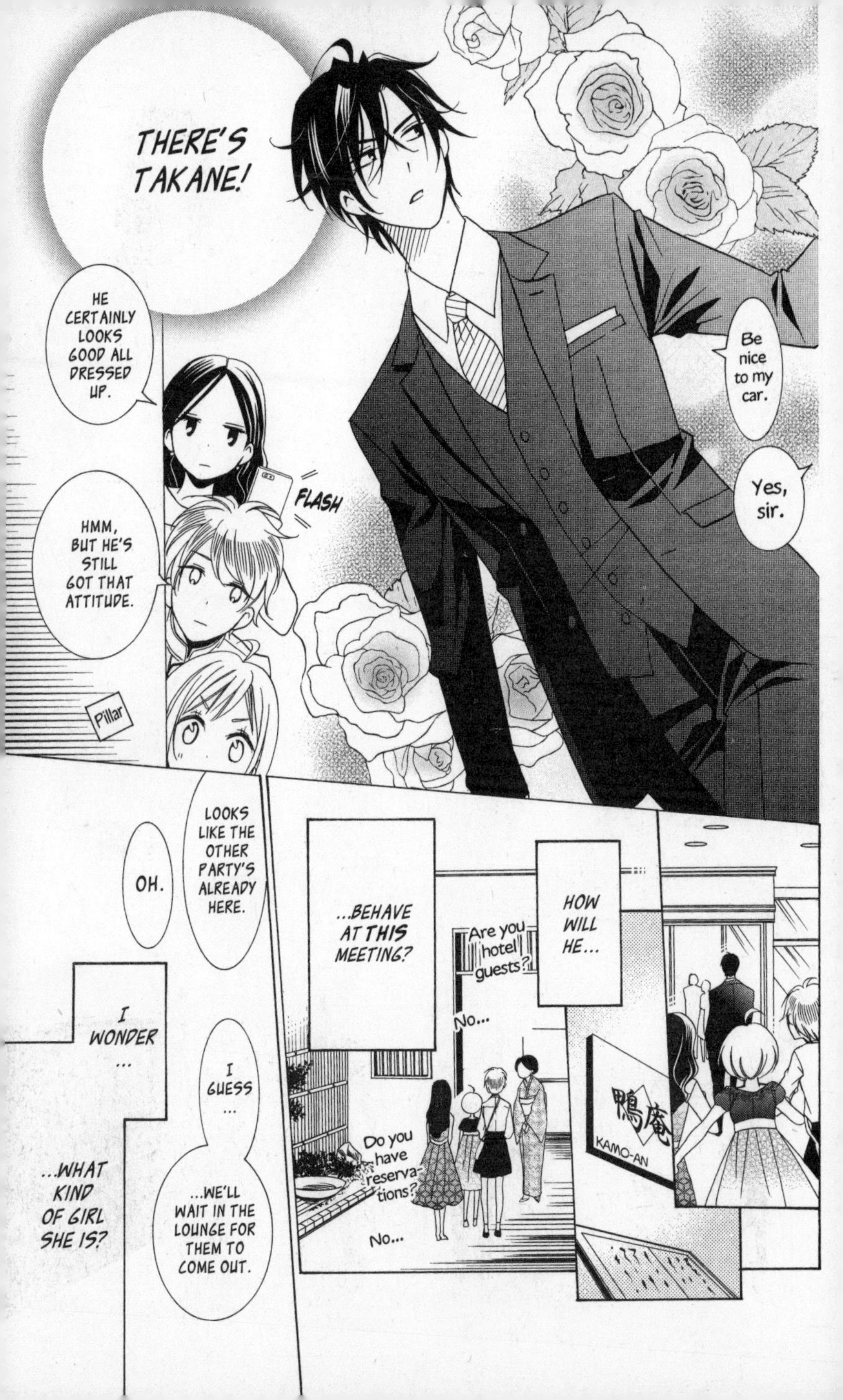

Be nice to my car.
Yes, sir.
THERE'S TAKANE!
HE CERTAINLY LOOKS GOOD ALL DRESSED UP.
FLASH
HMM, BUT HE'S STILL GOT THAT ATTITUDE.
Pillar
HOW WILL HE...
鴨庵
KAMO-AN
...BEHAVE AT THIS MEETING?
Are you hotel guests?
No...
Do you have reservations?
No...
LOOKS LIKE THE OTHER PARTY'S ALREADY HERE.
OH.
I GUESS...
...WE'LL WAIT IN THE LOUNGE FOR THEM TO COME OUT.
I WONDER...
...WHAT KIND OF GIRL SHE IS?

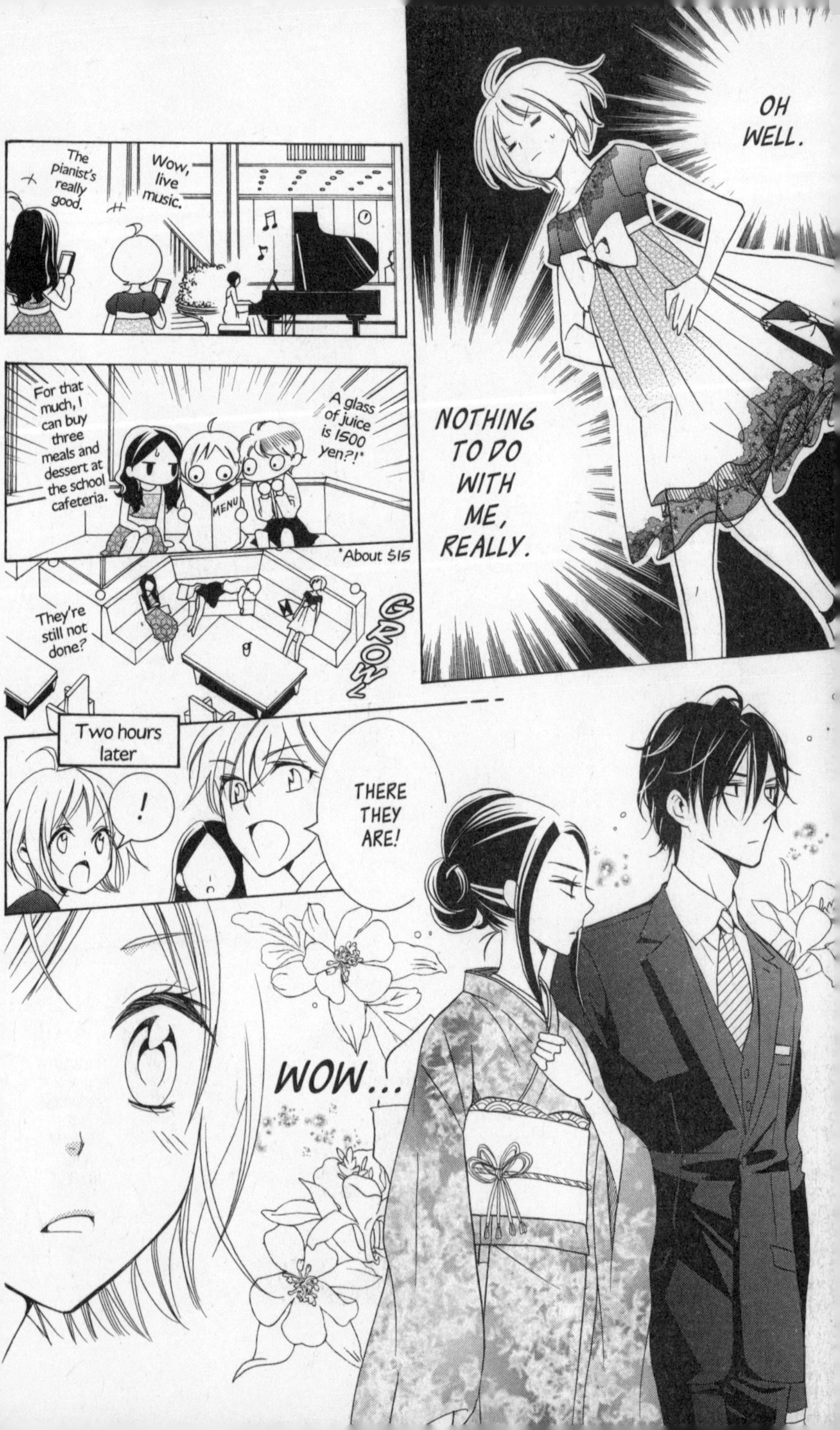
OH WELL.
NOTHING TO DO WITH ME, REALLY.
Wow, live music.
The pianist's really good.
A glass of juice is 1500 yen?!*
For that much, I can buy three meals and dessert at the school cafeteria.
MENU
*About $15
GROWL
They're still not done?
Two hours later
THERE THEY ARE!
!
WOW...

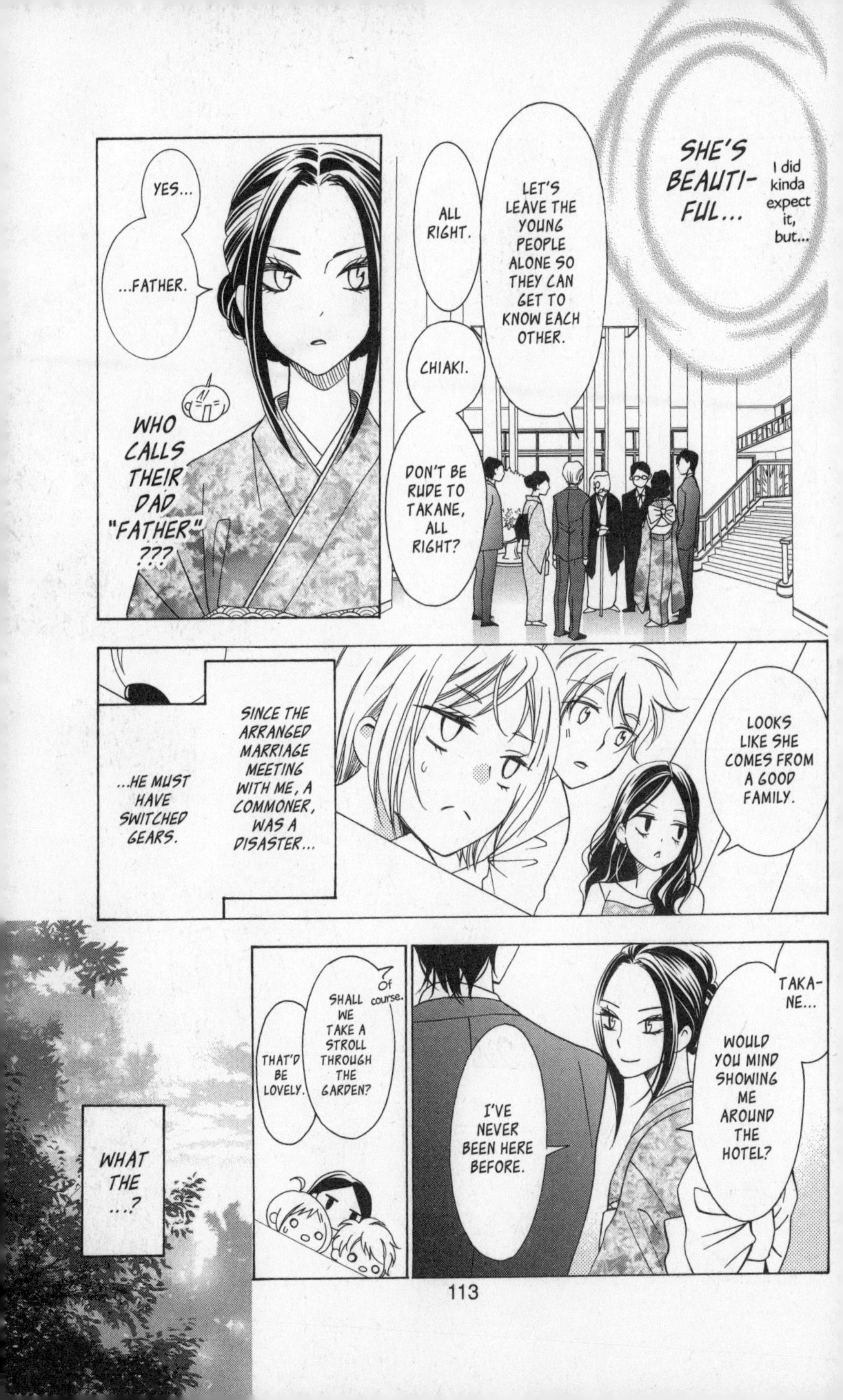
SHE'S BEAUTI-FUL...
I did kinda expect it, but...
LET'S LEAVE THE YOUNG PEOPLE ALONE SO THEY CAN GET TO KNOW EACH OTHER.
ALL RIGHT.
CHIAKI.
DON'T BE RUDE TO TAKANE, ALL RIGHT?
YES...
...FATHER.
WHO CALLS THEIR DAD "FATHER"???
LOOKS LIKE SHE COMES FROM A GOOD FAMILY.
SINCE THE ARRANGED MARRIAGE MEETING WITH ME, A COMMONER, WAS A DISASTER...
...HE MUST HAVE SWITCHED GEARS.
TAKA-NE...
WOULD YOU MIND SHOWING ME AROUND THE HOTEL?
I'VE NEVER BEEN HERE BEFORE.
Of course.
SHALL WE TAKE A STROLL THROUGH THE GARDEN?
THAT'D BE LOVELY.
WHAT THE ...?

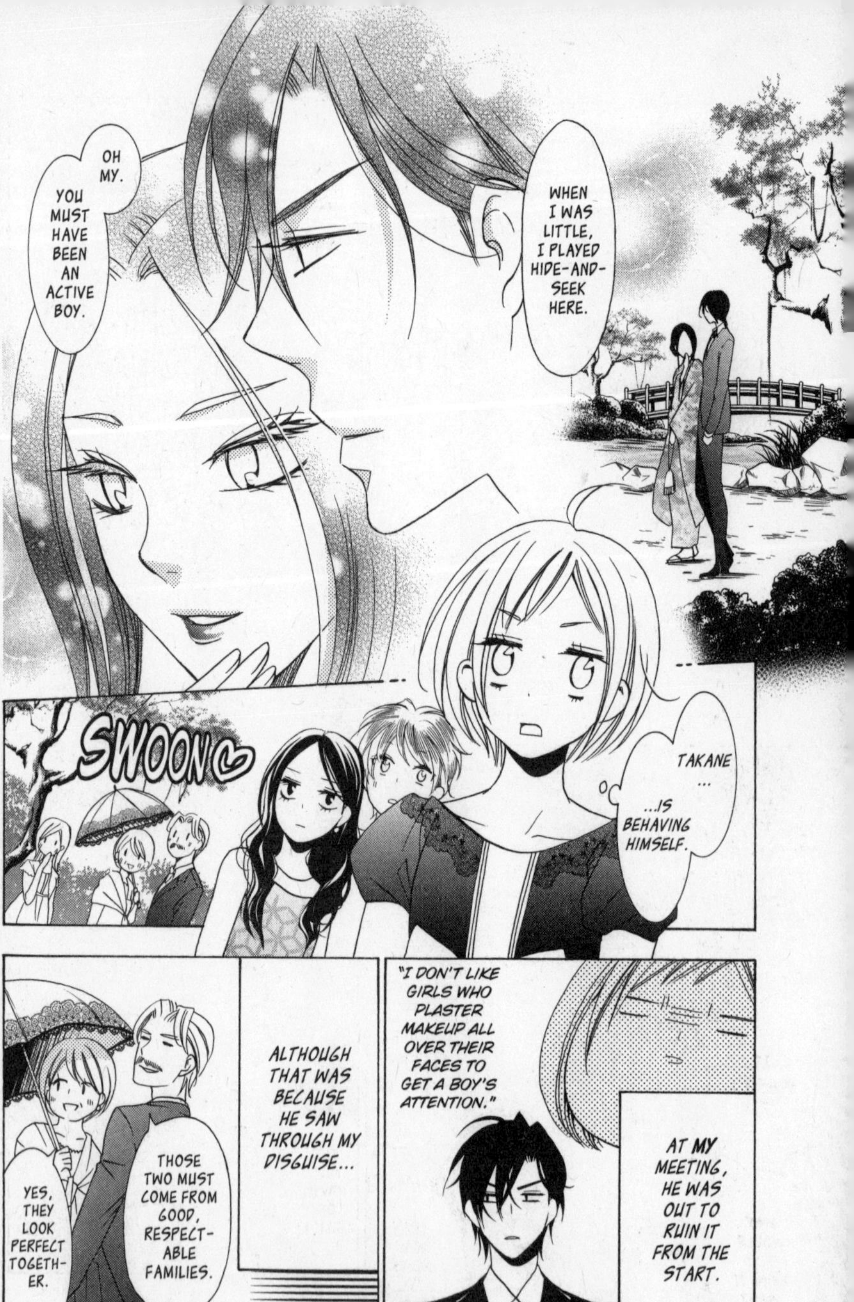
WHEN I WAS LITTLE, I PLAYED HIDE-AND-SEEK HERE.
OH MY. YOU MUST HAVE BEEN AN ACTIVE BOY.
TAKANE ...
...IS BEHAVING HIMSELF.
SWOON
"I DON'T LIKE GIRLS WHO PLASTER MAKEUP ALL OVER THEIR FACES TO GET A BOY'S ATTENTION."
AT MY MEETING, HE WAS OUT TO RUIN IT FROM THE START.
ALTHOUGH THAT WAS BECAUSE HE SAW THROUGH MY DISGUISE...
THOSE TWO MUST COME FROM GOOD, RESPECT-ABLE FAMILIES.
YES, THEY LOOK PERFECT TOGETH-ER.

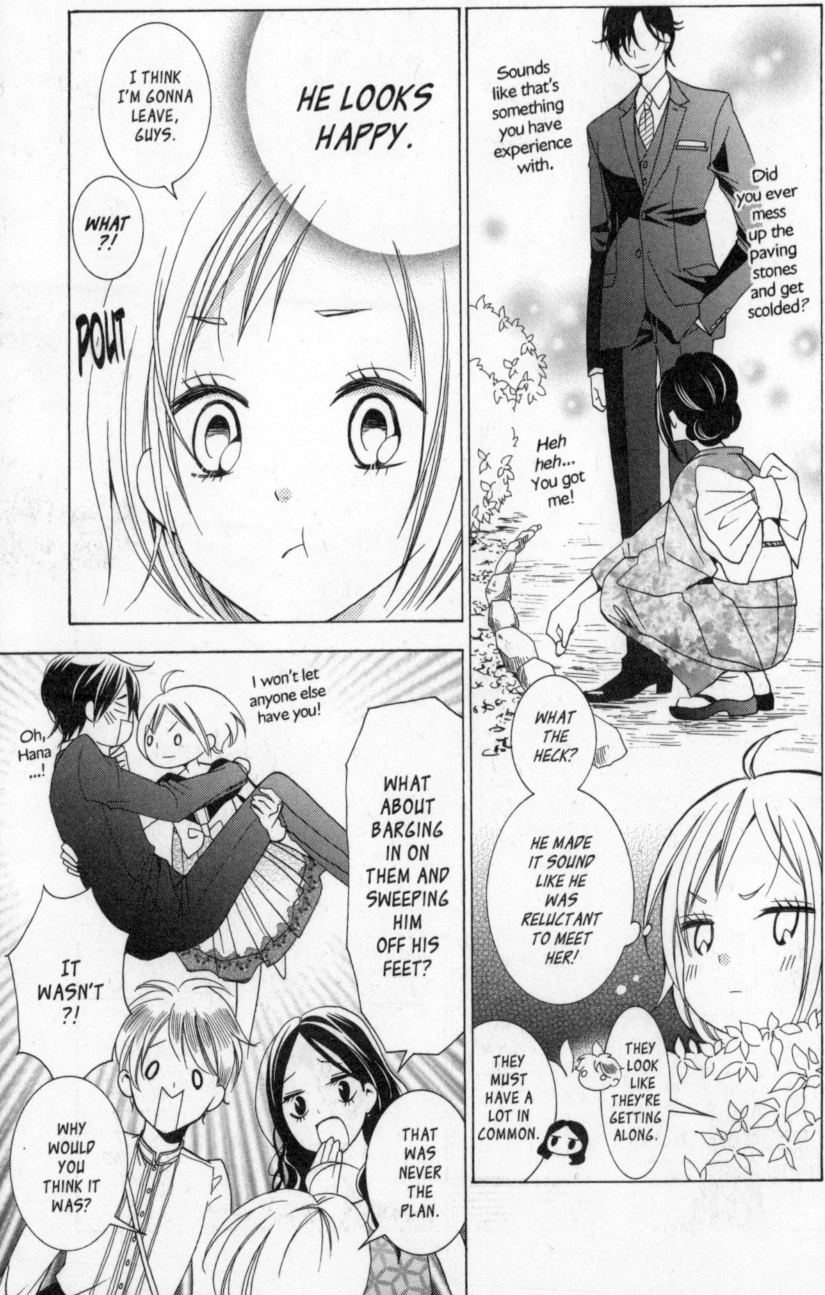
Sounds like that's something you have experience with.
Did you ever mess up the paving stones and get scolded?
Heh heh... You got me!
HE LOOKS HAPPY.
I THINK I'M GONNA LEAVE, GUYS.
WHAT ?!
POUT
WHAT THE HECK?
HE MADE IT SOUND LIKE HE WAS RELUCTANT TO MEET HER!
THEY LOOK LIKE THEY'RE GETTING ALONG.
THEY MUST HAVE A LOT IN COMMON.
WHAT ABOUT BARGING IN ON THEM AND SWEEPING HIM OFF HIS FEET?
I won't let anyone else have you!
Oh, Hana ...!
IT WASN'T ?!
THAT WAS NEVER THE PLAN.
WHY WOULD YOU THINK IT WAS?

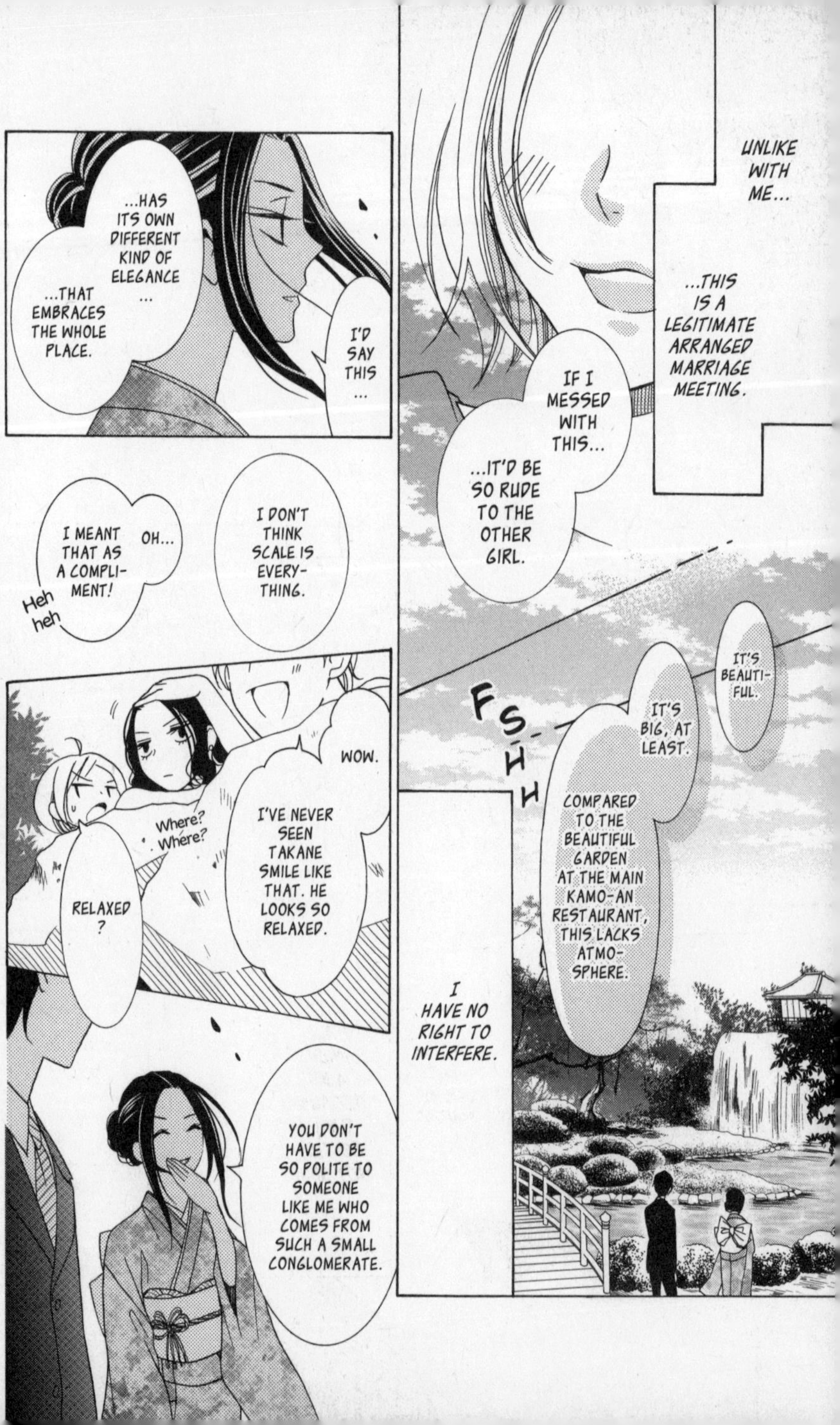
UNLIKE WITH ME...
...THIS IS A LEGITIMATE ARRANGED MARRIAGE MEETING.
IF I MESSED WITH THIS...
...IT'D BE SO RUDE TO THE OTHER GIRL.
IT'S BEAUTIFUL.
IT'S BIG, AT LEAST.
COMPARED TO THE BEAUTIFUL GARDEN AT THE MAIN KAMO-AN RESTAURANT, THIS LACKS ATMOSPHERE.
FSHH
I HAVE NO RIGHT TO INTERFERE.
I'D SAY THIS...
...HAS ITS OWN DIFFERENT KIND OF ELEGANCE...
...THAT EMBRACES THE WHOLE PLACE.
I DON'T THINK SCALE IS EVERYTHING.
OH...
I MEANT THAT AS A COMPLIMENT!
Heh heh
WOW.
I'VE NEVER SEEN TAKANE SMILE LIKE THAT. HE LOOKS SO RELAXED.
Where? Where?
RELAXED?
YOU DON'T HAVE TO BE SO POLITE TO SOMEONE LIKE ME WHO COMES FROM SUCH A SMALL CONGLOMERATE.

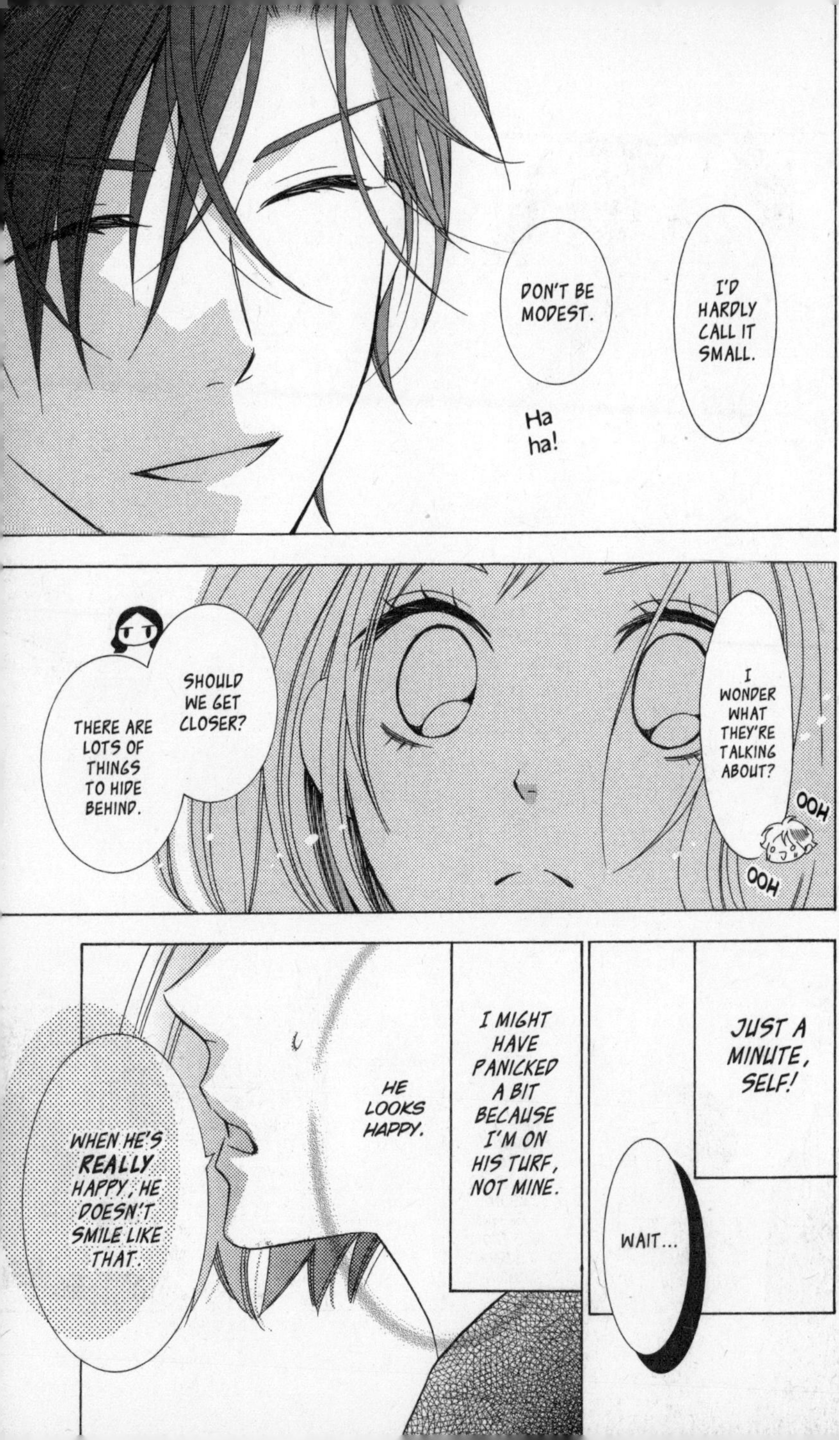

I'D HARDLY CALL IT SMALL.
DON'T BE MODEST.
Ha ha!
I WONDER WHAT THEY'RE TALKING ABOUT?
OOH
OOH
SHOULD WE GET CLOSER?
THERE ARE LOTS OF THINGS TO HIDE BEHIND.
JUST A MINUTE, SELF!
WAIT...
I MIGHT HAVE PANICKED A BIT BECAUSE I'M ON HIS TURF, NOT MINE.
HE LOOKS HAPPY.
WHEN HE'S **REALLY** HAPPY, HE DOESN'T SMILE LIKE THAT.

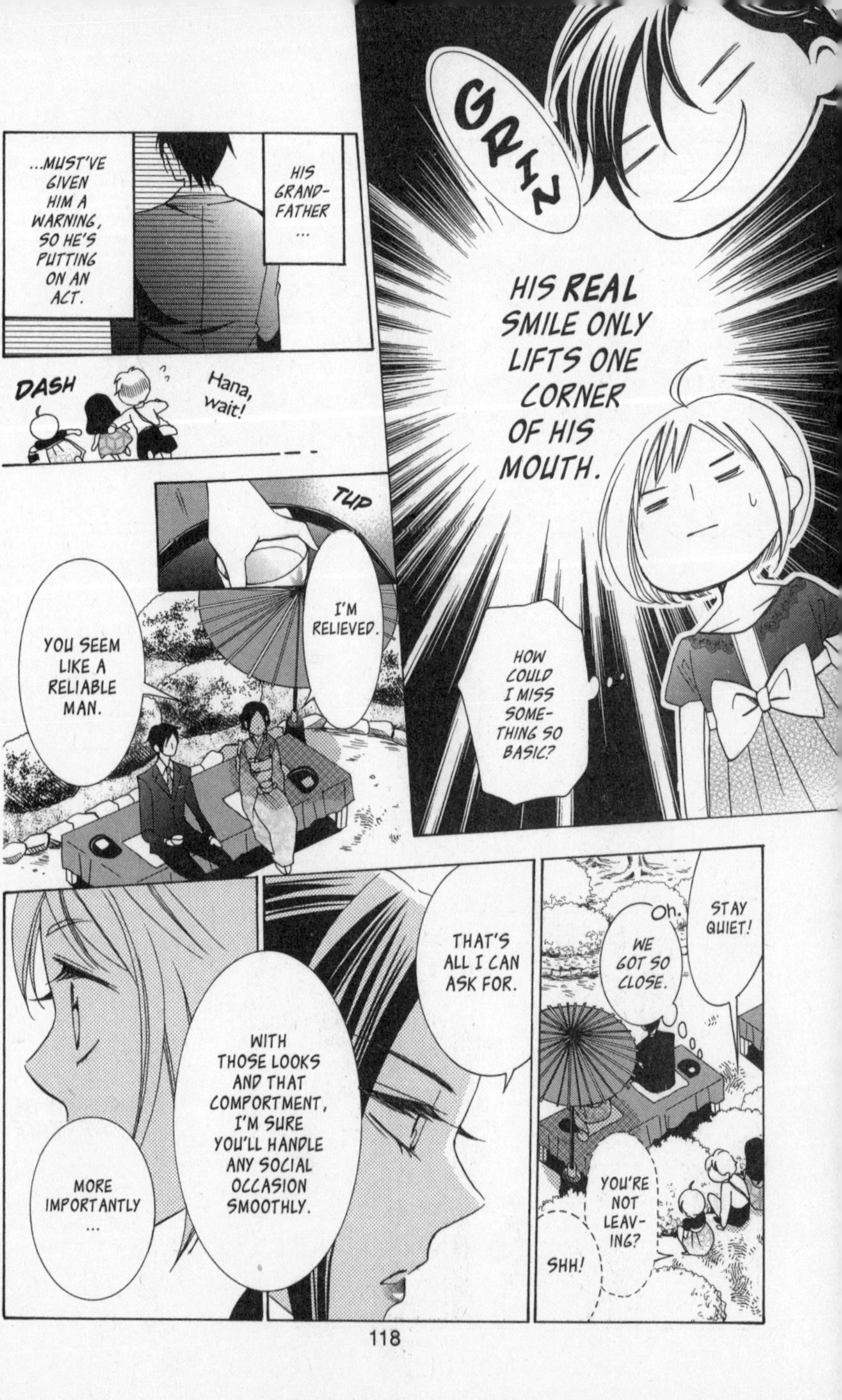
GRIN
HIS REAL SMILE ONLY LIFTS ONE CORNER OF HIS MOUTH.
HOW COULD I MISS SOME-THING SO BASIC?
HIS GRAND-FATHER ...
...MUST'VE GIVEN HIM A WARNING, SO HE'S PUTTING ON AN ACT.
Hana, wait!
DASH
TUP
I'M RELIEVED.
YOU SEEM LIKE A RELIABLE MAN.
STAY QUIET!
Oh.
WE GOT SO CLOSE.
YOU'RE NOT LEAV-ING?
SHH!
THAT'S ALL I CAN ASK FOR.
WITH THOSE LOOKS AND THAT COMPORTMENT, I'M SURE YOU'LL HANDLE ANY SOCIAL OCCASION SMOOTHLY.
MORE IMPORTANTLY ...

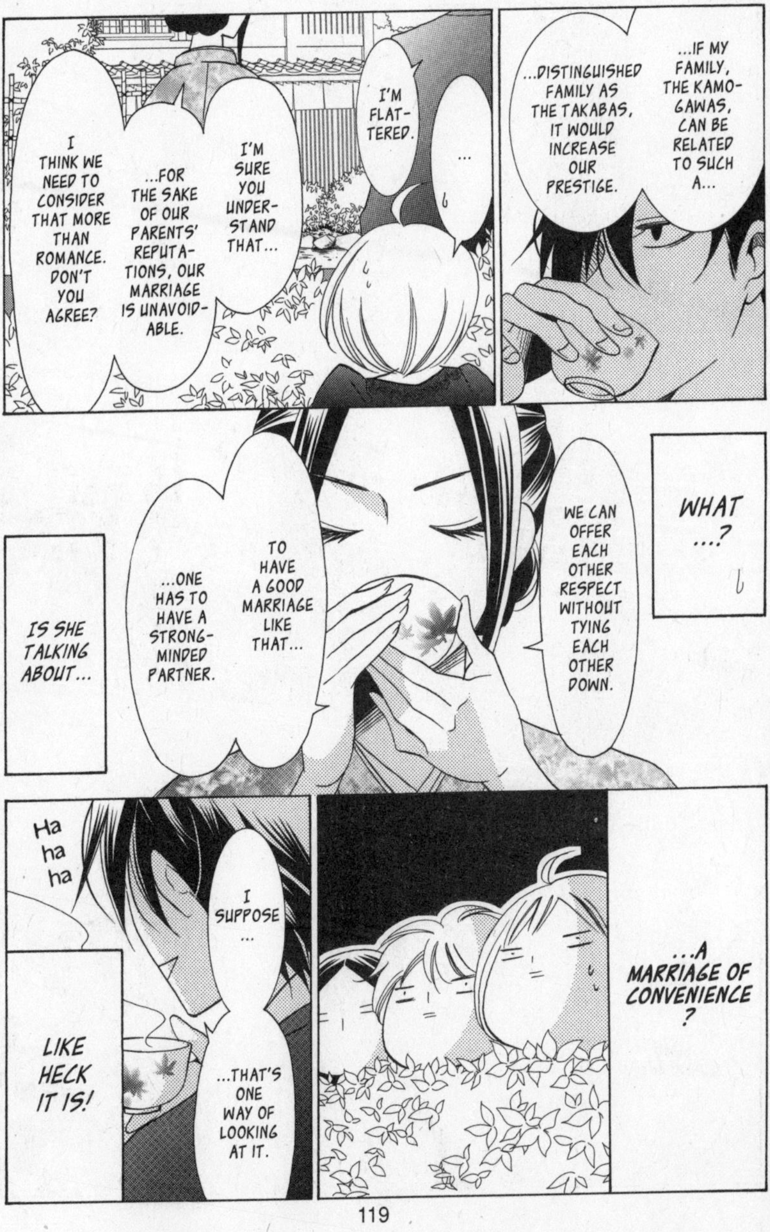
...IF MY FAMILY, THE KAMOGAWAS, CAN BE RELATED TO SUCH A...
...DISTINGUISHED FAMILY AS THE TAKABAS, IT WOULD INCREASE OUR PRESTIGE.
...
I'M FLATTERED.
I'M SURE YOU UNDERSTAND THAT...
...FOR THE SAKE OF OUR PARENTS' REPUTATIONS, OUR MARRIAGE IS UNAVOIDABLE.
I THINK WE NEED TO CONSIDER THAT MORE THAN ROMANCE. DON'T YOU AGREE?
WHAT ...?
WE CAN OFFER EACH OTHER RESPECT WITHOUT TYING EACH OTHER DOWN.
TO HAVE A GOOD MARRIAGE LIKE THAT...
...ONE HAS TO HAVE A STRONG-MINDED PARTNER.
IS SHE TALKING ABOUT...
...A MARRIAGE OF CONVENIENCE?
I SUPPOSE...
Ha ha ha
...THAT'S ONE WAY OF LOOKING AT IT.
LIKE HECK IT IS!

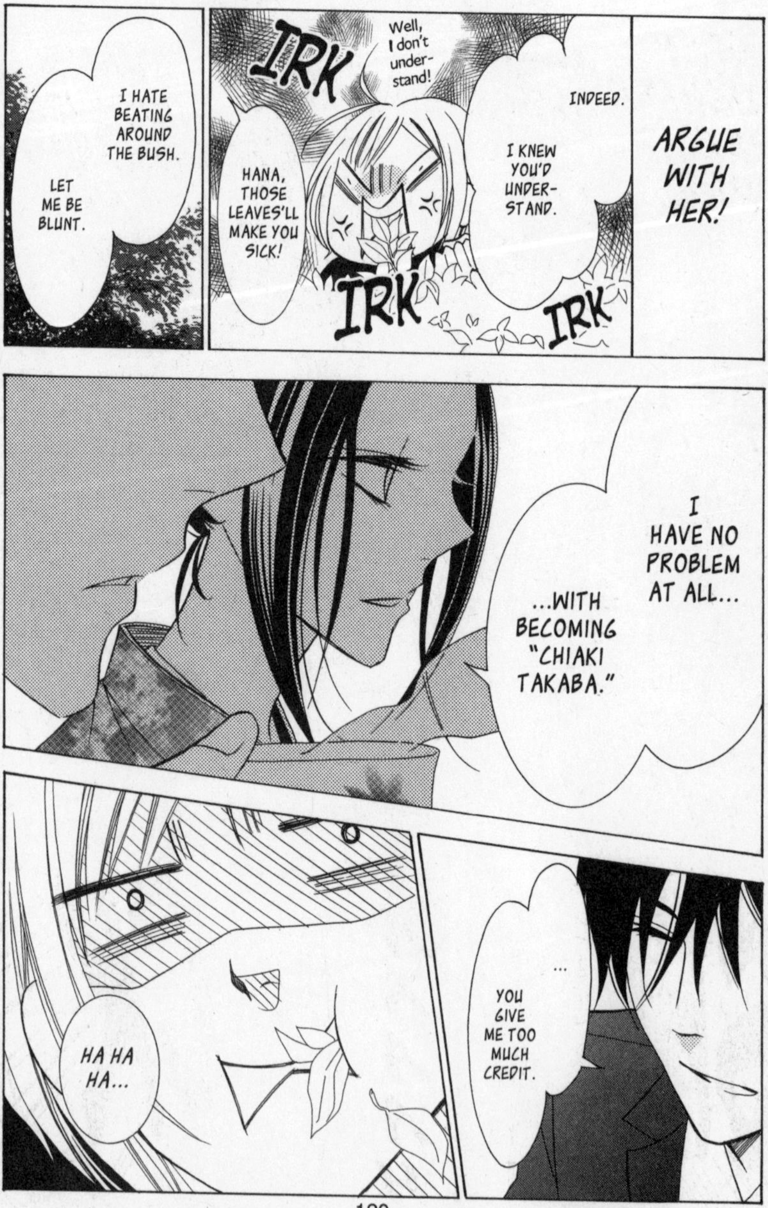
ARGUE WITH HER!
INDEED.
I KNEW YOU'D UNDER-STAND.
IRK
Well, I don't under-stand!
IRK
HANA, THOSE LEAVES'LL MAKE YOU SICK!
IRK
I HATE BEATING AROUND THE BUSH.
LET ME BE BLUNT.
I HAVE NO PROBLEM AT ALL...
...WITH BECOMING "CHIAKI TAKABA."
...
YOU GIVE ME TOO MUCH CREDIT.
HA HA HA...

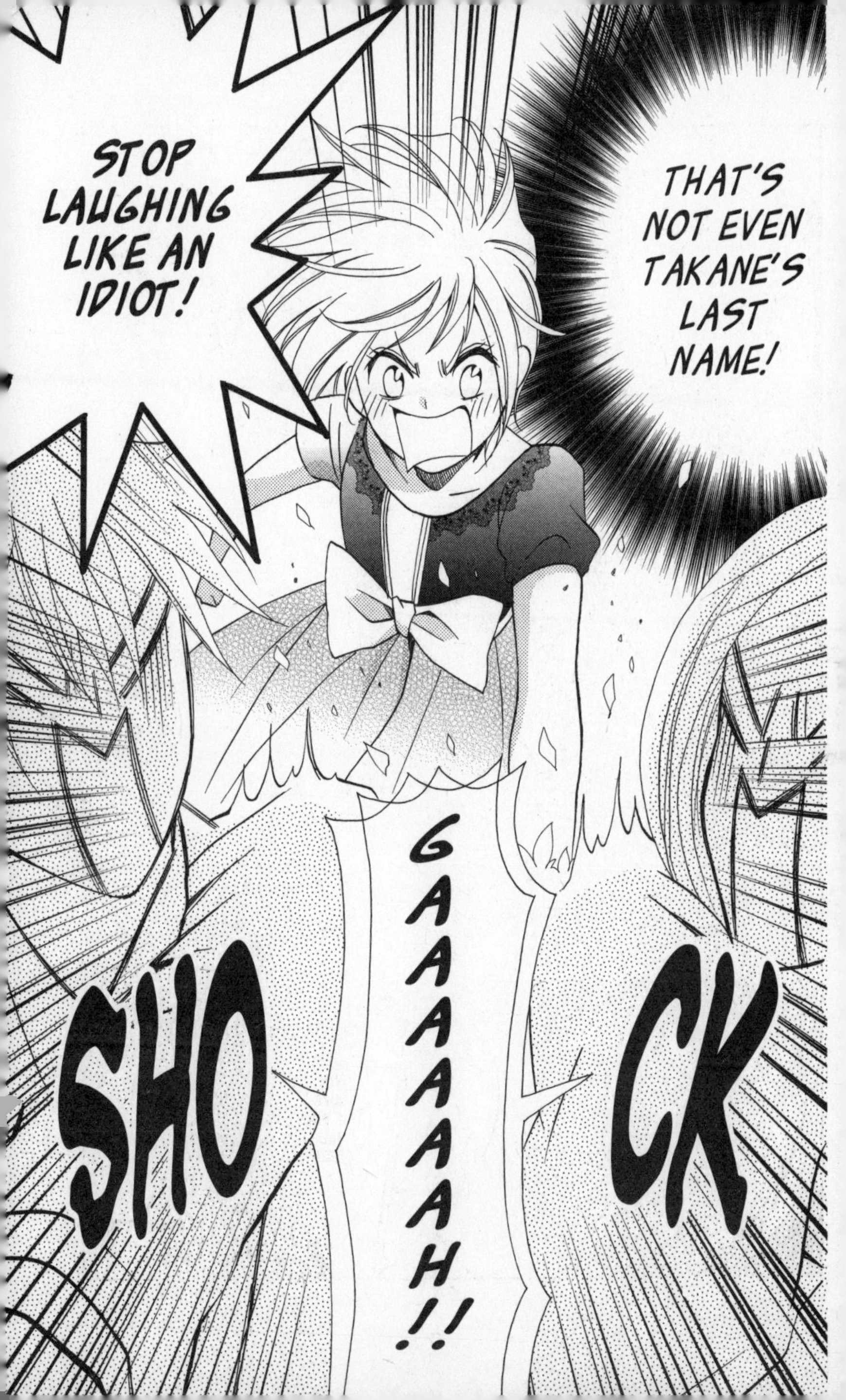
THAT'S NOT EVEN TAKANE'S LAST NAME!
STOP LAUGHING LIKE AN IDIOT!
GAAAAAAH!!
SHOCK

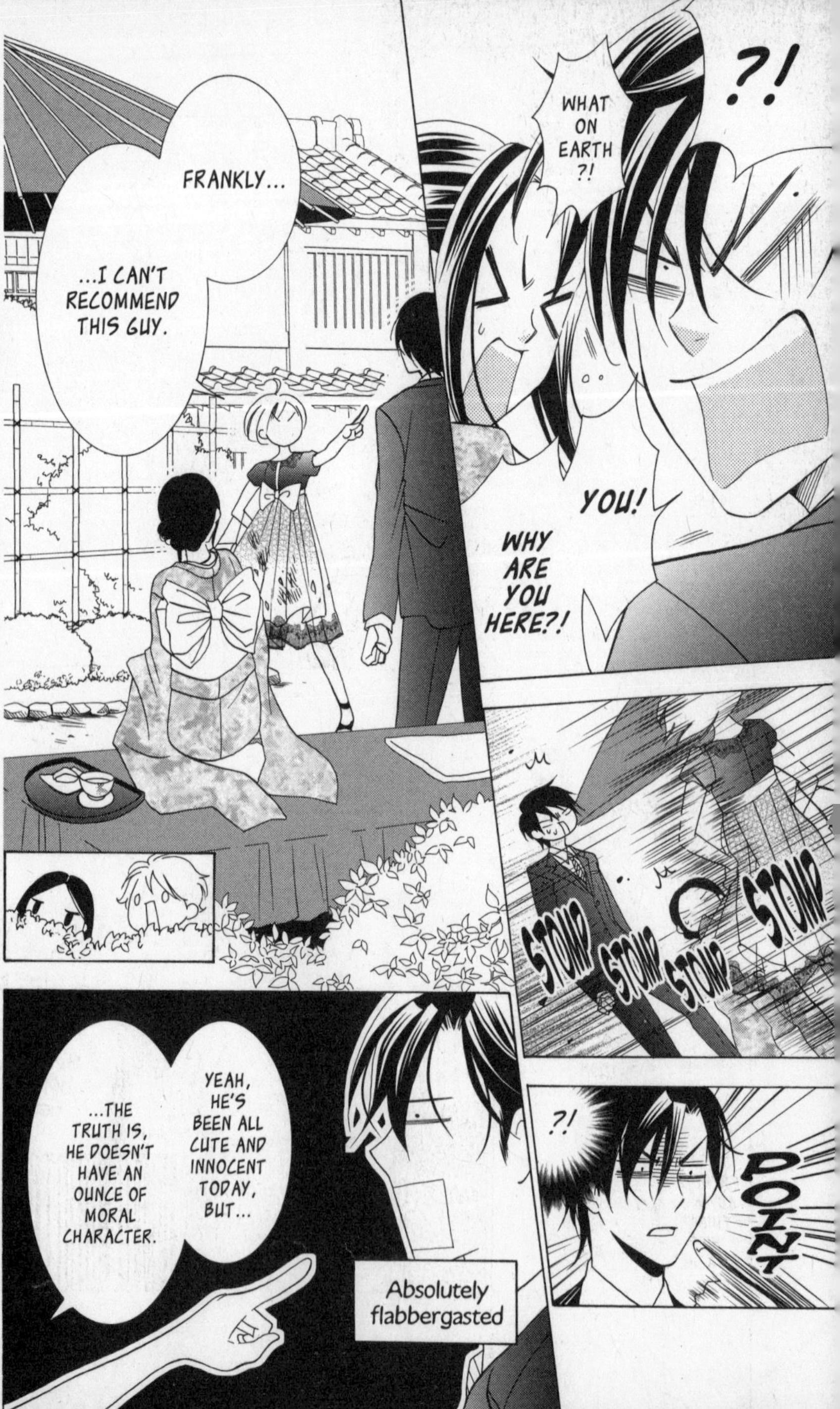
?!
WHAT ON EARTH?!
YOU!
WHY ARE YOU HERE?!
STOMP
STOMP
STOMP
STOMP
FRANKLY...
...I CAN'T RECOMMEND THIS GUY.
?!
POINT
YEAH, HE'S BEEN ALL CUTE AND INNOCENT TODAY, BUT...
...THE TRUTH IS, HE DOESN'T HAVE AN OUNCE OF MORAL CHARACTER.
Absolutely flabbergasted

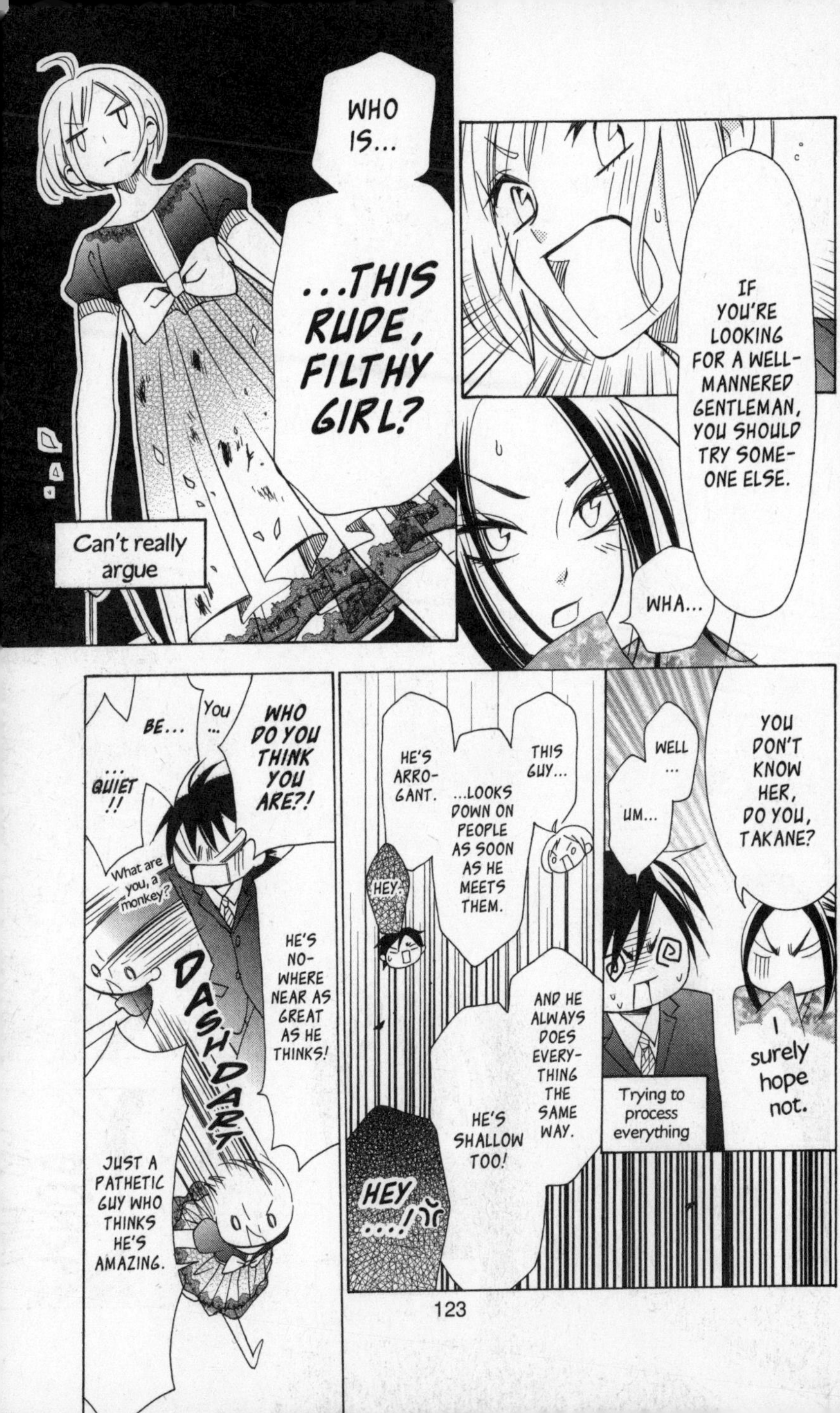
IF YOU'RE LOOKING FOR A WELL-MANNERED GENTLEMAN, YOU SHOULD TRY SOME-ONE ELSE.
WHA...
WHO IS...
...THIS RUDE, FILTHY GIRL?
Can't really argue
YOU DON'T KNOW HER, DO YOU, TAKANE?
WELL ...
UM...
I surely hope not.
Trying to process everything
THIS GUY...
HE'S ARRO-GANT.
...LOOKS DOWN ON PEOPLE AS SOON AS HE MEETS THEM.
HEY.
AND HE ALWAYS DOES EVERY-THING THE SAME WAY.
HE'S SHALLOW TOO!
HEY ...!
WHO DO YOU THINK YOU ARE?!
You ...
BE...
...QUIET!!
What are you, a monkey?
HE'S NO-WHERE NEAR AS GREAT AS HE THINKS!
DASH DART
JUST A PATHETIC GUY WHO THINKS HE'S AMAZING.

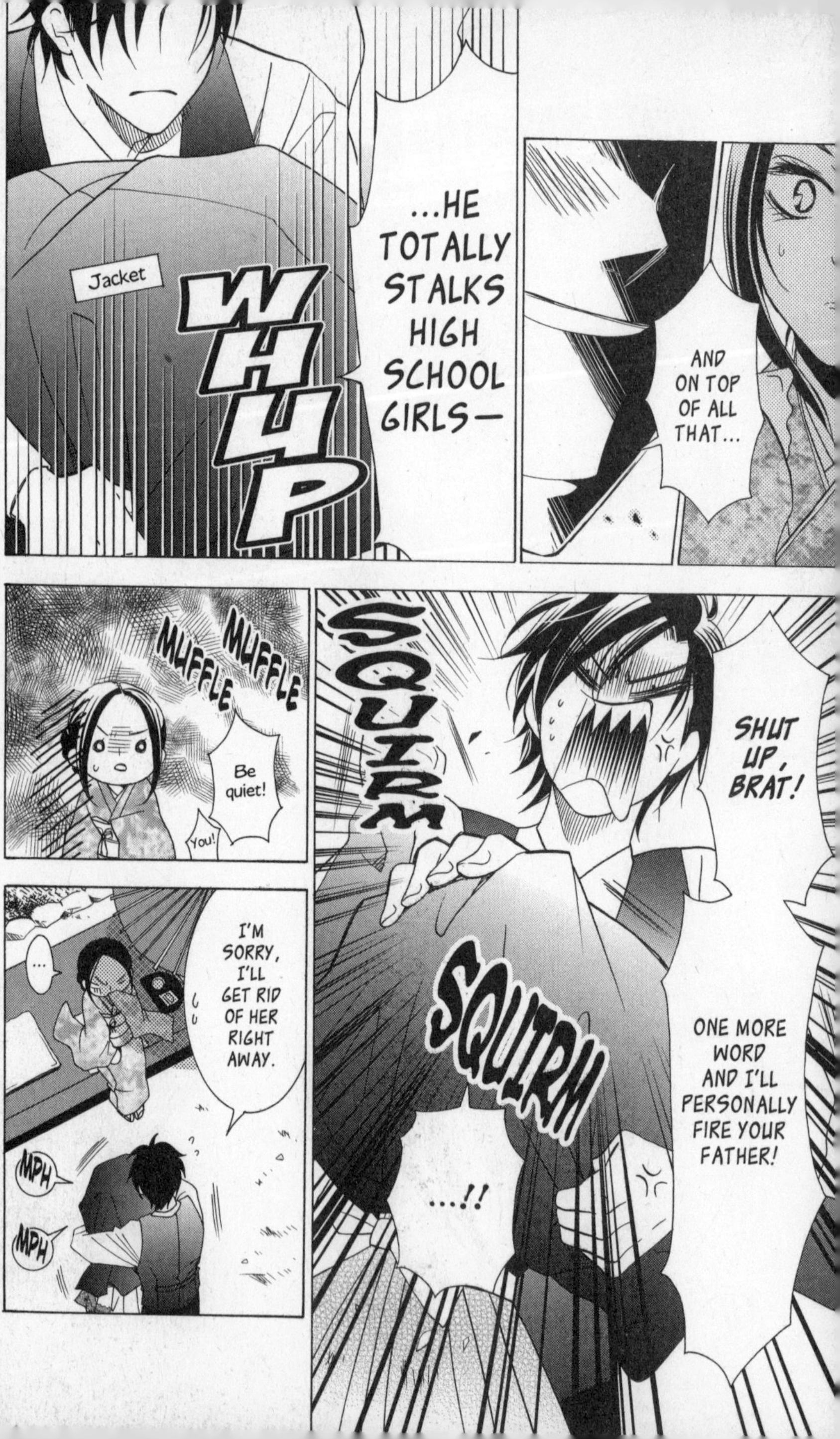
AND ON TOP OF ALL THAT...
...HE TOTALLY STALKS HIGH SCHOOL GIRLS—
WHUP
Jacket
SQUIRM
SHUT UP, BRAT!
SQUIRM
ONE MORE WORD AND I'LL PERSONALLY FIRE YOUR FATHER!
...!!
MUFFLE MUFFLE
Be quiet!
You!
I'M SORRY, I'LL GET RID OF HER RIGHT AWAY.
...
MPH
MPH

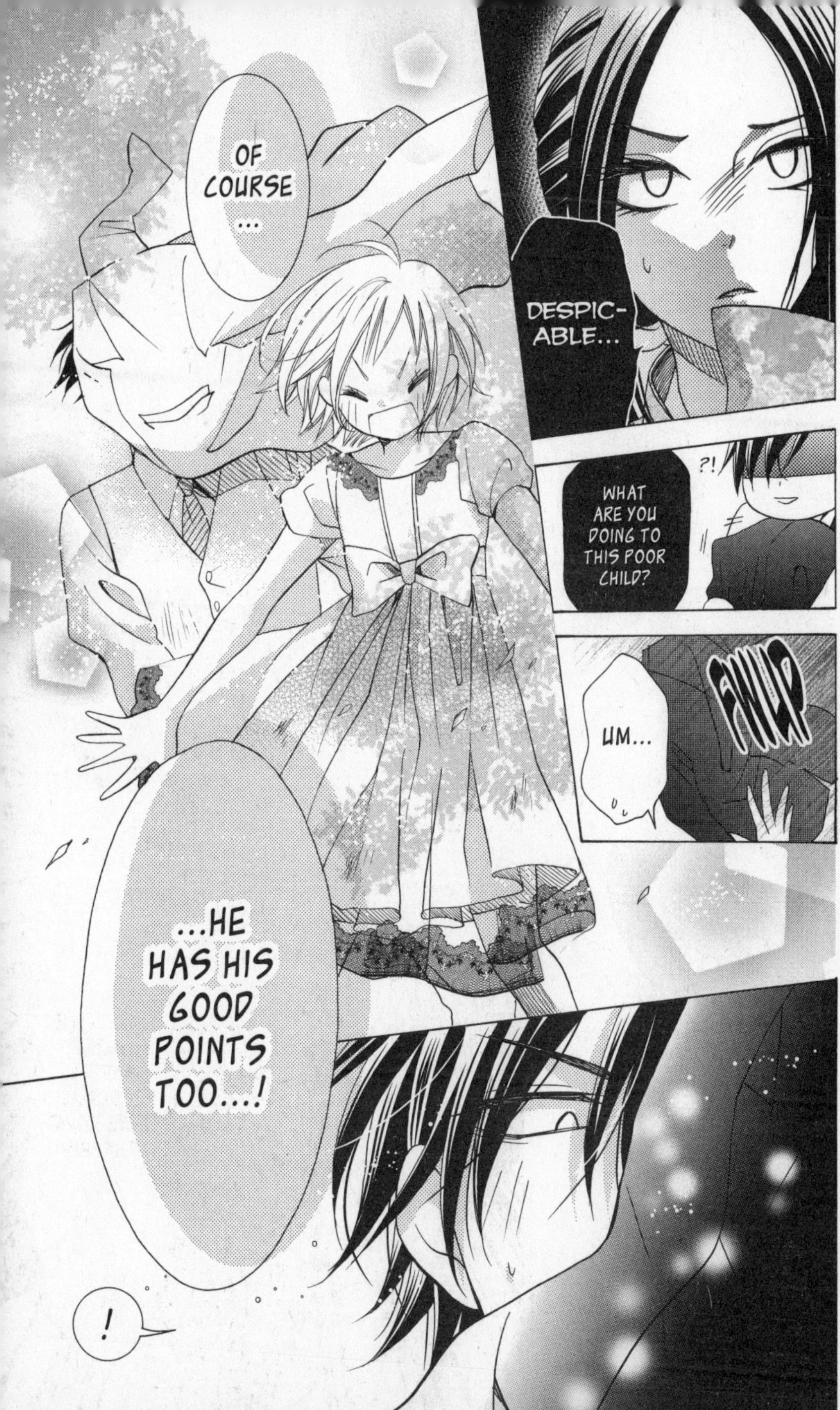
DESPIC-ABLE...
?!
WHAT ARE YOU DOING TO THIS POOR CHILD?
UM...
OF COURSE...
...HE HAS HIS GOOD POINTS TOO...!
!

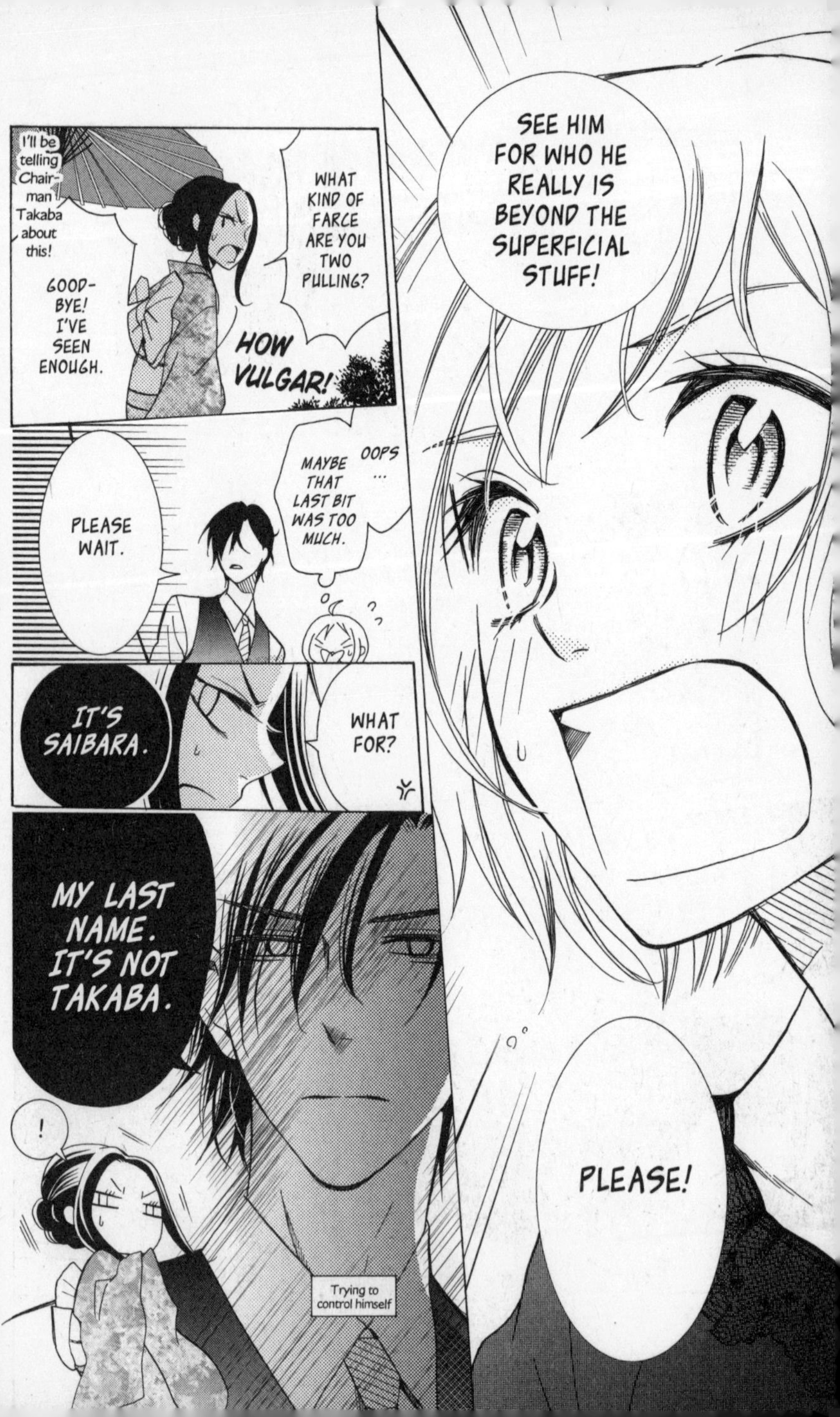
SEE HIM FOR WHO HE REALLY IS BEYOND THE SUPERFICIAL STUFF!
PLEASE!
WHAT KIND OF FARCE ARE YOU TWO PULLING?
HOW VULGAR!
GOOD-BYE! I'VE SEEN ENOUGH.
I'll be telling Chairman Takaba about this!
OOPS ...
MAYBE THAT LAST BIT WAS TOO MUCH.
PLEASE WAIT.
WHAT FOR?
IT'S SAIBARA.
MY LAST NAME. IT'S NOT TAKABA.
!
Trying to control himself

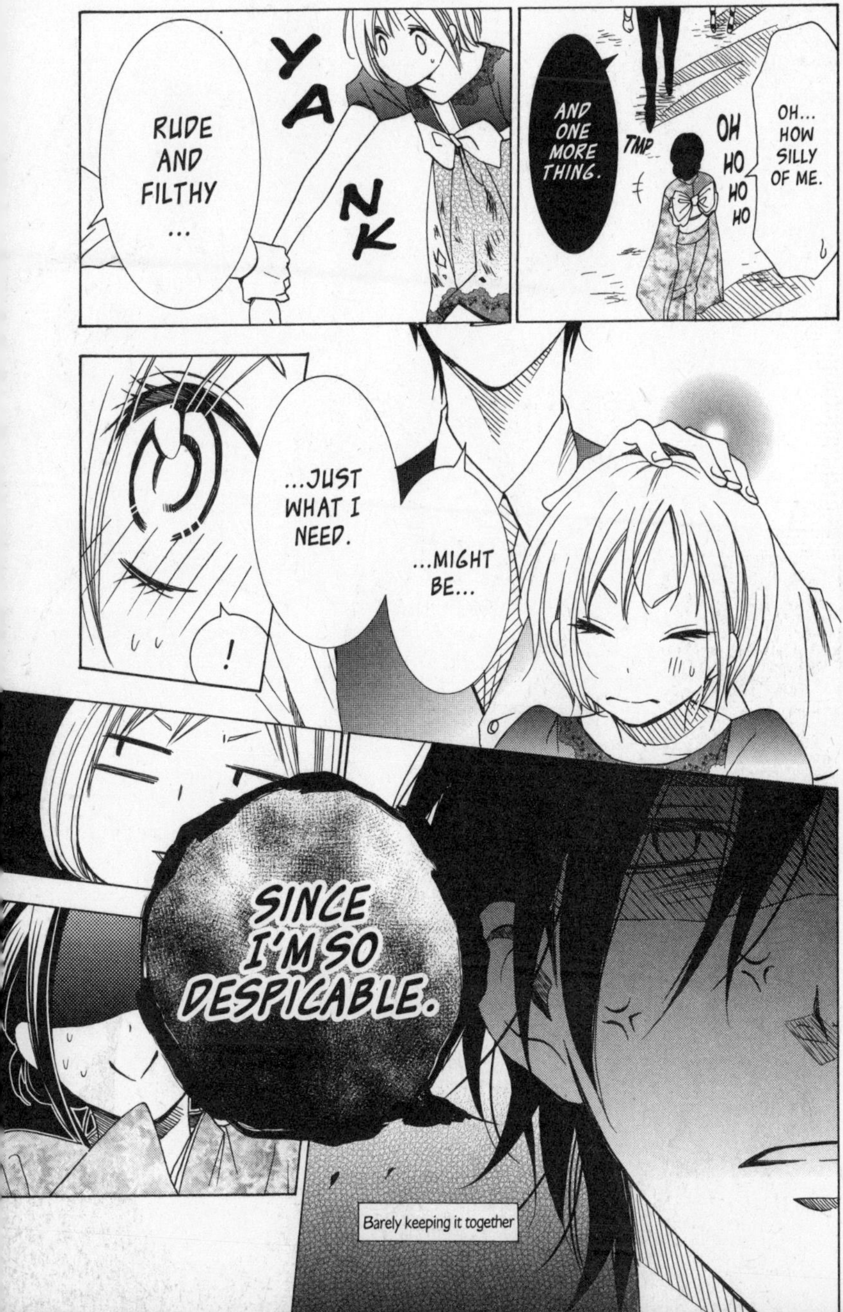
AND ONE MORE THING.
TMP
OH HO HO HO
OH... HOW SILLY OF ME.
YANK
RUDE AND FILTHY...
...MIGHT BE...
...JUST WHAT I NEED.
!
SINCE I'M SO DESPICABLE.
Barely keeping it together

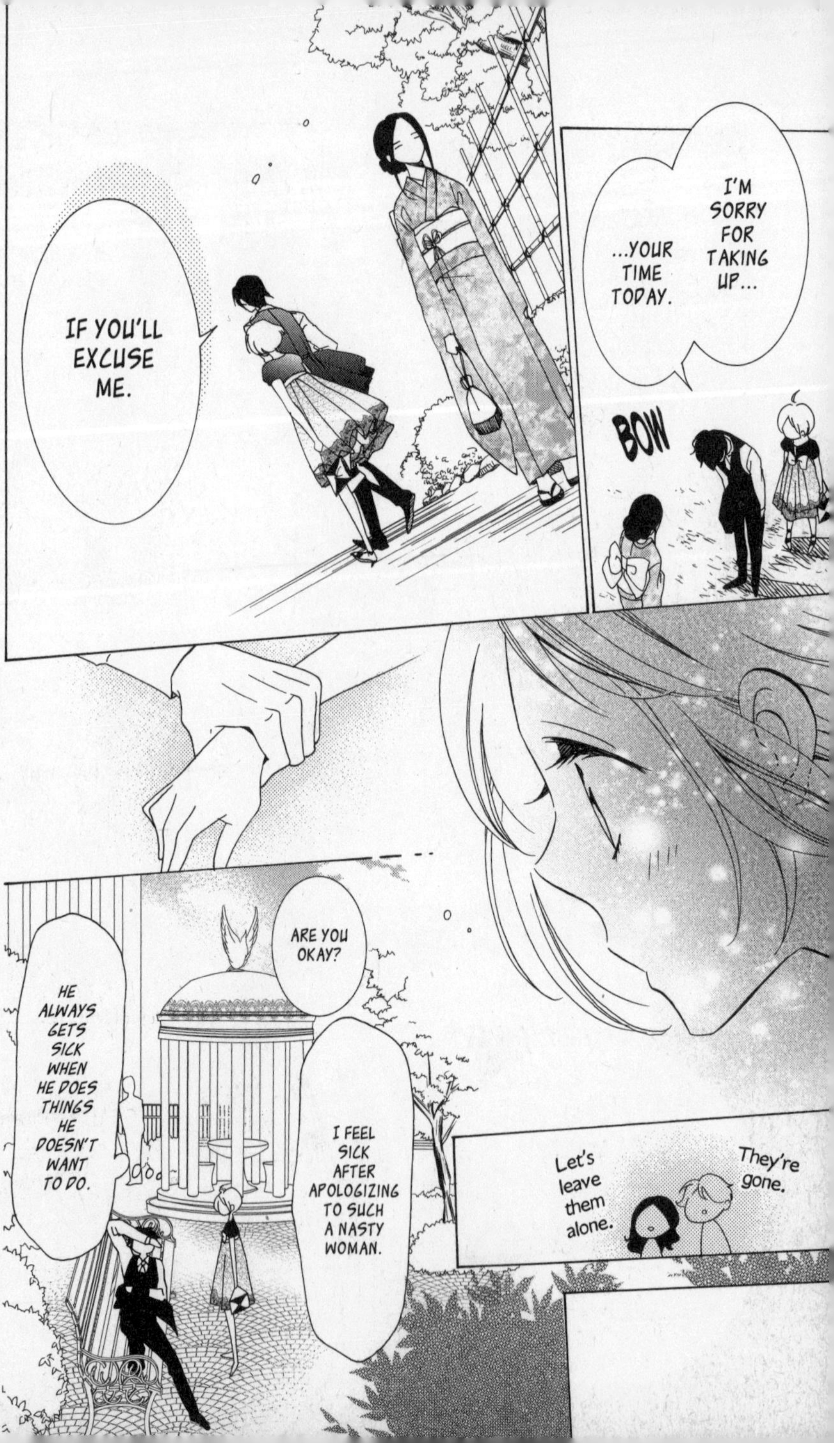
I'M SORRY FOR TAKING UP...
...YOUR TIME TODAY.
BOW
IF YOU'LL EXCUSE ME.
They're gone.
Let's leave them alone.
ARE YOU OKAY?
I FEEL SICK AFTER APOLOGIZING TO SUCH A NASTY WOMAN.
HE ALWAYS GETS SICK WHEN HE DOES THINGS HE DOESN'T WANT TO DO.

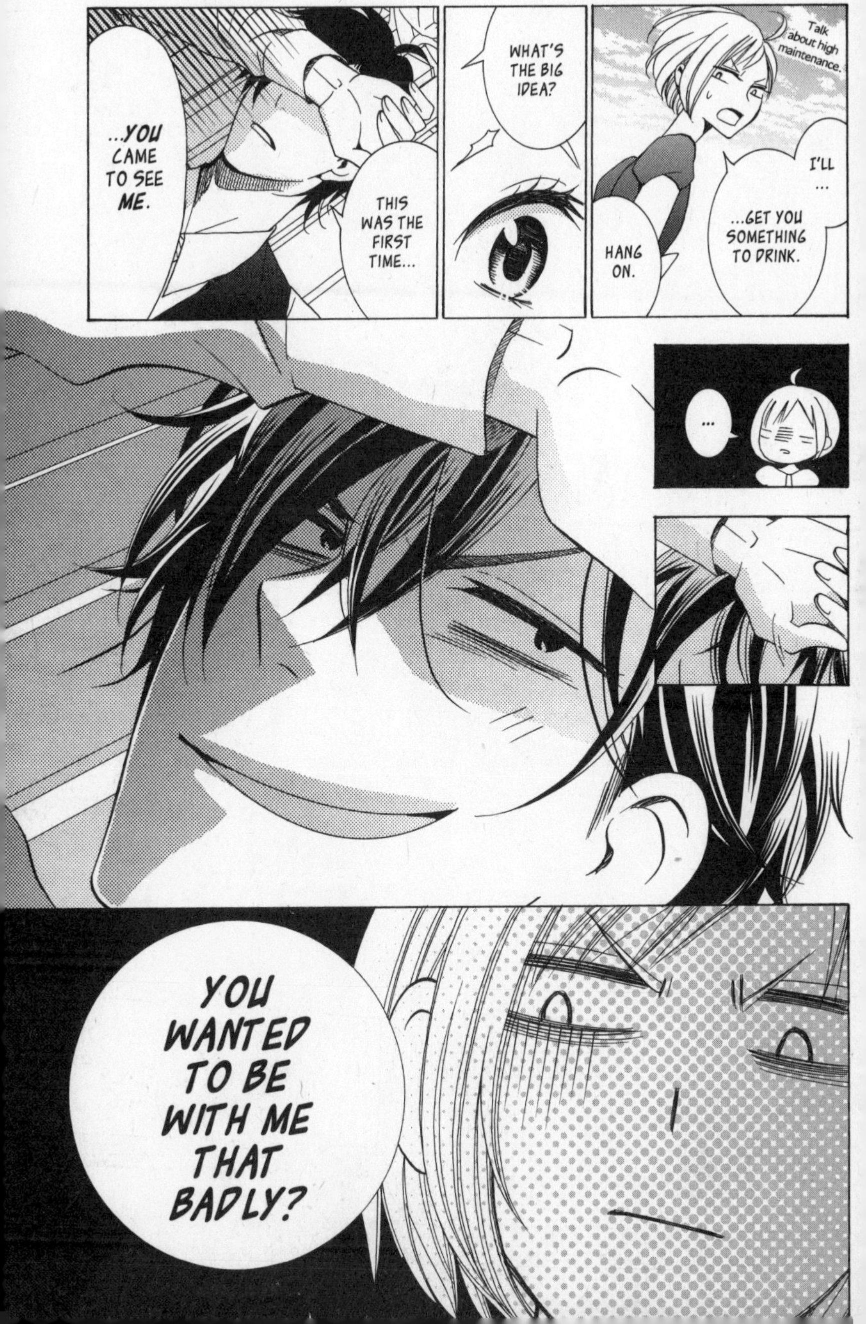
Talk about high maintenance.
I'LL ...
...GET YOU SOMETHING TO DRINK.
HANG ON.
WHAT'S THE BIG IDEA?
THIS WAS THE FIRST TIME...
...YOU CAME TO SEE ME.
...
YOU WANTED TO BE WITH ME THAT BADLY?

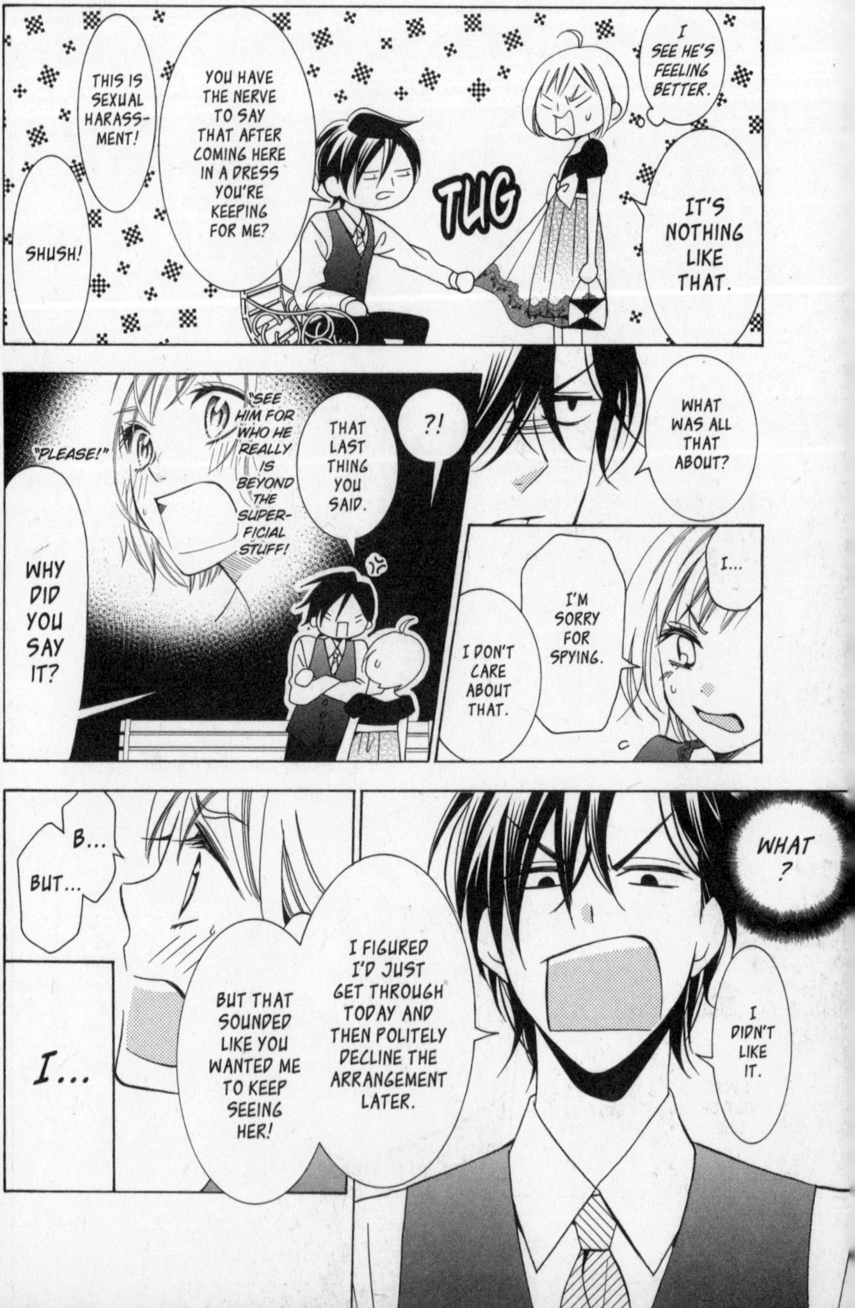
I SEE HE'S FEELING BETTER.
IT'S NOTHING LIKE THAT.
TUG
YOU HAVE THE NERVE TO SAY THAT AFTER COMING HERE IN A DRESS YOU'RE KEEPING FOR ME?
THIS IS SEXUAL HARASS-MENT!
SHUSH!
WHAT WAS ALL THAT ABOUT?
I...
I'M SORRY FOR SPYING.
I DON'T CARE ABOUT THAT.
?!
THAT LAST THING YOU SAID.
"SEE HIM FOR WHO HE REALLY IS BEYOND THE SUPER-FICIAL STUFF!
"PLEASE!"
WHY DID YOU SAY IT?
WHAT?
I DIDN'T LIKE IT.
I FIGURED I'D JUST GET THROUGH TODAY AND THEN POLITELY DECLINE THE ARRANGEMENT LATER.
BUT THAT SOUNDED LIKE YOU WANTED ME TO KEEP SEEING HER!
B...
BUT...
I...

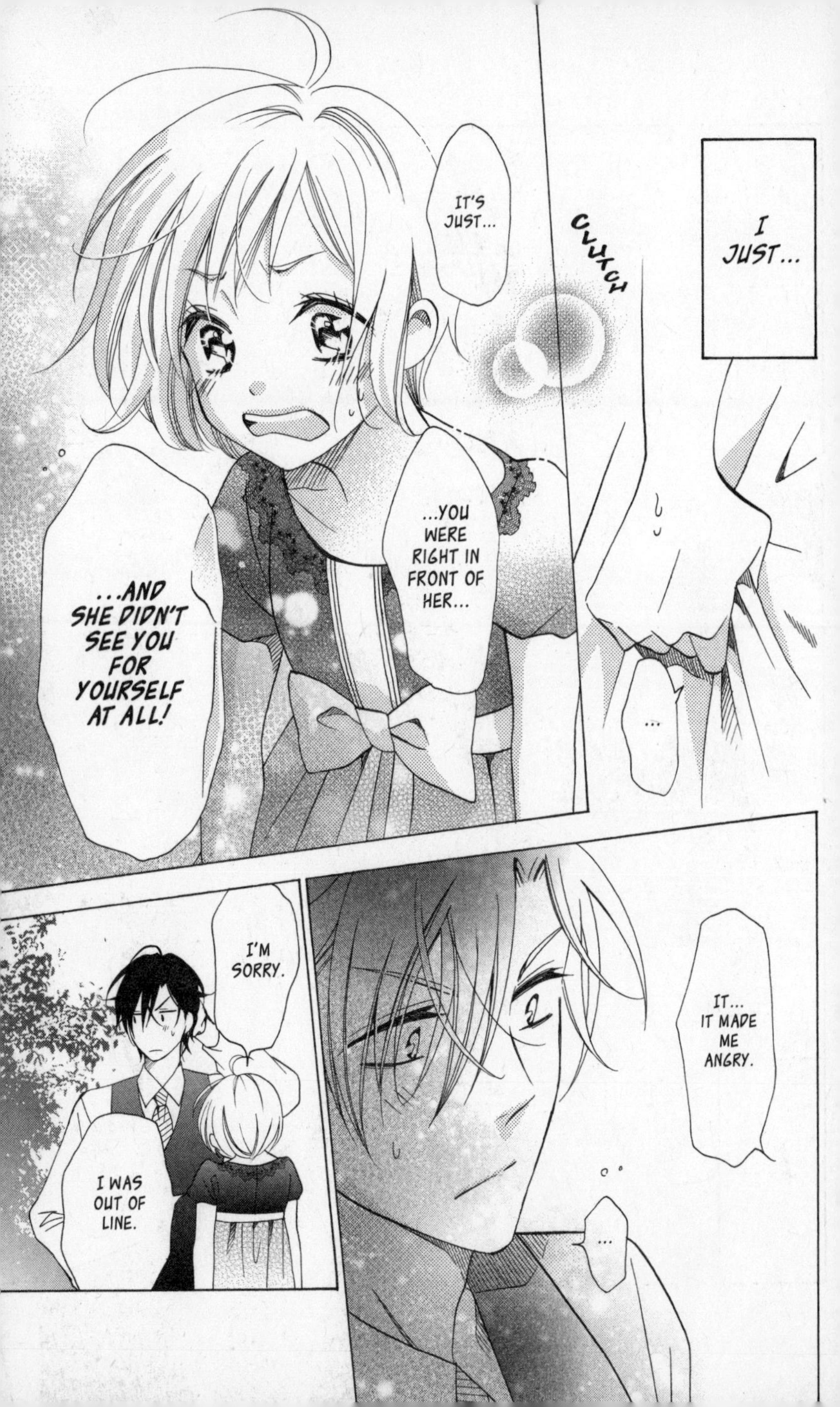
I JUST...
CLUTCH
...
IT'S JUST...
...YOU WERE RIGHT IN FRONT OF HER...
...AND SHE DIDN'T SEE YOU FOR YOURSELF AT ALL!
IT... IT MADE ME ANGRY.
...
I'M SORRY.
I WAS OUT OF LINE.

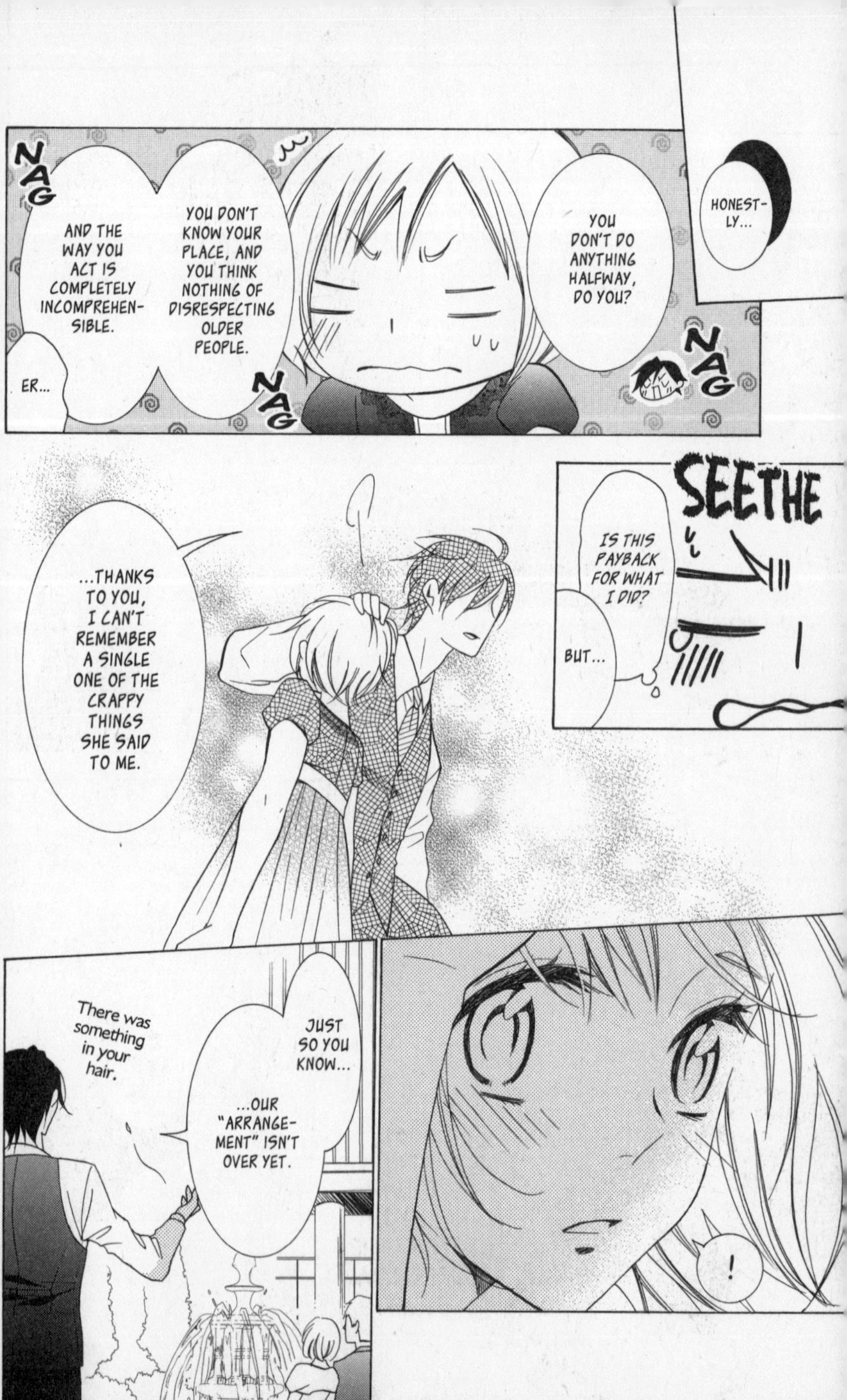
HONESTLY...
YOU DON'T DO ANYTHING HALFWAY, DO YOU?
NAG
YOU DON'T KNOW YOUR PLACE, AND YOU THINK NOTHING OF DISRESPECTING OLDER PEOPLE.
NAG
AND THE WAY YOU ACT IS COMPLETELY INCOMPREHENSIBLE.
NAG
ER...
SEETHE
IS THIS PAYBACK FOR WHAT I DID?
BUT...
...THANKS TO YOU, I CAN'T REMEMBER A SINGLE ONE OF THE CRAPPY THINGS SHE SAID TO ME.
!
JUST SO YOU KNOW...
...OUR "ARRANGEMENT" ISN'T OVER YET.
There was something in your hair.

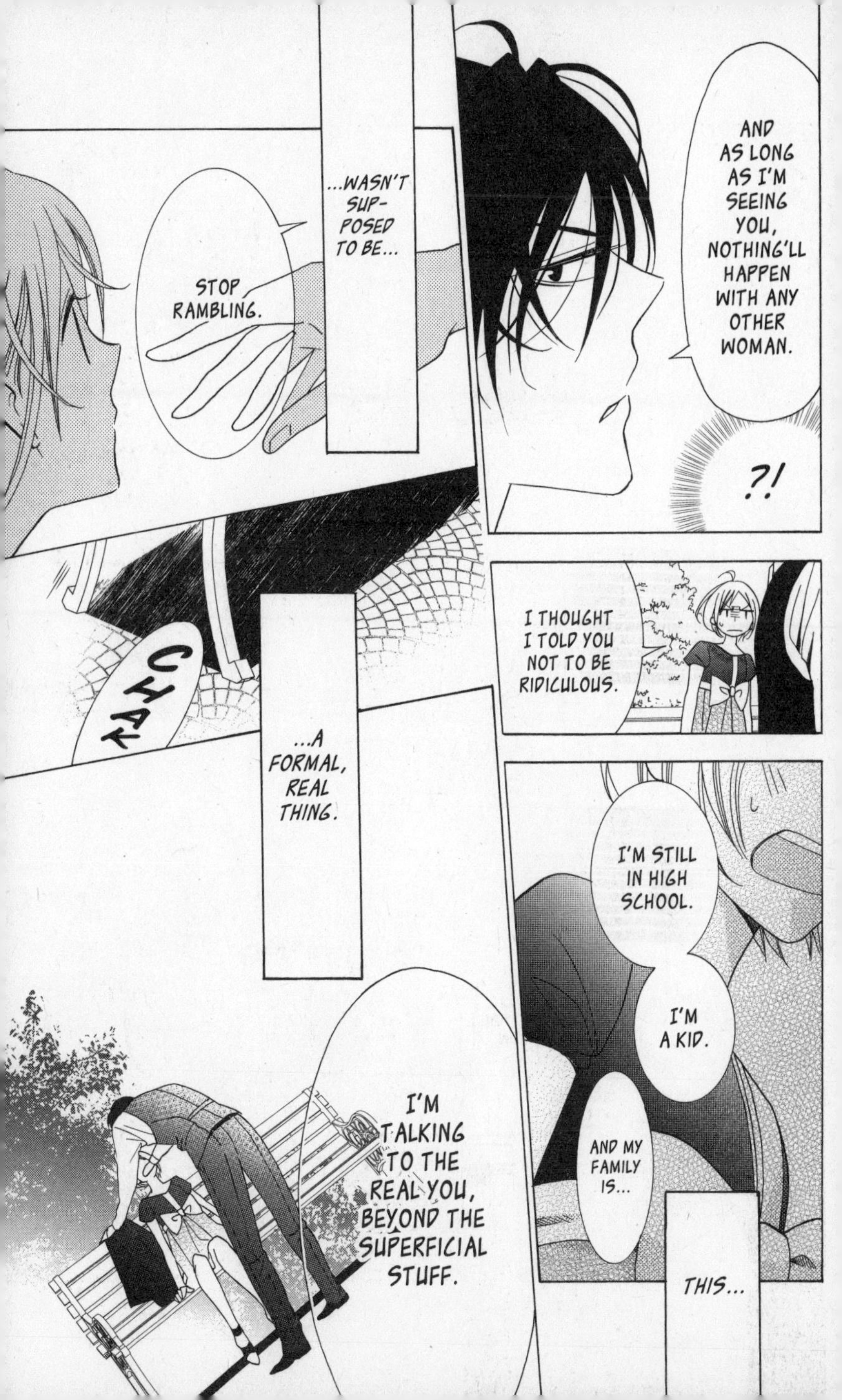
AND AS LONG AS I'M SEEING YOU, NOTHING'LL HAPPEN WITH ANY OTHER WOMAN.
?!
...WASN'T SUP-POSED TO BE...
STOP RAMBLING.
CHAK
I THOUGHT I TOLD YOU NOT TO BE RIDICULOUS.
I'M STILL IN HIGH SCHOOL.
I'M A KID.
AND MY FAMILY IS...
THIS...
...A FORMAL, REAL THING.
I'M TALKING TO THE REAL YOU, BEYOND THE SUPERFICIAL STUFF.

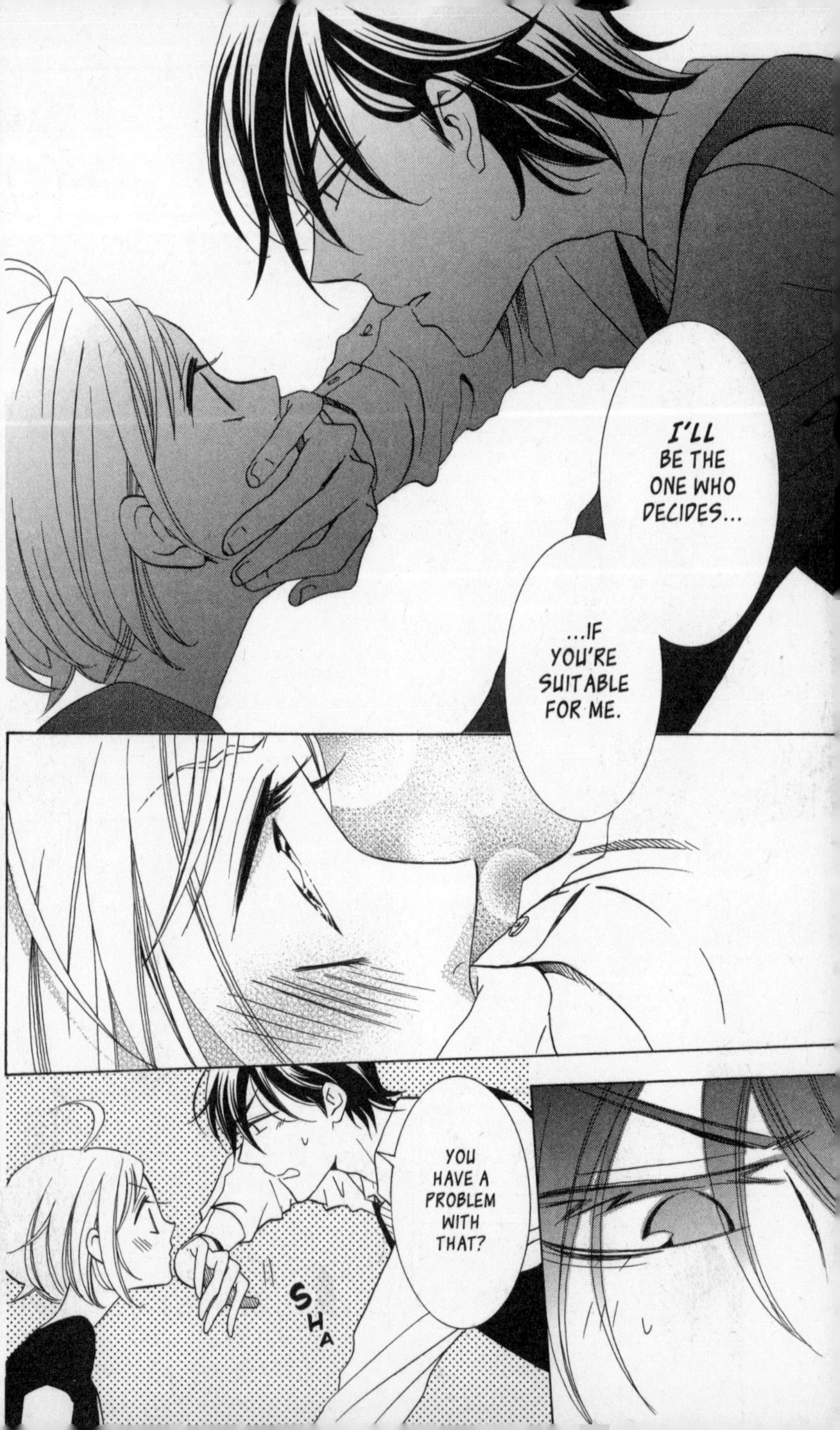
I'LL BE THE ONE WHO DECIDES...
...IF YOU'RE SUITABLE FOR ME.
YOU HAVE A PROBLEM WITH THAT?
SHA

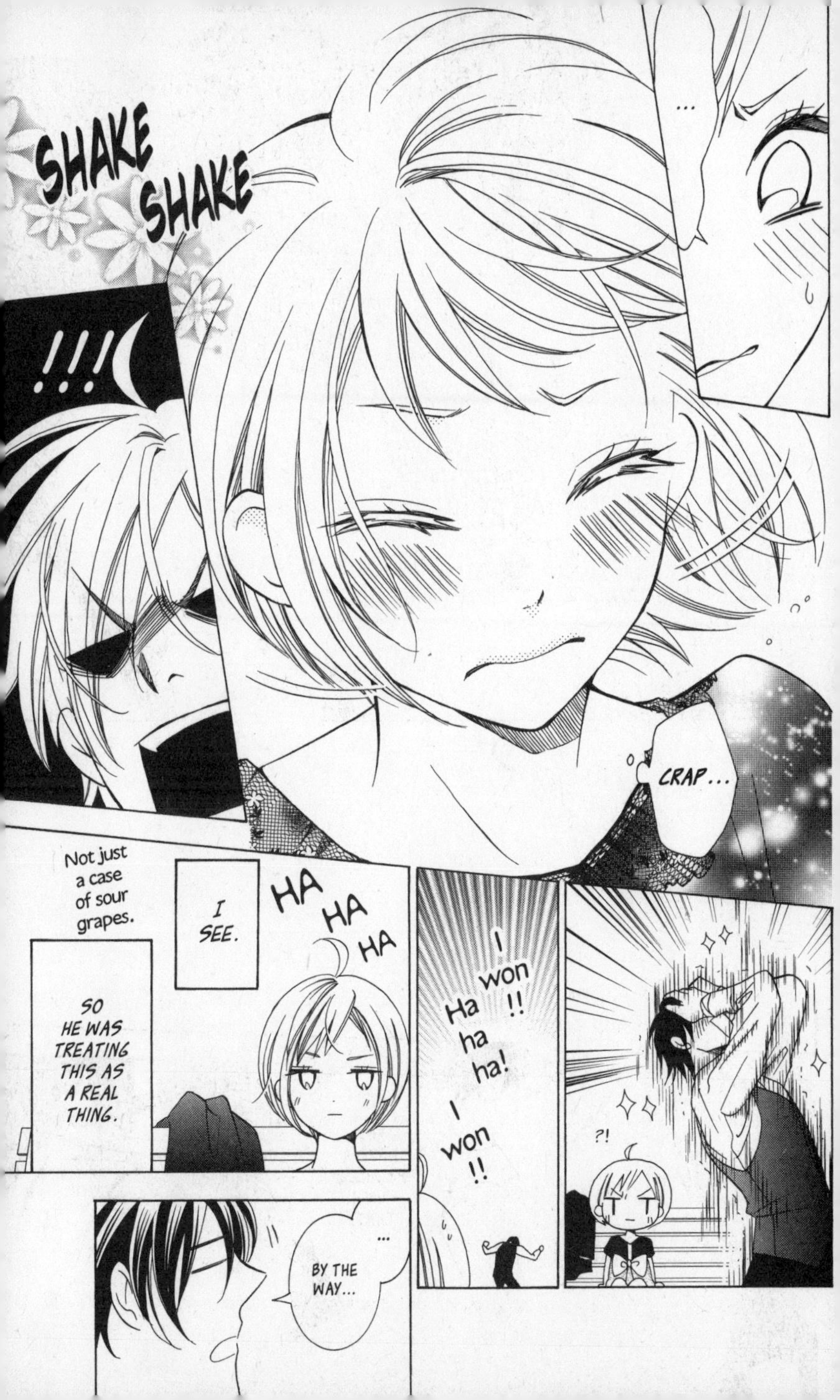
...
SHAKE SHAKE
!!!
CRAP...
?!
I won!!
Ha ha ha!
I won!!
HA HA HA
I SEE.
Not just a case of sour grapes.
SO HE WAS TREATING THIS AS A REAL THING.
...
BY THE WAY...

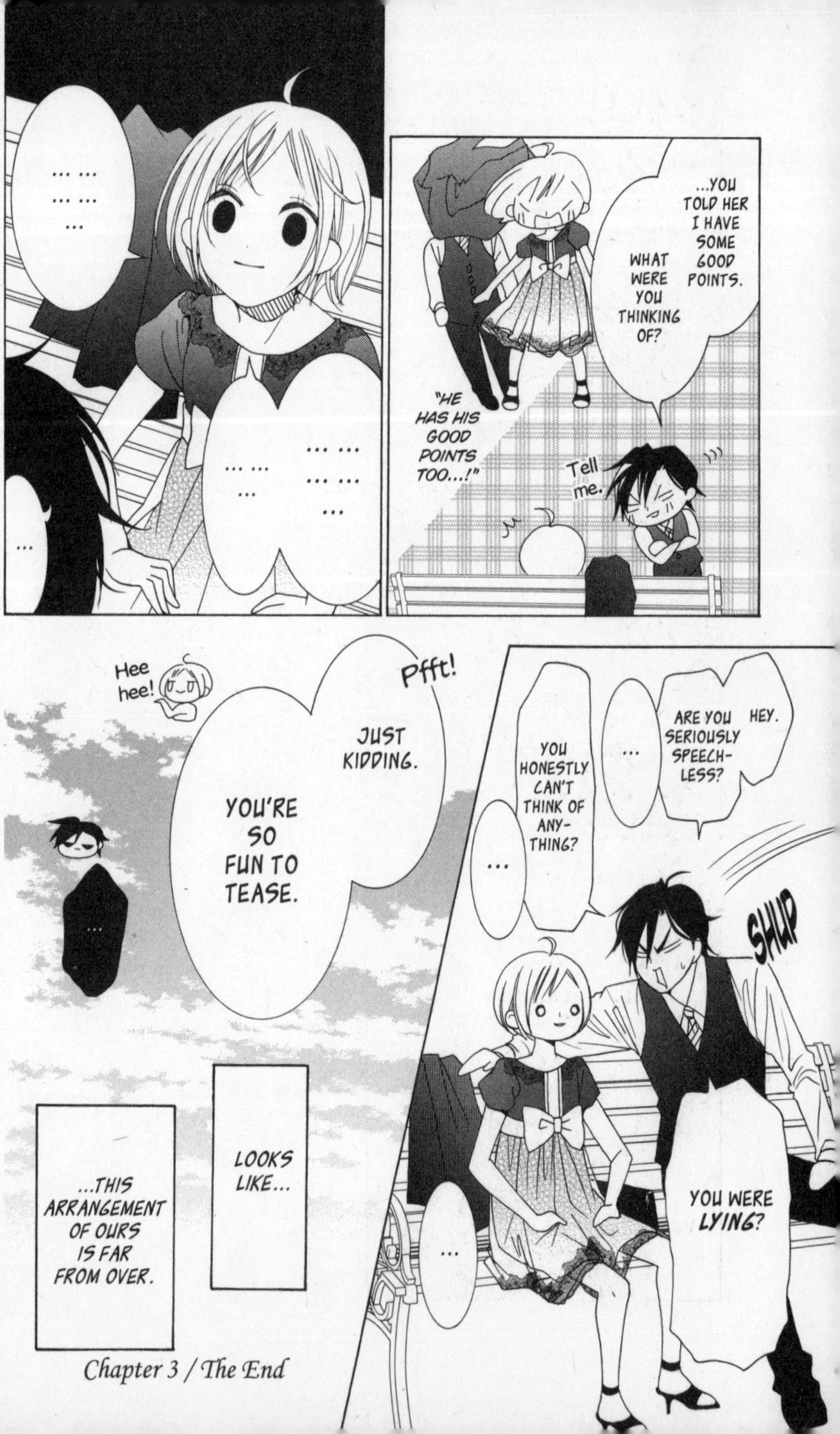
...You told her I have some good points.
What were you thinking of?
"He has his good points too...!"
Tell me.
... ...
... ...
...
Hey.
Are you seriously speech-less?
...
You honestly can't think of any-thing?
...
SHUP
You were lying?
...
Pfft!
Just kidding.
You're so fun to tease.
Hee hee!
...
Looks like...
...This arrangement of ours is far from over.

Chapter 3 / The End

Playing Catch with Words

PLAYING CATCH WITH WORDS WITH TAKANE GOES SOMETHING LIKE THIS...
WHOOSH
Pitches
WHACK
Hits
BOOM
Self-destruction
SIZZLE
SIZZLE
STAGGER
The next ball
Won't die

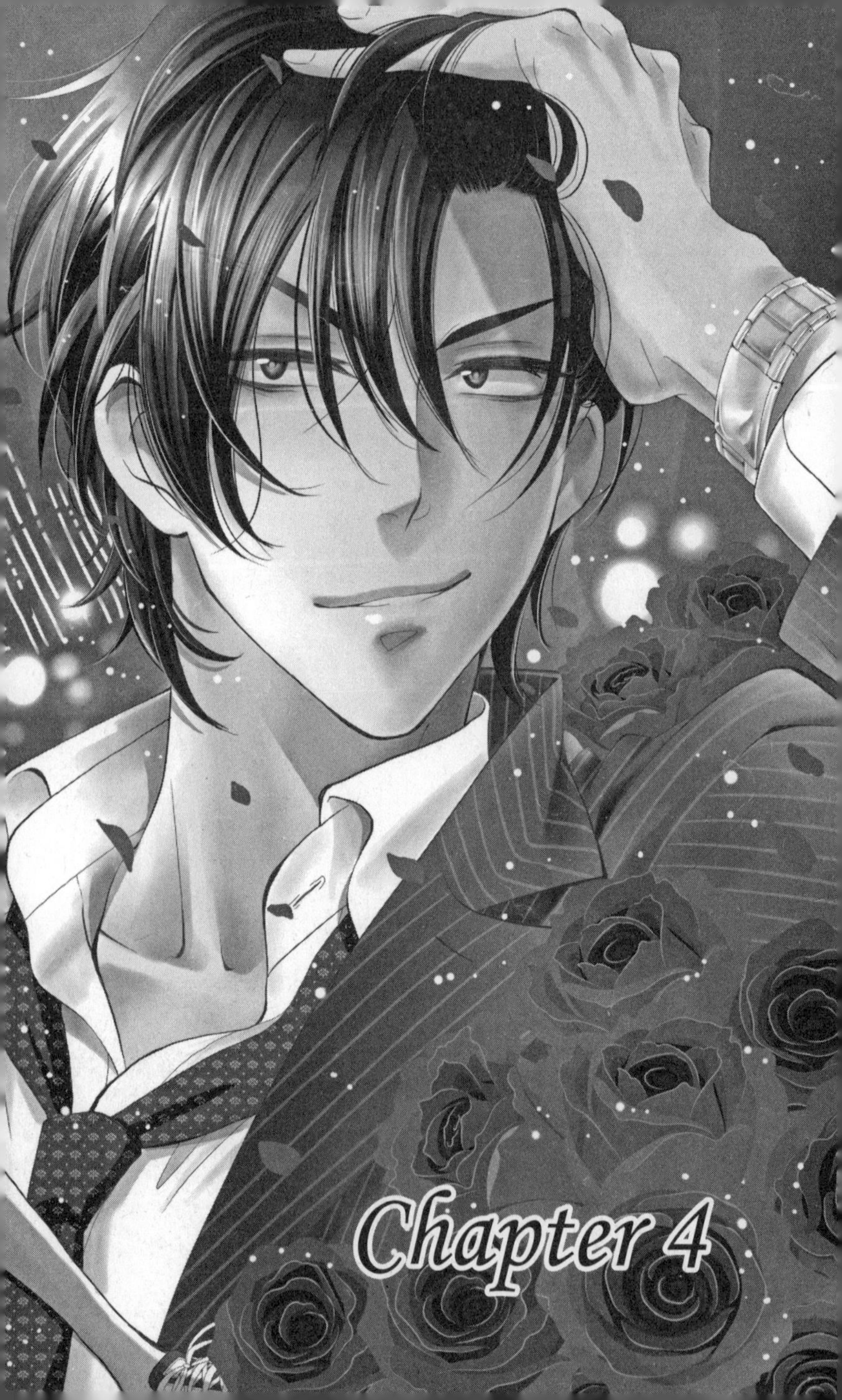
Chapter 4

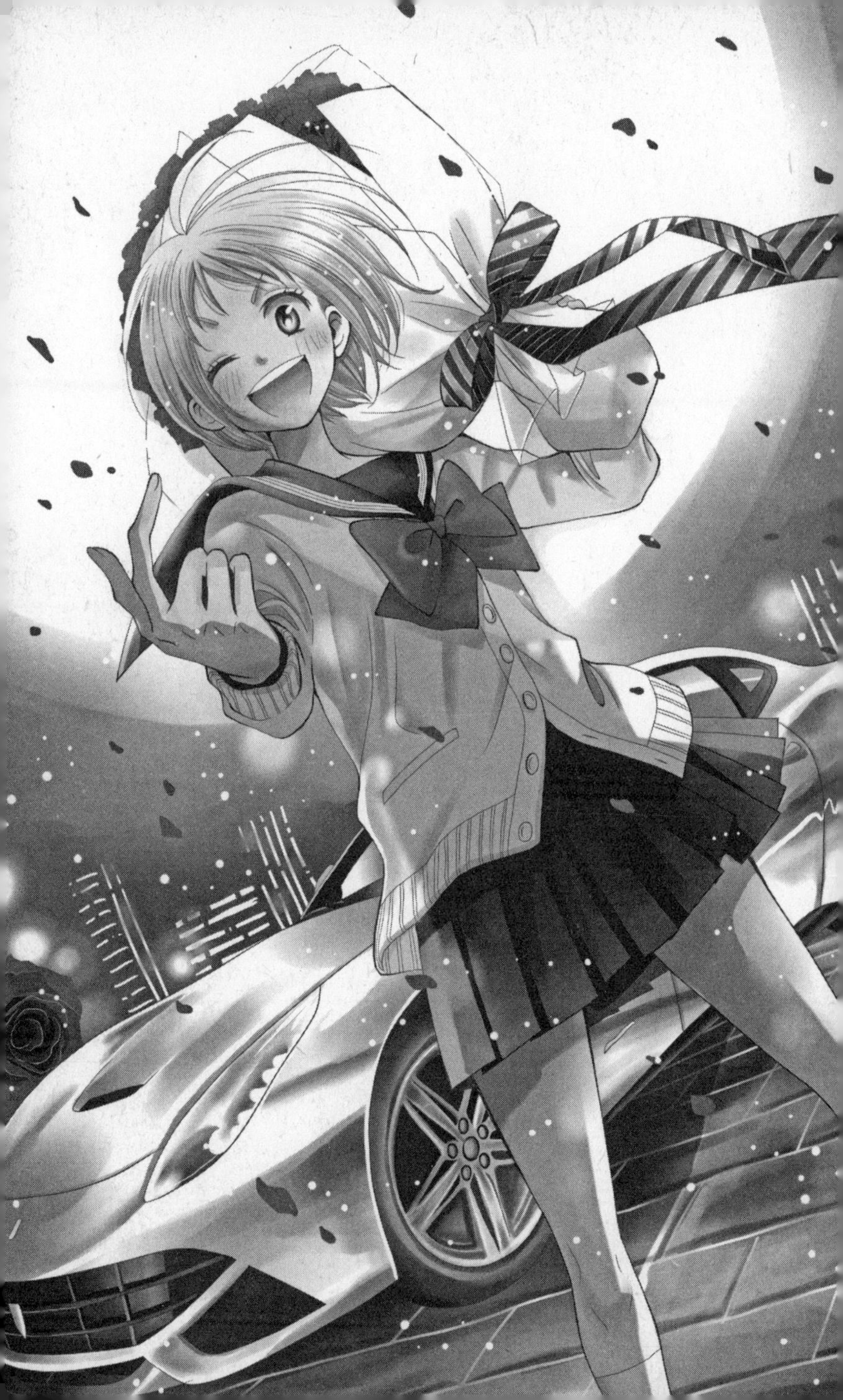

Captivated by Roses

TAKANE BRINGS ROSES EVERY TIME HE COMES OVER, SO OUR HOUSE IS FULL OF THEM.
WAFT
WHEN I FALL ASLEEP BREATHING IN THEIR SCENT...
...I CAN'T HELP DREAMING ABOUT HIM.
HA
EVERY SINGLE NIGHT, I HAVE A NIGHTMARE.
HA
HA
HA
HA
MAYBE HE KNOWS THAT, AND THIS IS ALL BECAUSE HE HAS A MEAN STREAK.
RUSTLE
I BROUGHT IRIDESCENT ONES TODAY.

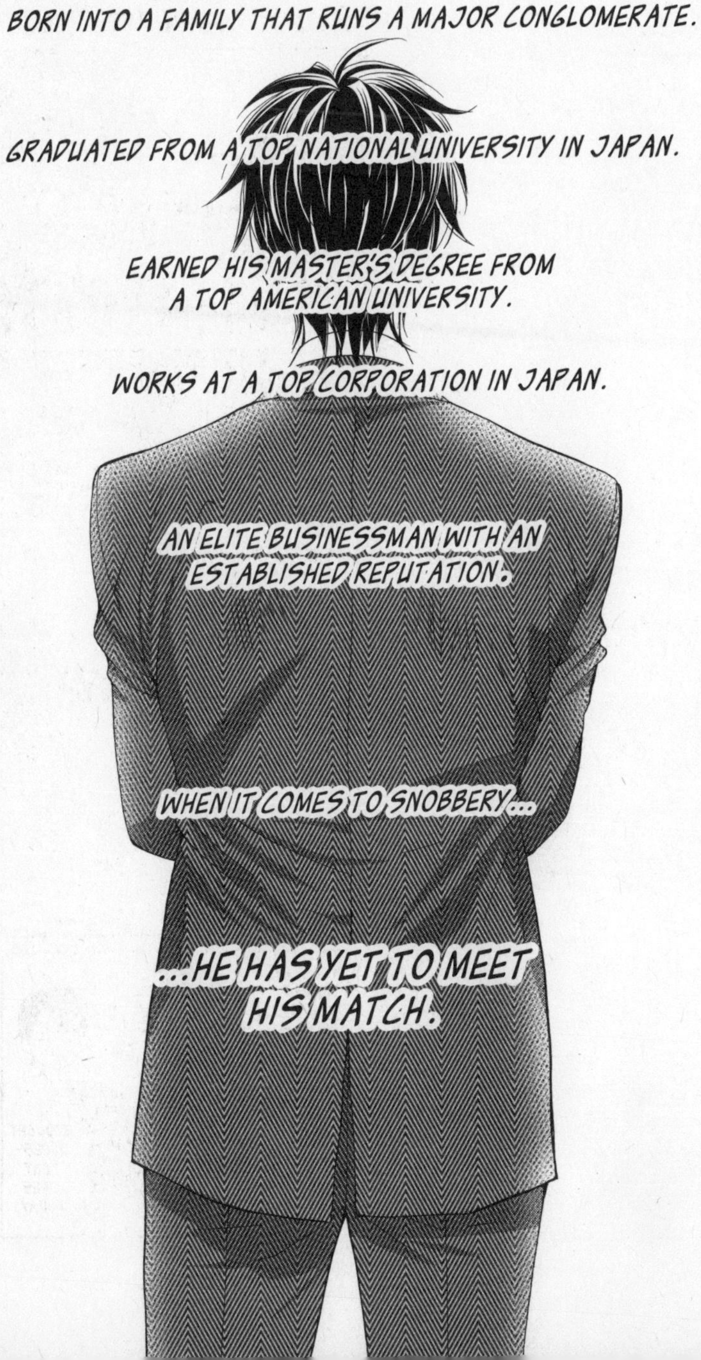
BORN INTO A FAMILY THAT RUNS A MAJOR CONGLOMERATE.
GRADUATED FROM A TOP NATIONAL UNIVERSITY IN JAPAN.
EARNED HIS MASTER'S DEGREE FROM A TOP AMERICAN UNIVERSITY.
WORKS AT A TOP CORPORATION IN JAPAN.
AN ELITE BUSINESSMAN WITH AN ESTABLISHED REPUTATION.
WHEN IT COMES TO SNOBBERY...
...HE HAS YET TO MEET HIS MATCH.

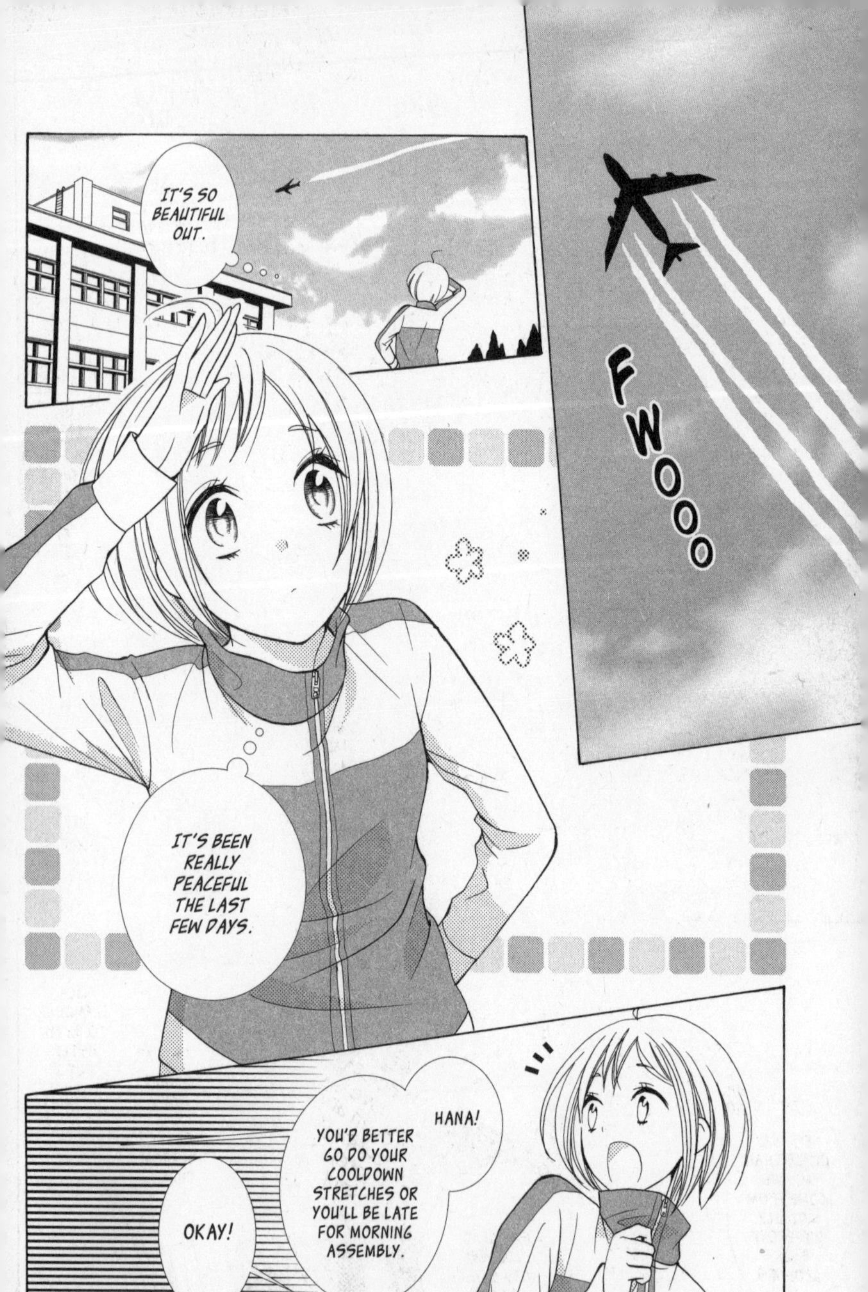
FWOOO
IT'S SO BEAUTIFUL OUT.
IT'S BEEN REALLY PEACEFUL THE LAST FEW DAYS.
HANA!
YOU'D BETTER GO DO YOUR COOLDOWN STRETCHES OR YOU'LL BE LATE FOR MORNING ASSEMBLY.
OKAY!

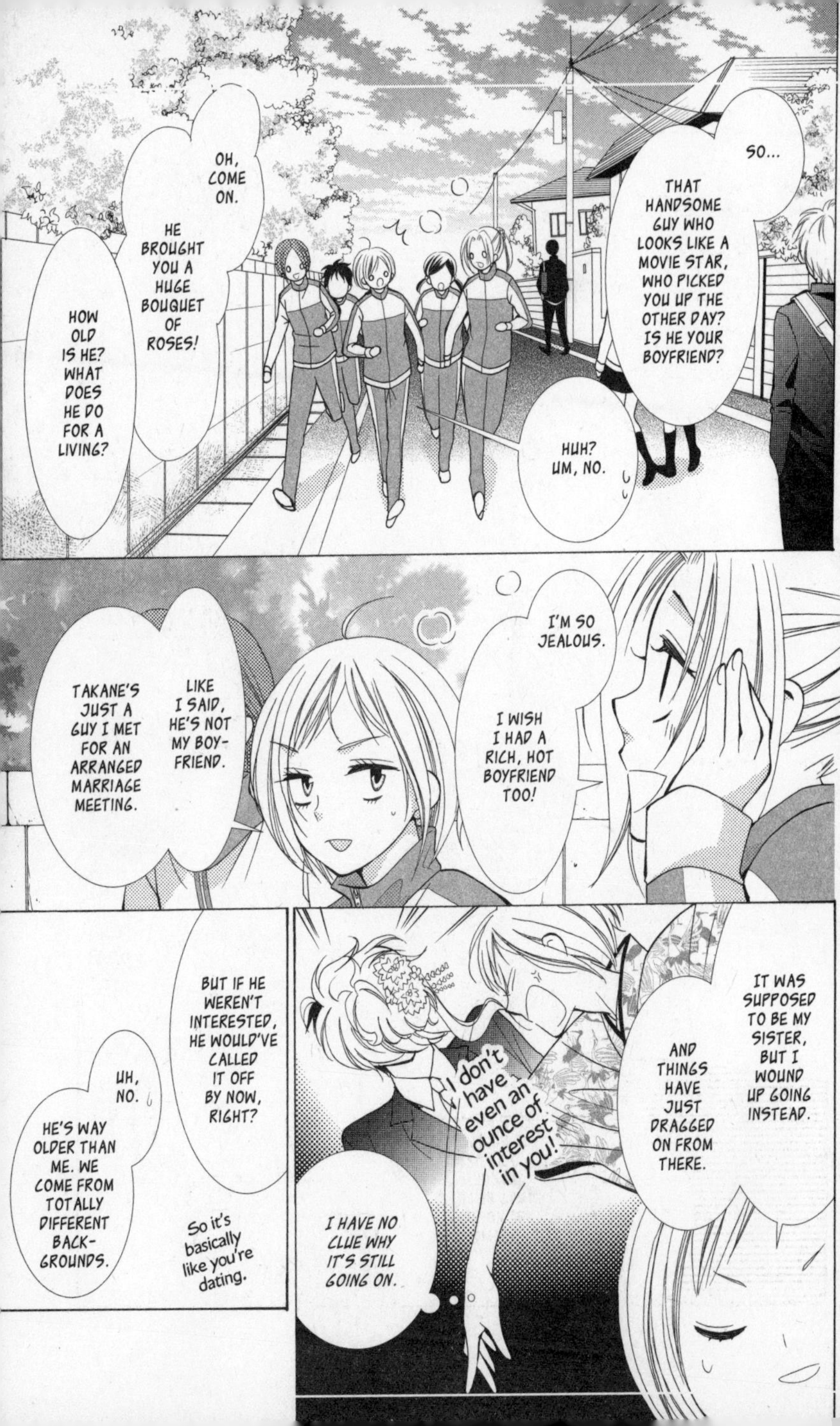
SO...
THAT HANDSOME GUY WHO LOOKS LIKE A MOVIE STAR, WHO PICKED YOU UP THE OTHER DAY? IS HE YOUR BOYFRIEND?
HUH? UM, NO.
OH, COME ON.
HE BROUGHT YOU A HUGE BOUQUET OF ROSES!
HOW OLD IS HE? WHAT DOES HE DO FOR A LIVING?
I'M SO JEALOUS.
I WISH I HAD A RICH, HOT BOYFRIEND TOO!
LIKE I SAID, HE'S NOT MY BOY-FRIEND.
TAKANE'S JUST A GUY I MET FOR AN ARRANGED MARRIAGE MEETING.
IT WAS SUPPOSED TO BE MY SISTER, BUT I WOUND UP GOING INSTEAD.
AND THINGS HAVE JUST DRAGGED ON FROM THERE.
I don't have even an ounce of interest in you!
I HAVE NO CLUE WHY IT'S STILL GOING ON.
BUT IF HE WEREN'T INTERESTED, HE WOULD'VE CALLED IT OFF BY NOW, RIGHT?
UH, NO.
HE'S WAY OLDER THAN ME. WE COME FROM TOTALLY DIFFERENT BACK-GROUNDS.
So it's basically like you're dating.

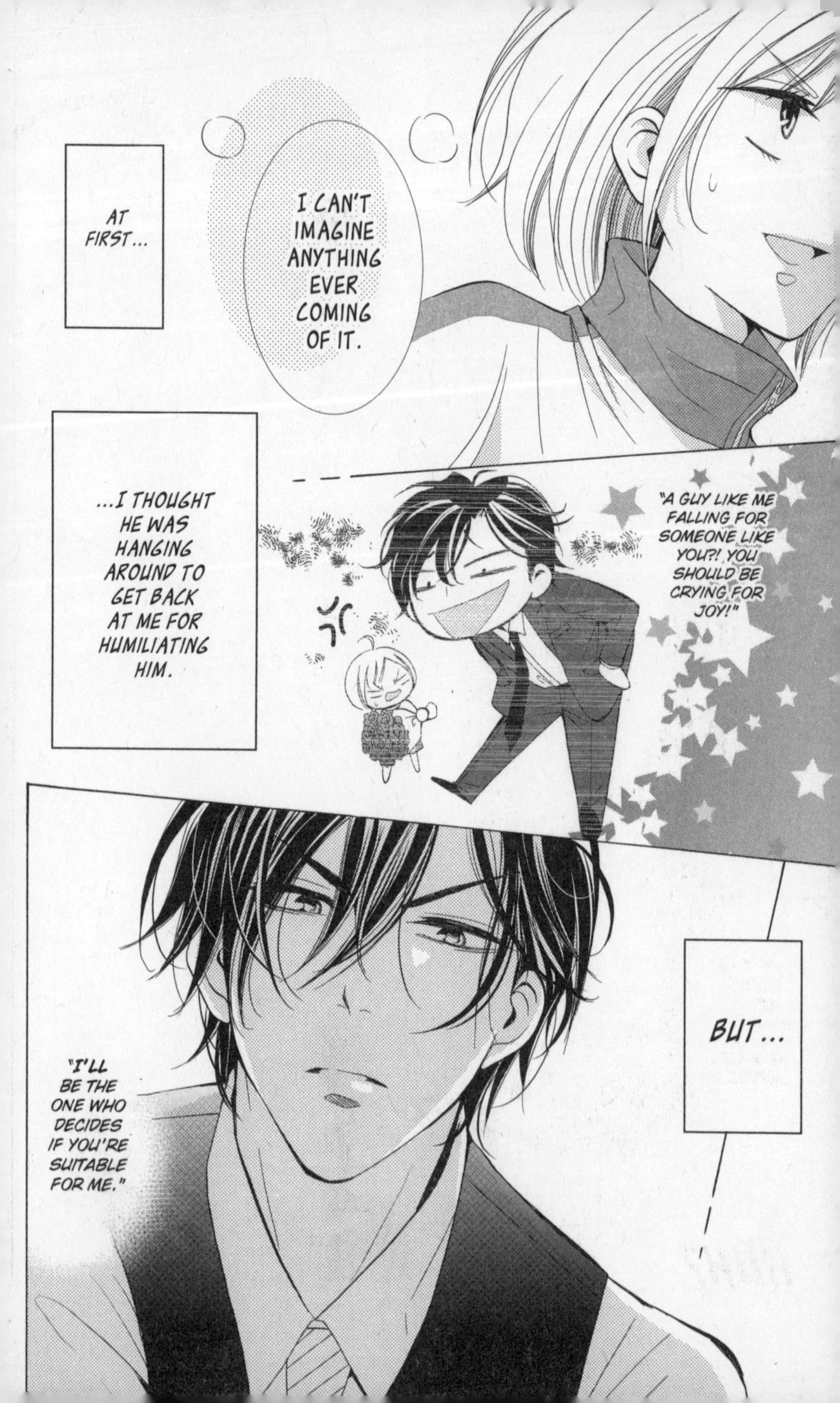

I CAN'T IMAGINE ANYTHING EVER COMING OF IT.
AT FIRST...
"A GUY LIKE ME FALLING FOR SOMEONE LIKE YOU?! YOU SHOULD BE CRYING FOR JOY!"
...I THOUGHT HE WAS HANGING AROUND TO GET BACK AT ME FOR HUMILIATING HIM.
BUT...
"I'LL BE THE ONE WHO DECIDES IF YOU'RE SUITABLE FOR ME."

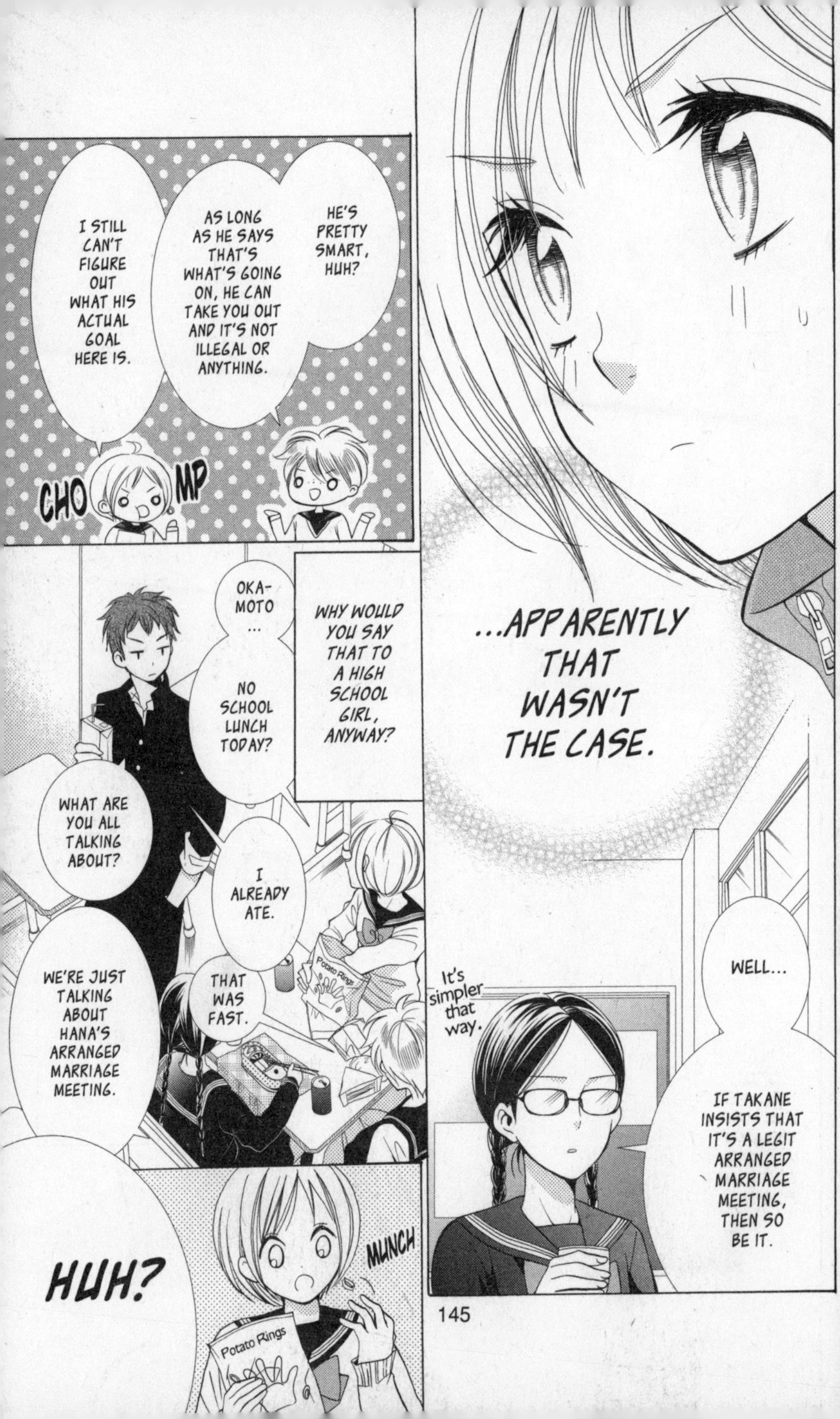
...APPARENTLY THAT WASN'T THE CASE.
WELL...
IF TAKANE INSISTS THAT IT'S A LEGIT ARRANGED MARRIAGE MEETING, THEN SO BE IT.
It's simpler that way.
HE'S PRETTY SMART, HUH?
AS LONG AS HE SAYS THAT'S WHAT'S GOING ON, HE CAN TAKE YOU OUT AND IT'S NOT ILLEGAL OR ANYTHING.
I STILL CAN'T FIGURE OUT WHAT HIS ACTUAL GOAL HERE IS.
CHOMP
WHY WOULD YOU SAY THAT TO A HIGH SCHOOL GIRL, ANYWAY?
OKA-MOTO...
NO SCHOOL LUNCH TODAY?
I ALREADY ATE.
THAT WAS FAST.
WHAT ARE YOU ALL TALKING ABOUT?
Potato Rings
WE'RE JUST TALKING ABOUT HANA'S ARRANGED MARRIAGE MEETING.
MUNCH
HUH?
Potato Rings

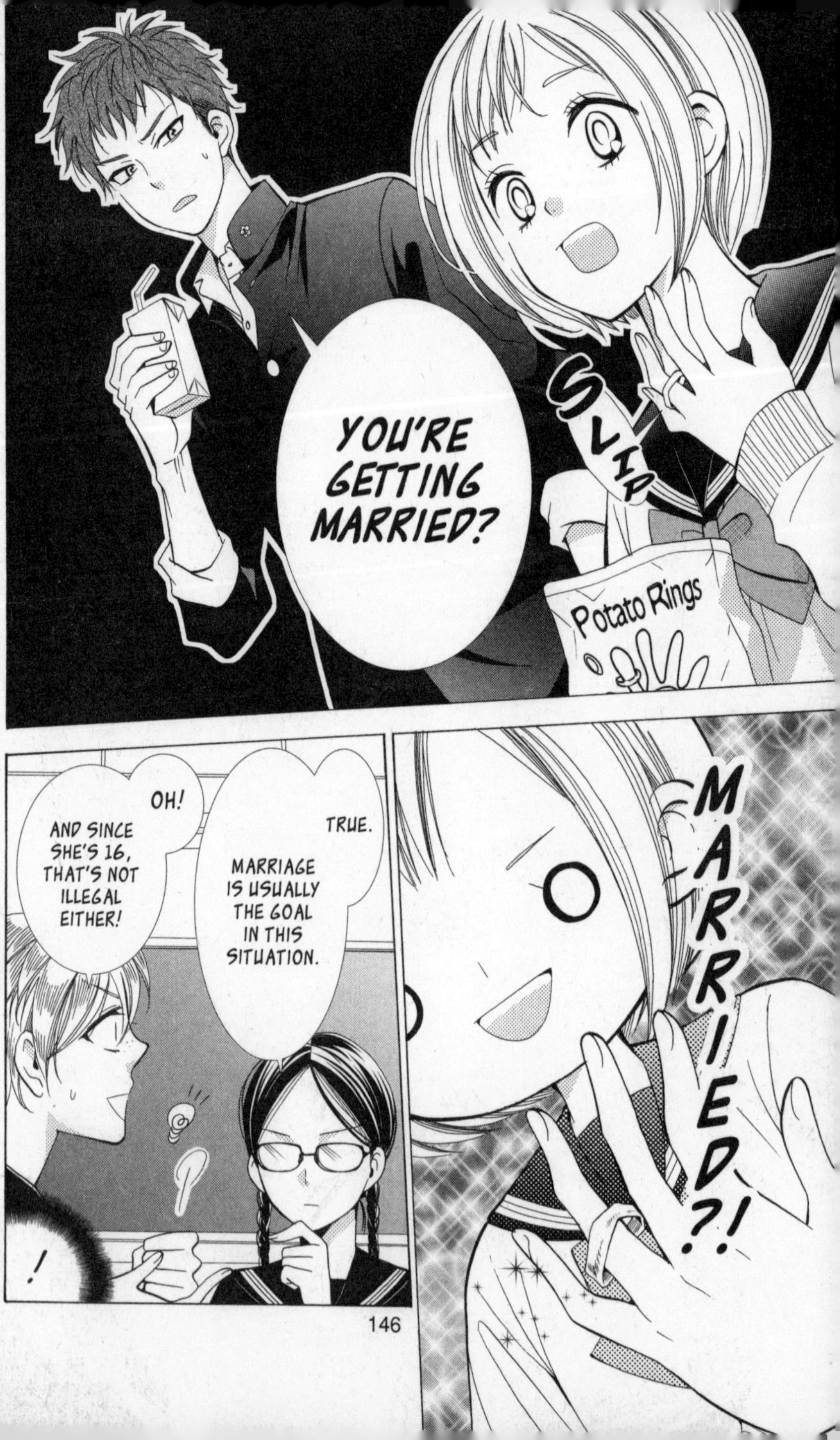

YOU'RE GETTING MARRIED?
SLIP
Potato Rings
MARRIED?!
TRUE.
MARRIAGE IS USUALLY THE GOAL IN THIS SITUATION.
OH!
AND SINCE SHE'S 16, THAT'S NOT ILLEGAL EITHER!
!

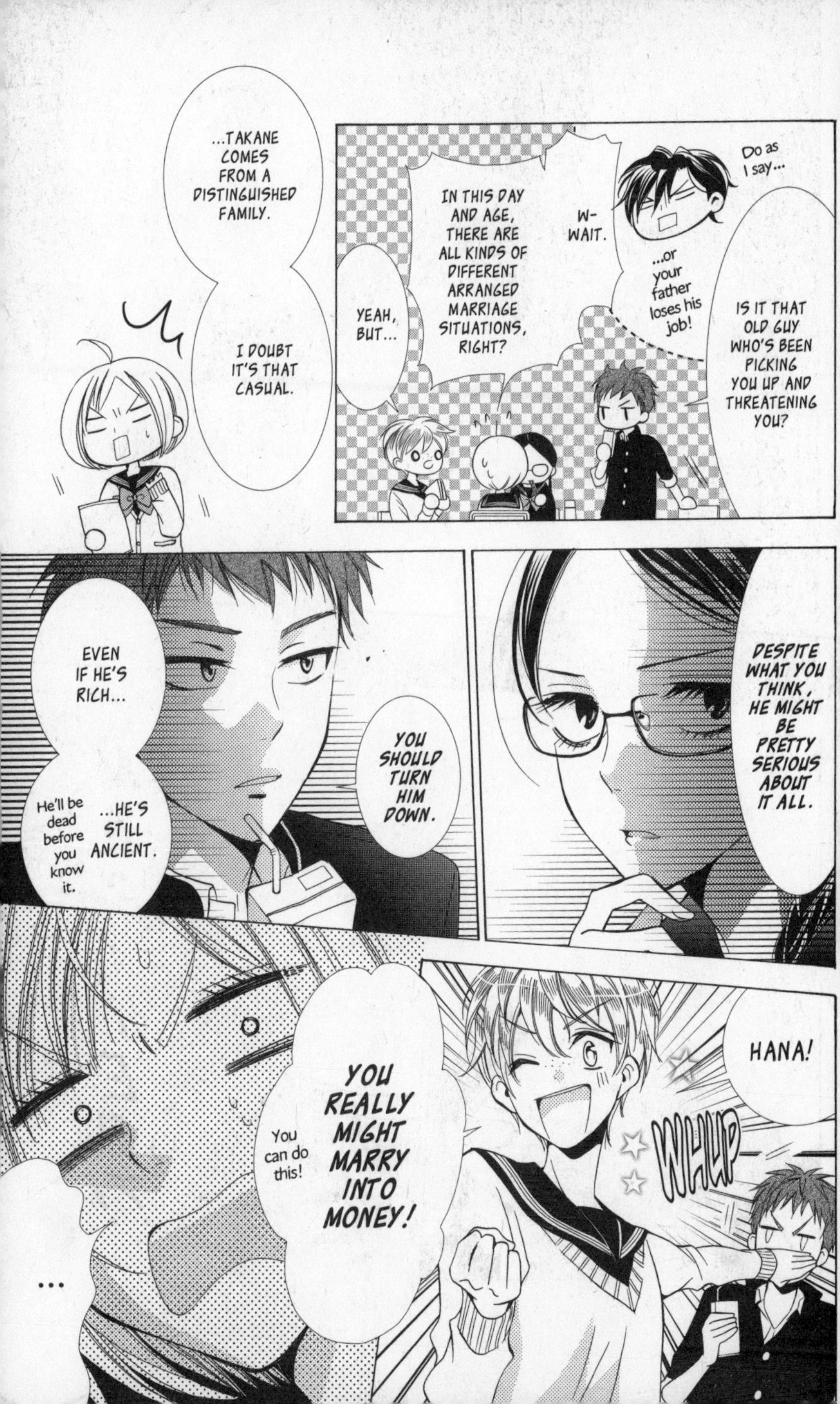
Do as I say...
...or your father loses his job!
IS IT THAT OLD GUY WHO'S BEEN PICKING YOU UP AND THREATENING YOU?
W-WAIT.
IN THIS DAY AND AGE, THERE ARE ALL KINDS OF DIFFERENT ARRANGED MARRIAGE SITUATIONS, RIGHT?
YEAH, BUT...
...TAKANE COMES FROM A DISTINGUISHED FAMILY.
I DOUBT IT'S THAT CASUAL.
DESPITE WHAT YOU THINK, HE MIGHT BE PRETTY SERIOUS ABOUT IT ALL.
EVEN IF HE'S RICH...
...HE'S STILL ANCIENT.
He'll be dead before you know it.
YOU SHOULD TURN HIM DOWN.
HANA!
WHUP
YOU REALLY MIGHT MARRY INTO MONEY!
You can do this!
...

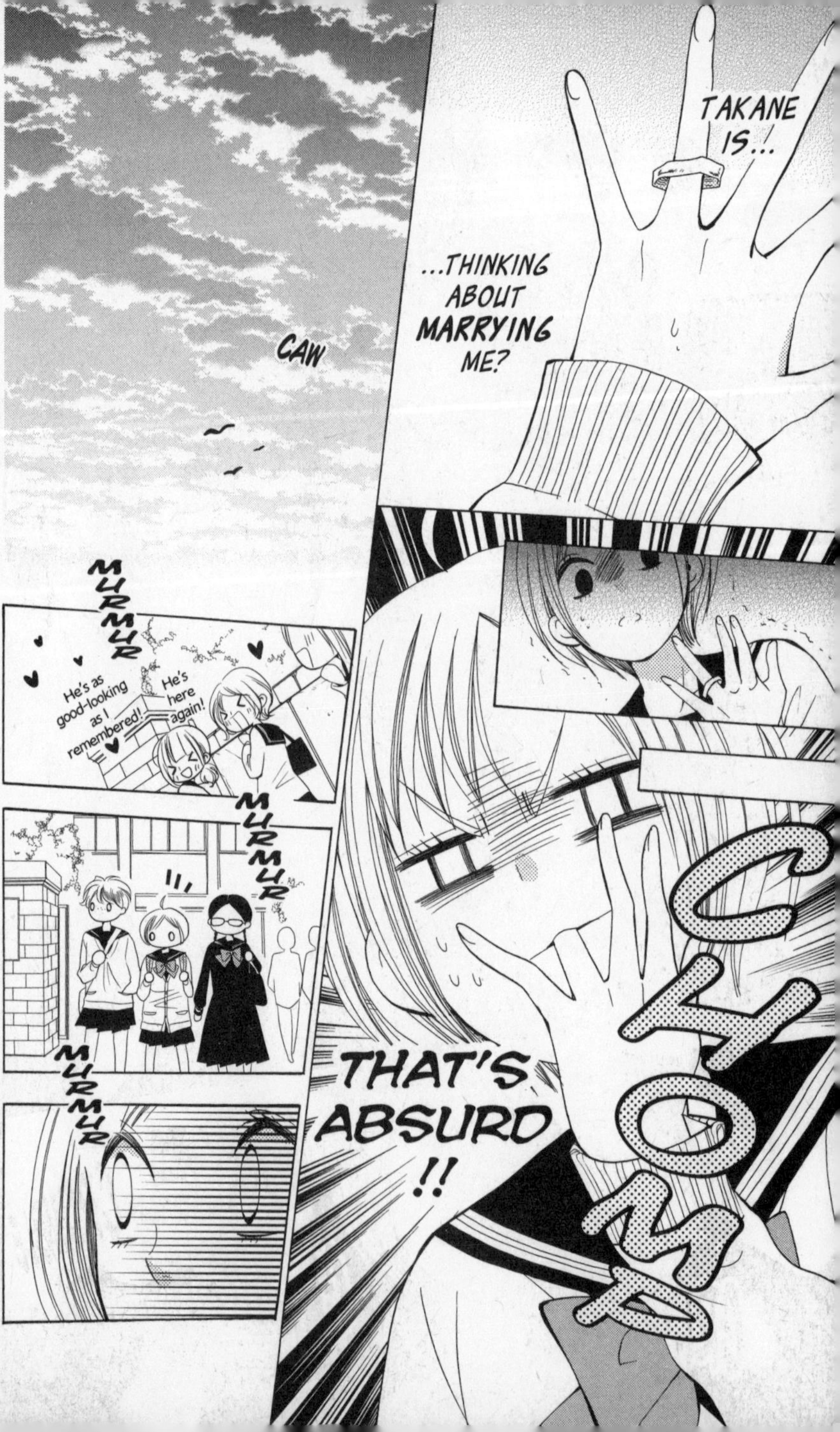
TAKANE IS...
...THINKING ABOUT MARRYING ME?
CHOMP
THAT'S ABSURD!!
CAW
MURMUR
He's here again!
He's as good-looking as I remembered!
MURMUR
MURMUR

!!!
HEH
IT'S BEEN A WHILE, HMM? I BET YOU MISSED ME.
PE ACE
CRUMBLE
CRUMBLE
CRUMBLE

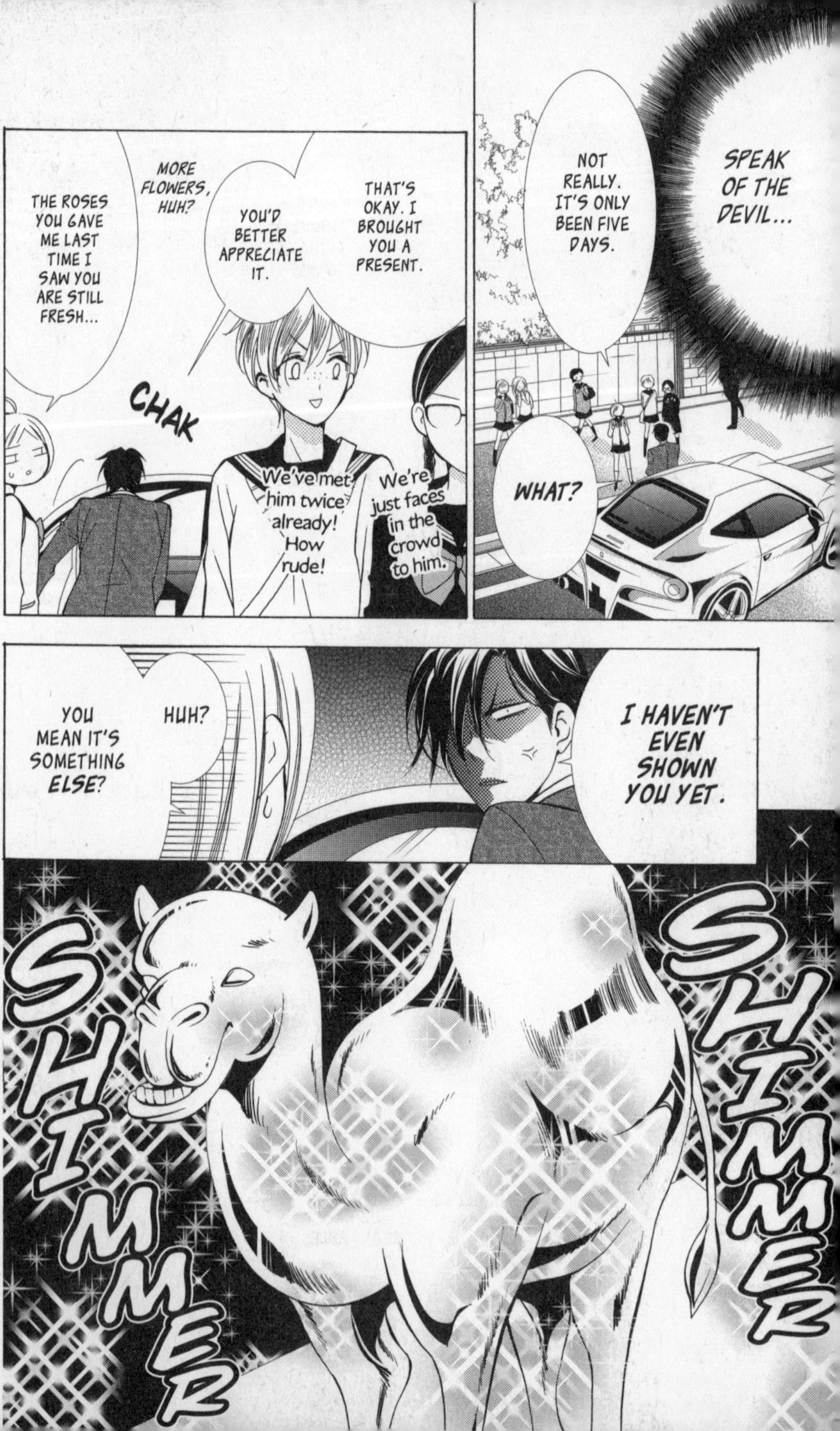
SPEAK OF THE DEVIL...
NOT REALLY. IT'S ONLY BEEN FIVE DAYS.
WHAT?
THAT'S OKAY. I BROUGHT YOU A PRESENT.
YOU'D BETTER APPRECIATE IT.
MORE FLOWERS, HUH?
THE ROSES YOU GAVE ME LAST TIME I SAW YOU ARE STILL FRESH...
CHAK
We're just faces in the crowd to him.
We've met him twice already! How rude!
I HAVEN'T EVEN SHOWN YOU YET.
HUH?
YOU MEAN IT'S SOMETHING ELSE?
SHIMMER
SHIMMER

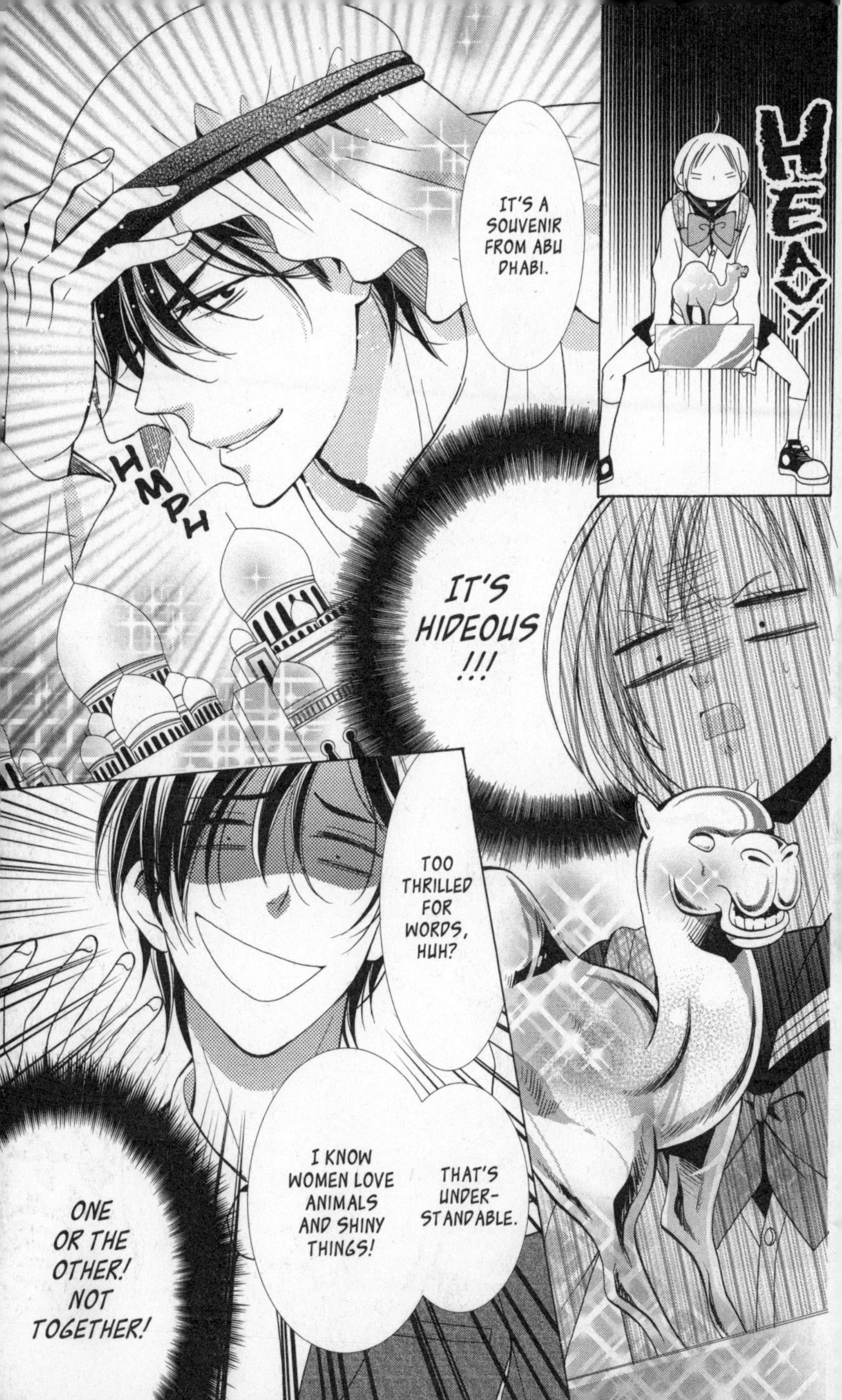
HEAVY
IT'S A SOUVENIR FROM ABU DHABI.
HMPH
IT'S HIDEOUS!!!
TOO THRILLED FOR WORDS, HUH?
THAT'S UNDER-STANDABLE.
I KNOW WOMEN LOVE ANIMALS AND SHINY THINGS!
ONE OR THE OTHER! NOT TOGETHER!

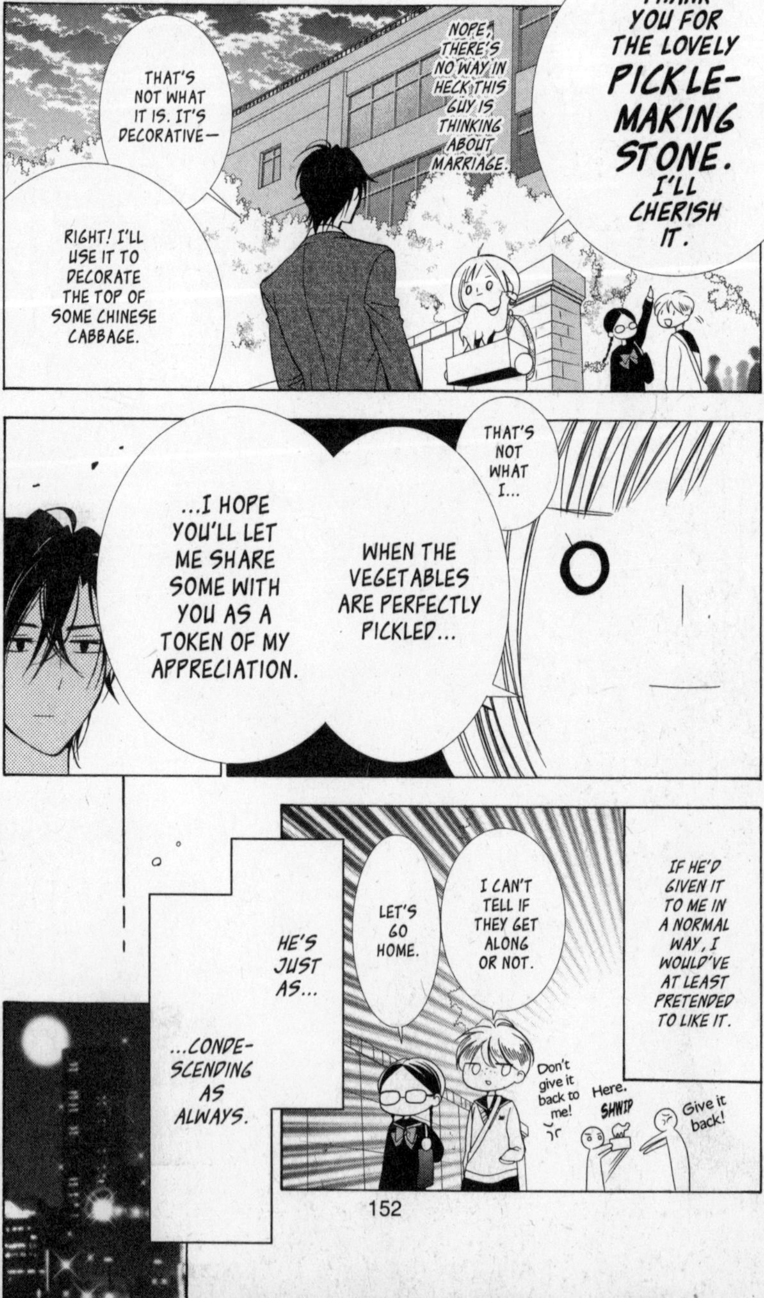
THANK YOU FOR THE LOVELY PICKLE-MAKING STONE. I'LL CHERISH IT.
NOPE, THERE'S NO WAY IN HECK THIS GUY IS THINKING ABOUT MARRIAGE.
THAT'S NOT WHAT IT IS. IT'S DECORATIVE—
RIGHT! I'LL USE IT TO DECORATE THE TOP OF SOME CHINESE CABBAGE.
THAT'S NOT WHAT I...
WHEN THE VEGETABLES ARE PERFECTLY PICKLED...
...I HOPE YOU'LL LET ME SHARE SOME WITH YOU AS A TOKEN OF MY APPRECIATION.
IF HE'D GIVEN IT TO ME IN A NORMAL WAY, I WOULD'VE AT LEAST PRETENDED TO LIKE IT.
Give it back!
SHWIP
Here.
Don't give it back to me!
I CAN'T TELL IF THEY GET ALONG OR NOT.
LET'S GO HOME.
HE'S JUST AS...
...CONDE-SCENDING AS ALWAYS.

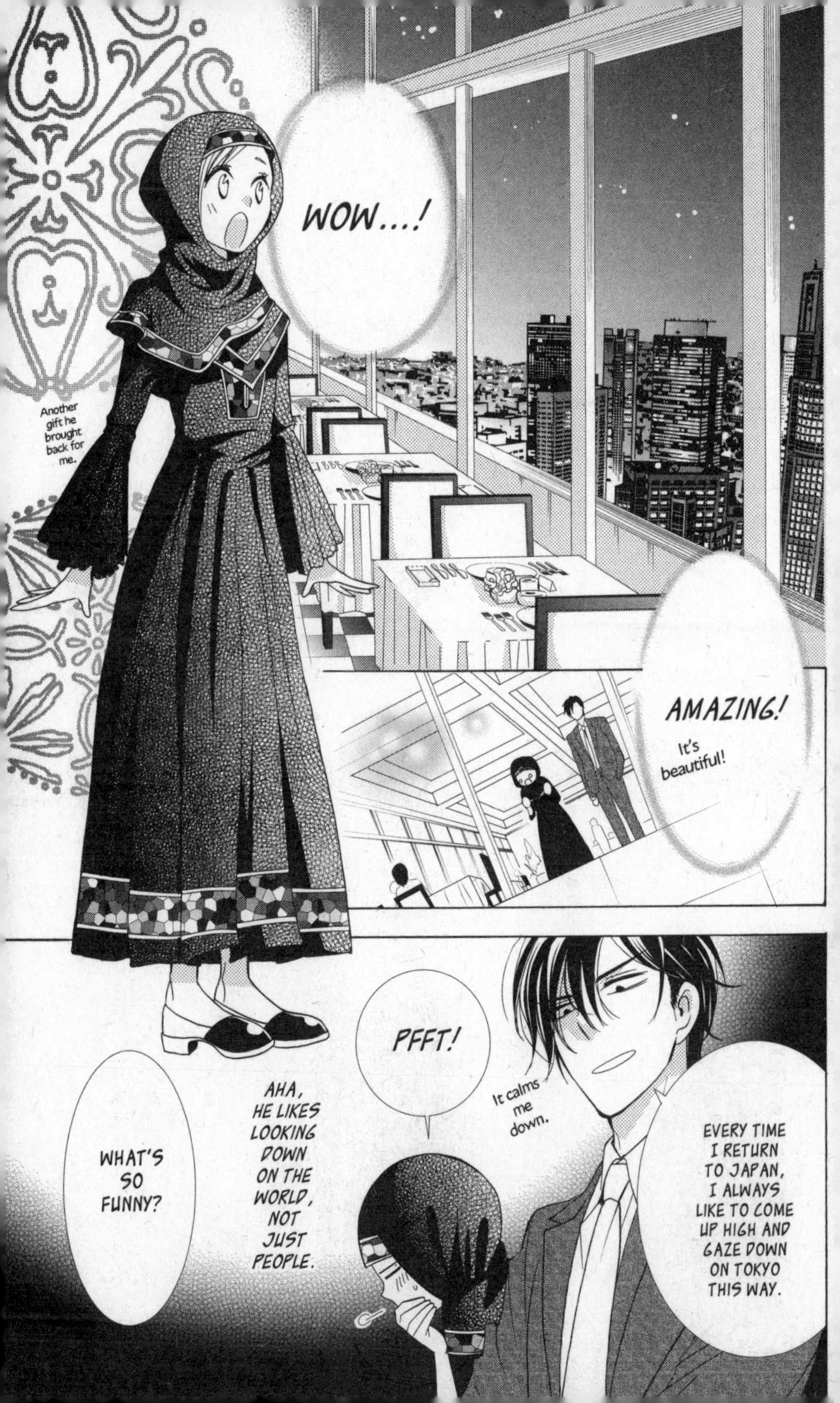
WOW...!
Another gift he brought back for me.
AMAZING!
It's beautiful!
EVERY TIME I RETURN TO JAPAN, I ALWAYS LIKE TO COME UP HIGH AND GAZE DOWN ON TOKYO THIS WAY.
It calms me down.
PFFT!
AHA, HE LIKES LOOKING DOWN ON THE WORLD, NOT JUST PEOPLE.
WHAT'S SO FUNNY?

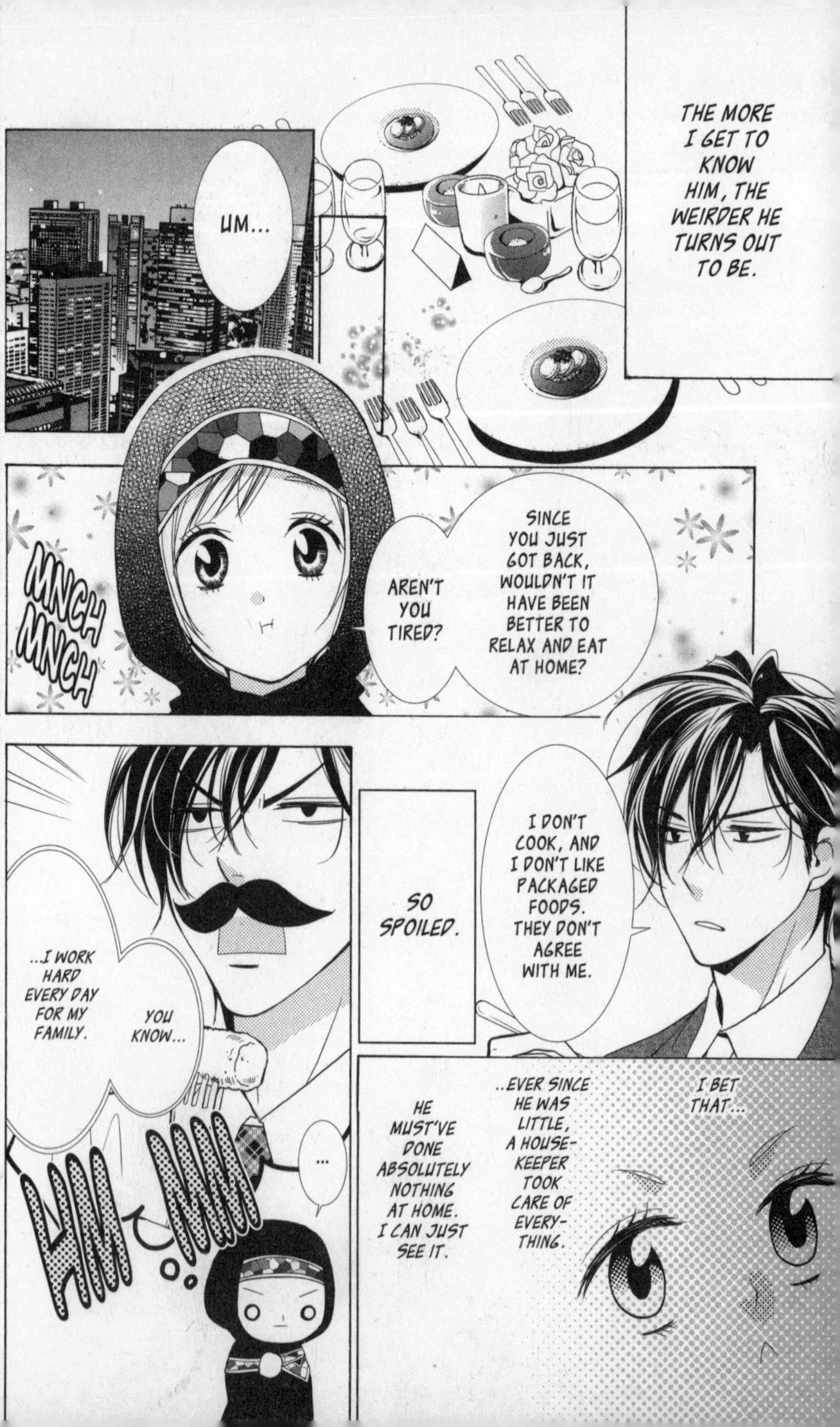
THE MORE I GET TO KNOW HIM, THE WEIRDER HE TURNS OUT TO BE.
UM...
SINCE YOU JUST GOT BACK, WOULDN'T IT HAVE BEEN BETTER TO RELAX AND EAT AT HOME?
AREN'T YOU TIRED?
MNCH MNCH
I DON'T COOK, AND I DON'T LIKE PACKAGED FOODS. THEY DON'T AGREE WITH ME.
SO SPOILED.
I BET THAT...
...EVER SINCE HE WAS LITTLE, A HOUSEKEEPER TOOK CARE OF EVERYTHING.
HE MUST'VE DONE ABSOLUTELY NOTHING AT HOME. I CAN JUST SEE IT.
YOU KNOW...
...I WORK HARD EVERY DAY FOR MY FAMILY.
...

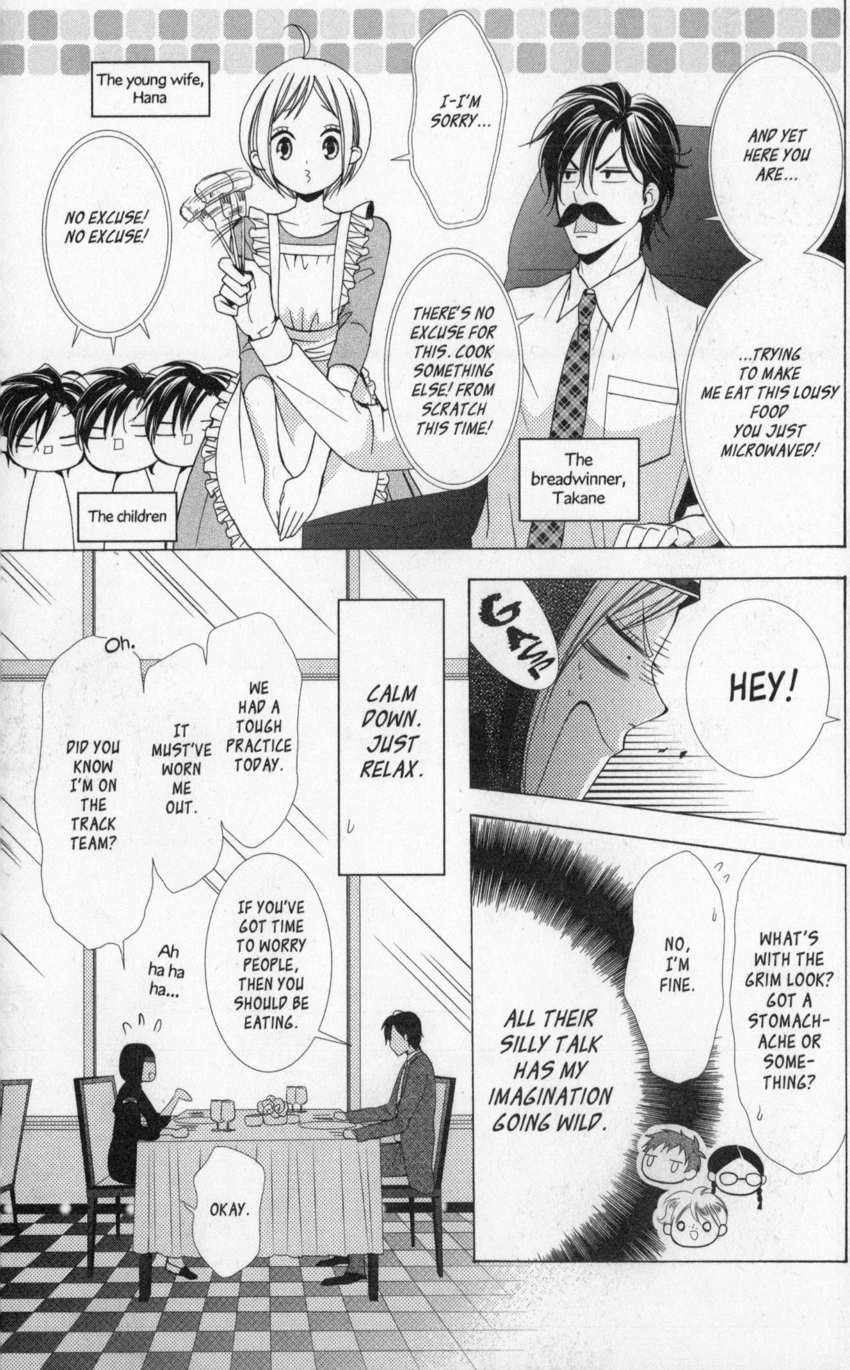
AND YET HERE YOU ARE...
...TRYING TO MAKE ME EAT THIS LOUSY FOOD YOU JUST MICROWAVED!
The breadwinner, Takane
I-I'M SORRY...
THERE'S NO EXCUSE FOR THIS. COOK SOMETHING ELSE! FROM SCRATCH THIS TIME!
The young wife, Hana
NO EXCUSE! NO EXCUSE!
The children
HEY!
WHAT'S WITH THE GRIM LOOK? GOT A STOMACH-ACHE OR SOME-THING?
NO, I'M FINE.
ALL THEIR SILLY TALK HAS MY IMAGINATION GOING WILD.
CALM DOWN. JUST RELAX.
WE HAD A TOUGH PRACTICE TODAY.
IT MUST'VE WORN ME OUT.
DID YOU KNOW I'M ON THE TRACK TEAM?
Oh.
IF YOU'VE GOT TIME TO WORRY PEOPLE, THEN YOU SHOULD BE EATING.
Ah ha ha ha...
OKAY.

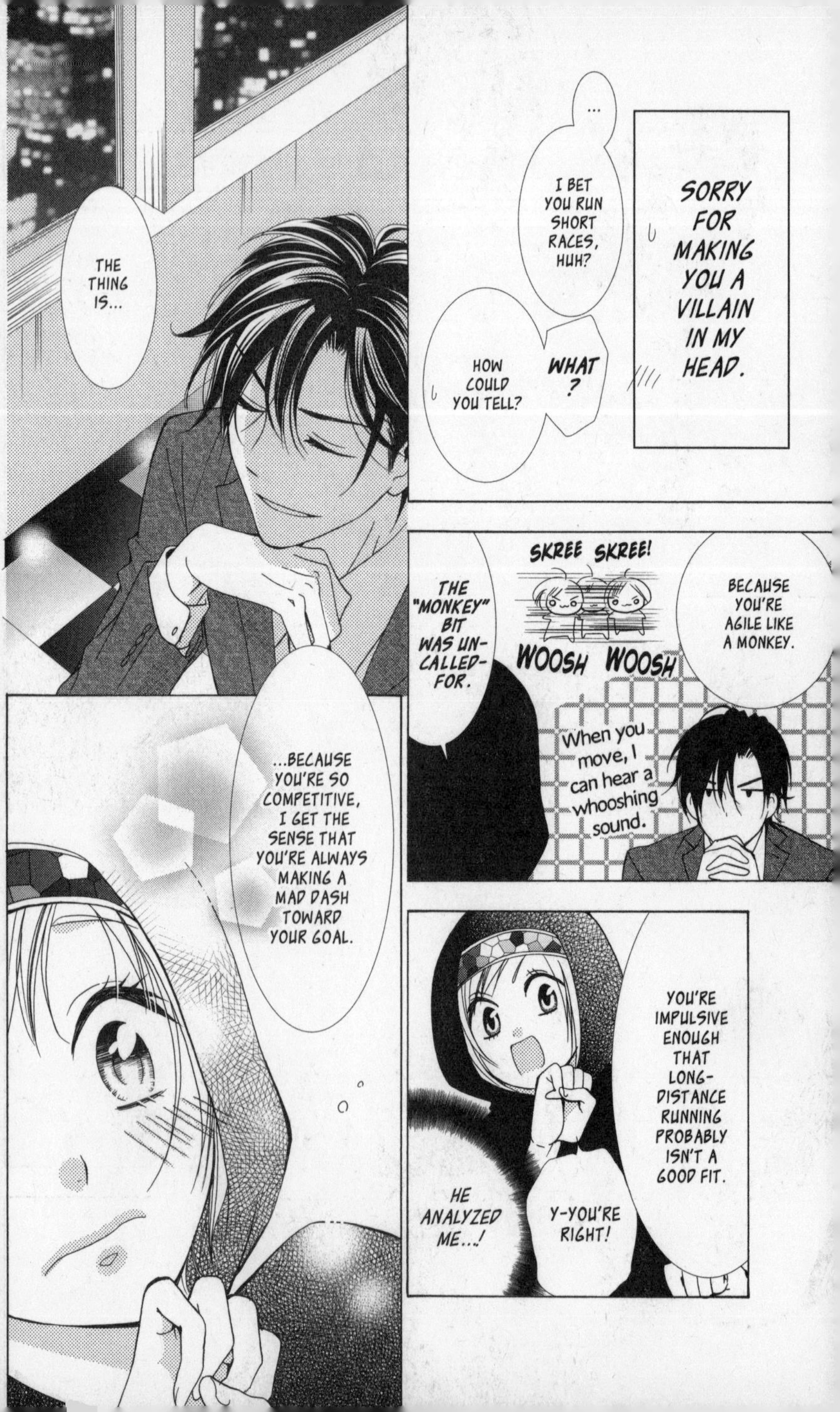

SORRY FOR MAKING YOU A VILLAIN IN MY HEAD.
...
I BET YOU RUN SHORT RACES, HUH?
WHAT?
HOW COULD YOU TELL?
THE THING IS...
BECAUSE YOU'RE AGILE LIKE A MONKEY.
SKREE SKREE!
WOOSH WOOSH
When you move, I can hear a whooshing sound.
THE "MONKEY" BIT WAS UNCALLED-FOR.
...BECAUSE YOU'RE SO COMPETITIVE, I GET THE SENSE THAT YOU'RE ALWAYS MAKING A MAD DASH TOWARD YOUR GOAL.
YOU'RE IMPULSIVE ENOUGH THAT LONG-DISTANCE RUNNING PROBABLY ISN'T A GOOD FIT.
Y-YOU'RE RIGHT!
HE ANALYZED ME...!

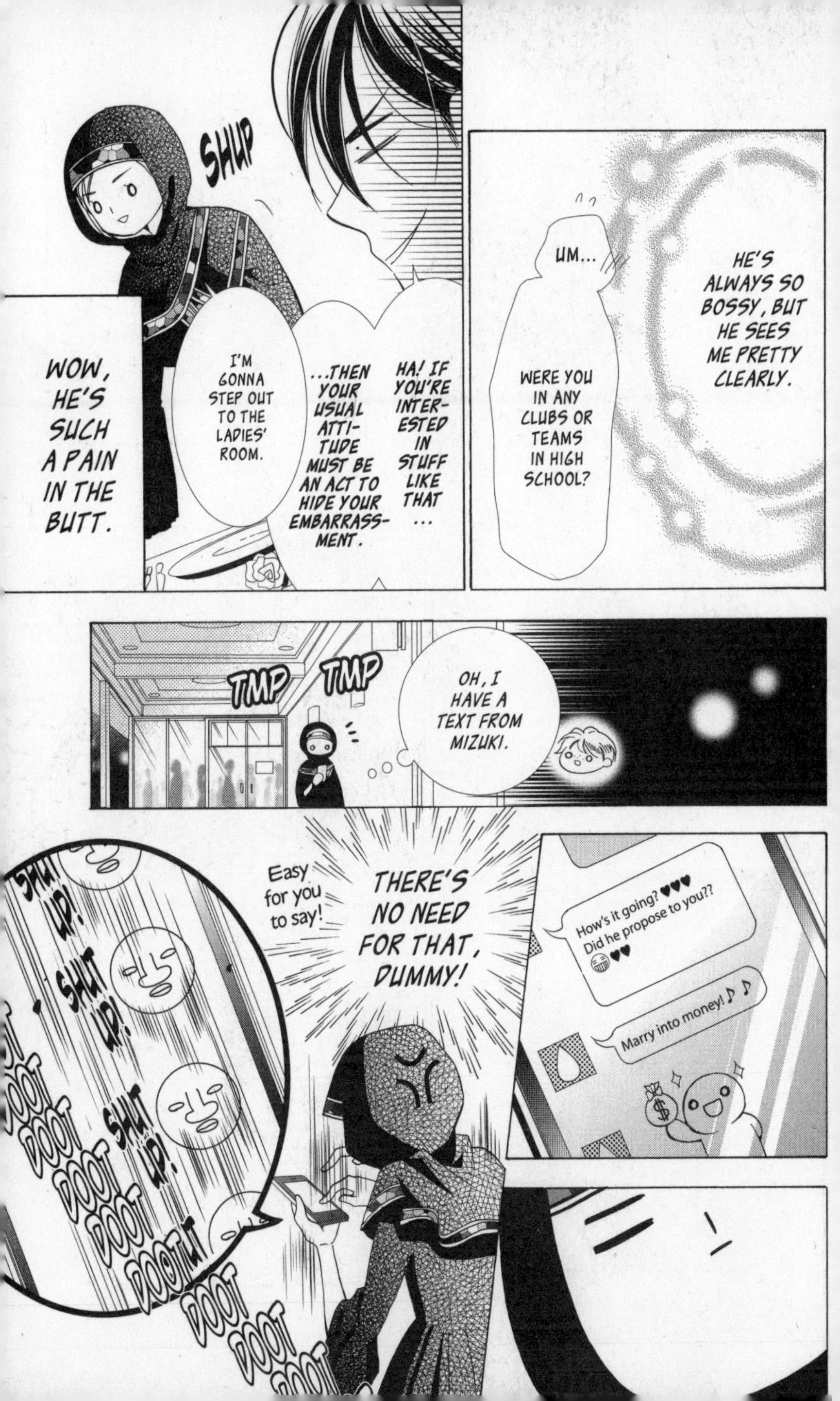

HE'S ALWAYS SO BOSSY, BUT HE SEES ME PRETTY CLEARLY.
UM...
WERE YOU IN ANY CLUBS OR TEAMS IN HIGH SCHOOL?
SHUP
HA! IF YOU'RE INTERESTED IN STUFF LIKE THAT...
...THEN YOUR USUAL ATTITUDE MUST BE AN ACT TO HIDE YOUR EMBARRASSMENT.
I'M GONNA STEP OUT TO THE LADIES' ROOM.
WOW, HE'S SUCH A PAIN IN THE BUTT.
OH, I HAVE A TEXT FROM MIZUKI.
TMP TMP
How's it going? ♥♥♥ Did he propose to you?? ♥♥
Marry into money! ♪♪
THERE'S NO NEED FOR THAT, DUMMY!
Easy for you to say!
SHUT UP!
SHUT UP!
SHUT UP!
DOOT DOOT DOOT DOOT DOOTUT DOOT DOOT

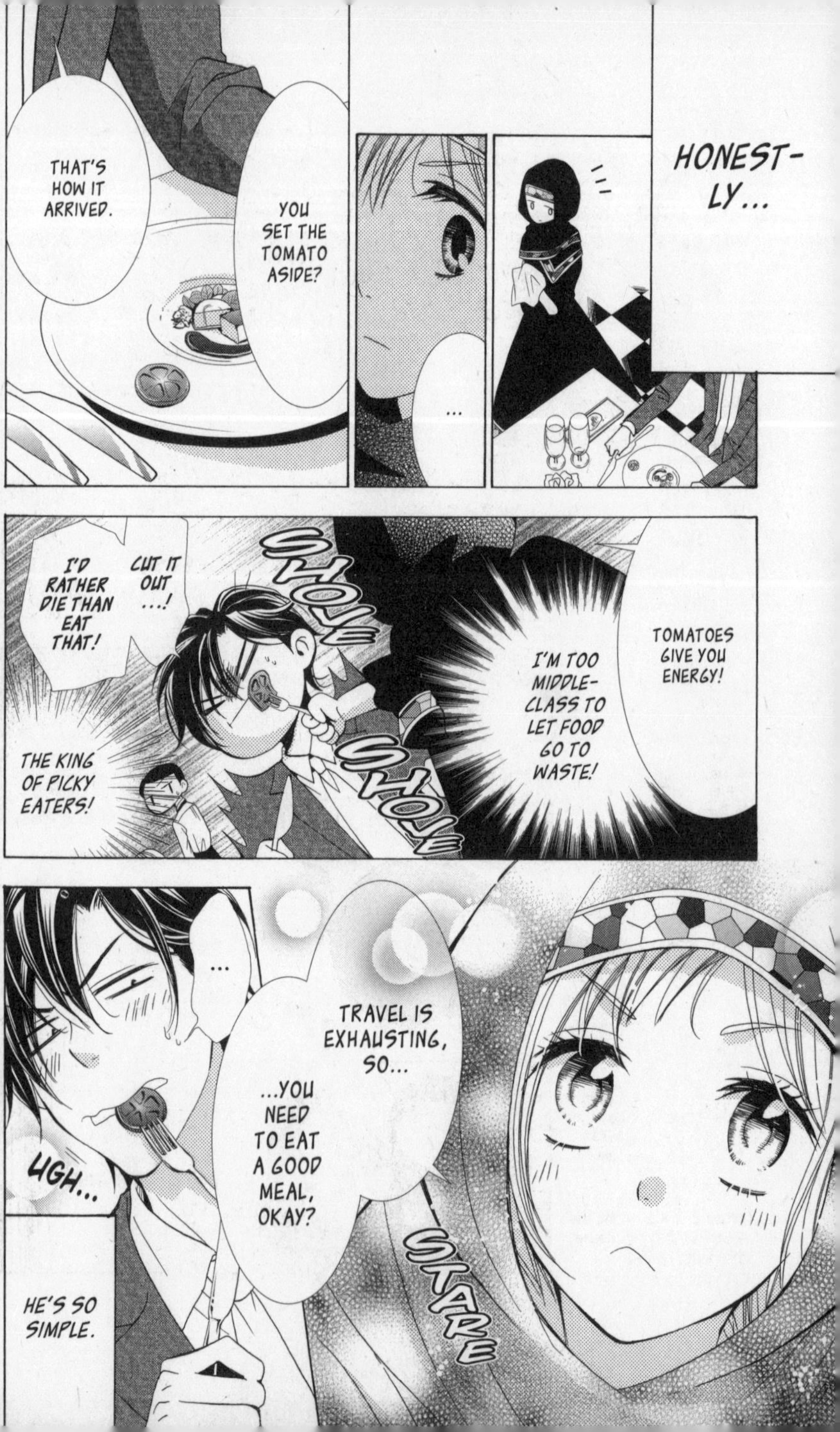
HONEST-LY...
...
YOU SET THE TOMATO ASIDE?
THAT'S HOW IT ARRIVED.
TOMATOES GIVE YOU ENERGY!
I'M TOO MIDDLE-CLASS TO LET FOOD GO TO WASTE!
SHOVE
SHOVE
SHOVE
CUT IT OUT ...!
I'D RATHER DIE THAN EAT THAT!
THE KING OF PICKY EATERS!
STARE
TRAVEL IS EXHAUSTING, SO...
...YOU NEED TO EAT A GOOD MEAL, OKAY?
...
UGH...
HE'S SO SIMPLE.

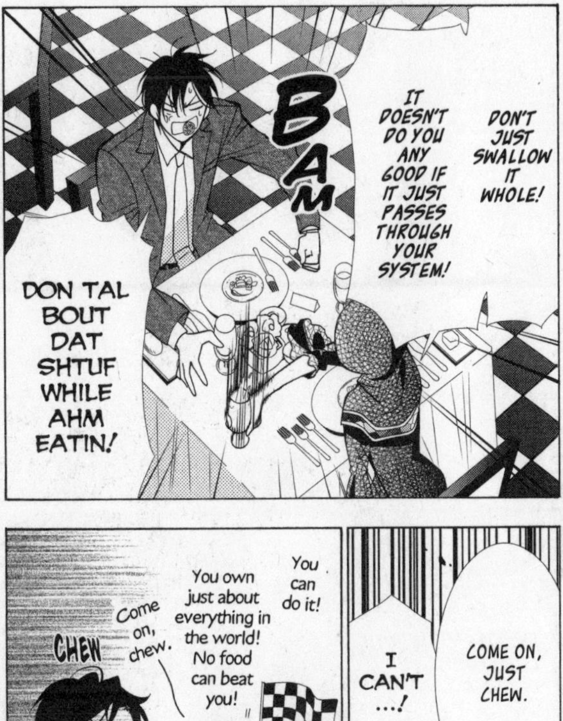
DON'T JUST SWALLOW IT WHOLE!
IT DOESN'T DO YOU ANY GOOD IF IT JUST PASSES THROUGH YOUR SYSTEM!
BAM
DON TAL BOUT DAT SHTUF WHILE AHM EATIN!
COME ON, JUST CHEW.
I CAN'T ...!
IT'S SQUISHY 'N' GROSS.
IT STINKS!
You can do it!
You own just about everything in the world! No food can beat you!
Come on, chew.
CHEW
CHEW
GULP!
I ate it...!
Good job!

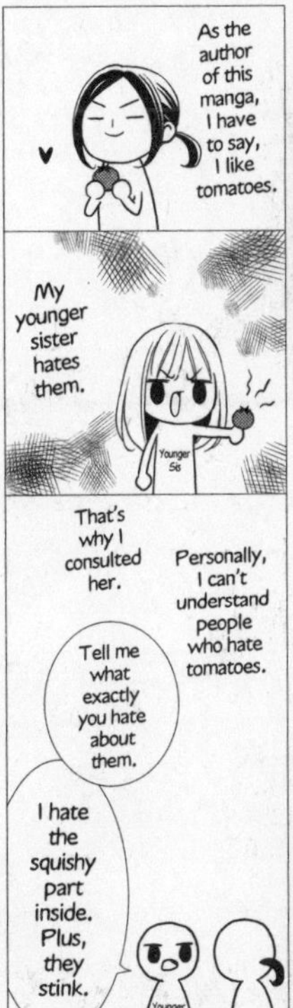
As the author of this manga, I have to say, I like tomatoes.
My younger sister hates them.
Younger Sis
That's why I consulted her.
Personally, I can't understand people who hate tomatoes.
Tell me what exactly you hate about them.
I hate the squishy part inside. Plus, they stink.
Younger Sis
So I still don't under-stand.
Okay, I'll grant that they're squishy, but...
...raw tomatoes have basically no smell.
They do too.
When she slices them, she holds her breath because they smell so bad.

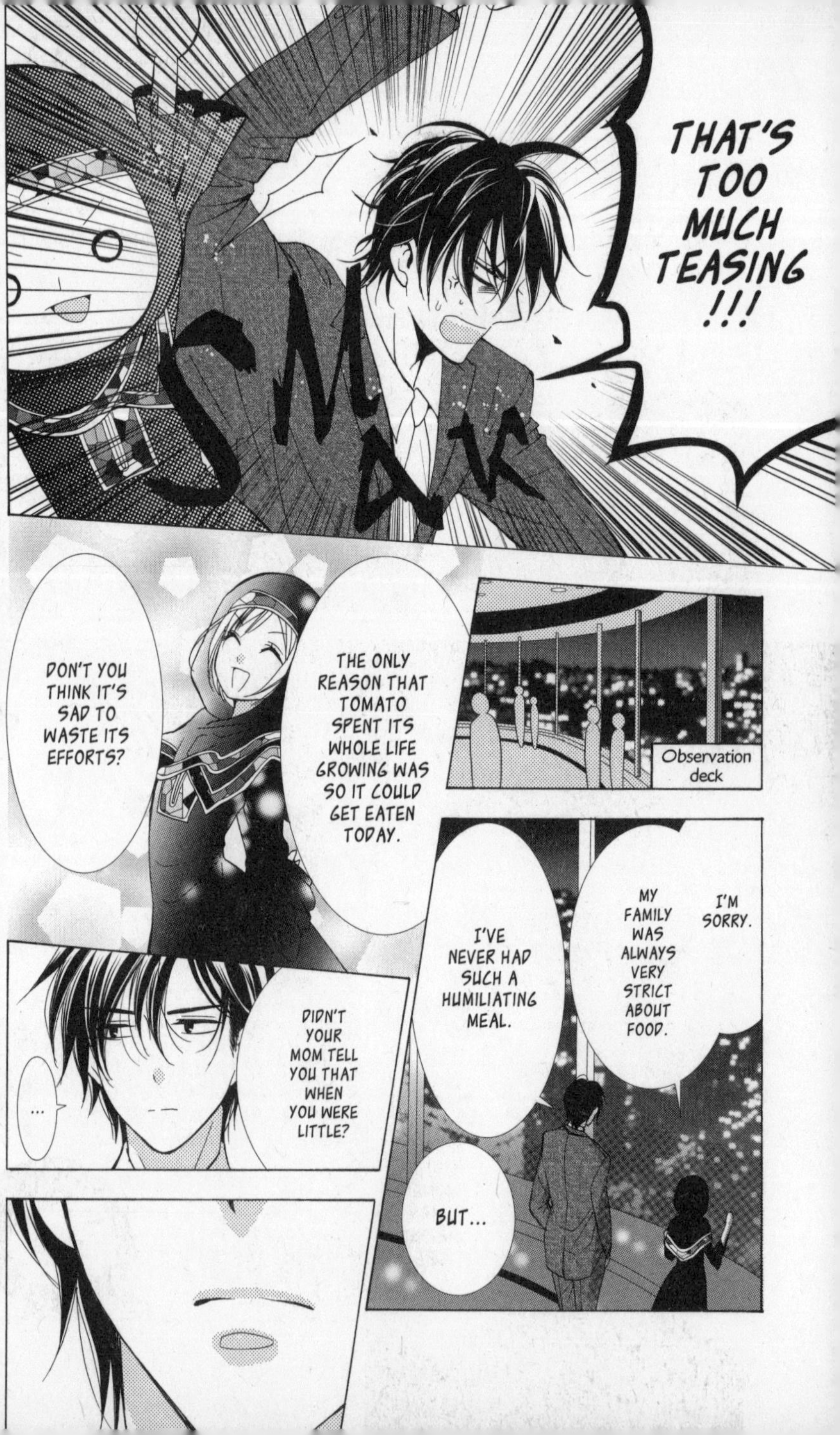
THAT'S TOO MUCH TEASING!!!
SMACK
Observation deck
THE ONLY REASON THAT TOMATO SPENT ITS WHOLE LIFE GROWING WAS SO IT COULD GET EATEN TODAY.
DON'T YOU THINK IT'S SAD TO WASTE ITS EFFORTS?
I'M SORRY.
MY FAMILY WAS ALWAYS VERY STRICT ABOUT FOOD.
I'VE NEVER HAD SUCH A HUMILIATING MEAL.
BUT...
DIDN'T YOUR MOM TELL YOU THAT WHEN YOU WERE LITTLE?
...

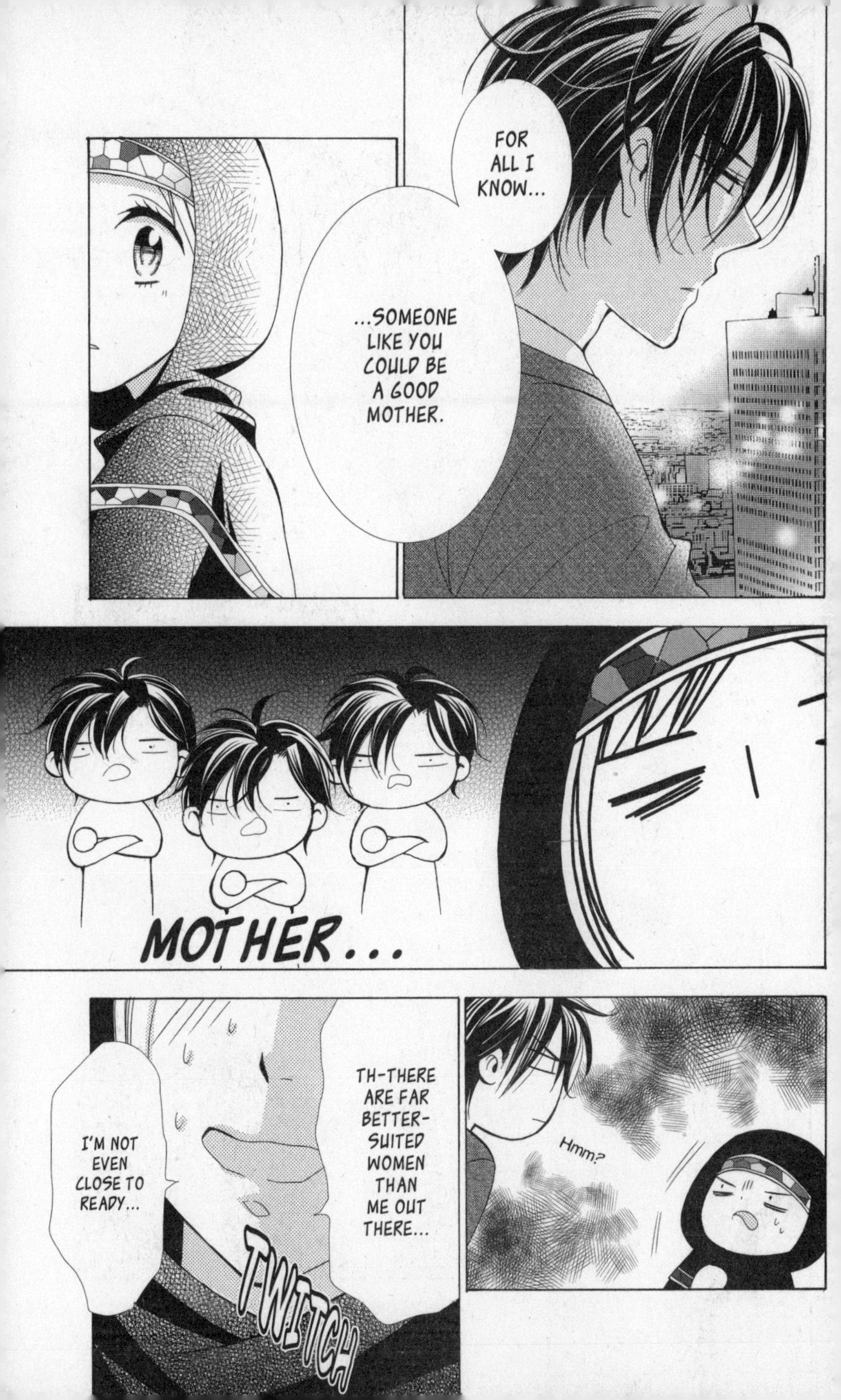
FOR ALL I KNOW...
...SOMEONE LIKE YOU COULD BE A GOOD MOTHER.
MOTHER...
Hmm?
TH-THERE ARE FAR BETTER-SUITED WOMEN THAN ME OUT THERE...
I'M NOT EVEN CLOSE TO READY...
TWITCH

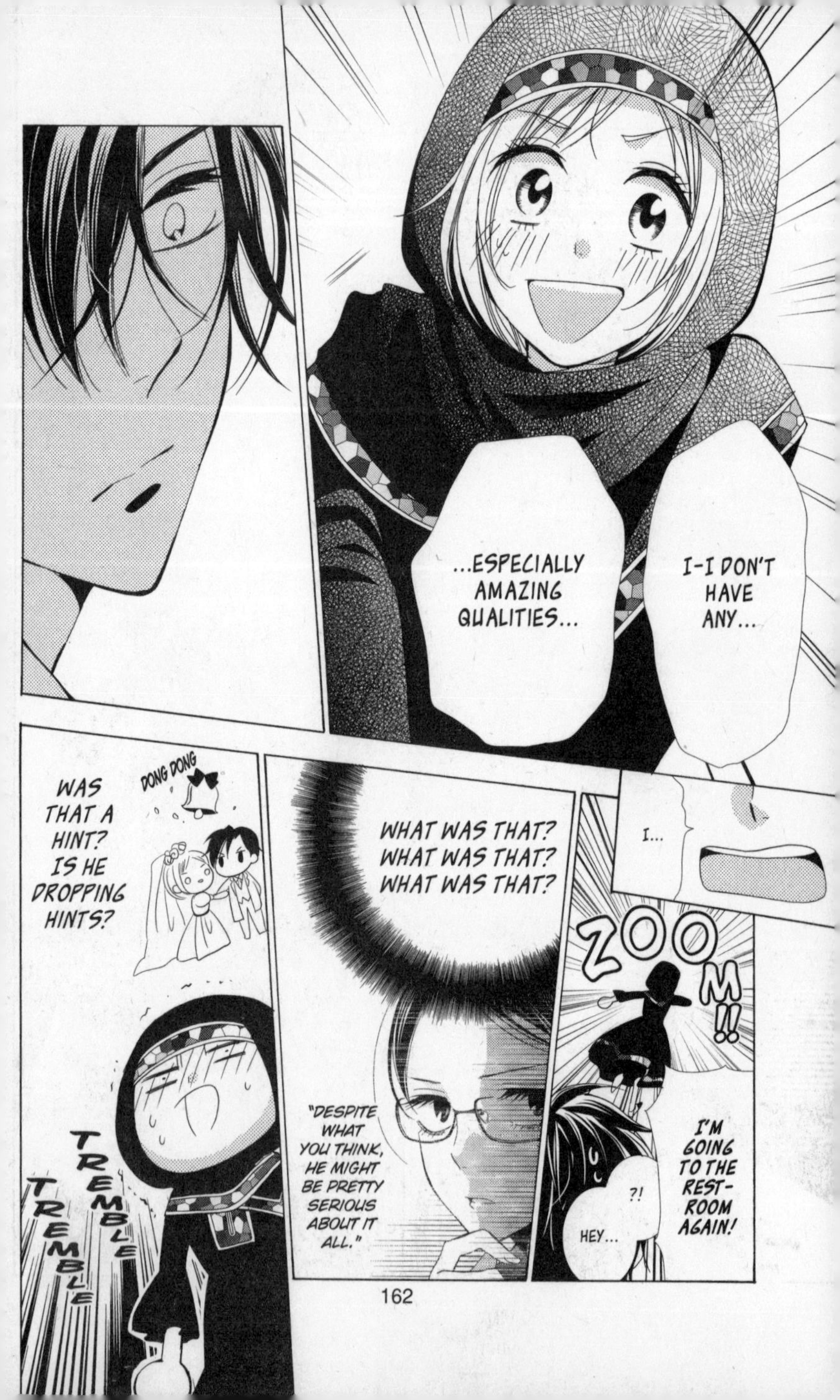
I-I DON'T HAVE ANY...
...ESPECIALLY AMAZING QUALITIES...
I...
ZOOM!!
I'M GOING TO THE REST-ROOM AGAIN!
?!
HEY...
WHAT WAS THAT? WHAT WAS THAT? WHAT WAS THAT?
"DESPITE WHAT YOU THINK, HE MIGHT BE PRETTY SERIOUS ABOUT IT ALL."
WAS THAT A HINT? IS HE DROPPING HINTS?
DONG DONG
TREMBLE
TREMBLE

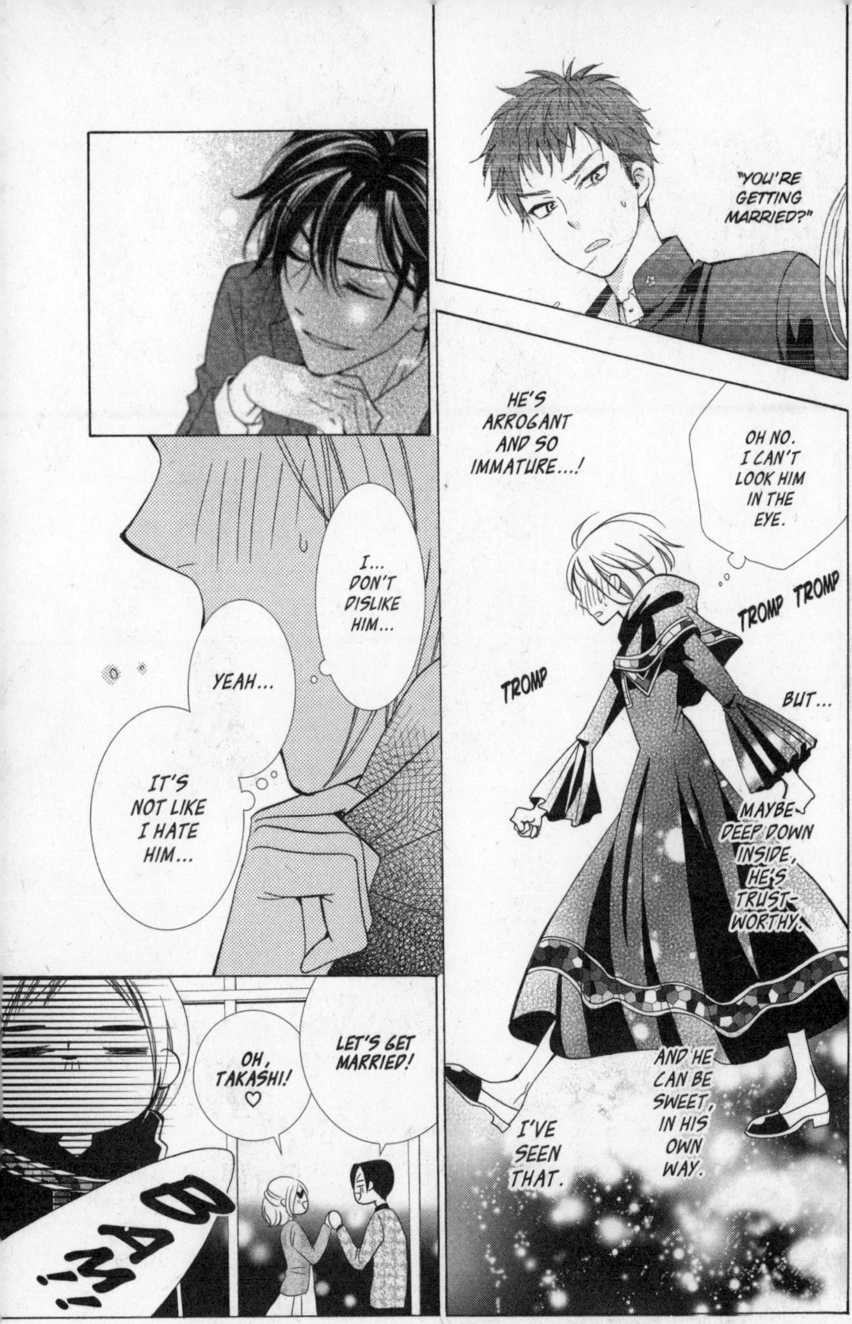
"YOU'RE GETTING MARRIED?"
OH NO. I CAN'T LOOK HIM IN THE EYE.
HE'S ARROGANT AND SO IMMATURE...!
TROMP TROMP
TROMP
BUT...
MAYBE DEEP DOWN INSIDE, HE'S TRUST-WORTHY.
AND HE CAN BE SWEET, IN HIS OWN WAY.
I'VE SEEN THAT.
I... DON'T DISLIKE HIM...
YEAH...
IT'S NOT LIKE I HATE HIM...
LET'S GET MARRIED!
OH, TAKASHI! ♡
BAM!!

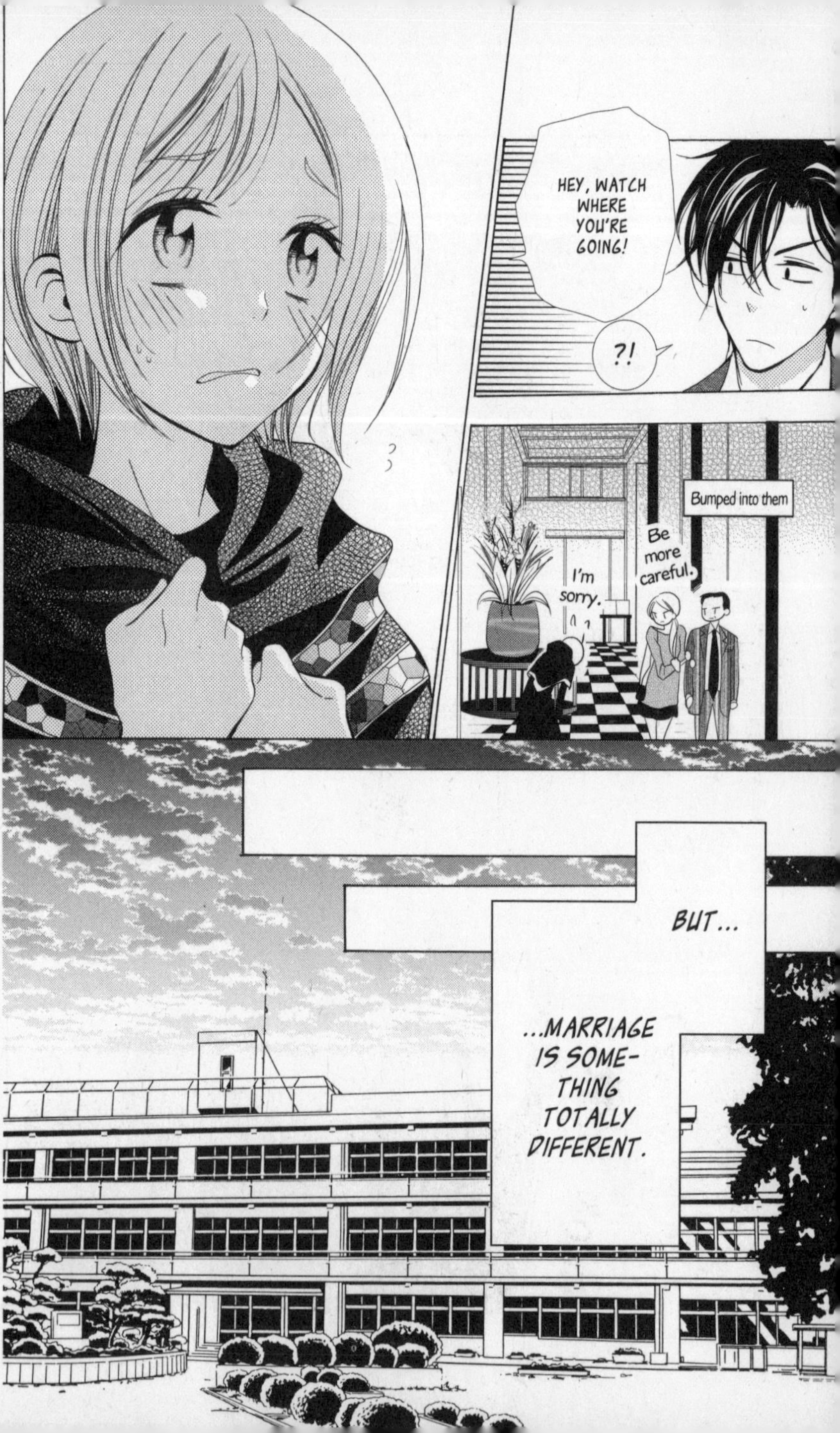
HEY, WATCH WHERE YOU'RE GOING!
?!
Bumped into them
Be more careful.
I'm sorry.
BUT...
...MARRIAGE IS SOME-THING TOTALLY DIFFERENT.

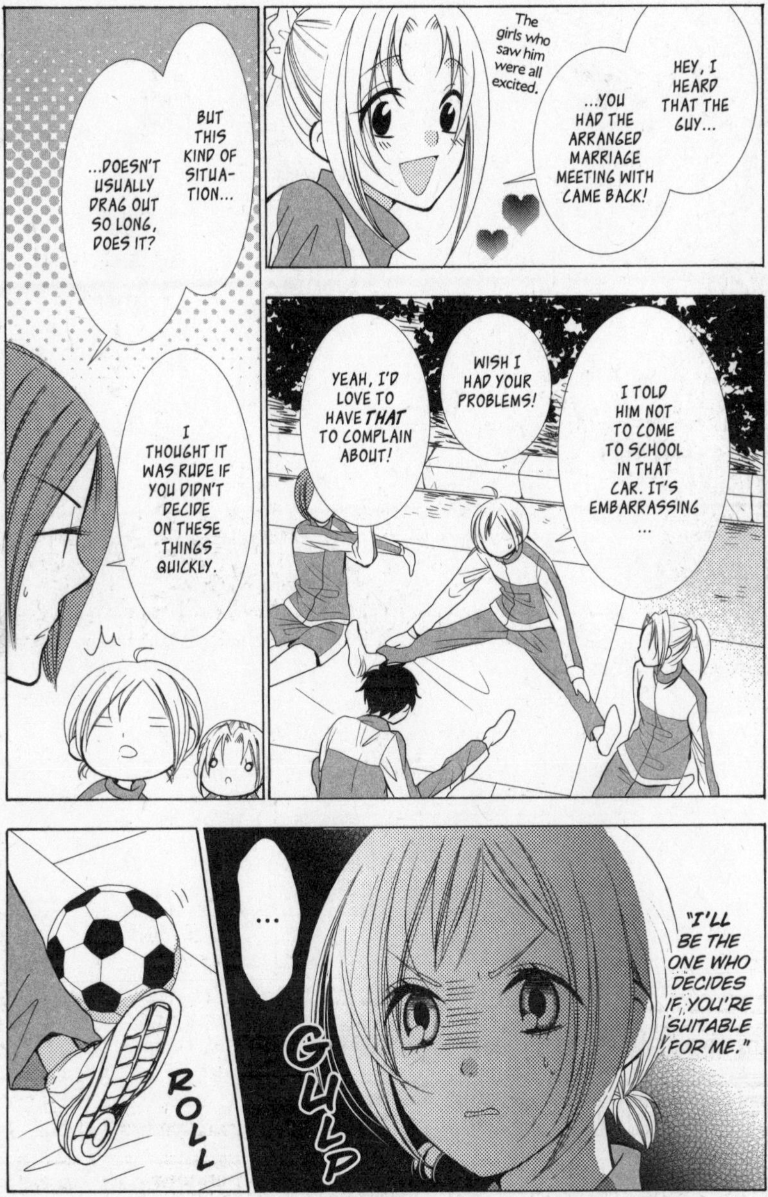
HEY, I HEARD THAT THE GUY...
...YOU HAD THE ARRANGED MARRIAGE MEETING WITH CAME BACK!
The girls who saw him were all excited.
I TOLD HIM NOT TO COME TO SCHOOL IN THAT CAR. IT'S EMBARRASSING ...
WISH I HAD YOUR PROBLEMS!
YEAH, I'D LOVE TO HAVE *THAT* TO COMPLAIN ABOUT!
BUT THIS KIND OF SITUATION...
...DOESN'T USUALLY DRAG OUT SO LONG, DOES IT?
I THOUGHT IT WAS RUDE IF YOU DIDN'T DECIDE ON THESE THINGS QUICKLY.
"I'LL BE THE ONE WHO DECIDES IF YOU'RE SUITABLE FOR ME."
...
GULP
ROLL

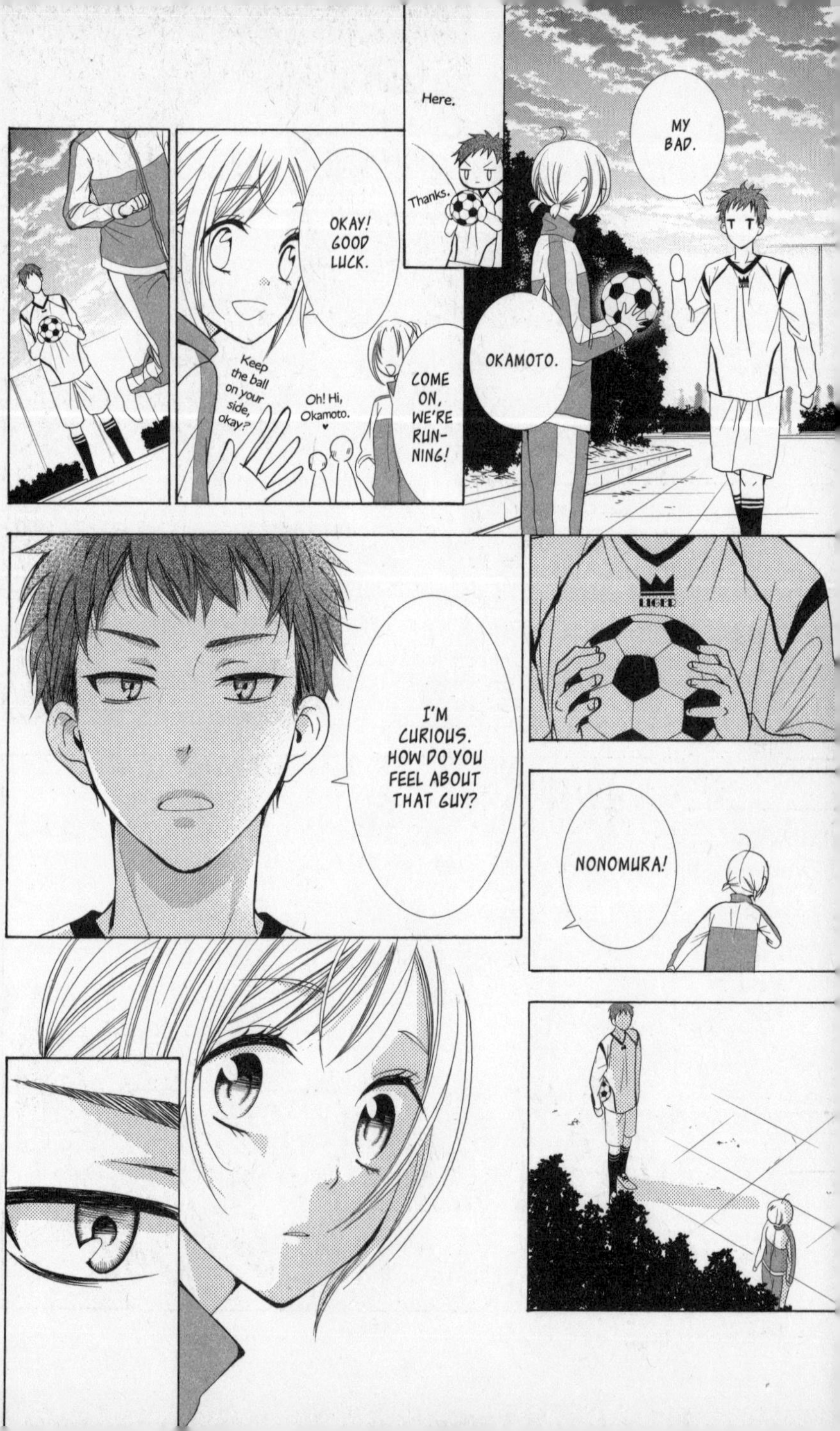
MY BAD.
OKAMOTO.
Here.
Thanks.
OKAY! GOOD LUCK.
COME ON, WE'RE RUN-NING!
Oh! Hi, Okamoto. ♥
Keep the ball on your side, okay?
NONOMURA!
I'M CURIOUS. HOW DO YOU FEEL ABOUT THAT GUY?

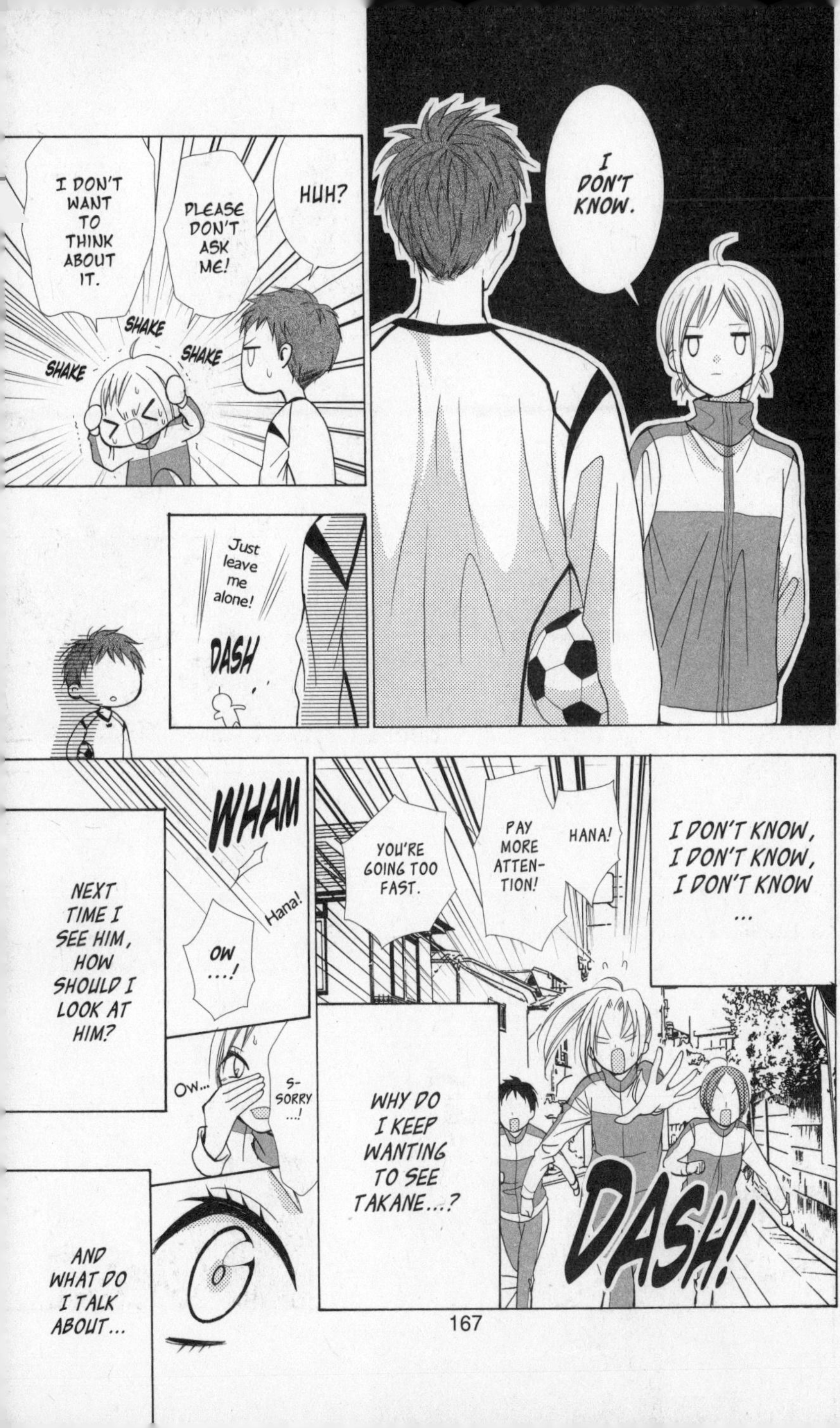
I DON'T KNOW.
HUH?
PLEASE DON'T ASK ME!
I DON'T WANT TO THINK ABOUT IT.
SHAKE
SHAKE
SHAKE
Just leave me alone!
DASH
I DON'T KNOW, I DON'T KNOW, I DON'T KNOW ...
HANA!
PAY MORE ATTENTION!
YOU'RE GOING TOO FAST.
DASH!
WHY DO I KEEP WANTING TO SEE TAKANE...?
WHAM
Hana!
OW ...!
S-SORRY ...!
Ow...
NEXT TIME I SEE HIM, HOW SHOULD I LOOK AT HIM?
AND WHAT DO I TALK ABOUT...

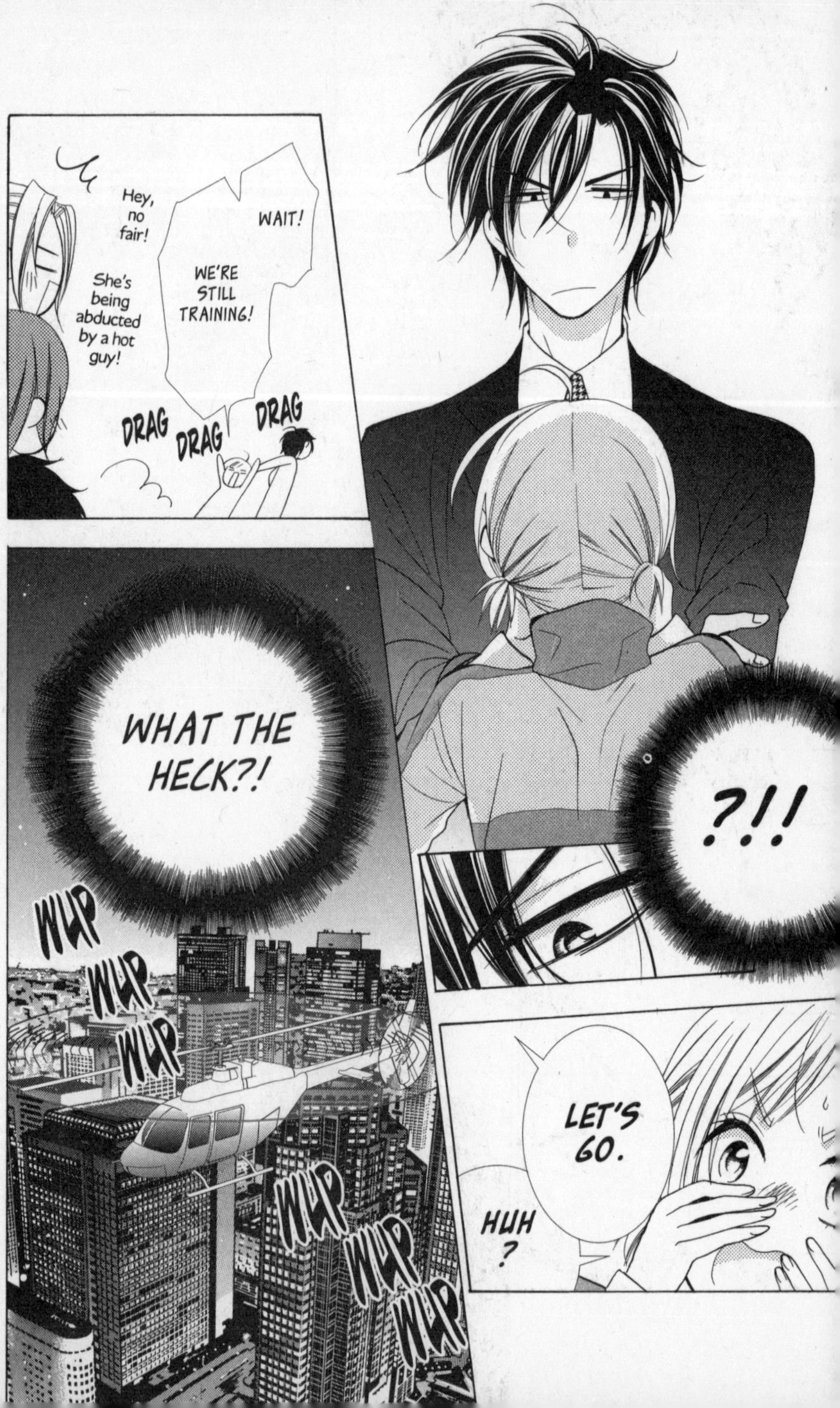

?!!
LET'S GO.
HUH?
WAIT!
WE'RE STILL TRAINING!
Hey, no fair!
She's being abducted by a hot guy!
DRAG
DRAG
DRAG
WHAT THE HECK?!
WUP WUP WUP
WUP WUP WUP

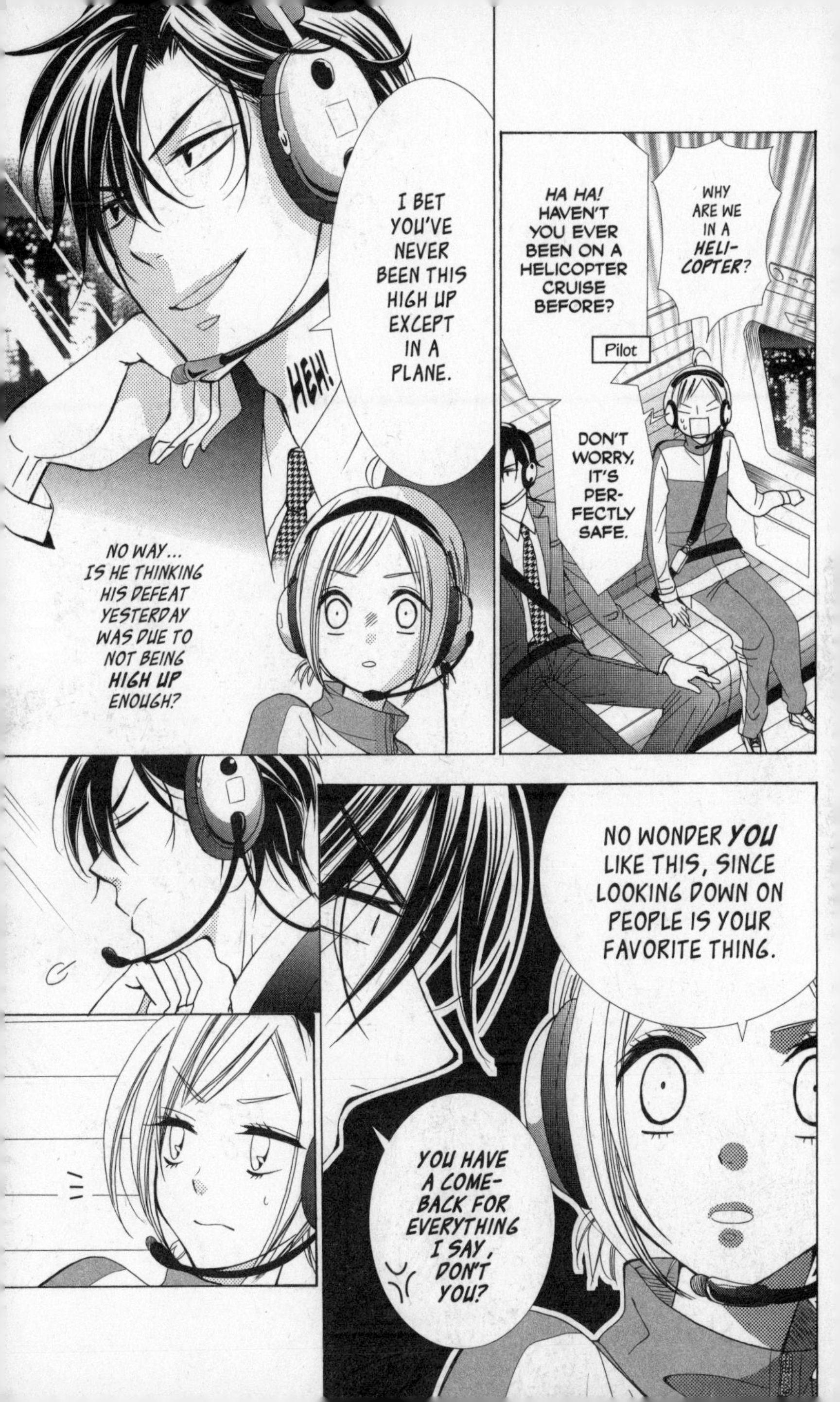
WHY ARE WE IN A HELICOPTER?
HA HA! HAVEN'T YOU EVER BEEN ON A HELICOPTER CRUISE BEFORE?
Pilot
DON'T WORRY, IT'S PERFECTLY SAFE.
I BET YOU'VE NEVER BEEN THIS HIGH UP EXCEPT IN A PLANE.
HEH!
NO WAY... IS HE THINKING HIS DEFEAT YESTERDAY WAS DUE TO NOT BEING HIGH UP ENOUGH?
NO WONDER YOU LIKE THIS, SINCE LOOKING DOWN ON PEOPLE IS YOUR FAVORITE THING.
YOU HAVE A COMEBACK FOR EVERYTHING I SAY, DON'T YOU?

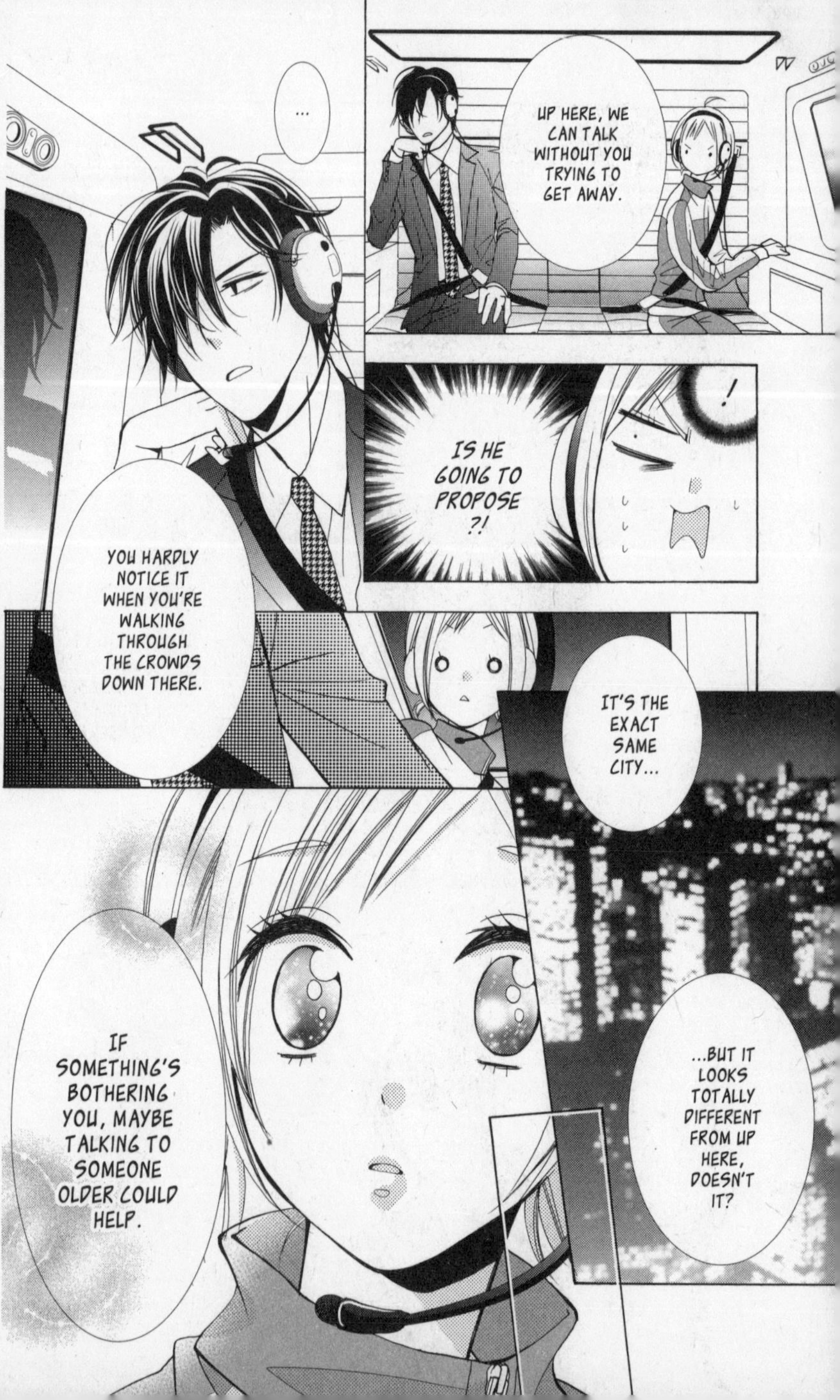
UP HERE, WE CAN TALK WITHOUT YOU TRYING TO GET AWAY.
!
IS HE GOING TO PROPOSE ?!
...
YOU HARDLY NOTICE IT WHEN YOU'RE WALKING THROUGH THE CROWDS DOWN THERE.
IT'S THE EXACT SAME CITY...
...BUT IT LOOKS TOTALLY DIFFERENT FROM UP HERE, DOESN'T IT?
IF SOMETHING'S BOTHERING YOU, MAYBE TALKING TO SOMEONE OLDER COULD HELP.

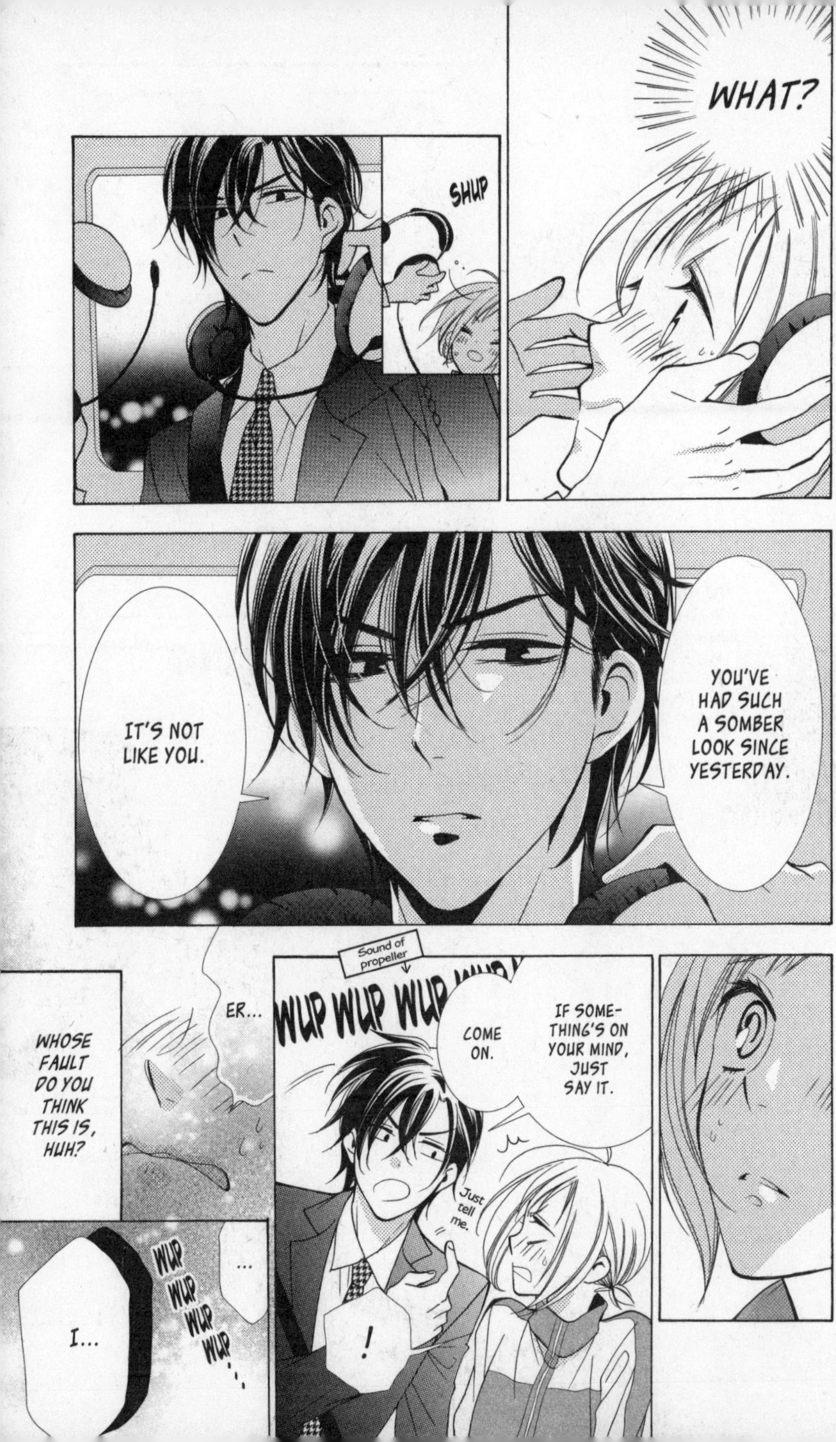
WHAT?
SHUP
YOU'VE HAD SUCH A SOMBER LOOK SINCE YESTERDAY.
IT'S NOT LIKE YOU.
IF SOME-THING'S ON YOUR MIND, JUST SAY IT.
COME ON.
Sound of propeller
WUP WUP WUP WUP
ER...
Just tell me.
!
WHOSE FAULT DO YOU THINK THIS IS, HUH?
...
I...
WUP WUP WUP WUP...

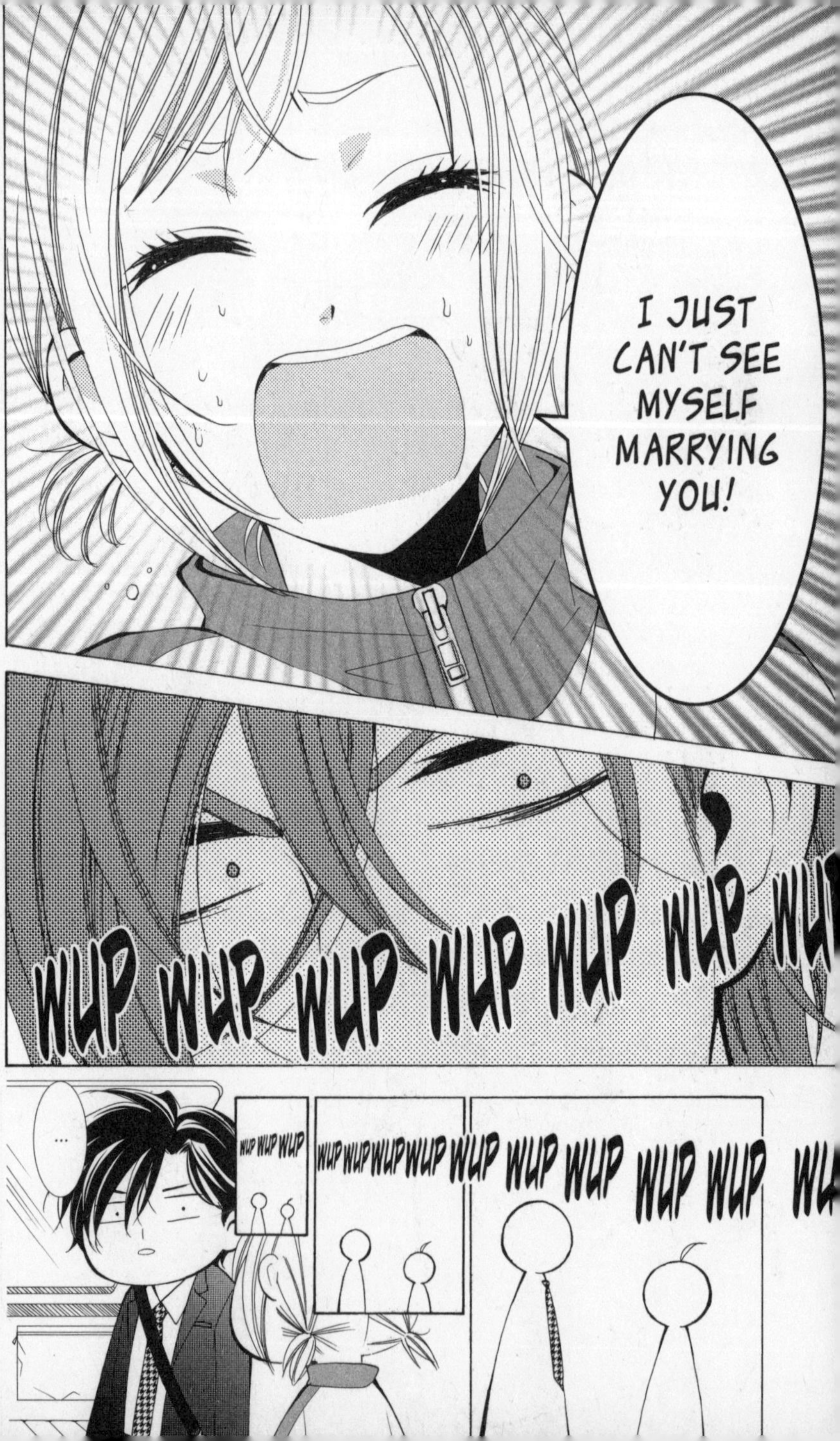
I JUST CAN'T SEE MYSELF MARRYING YOU!
WUP WUP WUP WUP WUP WUP
...
WUP WUP WUP WUP WUP WUP WUP WUP WUP
WUP WUP WUP

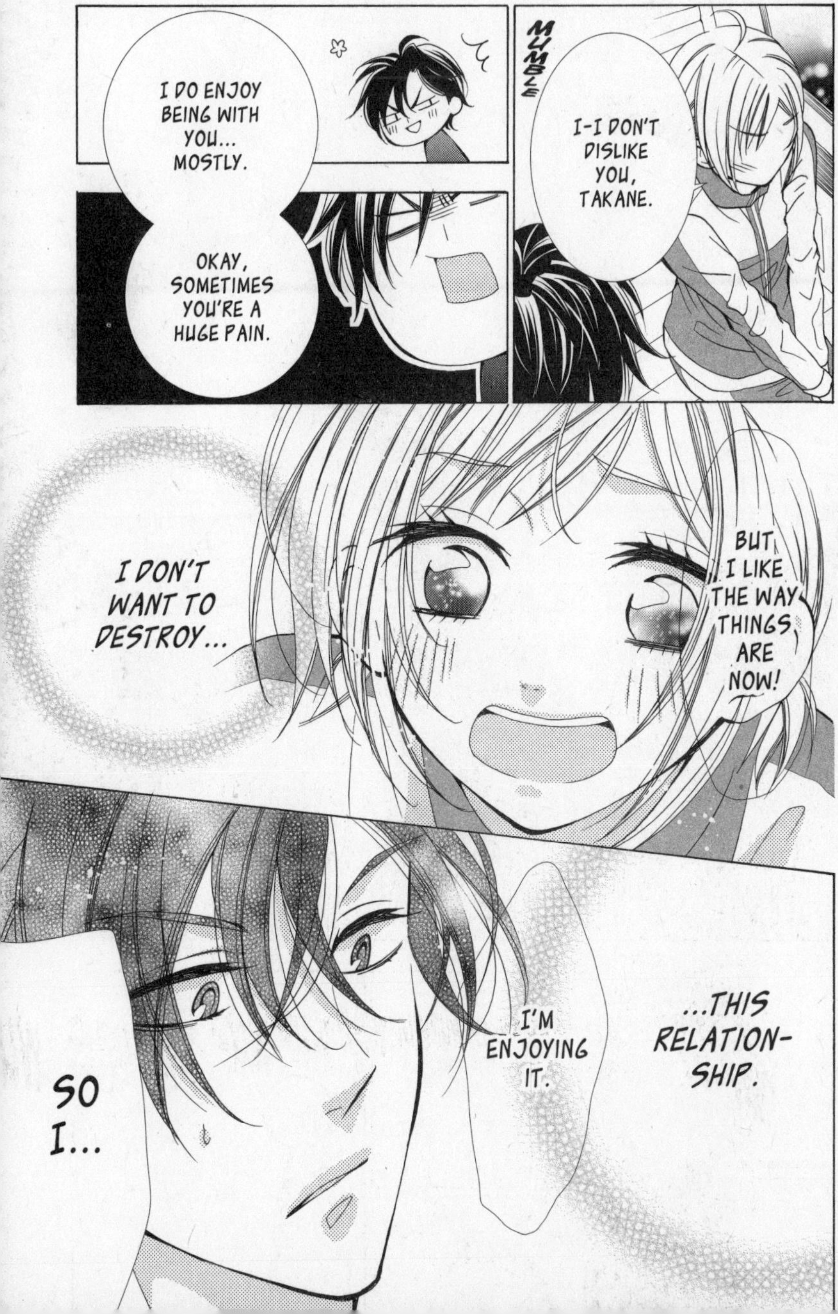
MUMBLE
I-I DON'T DISLIKE YOU, TAKANE.
I DO ENJOY BEING WITH YOU... MOSTLY.
OKAY, SOMETIMES YOU'RE A HUGE PAIN.
BUT I LIKE THE WAY THINGS ARE NOW!
I DON'T WANT TO DESTROY...
...THIS RELATION-SHIP.
I'M ENJOYING IT.
SO I...

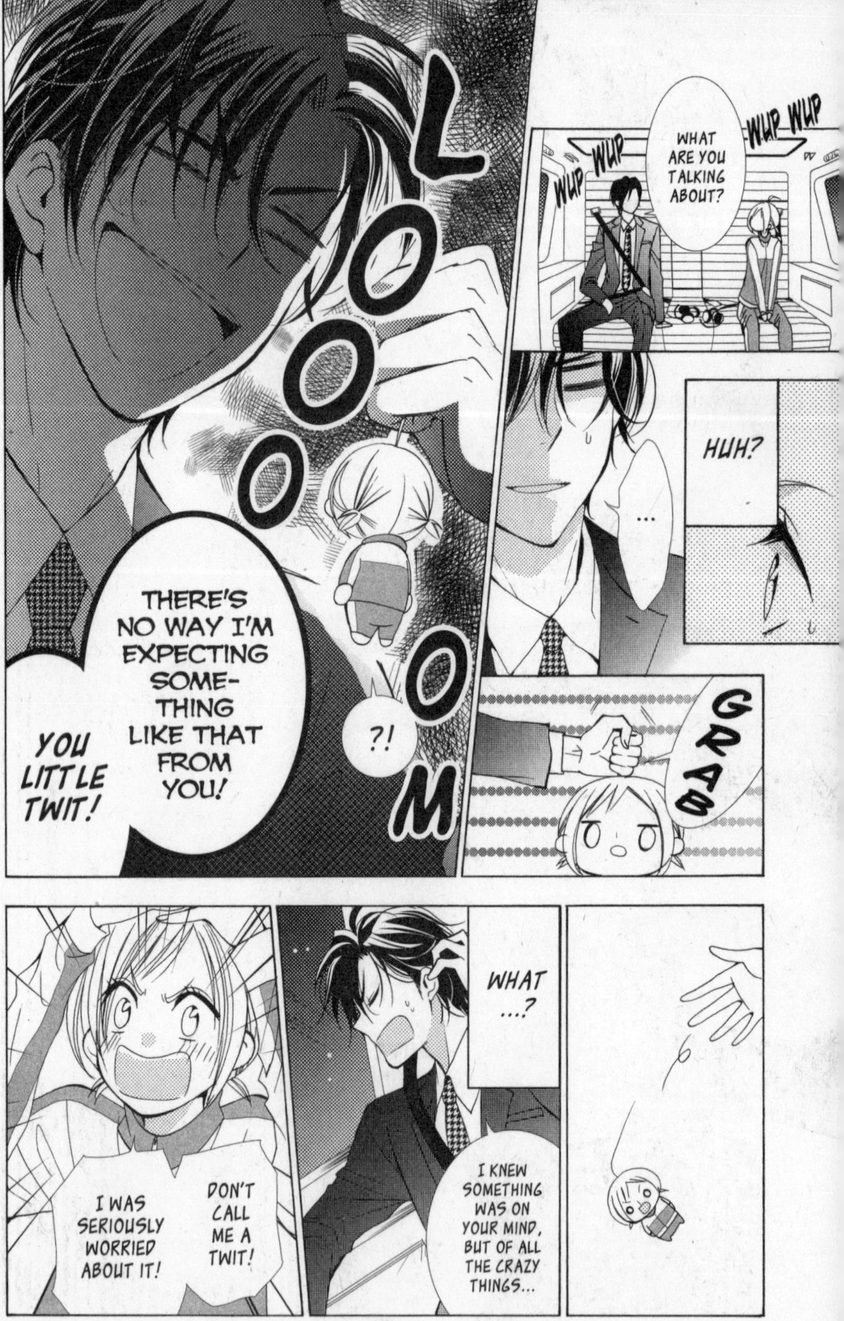
WUP WUP
WHAT ARE YOU TALKING ABOUT?
WUP WUP
HUH?
...
GRAB
LOOOOOOOM
?!
THERE'S NO WAY I'M EXPECTING SOME-THING LIKE THAT FROM YOU!
YOU LITTLE TWIT!
WHAT ...?
I KNEW SOMETHING WAS ON YOUR MIND, BUT OF ALL THE CRAZY THINGS...
DON'T CALL ME A TWIT!
I WAS SERIOUSLY WORRIED ABOUT IT!

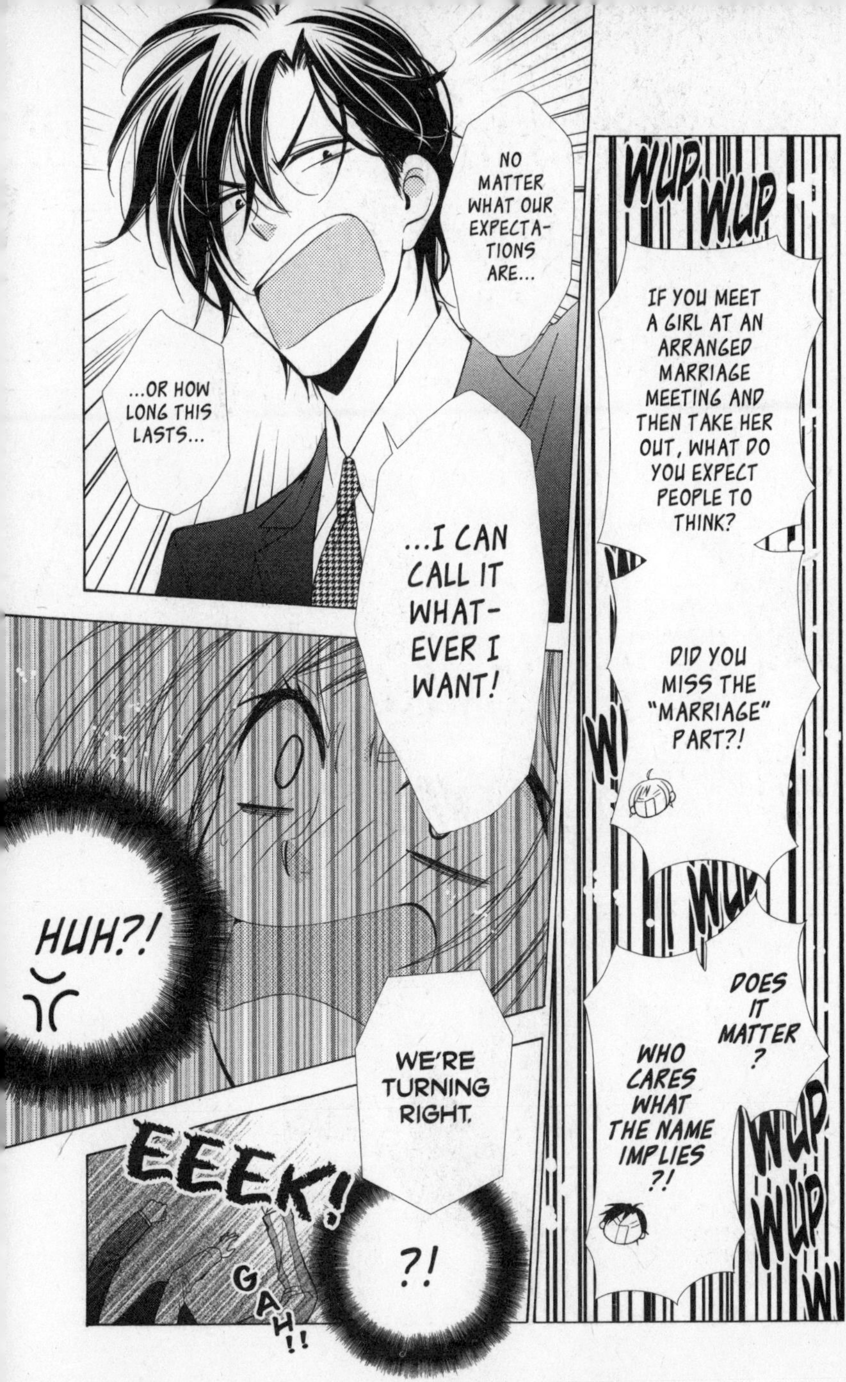
WUP WUP
IF YOU MEET A GIRL AT AN ARRANGED MARRIAGE MEETING AND THEN TAKE HER OUT, WHAT DO YOU EXPECT PEOPLE TO THINK?
DID YOU MISS THE "MARRIAGE" PART?!
WUP
DOES IT MATTER?
WHO CARES WHAT THE NAME IMPLIES?!
WUP WUP
NO MATTER WHAT OUR EXPECTATIONS ARE...
...OR HOW LONG THIS LASTS...
...I CAN CALL IT WHATEVER I WANT!
HUH?!
WE'RE TURNING RIGHT.
EEEK!
?!
GAH!!

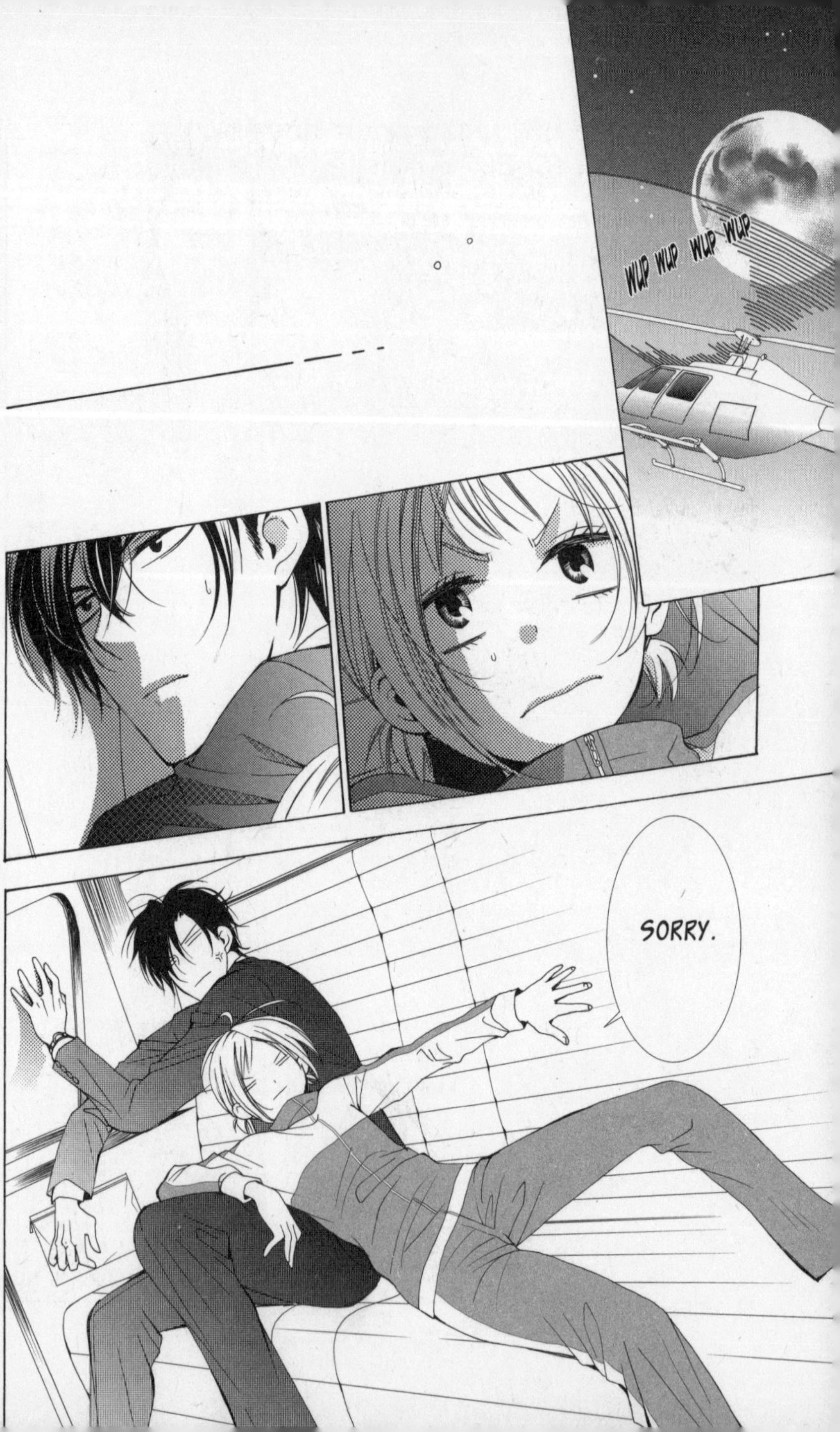
WUP WUP WUP WUP
SORRY.

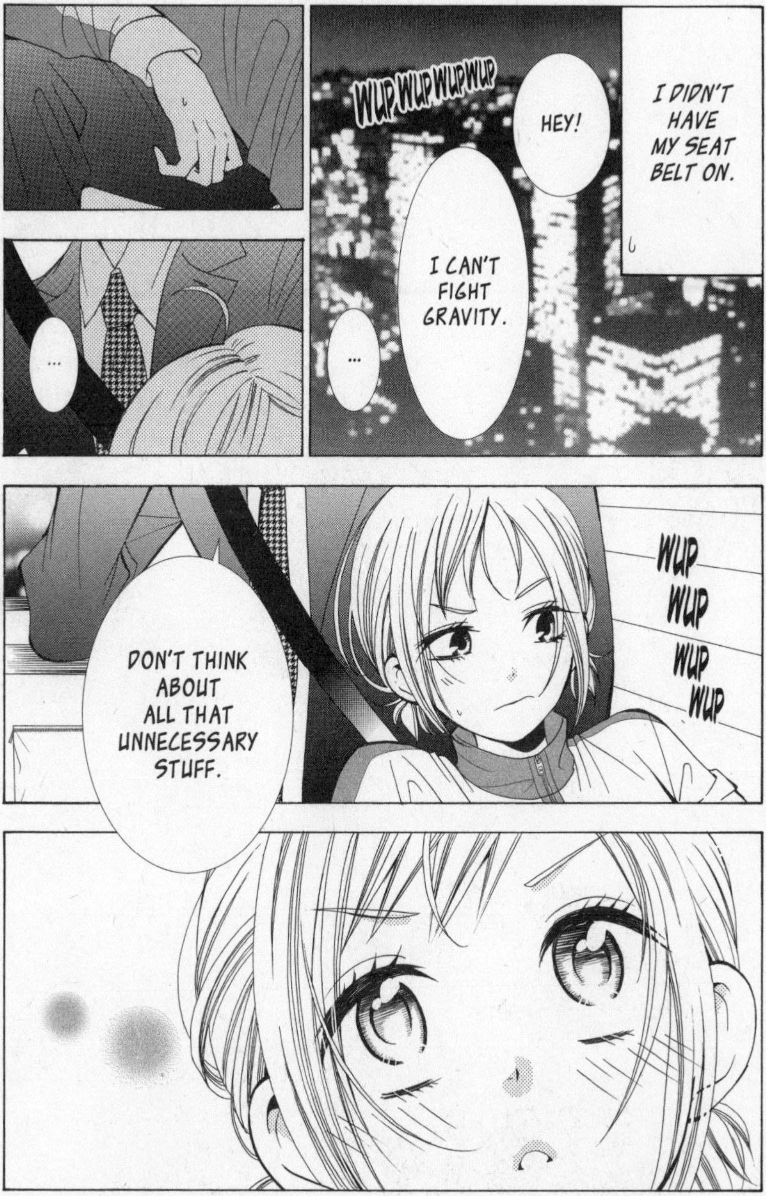
I DIDN'T HAVE MY SEAT BELT ON.
HEY!
WUP WUP WUP WUP
I CAN'T FIGHT GRAVITY.
...
...
WUP WUP WUP WUP
DON'T THINK ABOUT ALL THAT UNNECESSARY STUFF.

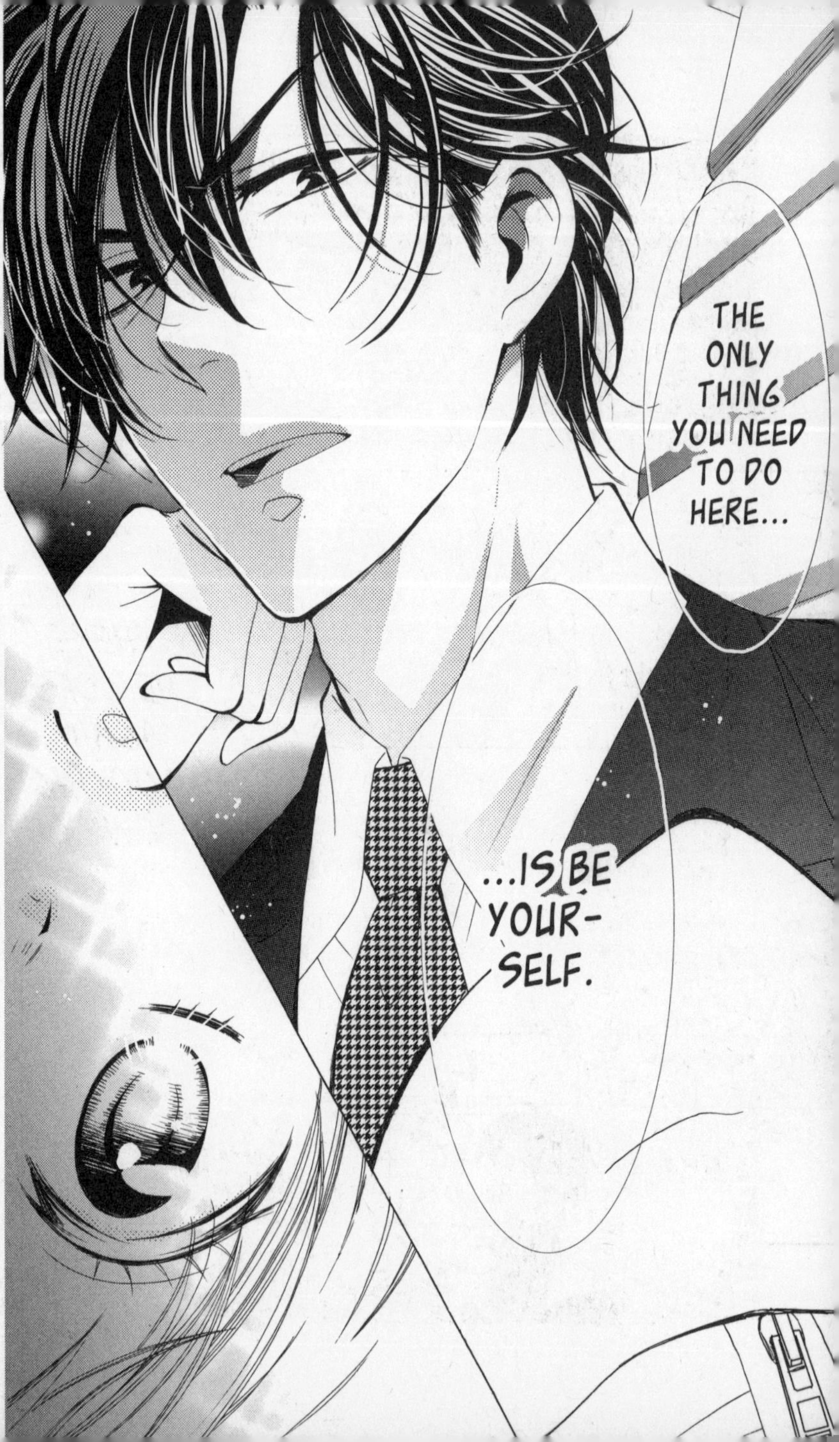
THE ONLY THING YOU NEED TO DO HERE...
...IS BE YOUR-SELF.

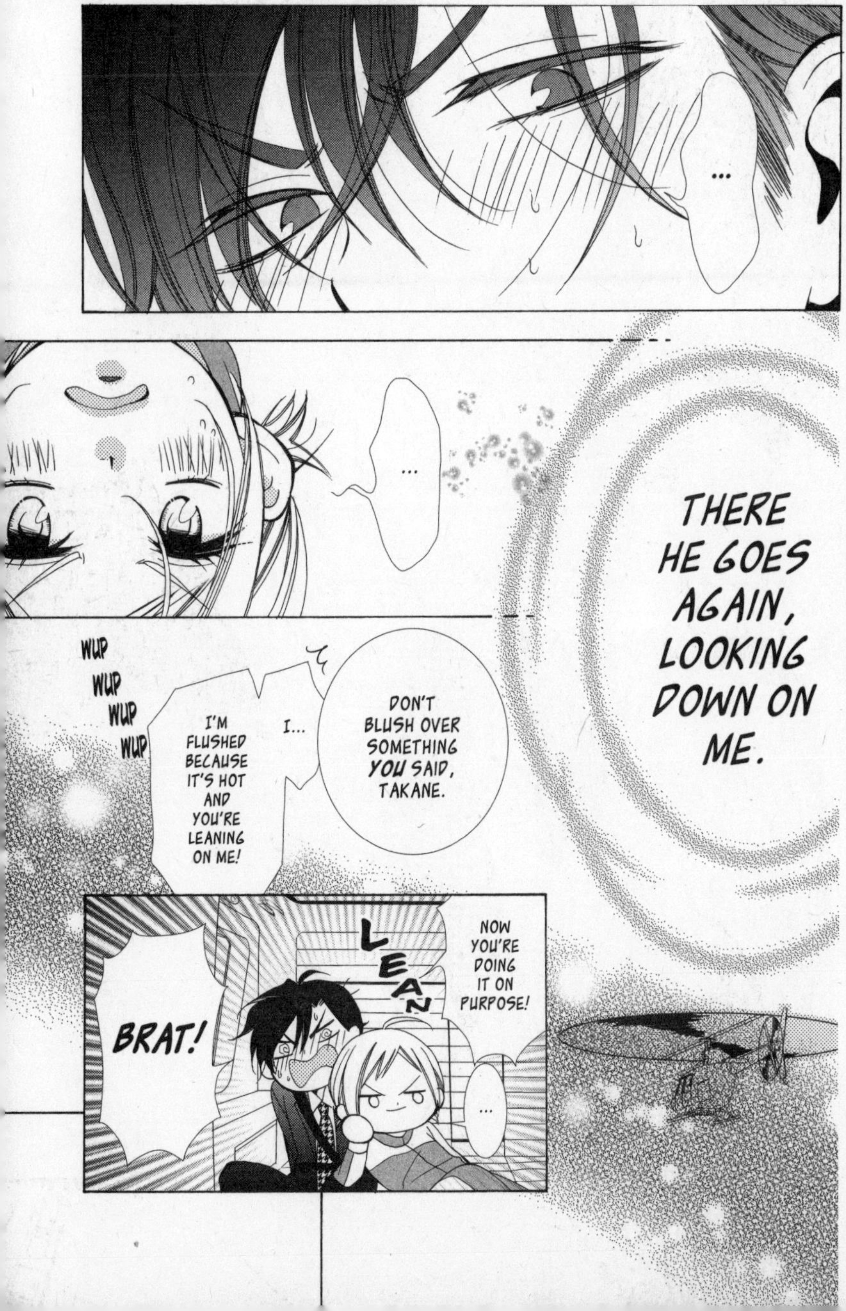
...
THERE HE GOES AGAIN, LOOKING DOWN ON ME.
...
DON'T BLUSH OVER SOMETHING YOU SAID, TAKANE.
I...
I'M FLUSHED BECAUSE IT'S HOT AND YOU'RE LEANING ON ME!
WUP WUP WUP WUP
NOW YOU'RE DOING IT ON PURPOSE!
LEAN
...
BRAT!

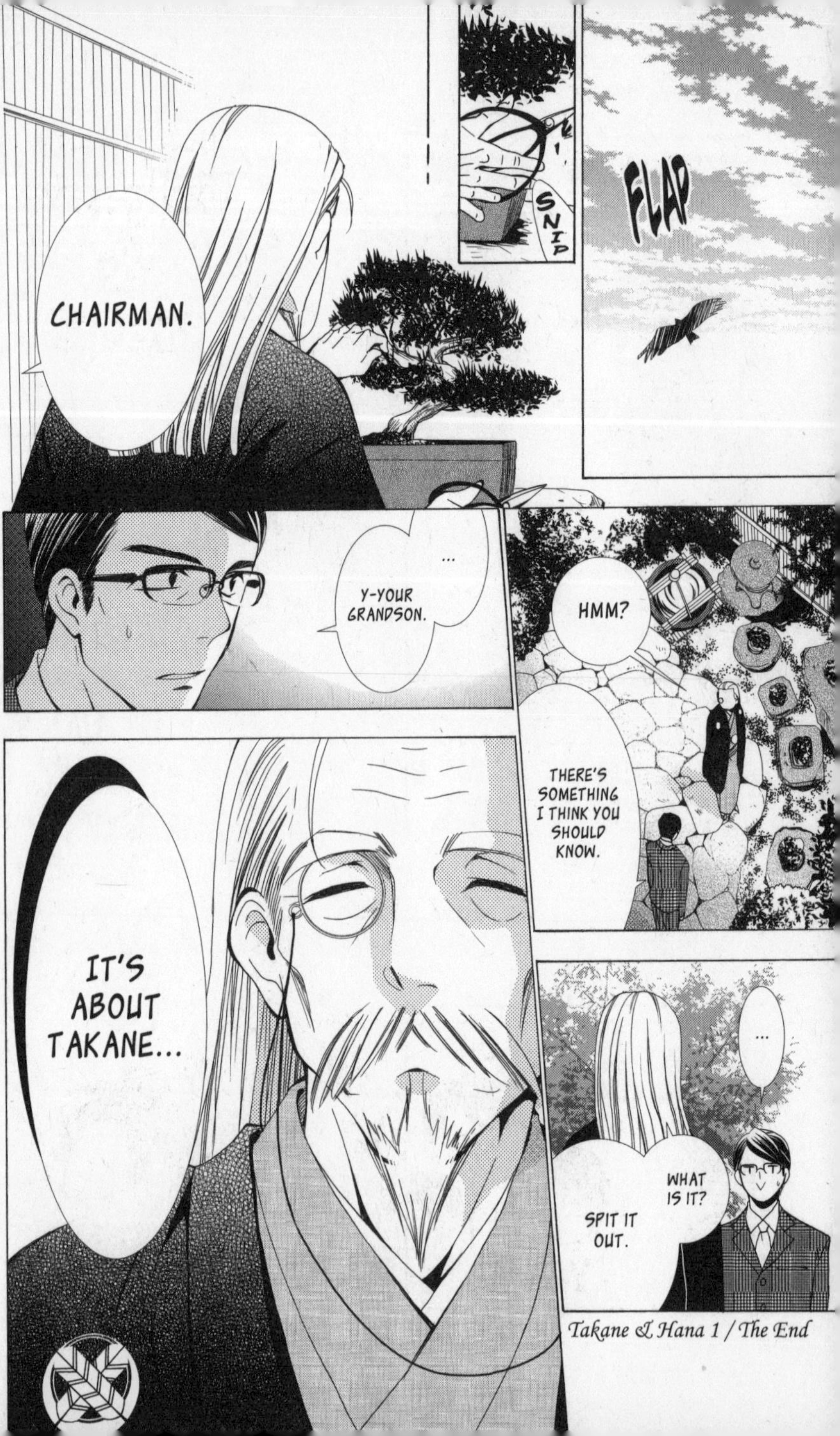
FLAP
SNIP
CHAIRMAN.
HMM?
THERE'S SOMETHING I THINK YOU SHOULD KNOW.
...
WHAT IS IT?
SPIT IT OUT.
...
Y-YOUR GRANDSON.
IT'S ABOUT TAKANE...

Takane & Hana 1 / The End

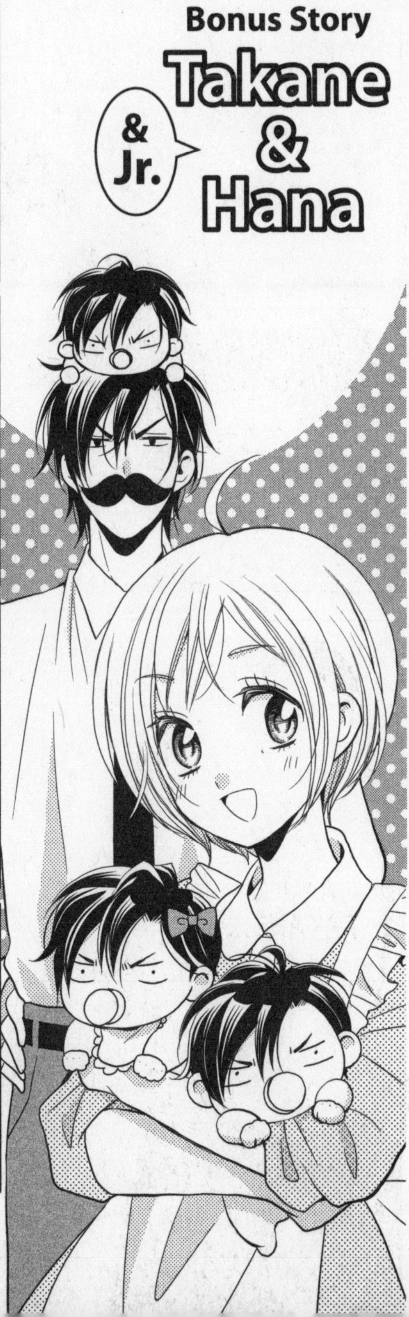
Bonus Story
Takane & Hana
& Jr.

Takane Jr. Is Born

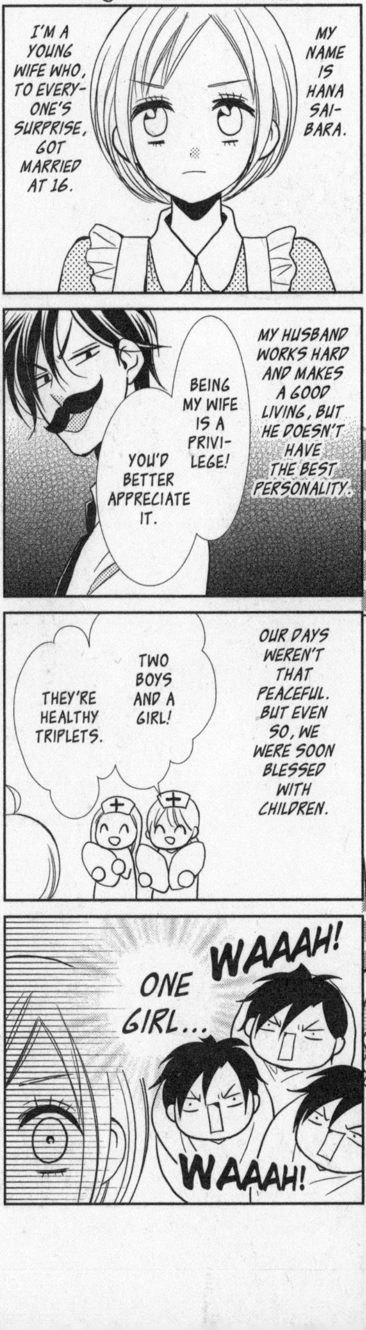
MY NAME IS HANA SAI-BARA.
I'M A YOUNG WIFE WHO, TO EVERY-ONE'S SURPRISE, GOT MARRIED AT 16.
MY HUSBAND WORKS HARD AND MAKES A GOOD LIVING, BUT HE DOESN'T HAVE THE BEST PERSONALITY.
BEING MY WIFE IS A PRIVI-LEGE!
YOU'D BETTER APPRECIATE IT.
OUR DAYS WEREN'T THAT PEACEFUL. BUT EVEN SO, WE WERE SOON BLESSED WITH CHILDREN.
TWO BOYS AND A GIRL!
THEY'RE HEALTHY TRIPLETS.
WAAAH!
ONE GIRL...
WAAAH!

The Only Girl

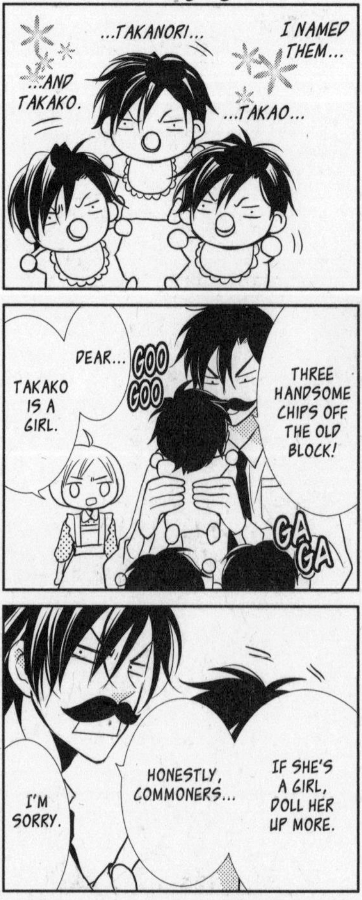
I NAMED THEM...
...TAKAO...
...TAKANORI...
...AND TAKAKO.
THREE HANDSOME CHIPS OFF THE OLD BLOCK!
GA GA
GOO GOO
DEAR...
TAKAKO IS A GIRL.
IF SHE'S A GIRL, DOLL HER UP MORE.
HONESTLY, COMMONERS...
I'M SORRY.
W-WHY IS SHE CRYING ...?!
WAA
DON'T PUT THAT ON HER HEAD!
SHE JUST LEARNED HOW TO HOLD IT UP!
MY HUSBAND ISN'T GOOD WITH WOM-EN.
WAAH

A Loving Parent

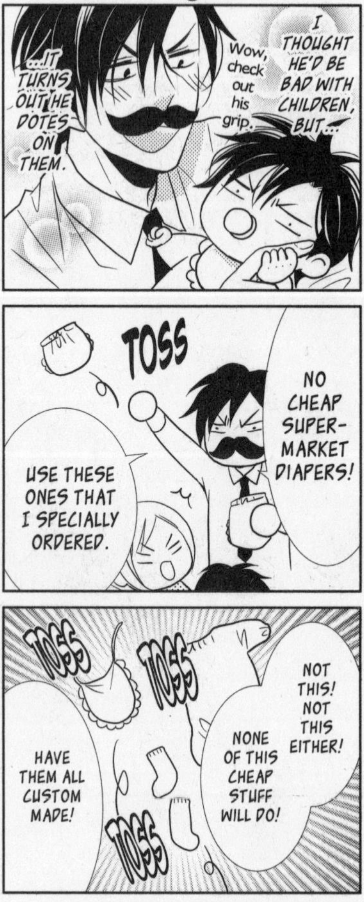
I THOUGHT HE'D BE BAD WITH CHILDREN, BUT...
Wow, check out his grip.
...IT TURNS OUT HE DOTES ON THEM.
NO CHEAP SUPER-MARKET DIAPERS!
TOSS
USE THESE ONES THAT I SPECIALLY ORDERED.
NOT THIS! NOT THIS EITHER!
TOSS
NONE OF THIS CHEAP STUFF WILL DO!
TOSS
HAVE THEM ALL CUSTOM MADE!
TOSS
KICK
LET'S CHANGE YOUR DIAPER, OKAY?
OH.
Discount diaper
THEY'RE MORE LIKE THEIR FATHER EVERY DAY.

First Word

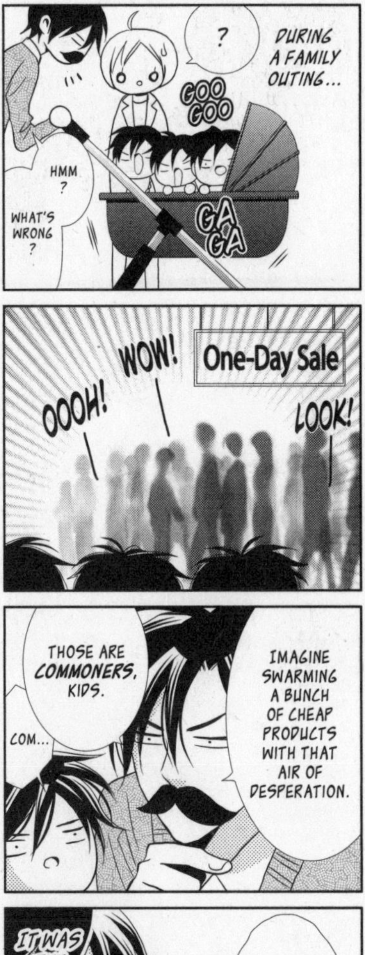
DURING A FAMILY OUTING...
?
GOO GOO
GA GA
HMM? WHAT'S WRONG?
One-Day Sale
LOOK!
WOW!
OOOH!
IMAGINE SWARMING A BUNCH OF CHEAP PRODUCTS WITH THAT AIR OF DESPERATION.
THOSE ARE *COMMONERS*, KIDS.
COM...
COMMON... ER...
IT WAS THE FIRST WORD THE KIDS LEARNED.
COMMON-ER.

Mother

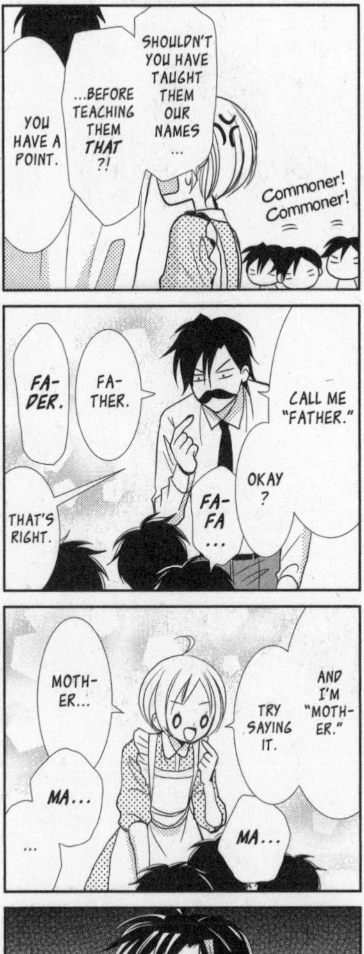
SHOULDN'T YOU HAVE TAUGHT THEM OUR NAMES...
...BEFORE TEACHING THEM *THAT*?!
YOU HAVE A POINT.
Commoner! Commoner!
CALL ME "FATHER."
OKAY?
FA-THER.
FA-FA...
FA-DER.
THAT'S RIGHT.
AND I'M "MOTH-ER."
TRY SAYING IT.
MA...
MOTH-ER...
MA...
...
COMMONER.

DNA

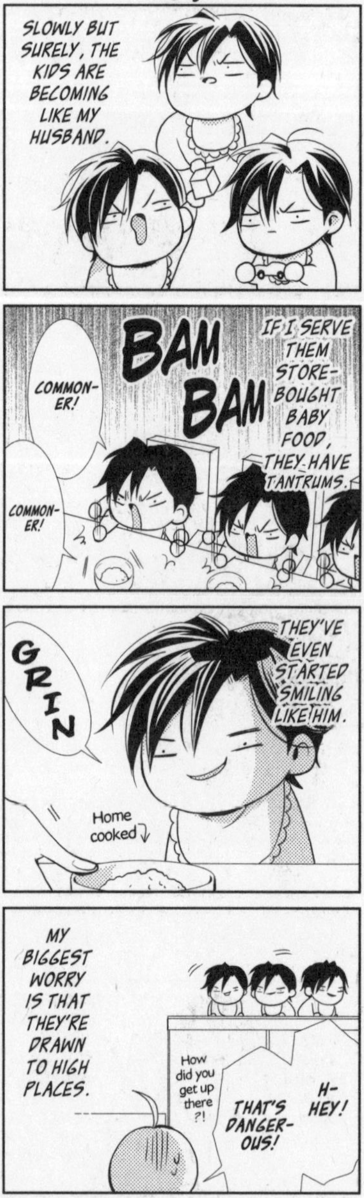
SLOWLY BUT SURELY, THE KIDS ARE BECOMING LIKE MY HUSBAND.
IF I SERVE THEM STORE-BOUGHT BABY FOOD, THEY HAVE TANTRUMS.
BAM BAM
COMMONER!
COMMONER!
THEY'VE EVEN STARTED SMILING LIKE HIM.
GRIN
Home cooked
H-HEY!
THAT'S DANGEROUS!
How did you get up there?!
MY BIGGEST WORRY IS THAT THEY'RE DRAWN TO HIGH PLACES.

My Husband Is Stressing Me Out

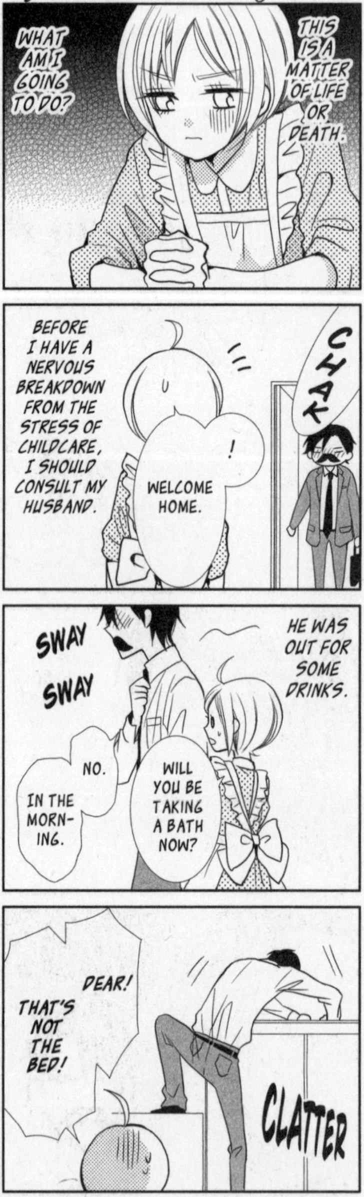
THIS IS A MATTER OF LIFE OR DEATH.
WHAT AM I GOING TO DO?
CHAK
!
WELCOME HOME.
BEFORE I HAVE A NERVOUS BREAKDOWN FROM THE STRESS OF CHILDCARE, I SHOULD CONSULT MY HUSBAND.
HE WAS OUT FOR SOME DRINKS.
WILL YOU BE TAKING A BATH NOW?
SWAY
SWAY
NO.
IN THE MORNING.
DEAR!
THAT'S NOT THE BED!
CLATTER

No Harm Intended

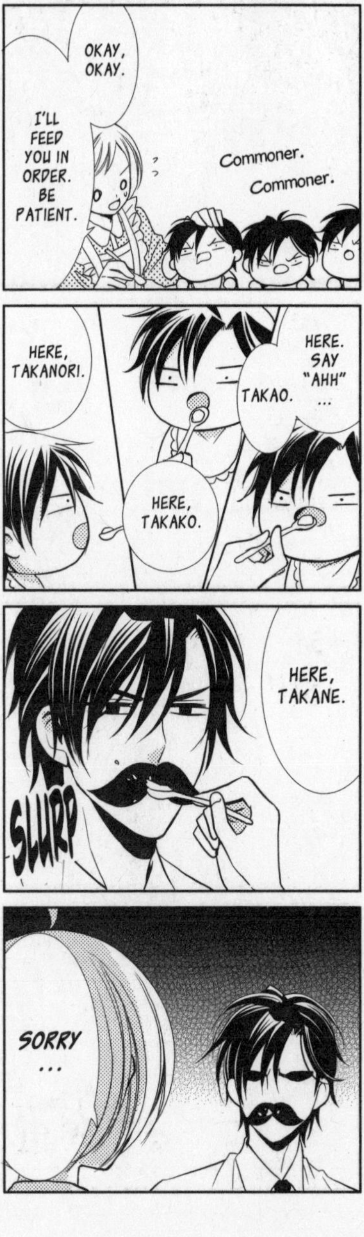
Commoner.
Commoner.
OKAY, OKAY.
I'LL FEED YOU IN ORDER. BE PATIENT.
HERE. SAY "AHH" ...
TAKAO.
HERE, TAKANORI.
HERE, TAKAKO.
HERE, TAKANE.
SLURP
SORRY ...

Underwear Costs as Much as Diapers

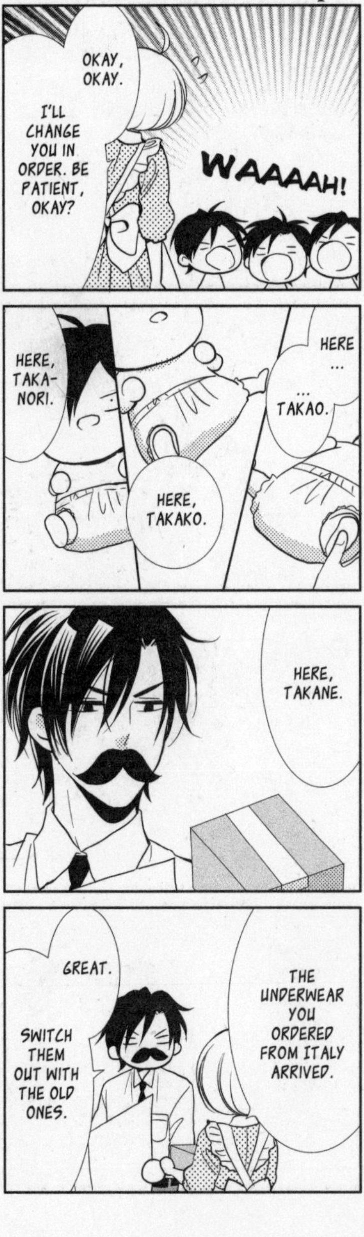
WAAAAH!
OKAY, OKAY.
I'LL CHANGE YOU IN ORDER. BE PATIENT, OKAY?
HERE ...
... TAKAO.
HERE, TAKANORI.
HERE, TAKAKO.
HERE, TAKANE.
THE UNDERWEAR YOU ORDERED FROM ITALY ARRIVED.
GREAT.
SWITCH THEM OUT WITH THE OLD ONES.

Daddy

TMP
TMP
?
WHERE'S HE TAKING JUST ONE BABY?
LISTEN, TAKAKO.
I TAUGHT YOU TO CALL ME "FATHER," BUT...
...I WANT YOU—ONLY YOU—TO CALL ME "DADDY."
DA ...?
Shh...
DON'T TELL MOTHER, OKAY?
DADDY ...
HOW SWEET.
HE WANTS HIS ONLY DAUGHTER TO CALL HIM "DADDY." HEE!
SWOON
DADDY!
AGAIN!
ALTHOUGH THAT'S TAKAO, NOT TAKAKO ...
SWOON
DADDY!

They're All Like My Husband

ZZZ...
FINALLY, THEY'RE ASLEEP.
SIGH...
I FINALLY GOT THROUGH THE DAY.
THEY'RE ONLY CUTE WHEN THEY'RE ASLEEP.
GRIN
GASP!

Bonus Story: Takane & Hana & Jr. / The End

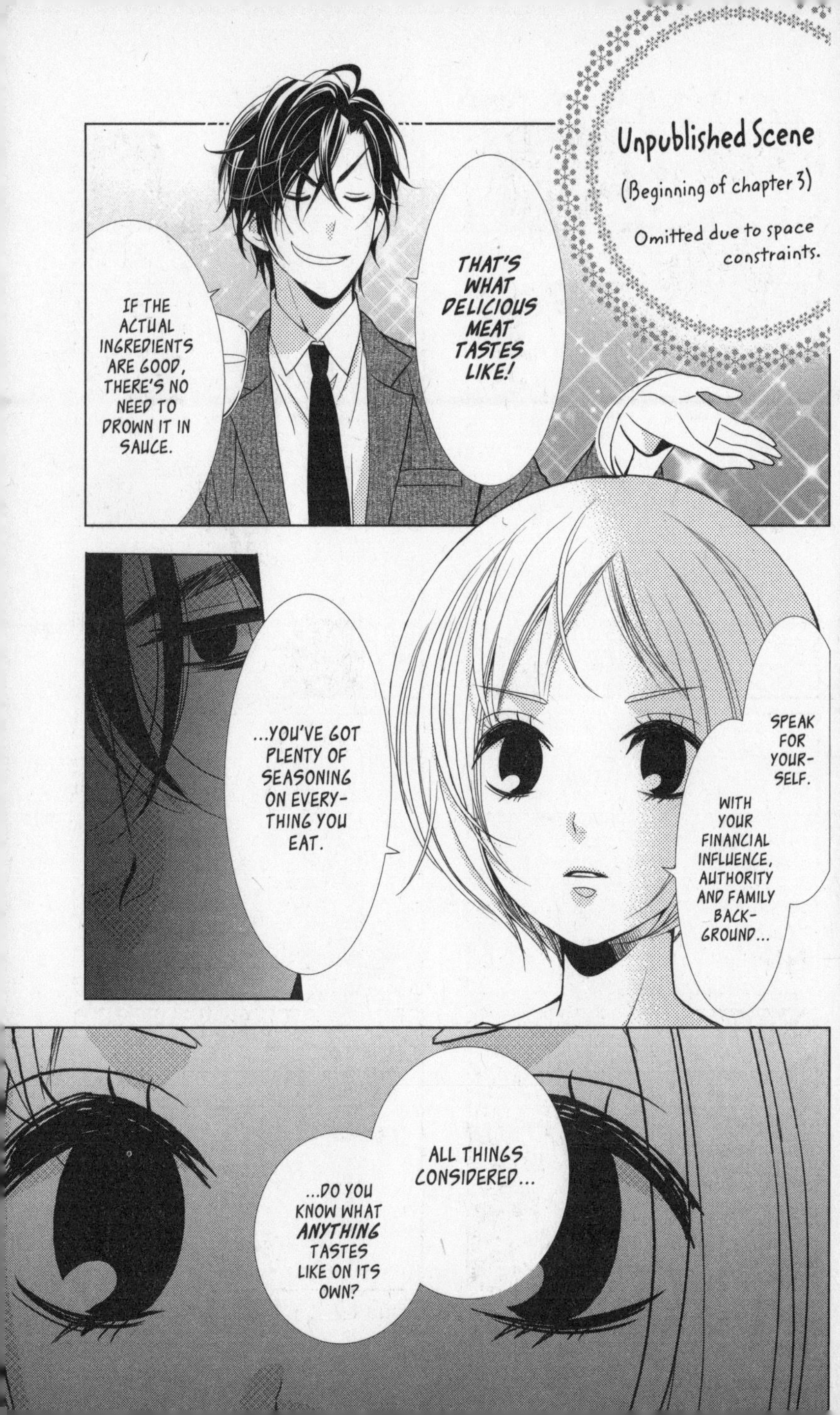
Unpublished Scene
(Beginning of chapter 3)
Omitted due to space constraints.
THAT'S WHAT DELICIOUS MEAT TASTES LIKE!
IF THE ACTUAL INGREDIENTS ARE GOOD, THERE'S NO NEED TO DROWN IT IN SAUCE.
SPEAK FOR YOUR-SELF.
WITH YOUR FINANCIAL INFLUENCE, AUTHORITY AND FAMILY BACK-GROUND...
...YOU'VE GOT PLENTY OF SEASONING ON EVERY-THING YOU EAT.
ALL THINGS CONSIDERED...
...DO YOU KNOW WHAT ANYTHING TASTES LIKE ON ITS OWN?

Takane Saibara

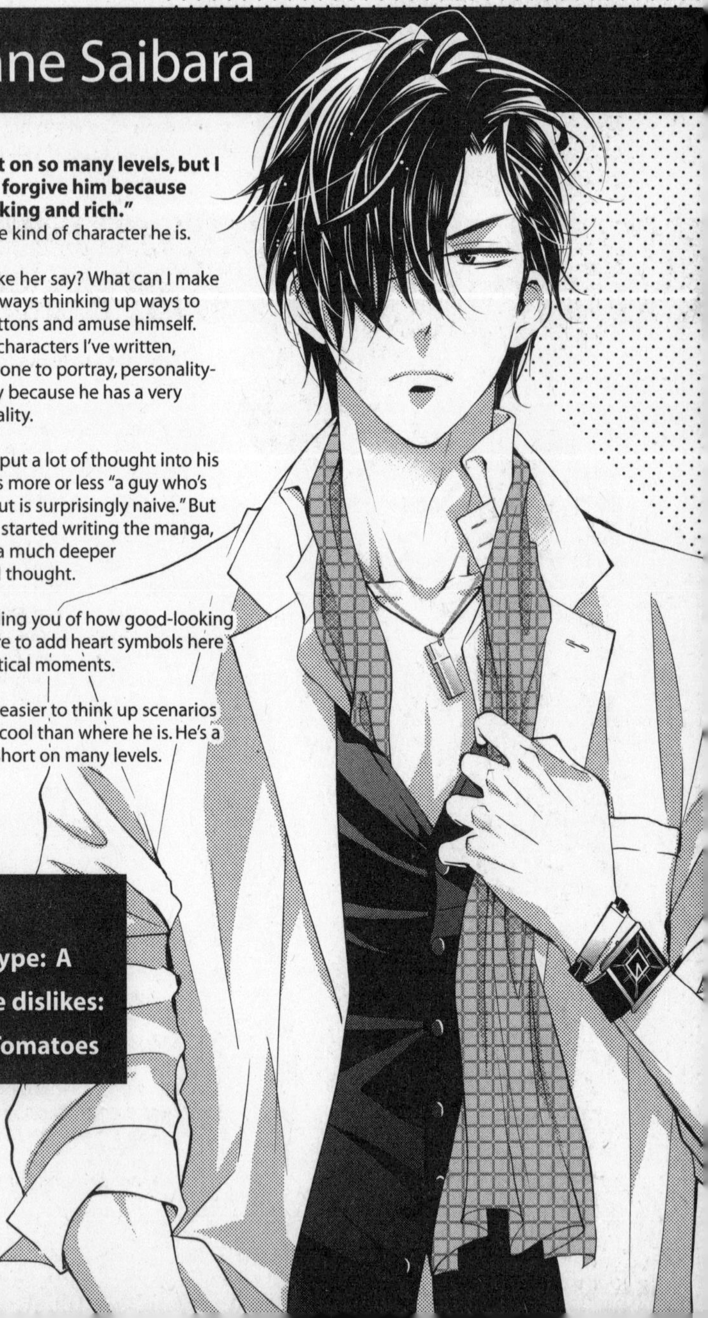

"He falls short on so many levels, but I hope you can forgive him because he's good-looking and rich."
That's the kind of character he is.

"What can I make her say? What can I make her do?" He's always thinking up ways to push Hana's buttons and amuse himself. Of all the male characters I've written, he's the easiest one to portray, personality-wise—probably because he has a very distinct personality.

Initially, I didn't put a lot of thought into his character. It was more or less "a guy who's usually bossy but is surprisingly naive." But when I actually started writing the manga, he turned into a much deeper character than I thought.

To keep reminding you of how good-looking he is, I make sure to add heart symbols here and there at critical moments.

It was so much easier to think up scenarios where he's **not** cool than where he is. He's a hero who falls short on many levels.

Age: 26

Blood type: A

Food he dislikes: Tomatoes

Age: 16
Blood type: O
Best trait:
Symmetrical

By the way, it may look like he's always wearing the same suit, but he actually wears a different one every day. (If you look closely, you'll see that the screen tone designs are different.) He's very particular and tends to buy similar suits. That's the impression I was trying to give.

Hana Nonomura

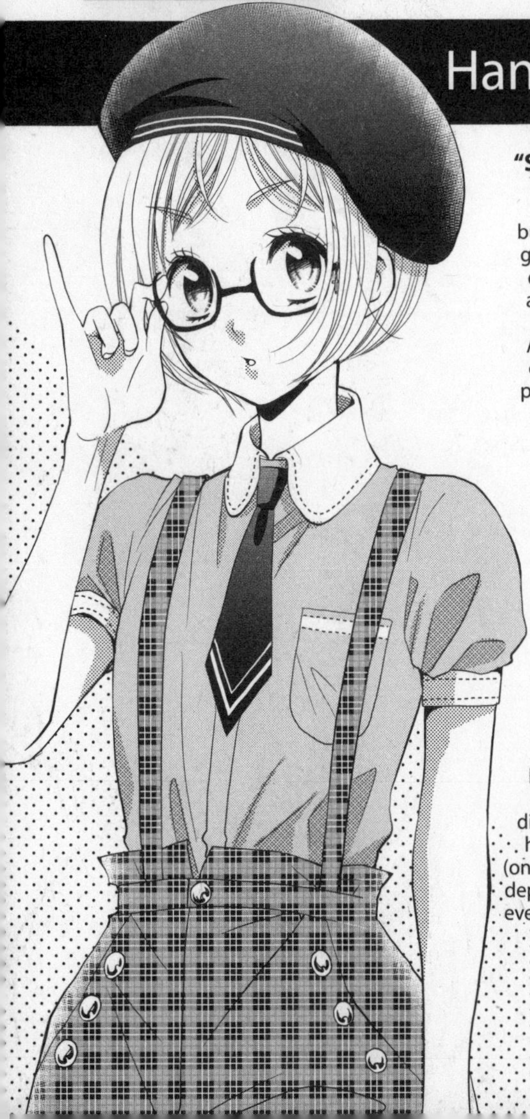

"She always has a comeback."

She's always been strong willed, but when she's with Takane, that trait goes into overdrive. (She does adjust depending on who she's with. After all, she's basically a sensible person.)

A main character we can trust to act on her natural instinct to lash out at people who piss her off. Like Takane, out of all the main characters I've written, she's one of the easiest to portray. Having said that, my brain is constantly working extra hard to think of clever comebacks. I find myself bouncing her dialogue off other people to make sure it's solid.

She's basically a good girl, but I'm hoping to portray her as someone who is grounded and can consider the interests of both parties without sacrificing herself.

Colorwise, with her pink hair and blue eyes, she may seem a bit funky, but I made her like that because I didn't want her to look too plain with her short hair. Her unruly lock of hair (on the top of her head) looks different depending on her mood. Sometimes it even stretches! Maybe someday it'll be able to attack things on its own.

I love drawing funny expressions.

Afterword

Thank you for reading all the way to the end. The bonus stories are all based on figments of Hana's imagination. I don't know how it would actually be if she and Takane got married.

If I get the chance, I think I want to continue writing about that... Things like seeing their children go off to elementary school, go through high school...even what they're like as adults in their own right! (LOL)

Special Thanks

- To my readers
- Family and friends
- My main editor, S
- Everyone in the editorial department
- Everyone who had a part in this book

Thank you very much!

Please send me your thoughts and impressions!

Yuki Shiwasu
c/o Takane & Hana Editor
VIZ Media
P.O. Box 77010
San Francisco, CA 94107

I'll be so happy to hear from you!

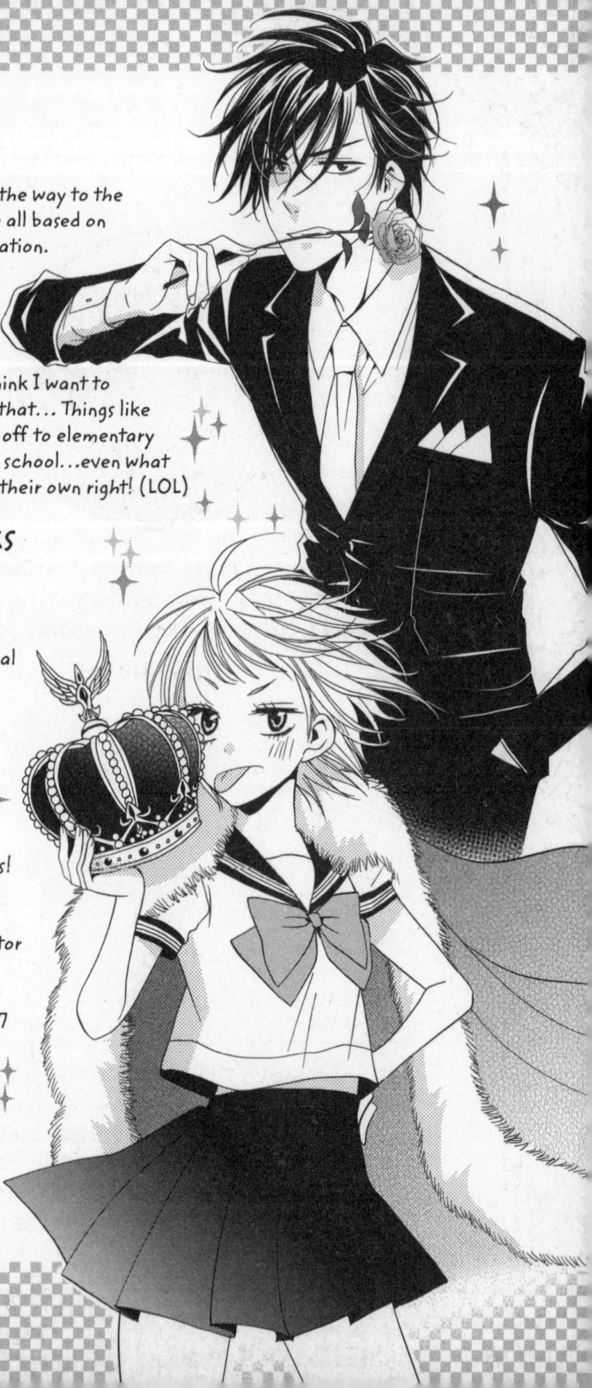

This is my fifth manga! Personally
I'm not really into pompous, arrogant
guys, but I tried to portray one here.

—YUKI SHIWASU

Born on March 7 in Fukuoka Prefecture, Japan,
Yuki Shiwasu began her career as a manga artist
after winning the top prize in the Hakusensha Athena
Newcomers' Awards from *Hana to Yume* magazine. She
is also the author of *Furou Kyoudai* (Immortal Siblings),
which was published by Hakusensha in Japan.

Takane & Hana

VOLUME 1
SHOJO BEAT EDITION

STORY & ART BY **YUKI SHIWASU**

ENGLISH ADAPTATION **Ysabet Reinhardt MacFarlane**
TRANSLATION **JN Productions**
TOUCH-UP ART & LETTERING **Freeman Wong**
DESIGN **Shawn Carrico**
EDITOR **Amy Yu**

Takane to Hana by Yuki Shiwasu
© Yuki Shiwasu 2015
All rights reserved.
First published in Japan in 2015 by HAKUSENSHA, Inc., Tokyo.
English language translation rights arranged with HAKUSENSHA, Inc., Tokyo.

Printed in Canada

Published by VIZ Media, LLC
P.O. Box 77010
San Francisco, CA 94107

10 9 8 7 6 5 4 3 2 1
First printing, February 2018

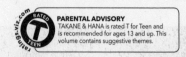

PARENTAL ADVISORY
TAKANE & HANA is rated T for Teen and
is recommended for ages 13 and up. This
volume contains suggestive themes.

viz.com   shojobeat.com

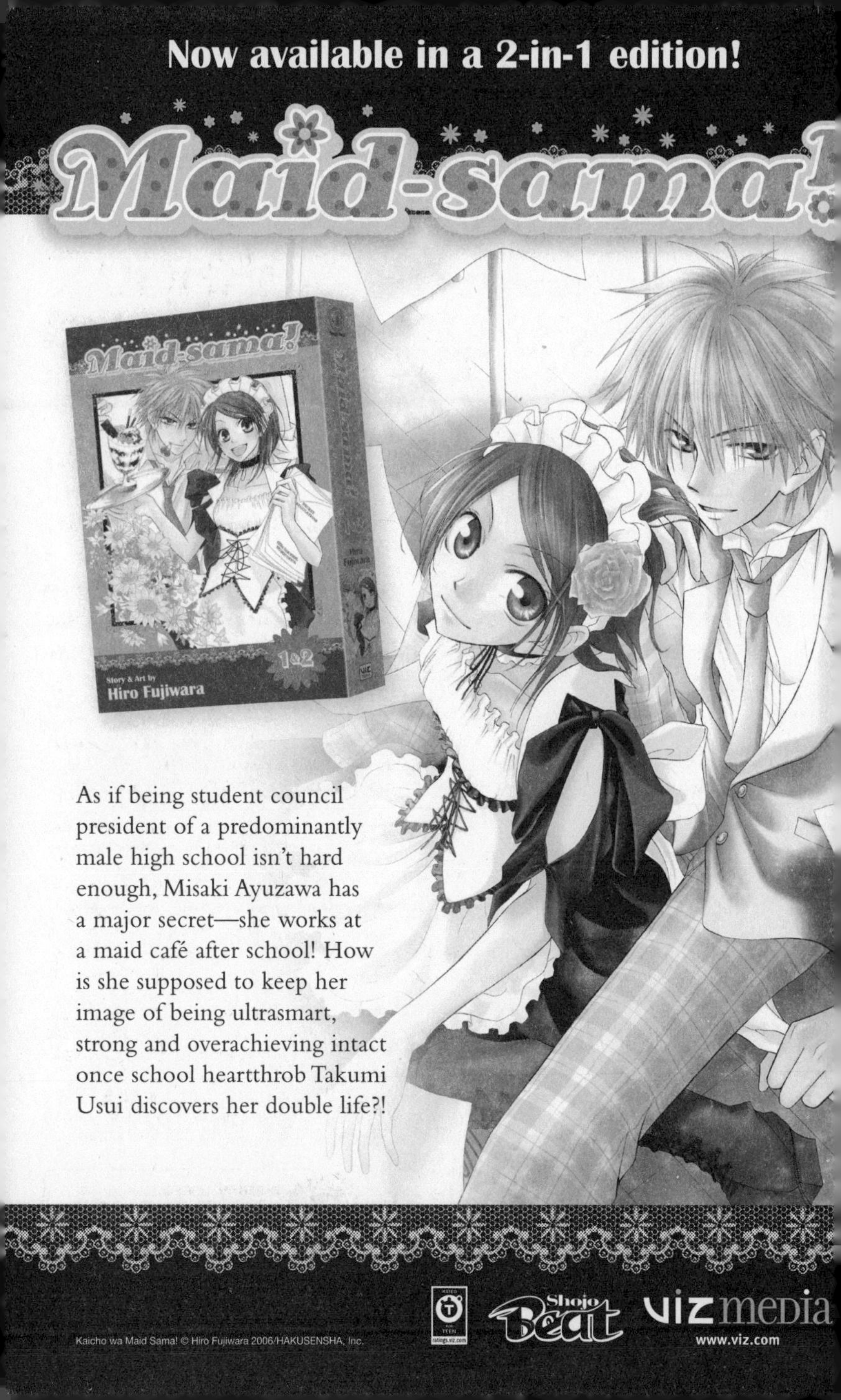
Now available in a 2-in-1 edition!
Maid-sama!
Maid-sama!
Story & Art by
Hiro Fujiwara
1&2
As if being student council president of a predominantly male high school isn't hard enough, Misaki Ayuzawa has a major secret—she works at a maid café after school! How is she supposed to keep her image of being ultrasmart, strong and overachieving intact once school heartthrob Takumi Usui discovers her double life?!
Kaicho wa Maid Sama! © Hiro Fujiwara 2006/HAKUSENSHA, Inc.
RATED T TEEN
ratings.viz.com
Shojo Beat
viz media
www.viz.com

Behind the Scenes!!

STORY AND ART BY **BISCO HATORI**

From the creator of Ouran High School Host Club

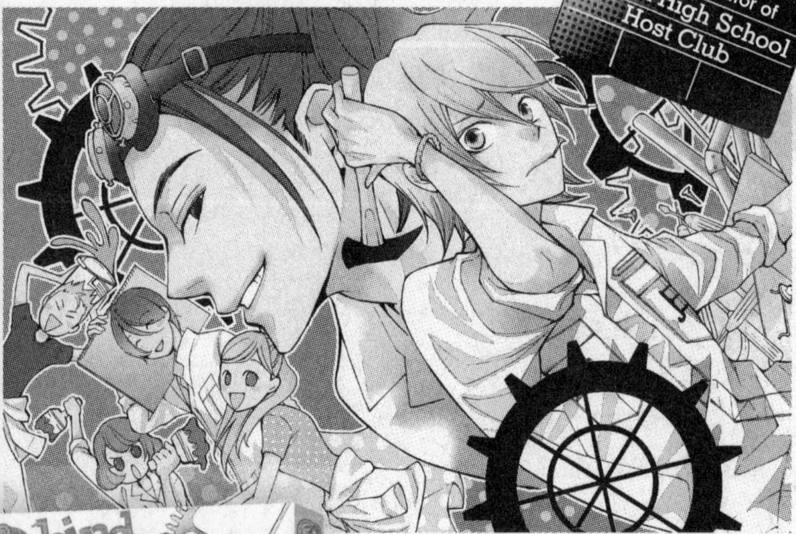

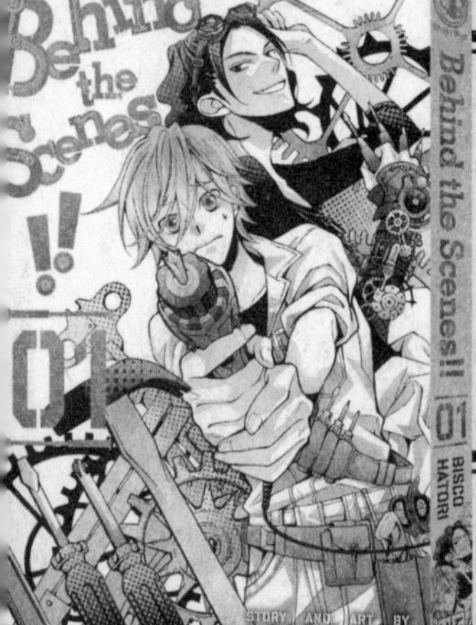

Behind the Scenes!!
01
Behind the Scenes!!
01
BISCO HATORI
STORY AND ART BY BISCO HATORI

Ranmaru Kurisu comes from a family of hardy, rough-and-tumble fisherfolk and he sticks out at home like a delicate, artistic sore thumb. It's given him a raging inferiority complex and a permanently pessimistic outlook. Now that he's in college, he's hoping to find a sense of belonging. But after a whole life of being left out, does he even know how to fit in?!

RATED T FOR TEEN ratings.viz.com

VIZ MEDIA www.viz.com

Shojo Beat

IDOL dreams

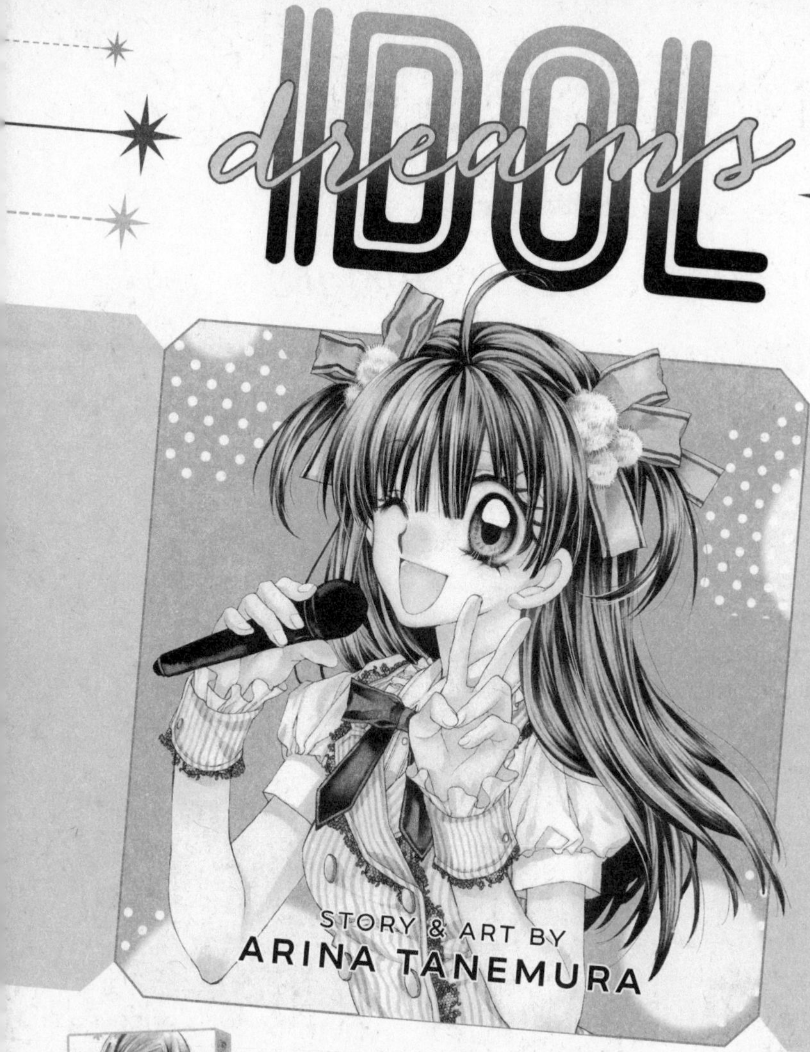
STORY & ART BY
ARINA TANEMURA

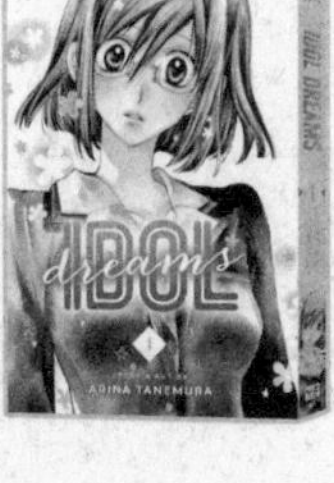
IDOL DREAMS
IDOL
dreams
1
ARINA TANEMURA

At age 31, office worker Chikage Deguchi feels she missed her chances at love and success. When word gets out that she's a virgin, Chikage is humiliated and wishes she could turn back time to when she was still young and popular. She takes an experimental drug that changes her appearance back to when she was 15. Now Chikage is determined to pursue everything she missed out on all those years ago—including becoming a star!

Shojo Beat VIZ media www.viz.com RATED T FOR TEEN ratings.viz.com

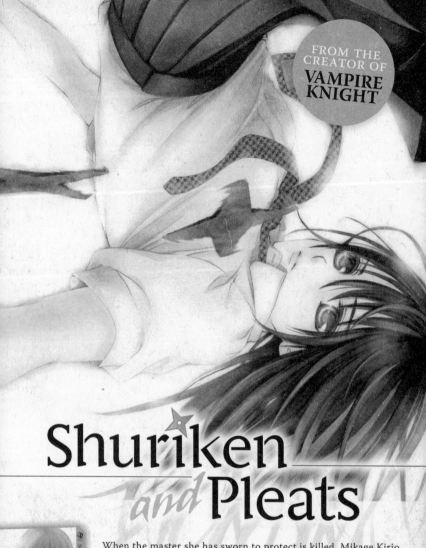

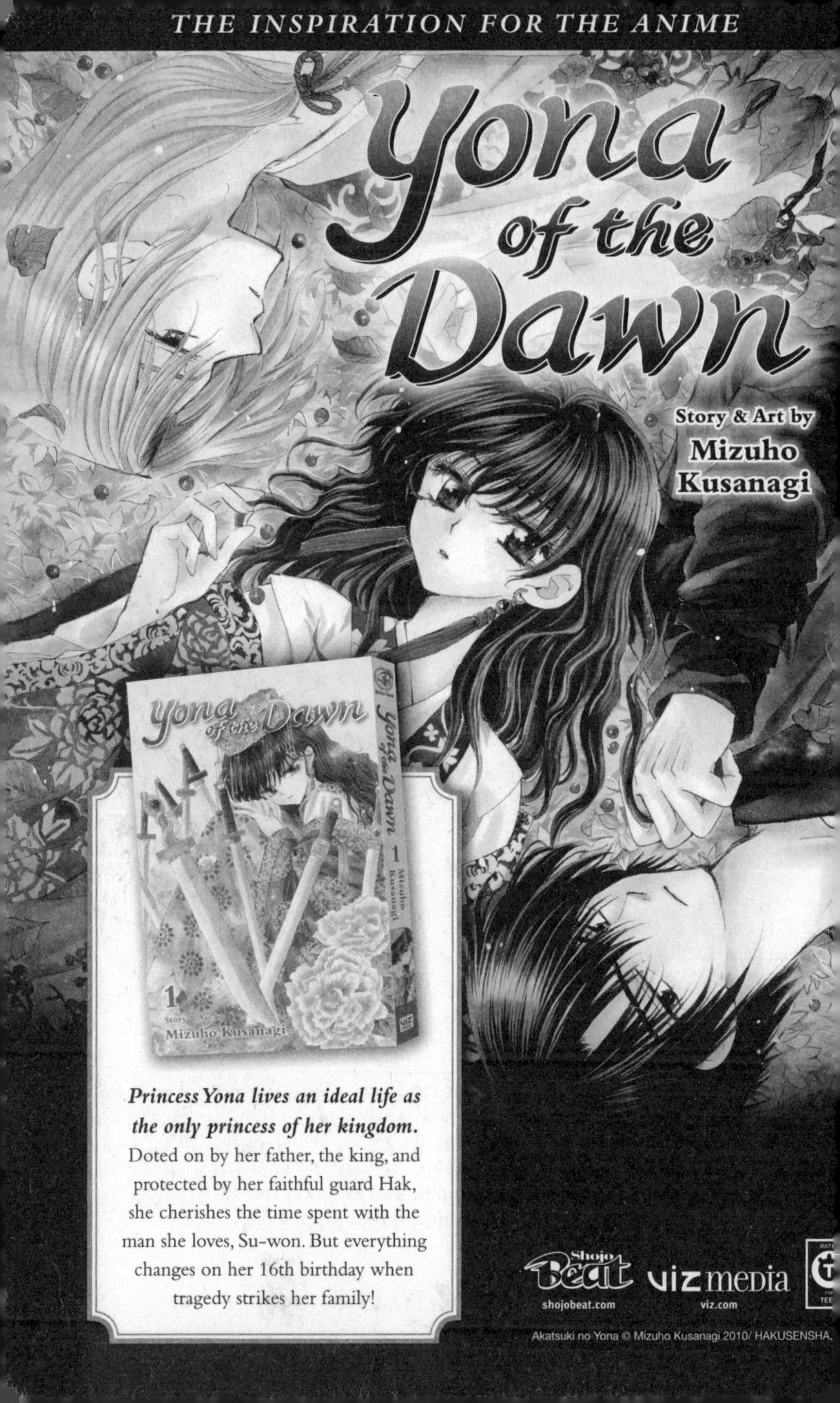
THE INSPIRATION FOR THE ANIME
Yona of the Dawn
Story & Art by
Mizuho Kusanagi
Yona of the Dawn
1
Story & Art by
Mizuho Kusanagi
Princess Yona lives an ideal life as the only princess of her kingdom.
Doted on by her father, the king, and protected by her faithful guard Hak, she cherishes the time spent with the man she loves, Su-won. But everything changes on her 16th birthday when tragedy strikes her family!
Shojo Beat
shojobeat.com
viz media
viz.com
Akatsuki no Yona © Mizuho Kusanagi 2010/ HAKUSENSHA,

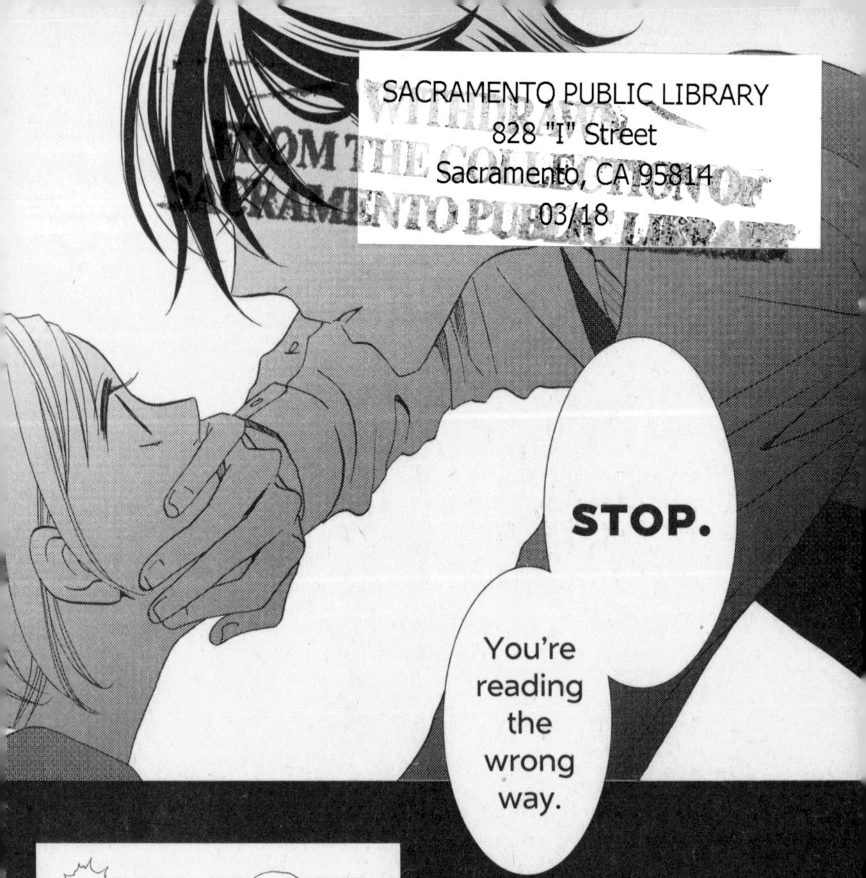
STOP.
You're reading the wrong way.

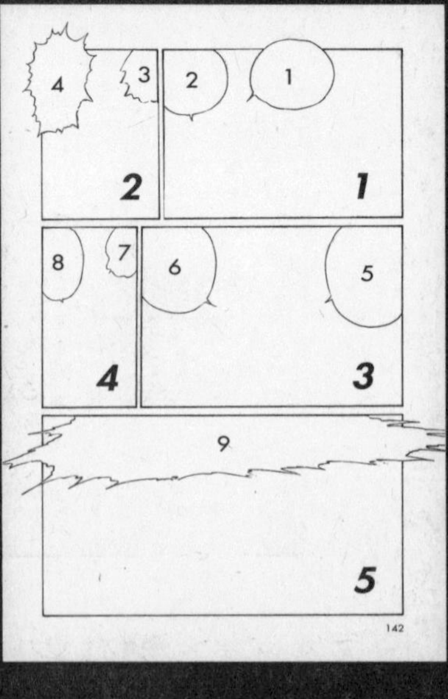
1
2
3
4
1
2
5
6
7
8
3
4
9
5
142

In keeping with the original Japanese comic format, this book reads from right to left—so action, sound effects and word balloons are completely reversed to preserve the orientation of the original artwork.

Check out the diagram shown here to get the hang of things, and then turn to the other side of the book to get started!